Social Insurance and Allied Services

REPORT BY
SIR WILLIAM BEVERIDGE

AMERICAN EDITION
REPRODUCED PHOTOGRAPHICALLY FROM
THE ENGLISH EDITION
AND PUBLISHED BY ARRANGEMENT WITH
HIS MAJESTY'S STATIONERY OFFICE

THE MACMILLAN COMPANY
NEW YORK · 1942

THE BEVERIDGE REPORT

SOCIAL INSURANCE AND ALLIED SERVICES

On the 10th June, 1941, the Minister without Portfolio (the Rt. Hon. Arthur Greenwood, M.P.) announced in the House of Commons that he had arranged with all the Departments concerned for a comprehensive survey of existing schemes of social insurance and allied services which would be considered in due course by the Committee on Reconstruction Problems of which he was chairman; and that Sir William Beveridge had accepted his invitation to become Chairman of an interdepartmental Committee which would conduct the survey, taking into account representations received from responsible organisations and persons connected with the problems involved.

The constitution of the Committee was as follows :—

Chairman—Sir William Beveridge, K.C.B.

Departmental Representatives—Mr. R. R. Bannatyne, C.B., Home Office; Mr. P. Y. Blundun, Ministry of Labour and National Service; Miss M. S. Cox, O.B.E., Ministry of Pensions; Sir George Epps, K.B.E., C.B., Government Actuary; Mr. R. Hamilton Farrell, Ministry of Health; Mr. E. Hale, C.B., Treasury; Mrs. M. A. Hamilton, Reconstruction Secretariat; Mr. A. W. McKenzie, Board of Customs and Excise; Sir George Reid, K.B.E., C.B., Assistance Board; Miss M. Ritson, C.B.E., Department of Health for Scotland; Mr. B. K. White, Registry of Friendly Societies and Office of the Industrial Assurance Commissioner.

Secretary—Mr. D. N. Chester.

The terms of reference were :—

> To undertake, with special reference to the inter-relation of the schemes, a survey of the existing national schemes of social insurance and allied services, including workmen's compensation, and to make recommendations.

The Minister without Portfolio announced in the House of Commons on 27th January, 1942, that "it will be within the power of the Committee to consider developments of the National Insurance Schemes in the way of adding death benefits with any other risks which are at present not covered by such schemes."

The following letter was sent to the Chairman on the 27th January, 1942, by the Minister without Portfolio.

My dear Beveridge,

I have discussed with the Chancellor of the Exchequer the position of the departmental representatives on the Inter-departmental Committee on Social Insurance and Allied Services. In view of the issues of high policy which will arise, we think that the departmental representatives should henceforward be regarded as your advisers and assessors on the various technical and administrative matters with which they are severally concerned. This means that the Report, when made, will be your own report; it will be signed by you alone, and the departmental representatives will not be associated in any way with the views and recommendations on questions of policy which it contains. It would be well that the Report should contain words to make it clear that this is the position.

Yours sincerely,

(Signed) ARTHUR GREENWOOD.

The estimated gross cost of the preparation of this Report is £4,625 0s. 0d., of which £3,150 0s. 0d. represents the estimated cost of printing and publishing the Report and the Volume of Memoranda from organisations.

The Rt. Hon. Sir William Jowitt, K.C., M.P.,
 His Majesty's Paymaster-General.

SIR,

I have the honour to submit the enclosed Report arising out of the work of the Inter-departmental Committee on Social Insurance and Allied Services appointed by your predecessor as Minister concerned with reconstruction problems, Mr. Arthur Greenwood, in June, 1941. For the reasons set out in the Report itself (paragraph 40), the Report is made by myself alone as Chairman.

It falls to me, therefore, on behalf of the Committee, in transmitting this Report to you, to express with more than conventional appreciation the gratitude of the Committee, as well as of myself, for the work of their Secretary, Mr. D. N. Chester. Without his able and untiring service and his orderly marshalling of our proceedings, the preparation of this Report could not have been accomplished. I take this opportunity of expressing at the same time my gratitude to my colleagues on the Committee who have so unreservedly placed at my disposal, in framing my Report and the recommendations for which I alone am responsible, their information and experience relating to the immense range of problems with which the work of the Committee was concerned.

I have the honour to be, Sir,

Your obedient servant,

W. H. BEVERIDGE,

Chairman.

20th November, 1942.

SOCIAL INSURANCE AND ALLIED SERVICES

REPORT BY SIR WILLIAM BEVERIDGE

CONTENTS

A detailed table of Contents, with a list of statistical tables, is given on pages 294–299.

SOCIAL INSURANCE AND ALLIED SERVICES

PART I

INTRODUCTION AND SUMMARY

1. The Inter-departmental Committee on Social Insurance and Allied Services were appointed in June, 1941, by the Minister without Portfolio, then responsible for the consideration of reconstruction problems. The terms of reference required the Committee " to undertake, with special reference to the inter-relation of the schemes, a survey of the existing national schemes of social insurance and allied services, including workmen's compensation and to make recommendations." The first duty of the Committee was to survey, the second to recommend. For the reasons stated below in paragraph 40 the duty of recommendation was confined later to the Chairman of the Committee.

THE COMMITTEE'S SURVEY AND ITS RESULTS

2. The schemes of social insurance and allied services which the Inter-departmental Committee have been called on to survey have grown piece-meal. Apart from the Poor Law, which dates from the time of Elizabeth, the schemes surveyed are the product of the last 45 years beginning with the Workmen's Compensation Act, 1897. That Act, applying in the first instance to a limited number of occupations, was made general in 1906. Compulsory health insurance began in 1912. Unemployment insurance began for a few industries in 1912 and was made general in 1920. The first Pensions Act, giving non-contributory pensions subject to a means test at the age of 70, was passed in 1908. In 1925 came the Act which started contributory pensions for old age, for widows and for orphans. Unemployment insurance, after a troubled history, was put on a fresh basis by the Unemployment Act of 1934, which set up at the same time a new national service of Unemployment Assistance. Meantime, the local machinery for relief of destitution, after having been exhaustively examined by the Royal Commission of 1905-1909, has been changed both by the new treatment of unemployment and in many other ways, including a transfer of the responsibilities of the Boards of Guardians to Local Authorities. Separate provision for special types of disability—such as blindness—has been made from time to time. Together with this growth of social insurance and impinging on it at many points have gone developments of medical treatment, particularly in hospitals and other institutions ; developments of services devoted to the welfare of children, in school and before it ; and a vast growth of voluntary provision for death and other contingencies, made by persons of the insured classes through Industrial Life Offices, Friendly Societies and Trade Unions.

3. In all this change and development, each problem has been dealt with separately, with little or no reference to allied problems. The first task of the Committee has been to attempt for the first time a comprehensive survey of the whole field of social insurance and allied services, to show just what provision is now made and how it is made for many different forms of need. The results of this survey are set out in Appendix B describing social insurance and the allied services as they exist today in Britain. The picture presented is impressive in two ways. First, it shows that provision for most of the many varieties of need through interruption of earnings and other causes that may arise in modern industrial communities has already been made in Britain on a scale not surpassed and hardly rivalled in any other country of the world. In one respect only of the first importance, namely limitation of medical service, both in the range of treatment which is provided as of right and in respect of the classes of persons for whom it is provided, does Britain's achievement fall seriously short of what has been accomplished elsewhere ; it falls

short also in its provision for cash benefit for maternity and funerals and through the defects of its system for workmen's compensation. In all other fields British provision for security, in adequacy of amount and in comprehensiveness, will stand comparison with that of any other country; few countries will stand comparison with Britain. Second, social insurance and the allied services, as they exist today, are conducted by a complex of disconnected administrative organs, proceeding on different principles, doing invaluable service but at a cost in money and trouble and anomalous treatment of identical problems for which there is no justification. In a system of social security better on the whole than can be found in almost any other country there are serious deficiencies which call for remedy.

4. Thus limitation of compulsory insurance to persons under contract of service and below a certain remuneration if engaged on non-manual work is a serious gap. Many persons working on their own account are poorer and more in need of State insurance than employees; the remuneration limit for non-manual employees is arbitrary and takes no account of family responsibility. There is, again, no real difference between the income needs of persons who are sick and those who are unemployed, but they get different rates of benefit involving different contribution conditions and with meaningless distinctions between persons of different ages. An adult insured man with a wife and two children receives 38/- per week should he become unemployed; if after some weeks of unemployment he becomes sick and not available for work, his insurance income falls to 18/-. On the other hand a youth of 17 obtains 9/- when he is unemployed, but should he become sick his insurance income rises to 12/- per week. There are, to take another example, three different means tests for non-contributory pensions, for supplementary pensions and for public assistance, with a fourth test—for unemployment assistance—differing from that for supplementary pensions in some particulars.

5. Many other such examples could be given; they are the natural result of the way in which social security has grown in Britain. It is not open to question that, by closer co-ordination, the existing social services could be made at once more beneficial and more intelligible to those whom they serve and more economical in their administration.

THREE GUIDING PRINCIPLES OF RECOMMENDATIONS

6. In proceeding from this first comprehensive survey of social insurance to the next task—of making recommendations—three guiding principles may be laid down at the outset.

7. The first principle is that any proposals for the future, while they should use to the full the experience gathered in the past, should not be restricted by consideration of sectional interests established in the obtaining of that experience. Now, when the war is abolishing landmarks of every kind, is the opportunity for using experience in a clear field. A revolutionary moment in the world's history is a time for revolutions, not for patching.

8. The second principle is that organisation of social insurance should be treated as one part only of a comprehensive policy of social progress. Social insurance fully developed may provide income security; it is an attack upon Want. But Want is one only of five giants on the road of reconstruction and in some ways the easiest to attack. The others are Disease, Ignorance, Squalor and Idleness.

9. The third principle is that social security must be achieved by co-operation between the State and the individual. The State should offer security for service and contribution. The State in organising security should

not stifle incentive, opportunity, responsibility; in establishing a national minimum, it should leave room and encouragement for voluntary action by each individual to provide more than that minimum for himself and his family.

10.   The Plan for Social Security set out in this Report is built upon these principles.   It uses experience but is not tied by experience.   It is put forward as a limited contribution to a wider social policy, though as something that could be achieved now without waiting for the whole of that policy. It is, first and foremost, a plan of insurance—of giving in return for contributions benefits up to subsistence level, as of right and without means test, so that individuals may build freely upon it.

The Way to Freedom from Want

11.   The work of the Inter-departmental Committee began with a review of existing schemes of social insurance and allied services.   The Plan for Social Security, with which that work ends, starts from a diagnosis of want— of the circumstances in which, in the years just preceding the present war, families and individuals in Britain might lack the means of healthy subsistence.   During those years impartial scientific authorities made social surveys of the conditions of life in a number of principal towns in Britain, including London, Liverpool, Sheffield, Plymouth, Southampton, York and Bristol.   They determined the proportions of the people in each town whose means were below the standard assumed to be necessary for subsistence, and they analysed the extent and causes of that deficiency.   From each of these social surveys the same broad result emerges.   Of all the want shown by the surveys, from three-quarters to five-sixths, according to the precise standard chosen for want, was due to interruption or loss of earning power.   Practically the whole of the remaining one-quarter to one-sixth was due to failure to relate income during earning to the size of the family.   These surveys were made before the introduction of supplementary pensions had reduced the amount of poverty amongst old persons.   But this does not affect the main conclusion to be drawn from these surveys : abolition of want requires a double re-distribution of income, through social insurance and by family needs.

12.   Abolition of want requires, first, improvement of State insurance, that is to say provision against interruption and loss of earning power. All the principal causes of interruption or loss of earnings are now the subject of schemes of social insurance.   If, in spite of these schemes, so many persons unemployed or sick or old or widowed are found to be without adequate income for subsistence according to the standards adopted in the social surveys, this means that the benefits amount to less than subsistence by those standards or do not last as long as the need, and that the assistance which supplements insurance is either insufficient in amount or available only on terms which make men unwilling to have recourse to it.   None of the insurance benefits provided before the war were in fact designed with reference to the standards of the social surveys.   Though unemployment benefit was not altogether out of relation to those standards, sickness and disablement benefit, old age pensions and widows' pensions were far below them, while workmen's compensation was below subsistence level for anyone who had family responsibilities or whose earnings in work were less than twice the amount needed for subsistence.   To prevent interruption or destruction of earning power from leading to want, it is necessary to improve the present schemes of social insurance in three directions : by extension of scope to cover persons now excluded, by extension of purposes to cover risks now excluded, and by raising the rates of benefit.

13.   Abolition of want requires, second, adjustment of incomes, in periods of earning as well as in interruption of earning, to family needs, that is to say

in one form or another it requires allowances for children. Without such allowances as part of benefit or added to it, to make provision for large families, no social insurance against interruption of earnings can be adequate. But, if children's allowances are given only when earnings are interrupted and are not given during earning also, two evils are unavoidable. First, a substantial measure of acute want will remain among the lower paid workers as the accompaniment of large families. Second, in all such cases, income will be greater during unemployment or other interruptions of work than during work.

14. By a double re-distribution of income through social insurance and children's allowances, want, as defined in the social surveys, could have been abolished in Britain before the present war. As is shown in para. 445, the income available to the British people was ample for such a purpose. The Plan for Social Security set out in Part V of this Report takes abolition of want after this war as its aim. It includes as its main method compulsory social insurance, with national assistance and voluntary insurance as subsidiary methods. It assumes allowances for dependent children, as part of its background. The plan assumes also establishment of comprehensive health and rehabilitation services and maintenance of employment, that is to say avoidance of mass unemployment, as necessary conditions of success in social insurance. These three measures—of children's allowances, health and rehabilitation services, and maintenance of employment—are described as assumptions A, B and C of the plan; they fall partly within and partly without the plan itself, extending into other fields of social policy. They are discussed, therefore, not in the detailed exposition of the plan in Part V of the Report, but in Part VI, which is concerned with social security in relation to wider issues.

15. The plan is based on a diagnosis of want. It starts from facts, from the condition of the people as revealed by social surveys between the two wars. It takes account of two other facts about the British community, arising out of past movements of the birth rate and the death rate, which should dominate planning for its future; the main effects of these movements in determining the present and future of the British people are shown by Table XI in para. 234. The first of the two facts is the age constitution of the population, making it certain that persons past the age that is now regarded as the end of working life will be a much larger proportion of the whole community than at any time in the past. The second fact is the low reproduction rate of the British community today; unless this rate is raised very materially in the near future, a rapid and continuous decline of the population cannot be prevented. The first fact makes it necessary to seek ways of postponing the age of retirement from work rather than of hastening it. The second fact makes it imperative to give first place in social expenditure to the care of childhood and to the safeguarding of maternity.

16. The provision to be made for old age represents the largest and most rapidly growing element in any social insurance scheme. The problem of age is discussed accordingly in Part III of the Report as one of three special problems; the measures proposed for dealing with this problem are summarised in paras. 254–257. Briefly, the proposal is to introduce for all citizens adequate pensions without means test by stages over a transition period of twenty years, while providing immediate assistance pensions for persons requiring them. In adopting a transition period for pensions as of right, while meeting immediate needs subject to consideration of means, the Plan for Social Security in Britain follows the precedent of New Zealand. The final rate of pensions in New Zealand is higher than that proposed in this Plan, but is reached only after a transition period of

twenty-eight years as compared with twenty years suggested here ; after twenty years, the New Zealand rate is not very materially different from the basic rate proposed for Britain. The New Zealand pensions are not conditional upon retirement from work ; for Britain it is proposed that they should be retirement pensions and that persons who continue at work and postpone retirement should be able to increase their pensions above the basic rate. The New Zealand scheme is less favourable than the plan for Britain in starting at a lower level ; it is more favourable in some other respects. Broadly the two schemes for two communities of the British race are plans on the same lines to solve the same problem of passage from pensions based on need to pensions paid as of right to all citizens in virtue of contribution.

Summary of Plan for Social Security

17. The main feature of the Plan for Social Security is a scheme of social insurance against interruption and destruction of earning power and for special expenditure arising at birth, marriage or death. The scheme embodies six fundamental principles : flat rate of subsistence benefit ; flat rate of contribution ; unification of administrative responsibility ; adequacy of benefit ; comprehensiveness ; and classification. These principles are explained in paras. 303–309. Based on them and in combination with national assistance and voluntary insurance as subsidiary methods, the aim of the Plan for Social Security is to make want under any circumstances unnecessary.

18. A plan which is designed to cover so many varieties of human circumstance must be long and detailed. It must contain proposals of differing orders of certainty and importance. In preparing the Report, the question arose naturally as to how far it was necessary at this stage to enter into details, and whether it might not be preferable to deal with principles only. For two reasons it has appeared desirable, in place of giving an outline only, to set the proposals out in as much detail as the time allowed. The first reason is that the principles underlying any practical reform can be judged only by seeing how they would work in practice. The second reason is that if a Plan for Social Security is to come into operation when the war ends or soon after, there is no time to lose in getting the plan prepared as fully as possible. The many details set forth in Part V are neither exhaustive nor final ; they are put forward as a basis of discussion, but their formulation will, it is hoped, shorten subsequent discussion. Even among the major proposals of the Report there are differences of importance and of relevance to the scheme as a whole. There are some proposals which, though important and desirable in themselves, could be omitted without changing anything else in the scheme. Three in particular in the list of major changes in para. 30 have this character and are placed in square brackets to indicate it. This does not mean that everything not bracketed is essential and must be taken or left as a whole. The six principles named above and all that is implied in them are fundamental ; the rest of the scheme can be adjusted without changing its character ; all rates of benefit and all details are by nature subject to amendment.

19. The main provisions of the plan may be summarised as follows :

(i) The plan covers all citizens without upper income limit, but has regard to their different ways of life ; it is a plan all-embracing in scope of persons and of needs, but is classified in application.

(ii) In relation to social security the population falls into four main classes of working age and two others below and above working age respectively, as follows :

    I. Employees, that is, persons whose normal occupation is employment under contract of service.

    II. Others gainfully occupied, including employers, traders and independent workers of all kinds.

    III. Housewives, that is married women of working age.

    IV. Others of working age not gainfully occupied.

    V. Below working age.

    VI. Retired above working age.

(iii) The sixth of these classes will receive retirement pensions and the fifth will be covered by children's allowances, which will be paid from the National Exchequer in respect of all children when the responsible parent is in receipt of insurance benefit or pension, and in respect of all children except one in other cases. The four other classes will be insured for security appropriate to their circumstances. All classes will be covered for comprehensive medical treatment and rehabilitation and for funeral expenses.

(iv) Every person in Class I, II or IV will pay a single security contribution by a stamp on a single insurance document each week or combination of weeks. In Class I the employer also will contribute, affixing the insurance stamp and deducting the employee's share from wages or salary. The contribution will differ from one class to another, according to the benefits provided, and will be higher for men than for women, so as to secure benefits for Class III.

(v) Subject to simple contribution conditions, every person in Class I will receive benefit for unemployment and disability, pension on retirement, medical treatment and funeral expenses. Persons in Class II will receive all these except unemployment benefit and disability benefit during the first 13 weeks of disability. Persons in Class IV will receive all these except unemployment and disability benefit. As a substitute for unemployment benefit, training benefit will be available to persons in all classes other than Class I, to assist them to find new livelihoods if their present ones fail. Maternity grant, provision for widowhood and separation and qualification for retirement pensions will be secured to all persons in Class III by virtue of their husbands' contributions ; in addition to maternity grant, housewives who take paid work will receive maternity benefit for thirteen weeks to enable them to give up working before and after childbirth.

(vi) Unemployment benefit, disability benefit, basic retirement pension after a transition period, and training benefit will be at the same rate, irrespective of previous earnings. This rate will provide by itself the income necessary for subsistence in all normal cases. There will be a joint rate for a man and wife who is not gainfully occupied. Where there is no wife or she is gainfully occupied, there will be a lower single rate ; where there is no wife but a dependant above the age for children's allowance, there will be a dependant allowance. Maternity benefit for housewives who work also for gain will be at a higher rate than the single rate in unemployment or disability, while their unemployment and disability benefit will be at a lower rate ; there are special rates also for widowhood as described below. With these exceptions all rates of benefit will be the same for men and for women. Disability due to industrial accident or disease will be treated like all other disability for the first thirteen weeks ; if disability continues thereafter, disability benefit at a flat rate will be replaced by an industrial pension related to the earnings of the individual subject to a minimum and a maximum.

(vii) Unemployment benefit will continue at the same rate without means test so long as unemployment lasts, but will normally be subject to a condition of attendance at a work or training centre after a certain period. Disability benefit will continue at the same rate without means test, so long as disability lasts or till it is replaced by industrial pension, subject to acceptance of suitable medical treatment or vocational training.

(viii) Pensions (other than industrial) will be paid only on retirement from work. They may be claimed at any time after the minimum age of retirement, that is 65 for men and 60 for women. The rate of pension will be increased above the basic rate if retirement is postponed. Contributory pensions as of right will be raised to the full basic rate gradually during a transition period of twenty years, in which adequate pensions according to needs will be paid to all persons requiring them. The position of existing pensioners will be safeguarded.

(ix) While permanent pensions will no longer be granted to widows of working age without dependent children, there will be for all widows a temporary benefit at a higher rate than unemployment or disability benefit, followed by training benefit where necessary. For widows with the care of dependent children there will be guardian benefit, in addition to the children's allowances, adequate for subsistence without other means. The position of existing widows on pension will be safeguarded.

(x) For the limited number of cases of need not covered by social insurance, national assistance subject to a uniform means test will be available.

(xi) Medical treatment covering all requirements will be provided for all citizens by a national health service organised under the health departments and post-medical rehabilitation treatment will be provided for all persons capable of profiting by it.

(xii) A Ministry of Social Security will be established, responsible for social insurance, national assistance and encouragement and supervision of voluntary insurance and will take over, so far as necessary for these purposes, the present work of other Government Departments and of Local Authorities in these fields.

THE NATURE OF SOCIAL INSURANCE

20. Under the scheme of social insurance, which forms the main feature of this plan, every citizen of working age will contribute in his appropriate class according to the security that he needs, or as a married woman will have contributions made by the husband. Each will be covered for all his needs by a single weekly contribution on one insurance document. All the principal cash payments—for unemployment, disability and retirement will continue so long as the need lasts, without means test, and will be paid from a Social Insurance Fund built up by contributions from the insured persons, from their employers, if any, and from the State. This is in accord with two views as to the lines on which the problem of income maintenance should be approached.

21. The first view is that benefit in return for contributions, rather than free allowances from the State, is what the people of Britain desire. This desire is shown both by the established popularity of compulsory insurance,

and by the phenomenal growth of voluntary insurance against sickness, against death and for endowment, and most recently for hospital treatment. It is shown in another way by the strength of popular objection to any kind of means test. This objection springs not so much from a desire to get everything for nothing, as from resentment at a provision which appears to penalise what people have come to regard as the duty and pleasure of thrift, of putting pennies away for a rainy day. Management of one's income is an essential element of a citizen's freedom. Payment of a substantial part of the cost of benefit as a contribution irrespective of the means of the contributor is the firm basis of a claim to benefit irrespective of means.

22. The second view is that whatever money is required for provision of insurance benefits, so long as they are needed, should come from a Fund to which the recipients have contributed and to which they may be required to make larger contributions if the Fund proves inadequate. The plan adopted since 1930 in regard to prolonged unemployment and sometimes suggested for prolonged disability, that the State should take this burden off insurance, in order to keep the contribution down, is wrong in principle. The insured persons should not feel that income for idleness, however caused, can come from a bottomless purse. The Government should not feel that by paying doles it can avoid the major responsibility of seeing that unemployment and disease are reduced to the minimum. The place for direct expenditure and organisation by the State is in maintaining employment of the labour and other productive resources of the country, and in preventing and combating disease, not in patching an incomplete scheme of insurance.

23. The State cannot be excluded altogether from giving direct assistance to individuals in need, after examination of their means. However comprehensive an insurance scheme, some, through physical infirmity, can never contribute at all and some will fall through the meshes of any insurance. The making of insurance benefit without means test unlimited in duration involves of itself that conditions must be imposed at some stage or another as to how men in receipt of benefit shall use their time, so as to fit themselves or to keep themselves fit for service ; imposition of any condition means that the condition may not be fulfilled and that a case of assistance may arise. Moreover for one of the main purposes of social insurance—provision for old age or retirement—the contributory principle implies contribution for a substantial number of years ; in the introduction of adequate contributory pensions there must be a period of transition during which those who have not qualified for pension by contribution but are in need have their needs met by assistance pensions. National assistance is an essential subsidiary method in the whole Plan for Social Security, and the work of the Assistance Board shows that assistance subject to means test can be administered with sympathetic justice and discretion taking full account of individual circumstances. But the scope of assistance will be narrowed from the beginning and will diminish throughout the transition period for pensions. The scheme of social insurance is designed of itself when in full operation to guarantee the income needed for subsistence in all normal cases.

24. The scheme is described as a scheme of insurance, because it preserves the contributory principle. It is described as social insurance to mark important distinctions from voluntary insurance. In the first place, while adjustment of premiums to risks is of the essence of voluntary insurance, since without this individuals would not of their own will insure, this adjustment is not essential in insurance which is made compulsory by the power of the State. In the second place, in providing for actuarial risks such as those of death, old age or sickness, it is necessary in voluntary insurance to fund contributions paid in early life in order to provide for the increasing risks of

later life and to accumulate reserves against individual liabilities. The State with its power of compelling successive generations of citizens to become insured and its power of taxation is not under the necessity of accumulating reserves for actuarial risks and has not, in fact, adopted this method in the past. The second of these two distinctions is one of financial practice only ; the first raises important questions of policy and equity. Though the State, in conducting compulsory insurance, is not under the necessity of varying the premium according to the risk, it may decide as a matter of policy to do so.

25. When State insurance began in Britain, it was felt that compulsory insurance should be like voluntary insurance in adjusting premiums to risks. This was secured in health insurance by the system of Approved Societies. It was intended to be secured in unemployment insurance by variation of contribution rates between industries as soon as accurate valuation became possible, by encouragement of special schemes of insurance by industry, and by return of contributions to individuals who made no claims. In the still earlier institution of workmen's compensation, adjustment of premiums to industrial risks was a necessary consequence of the form in which provision for industrial accidents was made, by placing liability on employers individually and leaving them to insure voluntarily against their liability. In the thirty years since 1912, there has been an unmistakable movement of public opinion away from these original ideas, that is to say, away from the principle of adjusting premiums to risks in compulsory insurance and in favour of pooling risks. This change has been most marked and most complete in regard to unemployment, where, in the general scheme, insurance by industry, in place of covering a large part of the field, has been reduced to historical exceptions ; today the common argument is that the volume of unemployment in an industry is not to any effective extent within its control ; that all industries depend upon one another, and that those which are fortunate in being regular should share the cost of unemployment in those which are less regular. The same tendency of opinion in favour of pooling of social risks has shown itself in the views expressed by the great majority of witnesses to the present Committee in regard to health insurance. In regard to workmen's compensation, the same argument has been put by the Mineworkers' Federation to the Royal Commission on Workmen's Compensation ; as other industries cannot exist without coalmining, they have proposed that employers in all industries should bear equally the cost of industrial accidents and disease, in coalmining as elsewhere.

26. There is here an issue of principle and practice on which strong arguments can be advanced on each side by reasonable men. But the general tendency of public opinion seems clear. After trial of a different principle, it has been found to accord best with the sentiments of the British people that in insurance organised by the community by use of compulsory powers each individual should stand in on the same terms ; none should claim to pay less because he is healthier or has more regular employment. In accord with that v.ew, the proposals of the Report mark another step forward to the development of State insurance as a new type of human institution, differing both from the former methods of preventing or alleviating distress and from voluntary insurance. The term " social insurance " to describe this institution implies both that it is compulsory and that men stand together with their fellows. The term implies a pooling of risks except so far as separation of risks serves a social purpose. There may be reasons of social policy for adjusting premiums to risks, in order to give a stimulus for avoidance of danger, as in the case of industrial accident and disease. There is no longer an admitted claim of the individual citizen to share in national insurance and yet to stand outside it, keeping the advantage of his individual lower risk whether of unemployment or of disease or accident.

PROVISIONAL RATES OF BENEFIT AND CONTRIBUTION

27. Social insurance should aim at guaranteeing the minimum income needed for subsistence. What the actual rates of benefit and contribution should be in terms of money cannot be settled now, and that for two reasons. First, it is impossible today to forecast with assurance the level of prices after the war. Second, determination of what is required for reasonable human subsistence is to some extent a matter of judgment ; estimates on this point change with time, and generally, in a progressive community, change upwards. The procedure adopted to deal with this problem has been : first, from consideration of subsistence needs, as given by impartial expert authorities, to determine the weekly incomes which would have been sufficient for subsistence in normal cases at prices ruling in 1938 ; second, to derive from these the rates appropriate to a cost of living about 25% above that of 1938. These rates of benefit, pension and grant are set out in para. 401 as provisional post-war rates ; by reference to them it is possible to set forth simply what appears to be the most appropriate relation between different benefits and what would be the cost of each benefit and of all benefits together ; it is possible to show benefits in relation to contributions and taxation. But the provisional rates themselves are not essential. If the value of money when the scheme comes into operation differs materially from the assumptions on which the provisional rates are based, the rates could be changed without affecting the scheme in any important particular. If social policy should demand benefits on a higher scale than subsistence, the whole level of benefit and contribution rates could be raised without affecting the structure of the scheme. If social policy or financial stringency should dictate benefits on a lower scale, benefits and contributions could be lowered, though not perhaps so readily or without some adjustments within the scheme.

28. The most important of the provisional rates is the rate of 40/– a week for a man and wife in unemployment and disability and after the transition period as retirement pension, in addition to allowances for children at an average of 8/– per head per week. These amounts represent a large addition to existing benefits. They will mean that in unemployment and disability a man and wife, if she is not working, with two children, will receive 56/– a week without means test so long as unemployment or disability lasts, as compared with the 33/– in unemployment and the 15/– or 7/6 in sickness, with additional benefit in some Approved Societies, which they were getting before the war. For married women gainfully occupied, there will be a maternity benefit at the rate of 36/– a week for 13 weeks, in addition to the maternity grant of £4 available for all married women. Other rates, as for widowhood and for industrial disability, show similar increases, as set out in detail in para. 284, in dealing with the Social Security Budget. There will be new benefits for funerals, marriage and other needs, as well as comprehensive medical treatment, both domiciliary and institutional, for all citizens and their dependants which, subject to further enquiry suggested in para. 437, will be without a charge on treatment at any point. At these provisional rates, the total Security Budget, including children's allowances and free health and rehabilitation services, is estimated to amount to £697,000,000 in 1945 as the first year of the plan, and £858,000,000 twenty years after, in 1965. The extent to which these sums represent new expenditure which is not now being incurred and the division of the total cost between insured persons, their employers and the Exchequer are discussed in Part IV of the Report and provisional rates of contribution are suggested in para. 403. The most important of these is the contribution of 4/3 a week by an adult man in employment and 3/3 a week from his employer. At this rate, with corresponding rates for other classes, the contribution of insured employees in

Class I for cash benefits, when the plan, including contributory pensions, is in full operation, is estimated to amount to about 25 per cent. of the cost of their cash benefits exclusive of allowances for children ; the balance will be provided by the employers' contributions and by taxation based on capacity to pay. At the outset, the contributions of insured persons will represent a larger proportion of the total cost ; the net addition to the burden on the National Exchequer in the first year, as compared with expenditure under the existing arrangements, will be about £86,000,000.

29. The attempt to fix rates of insurance benefit and pension on a scientific basis with regard to subsistence needs has brought to notice a serious difficulty in doing so in the conditions of modern Britain. This is the problem of rent discussed in paras. 197–216. In this as in other respects, the framing of a satisfactory scheme of social security depends on the solution of other problems of economic and social organisation. But subject to unavoidable difficulties in giving a numerical value to the conception of a subsistence minimum, the scheme of social insurance outlined in this Report provides insurance benefit adequate to all normal needs, in duration and in amount. It is at the same time a scheme from which the anomalies and overlapping, the multiplicity of agencies and the needless administrative cost which mark the British Social Services today, have been removed and have been replaced by co-ordination, simplicity and economy.

Unified Social Security and the Changes Involved

30. The advantages of unified social security are great and unquestionable. They can be obtained only at the cost of changes in the present administrative machinery whose necessity needs to be proved and can be proved case by case. The principal changes from present practice that are involved in the plan are set out below. The reasons for each of these changes are given in Part II ; in one or two cases they are set out there only briefly, in anticipation of fuller discussion.

1. Unification of social insurance in respect of contributions, that is to say, enabling each insured person to obtain all benefits by a single weekly contribution on a single document (paras. 41–43).

2. Unification of social insurance and assistance in respect of administration in a Ministry of Social Security with local Security Offices within reach of all insured persons (paras. 44–47).

3. Supersession of the present system of Approved Societies giving unequal benefits for equal compulsory contributions [combined with retention of Friendly Societies and Trade Unions giving sickness benefit as responsible agents for the administration of State benefit as well as voluntary benefit for their members] (paras. 48–76).

4. Supersession of the present scheme of workmen's compensation and inclusion of provision for industrial accident or disease within the unified social insurance scheme, subject to (a) a special method of meeting the cost of this provision, and (b) special pensions for prolonged disability and grants to dependants in cases of death due to such causes (paras. 77–105).

5. Separation of medical treatment from the administration of cash benefits and the setting up of a comprehensive medical service for every citizen, covering all treatment and every form of disability under the supervision of the Health Departments (para. 106).

6. Recognition of housewives as a distinct insurance class of occupied persons with benefits adjusted to their special needs, including (a) in all cases [marriage grant], maternity grant, widowhood and separation

provisions and retirement pensions ; (*b*) if not gainfully occupied, benefit during husband's unemployment or disability ; (*c*) if gainfully occupied, special maternity benefit in addition to grant, and lower unemployment and disability benefits, accompanied by abolition of the Anomalies Regulations for Married Women (paras. 107–117).

7. Extension of insurance against prolonged disability to all persons gainfully occupied and of insurance for retirement pensions to all persons of working age, whether gainfully occupied or not (paras. 118–121).

8. Provision of training benefit to facilitate change to new occupations of all persons who lose their former livelihood, whether paid or unpaid (para. 122).

9. Assimilation of benefit and pension rates for unemployment, disability other than prolonged disability due to industrial accident or disease, and retirement (para. 123).

10. Assimilation of benefit conditions for unemployment and disability, including disability due to industrial accident or disease, in respect of waiting time (paras. 124–126).

11. Assimilation of contribution conditions for unemployment and disability benefit, except where disability is due to industrial accident or disease, and revision of contribution conditions for pension (paras. 127–128).

12. Making of unemployment benefit at full rate indefinite in duration, subject to requirement of attendance at a work or training centre after a limited period of unemployment (paras. 129–132).

13. Making of disability benefit at full rate indefinite in duration, subject to imposition of special behaviour conditions (paras. 129–132).

14. Making of pensions, other than industrial, conditional on retirement from work and rising in value with each year of continued contribution after the minimum age of retirement, that is to say, after 65 for men and 60 for women (paras. 133–136).

15. Amalgamation of the special schemes of unemployment insurance, for agriculture, banking and finance and insurance, with the general scheme of social insurance (paras. 137–148).

16. Abolition of the exceptions from insurance
    (*a*) of persons in particular occupations, such as the civil service, local government service, police, nursing, railways, and other pensionable employments, and, in respect of unemployment insurance, private indoor domestic service ;
    (*b*) of persons remunerated above £420 a year in non-manual occupations (paras. 149–152).

17. Replacement of unconditional inadequate widows' pensions by provision suited to the varied needs of widows, including temporary widows' benefit at a special rate in all cases, training benefit when required and guardian benefit so long as there are dependent children (paras. 153–156).

18. Inclusion of universal funeral grant in compulsory insurance (paras. 157–160).

19. Transfer to the Ministry of Social Security of the remaining functions of Local Authorities in respect of public assistance, other than treatment and services of an institutional character (paras. 161–165).

20. Transfer to the Ministry of Social Security of responsibility for the maintenance of blind persons and the framing of a new scheme for maintenance and welfare by co-operation between the Ministry, Local Authorities and voluntary agencies (paras. 166–170).

21. Transfer to the Ministry of Social Security of the functions of the Assistance Board, of the work of the Customs and Excise Department in respect of non-contributory pensions, and probably of the employment service of the Ministry of Labour and National Service, in addition to unemployment insurance, and the work of other departments in connection with the administration of cash benefits of all kinds, including workmen's compensation (paras. 171–175).

22. Substitution for the Unemployment Insurance Statutory Committee of a Social Insurance Statutory Committee with similar but extended powers (paras. 176–180).

[**23.** Conversion of the business of industrial assurance into a public service under an Industrial Assurance Board.] (paras. 181–192).

31. This considerable list of changes does not mean that, in the proposals of the Report, either the experience or the achievements of the past are forgotten. What is proposed today for unified social security springs out of what has been accomplished in building up security piece by piece. It retains the contributory principle of sharing the cost of security between three parties —the insured person himself, his employer, if he has an employer, and the State. It retains and extends the principle that compulsory insurance should provide a flat rate of benefit, irrespective of earnings, in return for a flat contribution from all. It retains as the best method of contribution the system of insurance documents and insurance stamps. It builds upon the experience gained in the administration of unemployment insurance and later of unemployment assistance, of a national administration which is not centralised at Whitehall but is carried out through responsible regional and local officers, acting at all points in close co-operation with representatives of the communities which they serve. It provides for retaining on a new basis the association of Friendly Societies with national health insurance. It provides for retaining within the general framework of a unified scheme some of the special features of workmen's compensation and for converting the associations for mutual indemnity in the industries chiefly concerned into new organs of industrial co-operation and self-government. While completing the transfer from local to national government of assistance by cash payments, it retains a vital place for Local Authorities in the provision of institutions and in the organisation and maintenance of services connected with social welfare. The scheme proposed here is in some ways a revolution, but in more important ways it is a natural development from the past. It is a British revolution.

32. The Plan for Social Security is put forward as something that could be in operation in the immediate aftermath of the war. In the Memorandum by the Government Actuary on the financial aspects of the plan, which is printed as Appendix A to the Report, it is assumed, for the purpose of relating the estimates of expenditure to the numbers of the population, that the plan will begin to operate on 1st July, 1944, so that the first full year of benefit will be the calendar year 1945. But in view of the legislative and administrative work involved in bringing the plan into force, so early a date as this will be possible only if a decision of principle on the plan is taken in the near future by the Government and by Parliament.

PROCEDURE OF COMMITTEE

33. Before concluding the Introduction, it is necessary to say something as to the procedure of the Committee. They were appointed in June, 1941, held their first meeting on 8th July, 1941, and gave immediate notice of their terms of reference to the principal organisations concerned with the various insurance schemes and allied services and invited the submission of memoranda of evidence. They gave general notice through the press and in other ways of their activities. While organisations outside the Government departments should be preparing their evidence, the Committee asked the departments themselves to furnish detailed memoranda describing each of the insurance schemes and allied services as it stood today and from this constructed the survey to which reference has been made and which is set out in detail in Appendix B. The first of the interested organisations to appear before the Committee gave evidence on 26th November, 1941, and from then till the end of September, 1942, the Committee received memoranda from more than a hundred representative organisations whose names are given in Appendix C. The Minister without Portfolio (Mr. Arthur Greenwood) announced in the House of Commons on the 27th January, 1942, that " it will be within the power of the Committee to consider developments of the national insurance schemes in the way of adding death benefits or dealing with any other risks which are at present not covered by such schemes." In accord with this announcement, the Committee discussed problems affecting insurance for funeral benefit with the Industrial Life Offices which are concerned with such matters.

34. Those memoranda which appear to be of most general interest are given in Appendix G,* with any alterations made by their authors after submission ; certain other memoranda are summarised briefly. While Appendix B presents a general picture of the insurance schemes and allied services as they stand after forty years of piece-meal growth, Appendix G shows how those schemes and services and their problems are viewed by the persons outside Government departments who are most deeply concerned in their administration or interested in their results. A large number of those who presented written memoranda attended the Committee for oral examination. The minutes of these meetings will not be published as it was desired to make discussion on these occasions as informal and as informative as possible. In the case of several organisations whose interest in social insurance was of a general character the Committee have held more than one meeting with their representatives. In addition the Chairman has either individually or with particular members of the Committee directly interested in the particular aspect had many discussions with individuals and representatives of organisations. On two occasions, accompanied by members of the Committee, the Chairman held meetings in Edinburgh to hear oral evidence from Scottish organisations. Altogether the full Committee met on forty-eight occasions.

35. Social security is first and foremost an interest of the individual citizen, of the consumer of social insurance and allied services even more than of the administrator. With a view to obtaining, so far as possible, through persons engaged in forms of public and citizen service making them familiar with the working of the existing schemes, indications of the views, experiences and difficulties of the consumers of insurance, the Nuffield College Social Reconstruction Survey were invited to make an investigation of such matters and collected material for this purpose from many quarters.

36. The main problems of social security are common to all nations. In order to be sure that, in making their survey, the Committee had the benefit of the experience of other nations, so far as it could be made available in the abnormal circumstances of the time, they sought the help of the International Labour Office, which arranged for Dr. Oswald Stein, Head of the Social Insurance Section, and one of his chief assistants, Mr. Maurice Stack, to visit Britain for the purpose of conferring with the Committee. This visit was stimulating and informing in the highest degree. It is appropriate that the Committee should express in warm terms their gratitude for the help thus afforded by the International Labour Office. Some comparisons between the present British schemes, the proposals of this Report and the practice of other nations are given in Appendix F.

* Printed separately.

37. In regard to physical needs for subsistence, the Committee invited an independent Sub-Committee including Professor A. L. Bowley, Mr. Seebohm Rowntree, Mr. R. F. George and Dr. H. E. Magee to advise them. The results of this Sub-Committee's work are discussed in paras. 193–232 dealing with Benefit Rates and the Problem of Rent.

38. In regard to workmen's compensation, a Royal Commission on this subject, under the Chairmanship of Sir Hector Hetherington was appointed on 22nd December, 1938, and between February, 1939, and June, 1940, received a good deal of evidence which has been published. Some of the bodies most deeply interested, on the side of the employers, expressed their inability through pre-occupation with urgent war problems to give time to the preparation of evidence, and the Royal Commission suspended its sittings in July, 1940. Workmen's compensation, however, was expressly included in the reference to the Inter-departmental Committee, and it has been the duty of the Committee to deal with this question in their survey. The Report, with its wider reference, approaches the question from a different standpoint from that open to the Royal Commission, but taking into account both the printed evidence before the Commission and further evidence tendered to the Committee. It is recognised that, in this field particularly, there are many technical problems for which it would be premature now to suggest detailed final solutions. As to the general lines on which the results of industrial accident and disease should be treated in future, the Report is clear.

39. There will, it may be hoped, come a season when it is profitable to consider the practical relations of social insurance in Britain and of schemes for the same purpose in the Dominions, in the Colonies and in other countries of the world. On the assumption that once again it will be possible for men to move from one country to another to find the best use for their powers, it will be desirable to consider the making of reciprocal arrangements between the schemes of different countries facilitating transfer from one to the other, that is to say, arrangements enabling men on migration to avoid forfeiting security and allowing them to carry with them some of the rights that they have acquired in their former country. That should, in due course, become a practical problem. It is not possible today to do more then mention the problem to show that it has not been forgotten.

SIGNATURE OF REPORT

40. The Report is made by the Chairman alone. This calls for explanation and can be explained briefly. All the members of the Committee other than the Chairman are civil servants. Many of the matters dealt with in the Report raise questions of policy, on which it would be inappropriate for any civil servant to express an opinion except on behalf of the Minister to whom he is responsible ; some of these matters are so important as to call for decision by the Government as a whole. When the nature of the issues that would be raised before the Committee became apparent, the following letters were exchanged between the Minister without Portfolio who had appointed the Committee and the Chairman of the Committee.

27th January, 1942.

" My dear Beveridge,

" I have discussed with the Chancellor of the Exchequer the position of the departmental representatives on the Inter-departmental Committee on Social Insurance and Allied Services. In view of the issues of high policy which will arise, we think that the departmental representatives should henceforward be regarded as your advisers and assessors on the various technical and administrative matters with which they are severally concerned. This means that the Report, when made, will be your own report ; it will be signed by you alone, and the departmental representatives will not be associated in any way with the views and recommendations on questions of policy which it contains. It would be well that the Report should contain words to make it clear that this is the position.

Yours sincerely,
(Signed) ARTHUR GREENWOOD."

28th January, 1942.

" My dear Greenwood,

" Many thanks for your letter as to the work of the Committee on Social Insurance and Allied Services and the position of departmental representatives thereon. I had already communicated the substance of what you write to the Committee at their last meeting and will now circulate your letter.

" Needless to say I entirely accept the view taken by the Chancellor of the Exchequer and yourself. I believe that in this way the departmental representatives will be even more useful than if they had to sign the Report and I shall encourage them within the Committee itself to express their views with complete frankness to me so that whatever I may say I shall say after getting the best possible advice.

Yours sincerely,

(Signed)   W. H. BEVERIDGE."

In accord with the last sentence of the Chairman's letter, the departmental representatives have given their views within the Committee and have placed at the disposal of the Chairman their expert knowledge of the problems with which the Committee was concerned. In discussion and in examination of witnesses the Committee has functioned as a Committee. Through their representatives and otherwise the various Departments have been able to express views on questions arising in the course of the enquiry, but they have done so, if at all, without associating themselves or any Minister or the Government in any way whatever with anything that is written here. For every recommendation and every word in the Report and in Appendices D, E and F the Chairman alone is responsible. The Report stands or falls on its merits and its argument, with no authority behind it except that of a sincere attempt, with expert guidance from the departments and after consideration of views presented by interested bodies, to understand the innumerable problems of social security, to balance arguments and equities, to compare desires and resources, and to devise methods of making all the immense good that has been accomplished into something better still.

PART II

THE PRINCIPAL CHANGES PROPOSED AND THEIR REASONS

Change 1.   Unification of social insurance in respect of contributions, that is to say, enabling each insured person to obtain all benefits by a single weekly contribution on a single document.

41. The advantages of this are obvious. It means having one insurance document in place of two documents a year with stamps to correspond, for each of about 20,000,000 persons. This is a saving of paper, a saving of trouble to the insured persons and a saving of administration to the employers. The administrative costs of compulsory insurance, as they are usually reckoned, are not the whole costs. They show what the Government Departments or Local Authorities or Approved Societies spend on administration. They do not show the cost to employers of affixing insurance stamps, calculating and making deductions from wages, and dealing with insurance documents. The estimate made in Appendix E suggests that the employers' costs for the administration of the present schemes of compulsory social insurance are of the order of magnitude of about £1 200 000 a year, and that unification of insurance documents or stamps would reduce this by about £400 000 a year. Neither of these amounts is large in relation to the total sums involved in social insurance but the saving is worth making. The advantages of a single contribution on a single insurance document are so clear that the only question

that can be asked is whether the advantages would be bought too dear. What other changes in the present insurance schemes are involved in unifying the contribution ? The answer is in two stages.

42. In the first place, unification of contributions does not of itself involve any change in the present practice of keeping separate the money required for different purposes—unemployment or sickness or pensions. The proceeds of the single stamp which is now affixed to the health and pensions card are divided absolutely between health insurance and pensions insurance. It will be convenient, though not absolutely necessary, for all the contributions to go into a single Social Insurance Fund. But that is consistent with having fixed proportions of the contributions earmarked by Statute for named purposes, so that they can not be spent on anything else. Completely separate accounts could be kept in the Social Insurance Fund for unemployment, for sickness, for pensions, for widows and so on, as they are kept now in the single Unemployment Fund, in respect of the general and agricultural schemes respectively. It may be doubted whether this degree of separation in the Social Insurance Fund would be desirable or in the interests of the contributors ; it might mean that the Fund simultaneously had a surplus on one account— say, unemployment—so as to be able to increase that benefit, while a prospective deficiency on pensions or on sickness was making necessary a decrease of those benefits, bringing them out of line with other benefits, or a raising of contributions. To some extent a Social Insurance Fund raised to meet the various needs of the same general body of insured persons should be a common fund, and will be the stronger for being so. But some degree of separation is necessary and any desired degree of separation can be laid down by Parliament, either by earmarking most of the single contribution for specific purposes while leaving a fraction for allocation according to circumstances, or by fixing statutory minimum rates and periods of benefit for each purpose, so that the money needed for each purpose up to that minimum has to be kept available and cannot be absorbed by deficiency on another purpose. Whatever the procedure, there is no difficulty in providing safeguards for particular benefits under a scheme with a single contribution to a single fund.

43. In the second place, unification of contributions and insurance documents is hard to reconcile with administration of sickness benefit, as at present, through numerous financially separate societies. The approved society system means that the contributions of each individual insured person for health must be associated with a particular society ; the present and most practical way of doing this is to have a document for these particular contributions which gets into the hands of the society, and is used to establish the total number of its contributions, that is to say, its share of the proceeds from sales of insurance stamps. The administrators of unemployment insurance at the same time may need an individual's contribution record to determine his claim to unemployment benefit. The administrators of pensions will need it to determine the claim to pension. It is true that at present a single contribution card is used for health and for pensions. The card finds its way to the Approved Society and the society is required to keep records and furnish information to the pension authorities showing whether the contribution conditions for pension have been fulfilled. This is practicable with the present system, under which right to pension depends on contributions made in the last five years ; the Approved Societies need not keep records covering more than that period. If, however, with the making of contributory pensions universal, the right to such pensions is made conditional on payment of contributions throughout working life (as is proposed in para. 367), it will probably prove impracticable to rely upon Approved Societies for this information ; apart from differences in the organisation and efficiency of different

societies, difficulties would arise through the fact that any individual may have changed his society. If there is to be a single insurance contribution for all purposes on a single insurance document, the document, when stamped, must be retained by the central insurance administration. In order to assign the health insurance contributions on it to a particular society, either the document itself must show to what society the insured person belongs or he must have a separate membership card of which the central insurance administration takes note. The need for such additional work, as an alternative to having more than one insurance document to be stamped for each person under the approved society system, is one of the minor arguments set out in Change 3 below in favour of changing that system.

Change 2. Unification of social insurance and assistance in respect of administration in a Ministry of Social Security with local Security Offices within reach of all insured persons.

44.　The main advantage of this change is immensely improved efficiency, in the sense of greater satisfaction to insured persons as consumers of social insurance.　In detail, this advantage may be set out under several heads :—

(a) Convenience to the insured person of having one authority to deal with, in place of being bandied about from pillar to post.

(b) Avoidance of demarcation problems, that is to say, of disputes as to which authority is responsible for dealing with a particular case and on what principles.

(c) Avoidance of overlapping and duplication of benefits.

(d) Avoidance of gaps : unified insurance can become, even if it does not start as, " all-in insurance," covering fresh needs as they are recognised, without dispute as to which authority is responsible for dealing with them.

(e) Absolute security of benefit, such as is not now guaranteed in workmen's compensation.

(f) Uniformity of benefit rates and conditions, except in so far as differentiation is justifiable by real differences of need, or other circumstances.

(g) Uniformity of procedure for determination of claims to benefit, except in so far as differences of procedure are justified.

The main ground for this proposal, as stated above, is greater efficiency in satisfying the needs of citizens ; it is obvious that there can also be economies through concentration of administrative machinery.

45.　Unification of social insurance and assistance does not mean that the citizen must obtain all benefits in the same way or from the same place. Unification of administration is entirely consistent with the citizen getting money when sick in a different way from that in which he gets money when unemployed and, normally, he will do so. He can have disability benefit or pensions taken to him or posted to him just as at present. More than that, under the proposals made in Change 3, a man who is entitled to voluntary benefit as well as State benefit for sickness will be able to continue, if he desires, to obtain these benefits just as at present through his society. Unification, again, does not exclude an extension of such arrangements and the use of special schemes such as that now established for the insurance industry or for banking or finance to administer State benefit with their own benefit to their own members. Unification does not mean ruling out differences where differences are appropriate and in the interest of the consumer. It means avoidance of departmentalism which is of no conceivable advantage to him and often leads to his distress and confusion.

46. Unification of responsibility for administration involves the setting up of a Ministry of Social Security. This is one of the main proposals of the Report. Through this Ministry unified responsibility for administration is extended beyond social insurance to the sphere of assistance. This question is discussed further in connection with Change 21 below. That unification of departmental responsibility is in the interests of the consumer of social services is clear.

47. The obtaining of the full advantages of co-ordination is inconsistent with maintenance in its present form of the approved society system and also with maintenance of a separate scheme of compensation for industrial accident and disease. It is not inconsistent with giving to the consumers all the advantages which they now obtain from the approved society system ; it is not inconsistent with making special provision for the results of industrial accident or disease or with raising the funds required to meet the cost of this provision in part, at least, in a special way. These issues are dealt with in connection with Changes 3 and 4.

Change 3. Supersession of the present system of Approved Societies giving unequal benefits for equal compulsory contributions [combined with retention of Friendly Societies and Trade Unions giving sickness benefit as responsible agents for the administration of State benefit as well as voluntary benefit fo their members].

48. One of the most important features of the scheme of national health insurance, as established in 1911, is the administration of its cash benefits by autonomous Approved Societies, each with separate finance. In the first draft of the Bill of 1911, it was proposed that recognition as an Approved Society should be confined to Friendly Societies of a particular type, those giving sickness and other benefits for actuarial risks without division of any part of their funds on other occasions. This limitation was removed, through introduction of a proviso to Section 23 (1) of the Act of 1911, which allowed any society registered for any purpose to form a separate section as an Approved Society. Under the proviso it became possible, not only for the various types of dividing and deposit societies which would otherwise have been excluded, but also for the Industrial Life Offices, that is to say, the companies and Collecting Societies engaged in industrial assurance, to enter the field of national health insurance. Only two main conditions were imposed by Statute on all Approved Societies, namely :—

(i) that the Society should not be conducted for profit ; and
(ii) that its constitution should provide for its affairs being subject to the absolute control of its members.

Types of Approved Societies

49. The societies approved under these wide provisions are of every size and of many different types. They can be grouped under five main heads according to the kind of office or society with which they are associated, namely, Friendly Societies with branches, Friendly Societies without branches, Industrial Life Offices, Trade Unions and Employers' Provident Funds. Friendly Societies, whether with or without branches, are engaged in the main in voluntary insurance against sickness on a mutual basis. But many or most of them, in addition to sickness benefits, give benefits for death or maternity, and recently they have undertaken a growing amount of endowment and deposit insurance. The Industrial Life Offices are engaged primarily in insurance for burial expenses and other expenses connected with death, but like the Friendly Societies have developed in the direction of general life insurance and endowment insurance. The work of these Offices is examined

in more detail in Appendix D. The primary function of Trade Unions is in dealing, on behalf of their members, with employers in regard to terms and conditions of work. But a large number of them also provide insurance benefits of various kinds for unemployment, sickness, old age and other contingencies ; most, but not all, of the Trade Unions with which Approved Societies are associated have a friendly side. Employers' Provident Funds are societies consisting of persons entitled to rights under superannuation or other provident funds established for the benefit of persons employed by one or more particular employers.

50. Under each of the five heads there are great differences both of size and of method. As a whole, the Approved Societies range in membership from under 50 up to the 3,000,000 of the National Amalgamated Approved Society associated with a group of Industrial Life Offices, or the 4,000,000 of the four technically separate societies associated with the largest of these offices—the Prudential Assurance Company, Ltd. The number of Approved Societies is about 800, but some of these have branches which are separate financial units ; the total number of units which are valued separately and each of which, therefore, may give benefits differing from those of other units, is now about 6,600, a substantial reduction from the number at earlier valuations. The reduction has been most marked among the Friendly Societies with branches, from about 15,500 units in 1912, to less than 8,500 at the first valuation in 1918, and about 5,700 at the fifth valuation in 1938.* Some of these societies, while retaining separate branches for their own benefits, group the branches into larger units for administration of national health insurance, thus diminishing the number of valuations and the chance that two members of the same society in different neighbouring branches may receive different rates of national insurance benefit.

51. The Approved Societies are formed on many different bases, some with trade or local associations, but many without. Even where a society starts with a definite local association its members may move, so that any Approved Society may carry on business in any part of the country. In any moderate-sized town the insured persons are likely to be scattered among some hundreds of societies and branches, each of which has to make arrangements for administration of cash benefits to members entitled to them. The Royal Commission of 1926 obtained information as to the numbers of separate societies functioning in several typical towns, and this information has been brought up to date for the present Committee. The numbers of societies in each of those towns in 1942, with the corresponding figures from the Royal Commission Report of 1926 given in brackets, are as follows : in Liverpool 437 (488) societies had members ; in Bolton 248 (285) ; in Brighton 324 (304) ; in Norwich 241 (213) ; in Reading 361 (245) ; and in Tynemouth 181 (168).

52. The membership of a particular society in a particular town is often very small. Figures for some typical towns in 1941, with corresponding figures from the Royal Commission Report of 1926 in brackets, are as follows : in Glasgow in 1942 out of 396 (384) societies, 97 (98) had each one member only ; in Dundee, out of 219 (217) societies, 61 (52) had each one member, and another 54 (47) had each from 2 to 9 members. Almost any town would give similar results. The number and variety of administrative units functioning in each town is actually greater than is suggested by the above figures which relate to societies ; some of these societies have branches which

---

* After the first valuations at 1918 each subsequent series of valuations has been spread over several years; the quinquennial years 1923, 1928, 1933 and 1938 relate to the years at which the larger societies, comprising the bulk of the insured persons, were valued on the 2nd, 3rd, 4th and 5th occasions.

are financially separate. Though the number of financially separate branches of societies with branches is now only about a third of the original number. it still remains very large.

DISTRIBUTION OF INSURED PERSONS BY SOCIETIES

53. While in essentials the approved society system has remained the same as in 1912, there have been interesting changes in the relative importance of different types of society. In 1912, according to the not entirely adequate statistics which were compiled at the outset, the distribution of insured persons in Great Britain, according to the five principal types of Approved Society, was as follows :—

TABLE

NATIONAL HEALTH INSURANCE—DISTRIBUTION OF INSURED PERSONS IN GREAT BRITAIN BY TYPE OF APPROVED SOCIETY IN 1912

TYPE OF SOCIETY	Men		Women	
	Numbers (in 000's)	Percentage Distribution	Numbers (in 000's)	Percentage Distribution
Industrial Life Offices	2,971	34·1	2,172	59·1
Friendly Societies without branches ...	2,178	25·0	648	17·6
Friendly Societies with branches ...	2,348	27·0	587	15·9
Trade Unions	1,159	13·3	259	7·0
Employers' Provident Funds	53	0·6	15	0·4
TOTAL	8,709	100·0	3,681	100·0

54. The more precise statistics for later years, compiled in connection with the several valuations of Approved Societies, are not exactly comparable with those given above. The differences, e.g., the inclusion of Northern Ireland membership in the valuation statistics, affect particularly the actual numbers ; the percentage distributions may be regarded as broadly comparable. The following statement gives the numbers and percentage distributions for the second valuation (corresponding to the year 1923) and the fifth valuation (corresponding to 1938) :—

TABLE II

NATIONAL HEALTH INSURANCE—DISTRIBUTION OF INSURED PERSONS IN GREAT BRITAIN AND NORTHERN IRELAND BY TYPE OF APPROVED SOCIETY IN 1923 AND 1938

TYPE OF SOCIETY	Men				Women			
	Numbers (in 000's)		Percentage Distribution		Numbers (in 000's)		Percentage Distribution	
	1923	1938	1923	1938	1923	1938	1923	1938
Industrial Life Offices ...	3,810	5,120	37·7	42·5	3,060	3,350	59·9	54·7
Friendly Societies without branches	2,540	3,470	25·2	28·8	1,010	1,670	19·9	27·3
Friendly Societies with branches	2,390	2,230	23·7	18·5	760	770	14·8	12·7
Trade Unions	1,270	1,190	12·6	9·8	240	290	4·8	4·7
Employers' Provident Funds	80	50	0·8	0·4	30	30	0·6	0·6
TOTAL ...	10,090	12,060	100·0	100·0	5,100	6,110	100·0	100·0

These figures show a steady increase both in the number and in the proportion of insured men covered by the Industrial Life Offices and by the Friendly Societies without branches. In the case of women, however, the Industrial Life Offices have a declining proportion of the whole (though their women's membership has actually increased), whereas the Friendly Societies without branches have substantially increased their proportion of the female insured population. Taking men and women together, the Industrial Life Offices had nearly 42 per cent. of the total membership in 1912, and had nearly 47 per cent. in 1938 ; the Friendly Societies without branches had 22 per cent. of the membership in 1912 and had more than 28 per cent. in 1938. Taking these two types of centralised societies together, they accounted for about 64 per cent. of the total men's and women's membership in 1912, nearly 69 per cent. in 1923 and practically 75 per cent. in 1938. The two other principal types—Friendly Societies with branches and Trade Unions—each have a steadily declining proportion of the whole membership. They accounted for 35·2 per cent. of the insured population in 1912, 30·7 per cent. in 1923, and only 24·6 per cent. in 1938. It seems safe to say that of the total increase in the insured membership in Britain between 1912 and 1938 (probably about 5,400,000), practically the whole has taken place in the Approved Societies associated with Industrial Life Offices or with the Friendly Societies without branches. The other three groups—Friendly Societies with branches, Trade Unions and Employers' Provident Funds—have been retrograde or stationary.

55. Looking at the position in 1938, and taking men and women together, of the 18,170,000 insured persons who were members of Approved Societies, 8,470,000 or 46·6 per cent. were in Approved Societies associated with Industrial Life Offices ; 5,140,000 or 28·3 per cent. in Friendly Societies without branches ; 3,000,000 or 16·5 per cent. in Friendly Societies with branches ; 1,480,000 or 8·1 per cent. in Trade Union societies ; and 80,000 in Employers' Provident Funds.

ADDITIONAL BENEFITS

56. The essence of the approved society system is financial responsibility ; each society can realise a surplus or a deficiency for its members out of the administration of the contributions collected compulsorily from them. After each quinquennial valuation, surpluses, after retention of suitable reserves, are distributed in additional benefits. A deficiency means that the society can give no additional benefits ; deficiencies are in practice made up from a central pool reserved for that purpose from the contributions. The finance of the national health insurance scheme has been such as to yield surpluses in societies covering a large proportion of the whole insured population. At the fifth valuation, relating approximately to 1938, additional benefits were made available in societies with about 88 per cent. of all insured men and 81 per cent. of all the insured women ; that is to say, only 12 per cent. of the men and 19 per cent. of the women had no more than the statutory benefits.

57. The surpluses were very substantial in amount, as well as in the numbers covered. The annual allocation in schemes adopted on the fifth valuation amounted to £5,850,000 as compared with a total expenditure on benefit of all kinds, including additional benefits, of about £35,000 000. The distribution of this total of £5,850,000 between different purposes is shown in the following table :—

TABLE III

NATIONAL HEALTH INSURANCE—ANNUAL ALLOCATIONS FOR ADDITIONAL BENEFITS
(5TH VALUATION SCHEMES)

	Annual Allocation £000	Percentage of Total Allocation
Dental	2,420	41·4
Ophthalmic	630	10·8
Medical and Surgical Appliances	200	3·4
Convalescent Home Treatment	160	2·7
Hospital Treatment	90	1·5
Other Treatment	150	2·6
All Treatment Benefits	3,650	62·4
Cash Benefits	2,200	37·6
TOTAL	5,850	100·0

The cash benefits at £2,200,000 represent 37·6 per cent. of the whole allocation. Additional sickness and disablement benefits were given in societies containing 63 per cent. of all insured men, but only 28 per cent. of the spinsters and widows and 20 per cent. of the insured married women. That is to say, while rather over one-third of all the insured men got no more than the statutory sickness and disablement benefit, three-quarters of all the insured women were in the same position. The average weekly addition to sickness benefit in societies giving such an addition was 3·2s. for men and 2·2s. for women, but these averages, particularly for men, ·cover great differences in the actual addition. The additional sickness benefit ranged from 1/– a week to as much as 15/– a week, though this last is an abnormal figure applying only to a few hundred persons ; less than 3 per cent. of the men and practically none of the women received an increase of more than 5/– a week.

58. Of the £2,200,000 allotted to additional cash benefits about £250,000 was for maternity and practically the whole of the rest was for sickness or disablement. Of the money allocated to treatment benefits an overwhelmingly large proportion, more than four-fifths, was devoted to dental and ophthalmic benefit. Most of the remaining one-fifth of the money for treatment benefits was devoted to the provision of medical and surgical appliances, convalescent homes and hospital treatment.

VIEWS OF ROYAL COMMISSION OF 1924–26

59. The approved society system was examined at some length by the Royal Commission of 1924–26. The majority of the Commission, after considering a variety of criticisms, concluded that the Approved Societies should be retained as· an essential part of the health insurance scheme and submitted a recommendation to that effect. They added that " it must be clearly understood that our recommendation is made in relation to the scheme of National Health Insurance as it exists at present, and that our view in favour of the retention of Approved Societies does not necessarily imply that developments in the system of social insurance outside the range of present contemplation might 'not necessitate a reconsideration of the position."* The Minority of the Commission took the opposite view. They held " that it is undesirable to retain Approved Societies any longer as the agencies through which benefits paid in cash are distributed to insured persons " and recommended " that Local Authorities could and should take the place of Approved Societies as the

---

* Royal Commission on National Health Insurance, 1926. Majority Report, para. 223.

Authorities through whom sickness and disablement benefits should be administered."*

60. Today the question comes up once more at a time when, in the words of the Majority of the Commission of 1924–26, developments in the system of social insurance then outside the range of contemplation are in view. The case for reconsideration is clear. Reconsideration leads to the conclusion that the approved society system in its present form has served its purpose and had its day. Without belittling in any way the services rendered by all kinds of societies in the launching of health insurance, it is possible to decide that the time has come to make health insurance national. The reasons leading to this conclusion may be summed up under two heads : first, that the approved society system is inconsistent with the policy of a national minimum ; second, that the approved society system has disadvantages for insured persons and involves unnecessary administrative costs, while the compensating advantages which it may provide for such persons can be obtained in other ways.

APPROVED SOCIETY SYSTEM INCONSISTENT WITH THE POLICY OF A NATIONAL MINIMUM

61. If the Approved Societies are to have responsibility for administering cash benefits for sickness and disablement, they must be independent financially and have the possibility of giving or withholding according to their financial results, additional benefits, which must both be so valuable that it is right to spend upon them money collected compulsorily and at the same time not so important that they ought to be available for every insured person. These additional benefits must either be cash benefits or treatment benefits.

62. As regards cash benefits, with two exceptions, all the organisations directly concerned in the administration of national health insurance which gave evidence to the present Committee, including the National Conference of Friendly Societies, the National Conference of Industrial Assurance Approved Societies, the Prudential Assurance Company Limited, the Trade Union Approved Societies, the Association of Approved Societies, and the National Union of Holloway Friendly Societies, agreed in recommending that Approved Societies should no longer have power to add to the statutory sickness and disablement benefits ; the societies represented by these organisations include over 90 per cent. of the 18,000,000 members of Approved Societies. The only organisations which gave evidence in a contrary sense were the National Federation of Employees' Approved Societies, representing about 300,000 insured persons, and the National Federation of Rural Approved Societies, representing about 400,000 insured persons. This nearly unanimous agreement of the various groups of Approved Societies for the abolition of the principal additional cash benefits is clearly in accord with the general sentiment of insured persons and the development of social policy. It is felt to be inequitable that for uniform contributions under a national scheme different rates of cash benefit should emerge. If the State provides a minimum statutory benefit based upon assumed subsistence needs, it is felt to be anomalous that from contributions collected for these purposes particular groups should be able to secure benefits above that minimum. As regards treatment, to provide any form of treatment as an additional, rather than as a statutory benefit, means that it is given selectively, w th reference not to the degree to which it is wanted but according to valuation results. An overwhelmingly large proportion of the valuation surpluses devoted to treatment benefits in the past has been allocated for the provision of dental and ophthalmic treatment, showing a need for these services which led all the

* Royal Commission on National Health Insurance, 1926. Minority Report, paras. 3 and 7.

associations of Approved Societies which gave evidence to the present Committee to recommend that these particular forms of treatment should be made available for all insured persons.

63. The representatives of the principal groups of Approved Societies who urged the retention of their financial autonomy and separate valuation, combined with standardisation of all the benefits on which any substantial sums had been spent hitherto, were asked to suggest how they proposed that valuation surpluses should be distributed in future. The principal suggestions made were that surpluses could be used :—

(*a*) to give additional cash benefits other than for sickness and disablement, such as for maternity, paying for waiting time and making grants for relief of distress ;

(*b*) to provide medical treatment for rheumatism, or provide surgical appliances, convalescent homes or nursing services.

It is unlikely that all these suggestions together would make it possible to dispose with advantage of anything like the surplus which would be realised by some societies, if the present system were retained. Most of the organisations representative of Approved Societies which gave evidence to the Committee recognised that their proposals for standardising the principal cash benefits and for making statutory the principal treatment benefits involved further pooling of surpluses between societies. Eighty-five per cent. of the very substantial annual sum (about £5,850,000) allocated for additional benefits on the last valuation was devoted to the provision of benefits—sickness, disablement, dental and ophthalmic—which in the opinion of practically every one who gave evidence to the Committee ought now to be made statutory and universal. With the raising of the rates of contribution to provide the subsistence minimum in all cases, the surpluses of the more fortunate societies will be increased proportionately. But, apart from this practical difficulty of finding a means of disposing of surpluses which must remain large in total if they are to give an adequate motive for economical administration, the more serious objection of principle remains. Why should treatment for rheumatism, why should surgical appliances, convalescent homes and nurses be reserved for those classes of the community which are already the most healthy, and denied to others, by the results of a valuation surplus ? Why, if adequate maternity grants are important, should they be given selectively ? If the State, as a general principle, lays down one provision as to waiting time, why should that be modified for a particular group of individuals ? Once it is accepted that prolongation of illness means need for at least as much income, and not for less income, than at the beginning of illness, a policy of enabling persons with low risks of illness to get for their shorter periods of illness higher cash benefits or better treatment than those with less favourable sickness experience, becomes indefensible in a national insurance scheme.

DISADVANTAGES TO INSURED PERSONS OF APPROVED SOCIETY SYSTEM

64. Apart from inequality of benefits, the approved society system has five principal disadvantages for insured persons :—

(1) The Approved Societies are of every size and sort. Insured persons are continually liable to change their place of work and residence. Unless, therefore, an insured person belongs to one of the larger societies with agencies everywhere, he has no assurance of any persona treatment or contact, if he has to move his residence.

(2) Maintenance of the approved society system, involving separation of responsibility for ordinary sickness from responsibility for industrial accident and disease or for unemployment, involves, by consequence,

maintenance of the conflict of interests between different administrative authorities, each rightly endeavouring to reduce charges on its own fund, and referring any doubtful claims to some other agency.

(3) Maintenance of the approved society system involves maintenance of different procedures for determination of claims, different and often not well-known routine as to appeals, and different principles of decision.

(4) The approved society system, as explained in para. 43, requires either the keeping of separate contribution cards for health and unemployment insurance or special machinery for assigning health contributions to particular societies. Whichever method is adopted, there must be a separate valuation every five years of each of the financial units, now numbering about 6,600. Whether through duplication of insurance documents or through the setting up of alternative machinery, additional cost and trouble to all parties is involved, not for the purpose of enabling insured persons to pay for additional insurance, but in order to enable particular groups of such persons to obtain larger or smaller shares of a fund to which all alike have contributed compulsorily.

(5) No organised disinterested information is available to guide insured persons in the choice of an Approved Society, and no such information could be provided by any official or semi-official body, since this would mean favouring some societies and appearing to criticise others. Officially, all the societies must be allowed to compete for members on equal terms, and the insured persons must make their choice—which may affect their benefits very substantially over long periods of time—without systematic guidance or any easy means of comparing different societies.

65. Some of these disadvantages have become apparent only in the course of time. If they had all been realised in 1911, it might still have seemed worth while to adopt the approved society system at the launching of national health insurance. The system made it possible to build State insurance upon the foundations of voluntary insurance, and brought to the service of the community in a wider field the experience and the organisation of the great friendly society movement. There was no suggestion, at that time, that State insurance of itself should give benefits up to subsistence level, that is to say, there was no policy of a national minimum ; the benefit provided when the approved society system began was 10/– a week for men and 7/6 a week for women for 26 weeks of sickness, and 5/– a week thereafter.

NEW BASIS FOR CO-OPERATION BETWEEN STATE AND FRIENDLY SOCIETIES

66. Today, views on social policy differ in two respects from those accepted in 1911. There is wide-spread acceptance of a principle of a national minimum. There is growing support for the principle discussed in paras. 24–26 that in compulsory insurance all men should stand in together on equal terms, that no individual should be entitled to claim better terms because he is healthier or in more regular employment. With both these principles the approved society system, in its present form, is in irreconcilable conflict. If the combination of State insurance and voluntary insurance against sickness which was the corner-stone of the plan of 1911 is to be retained, it must be on a different basis. The attempt to find such a basis is well worth making for several reasons. As against the disadvantages named above, it can be claimed that two advantages are secured by the approved society system to the insured person. First, if in addition to the benefits of compulsory insurance he wishes to increase his provision against sickness by voluntary insurance through a society giving sickness benefit, it is possible for him now to obtain both the compulsory and the voluntary benefit through the same source. Second, combination of

compulsory health insurance with voluntary insurance for other purposes, such as sickness benefit through a Friendly Society or Trade Union or funeral expenses through an Industrial Life Office, may make it possible for the combined insurance to be administered at lower cost than if each was dealt with by a separate organisation ; there is here a possible saving to set against the additional administrative cost of the approved society system.

67. Each of these possibilities is a real advantage secured today under the approved society system, though neither is of first-rate importance, or comparable to the disadvantages. If both had to be sacrificed in making national health insurance truly national, the gain would outweigh the loss. But no such sacrifice is necessary. The first advantage, of enabling insured persons to obtain State and voluntary sickness benefit through the same agency, can be retained completely, and the second advantage, of possible administrative economy through combination of services, can be retained wholly or in large measure, without maintaining Approved Societies as separate financial units giving unequal benefits in compulsory insurance. The purpose in view in giving each Approved Society its separate finance is to give it an interest in the results of its management. This is a necessary purpose ; it would be impossible to entrust the administration of national sickness benefit to independent bodies under arrangements which did not make them feel direct responsibility for careful administration. But in the case of societies giving voluntary sickness benefit from their own funds in addition to benefits provided by compulsory insurance, it is possible to give a motive for care in administration in another way than that adopted in 1911. This other way depends on requiring the societies to expend money from their own funds in some reasonable proportion to the money which they pay as State benefit on behalf of the Social Insurance Fund.

68. This leads to a proposal that the Department concerned with social insurance—that is to say, the Ministry of Social Security—should be prepared to make arrangements with societies fulfilling certain conditions, under which these societies could act as responsible agents for the administration of disability benefit to their members. The conditions to be fulfilled by any society desiring to make an arrangement would include the following :—

(a) That it gave a substantial disability benefit from its own resources, i.e. from the voluntary contributions of its members.

(b) That it had an efficient system for sick visiting its members wherever they might be.

(c) That it was effectively self-governing.

(d) That it did not work for profit and was not associated with any body working for profit.

(e) That it was registered under the Friendly Societies Acts or the Trade Union Acts or if not registered that it conformed substantially to the requirements for registration.

How closely payment of State benefit would have to be associated with payment of voluntary benefit is a matter for further consideration. It does not seem necessary to require that for each individual payment of State benefit there should be a simultaneous payment of voluntary benefit ; some general condition relating the expenditures on the two purposes should be sufficient to give the society a motive for careful administration of State benefit, and to make it possible to trust it as a responsible agent, taking decisions in individual cases, subject only to general supervision. It would no doubt be necessary for the Ministry of Social Security, before making arrangements, to be satisfied that the voluntary side of any society desiring to administer State benefit had an adequate financial basis ; the prestige of being recognised as agent for the national scheme should not be used to attract voluntary contributions to an unsound society. But no question on this would be likely to arise in regard to most of the societies which might contemplate making arrangements.

69   By arrangements on the lines suggested above, even if the approved society system as such is ended, a responsible function in the administration of social security benefits can remain for societies which give sickness benefit of their own.   This would secure the first of the advantages claimed above for the approved society system, and, would secure the second advantage also so far as the members of these societies are concerned.   Most of these members would not notice any difference between the present system and what is now proposed, except in higher benefits.   The proposal has other objects even more important.   One is to enlist the help of the Friendly Societies in ensuring that individual problems are handled with local knowledge and that the general welfare of sick persons, as well as provision of cash benefits, receives adequate consideration.   The second object is that of encouraging voluntary insurance to supplement the subsistence benefits provided by compulsory insurance.   With this in view, it might well be provided that societies making arrangements as proposed, should be allowed to recruit juvenile members for State benefits only, with a view to their subscribing for voluntary benefits on becoming adults.

The Problem of Industrial Life Offices

70.   Arrangements on these lines could be made with Friendly Societies and with Trade Unions giving friendly benefits. They could not be made with bodies like the industrial assurance companies and collecting societies, in which the administration of health insurance is now associated, not with the payment of voluntary sickness benefits, but with industrial assurance, that is to say, life assurance through collectors. It is not easy, indeed, to see how supersession of Approved Societies as separate financial units, with a view to standardisation of adequate benefits both of cash and of treatment, can be combined with giving to the Industrial Life Offices in their present form any continuing association with the administration of health insurance. To say this is not to belittle the service rendered by these offices in the past, in providing efficiently and on reasonable terms the machinery of health insurance for the large numbers of insured persons who were not members of Friendly Societies ; this service was acknowledged in emphatic and generous terms by the originator of national health insurance in 1933. But this service to national health insurance is directly associated with the purpose of securing customers for industrial assurance, and has undoubtedly been of great advantage to the Industrial Life Offices in the extension of their business. Whether or not this association of social insurance with private business was necessary or desirable in the past, there can be no justification for continuing it in the future, under a system of uniform adequate benefits for disability. It is impossible to contemplate an arrangement under which bodies working for private profit were allowed to act as agents of the Social Insurance Fund at the risk of the Fund, and to use this agency as a means of extending their business ; on these terms the Industrial Life Offices, so far from having any motive for careful administration of disability benefit, would have a direct economic motive to be liberal with the money of the Social Insurance Fund, in order to obtain or retain customers for industrial assurance and to increase the profits of their shareholders or the pay of their staff. The third and fourth of the conditions suggested above for societies desiring to make agency arrangements are fundamental.

71. If the facts of the situation are faced, it becomes clear that for the future of national health insurance there are three possibilities alone : (i) to keep the approved society system with substantial inequalities of benefit and therefore with substantial inadequacy of benefit, either of cash or of treatment, for those who are not fortunate in their society ; (ii) to break the association established in 1911 between national health insurance and industrial assurance, extending now to nearly half the insured population ; (iii) to convert industrial assurance itself from a competitive business into a public service. The first possibility should by now be regarded as excluded by argument and evidence. The choice between the second and third possibilities depends upon many considerations, some of which are unconnected with health insurance ; they are discussed in Change **23** below and in Appendix D, and reasons, both of public policy and of administrative convenience, are given for preferring the third. Not the least of the reasons is that this third course, more fully than any other course, would make it possible to retain for the service of insured persons the organising ability and the experience of the staff of all grades who now serve the Industrial Life Offices.

72. As is shown above, there is no need, in ending the present approved society system, to break or even to weaken appreciably the close relation that has existed hitherto between the administration of State insurance for sickness and of voluntary insurance for the same purpose. If the reasons given for bringing the approved society system as such to an end are accepted by the Government and Parliament, it is to be hoped that those voluntary organisations with which the arrangements suggested could appropriately be made will be willing to join in them and to continue to serve the people both in voluntary and in State insurance. But these arrangements, though desirable, are not an essential part of the scheme. If it should appear to the Friendly Societies and Trade Unions that, under the new scheme of social security, they could serve their members best by confining themselves to voluntary insurance, managing their own affairs only and not those of the State as well, they would be free to take this course. In that event, in place of the suggested arrangements there would be no difficulty in organising, for these members and for all other insured persons, decentralised administration of disability benefit as part of the work of the Ministry of Social Security, taking over whatever staffs were available for this purpose from Approved Societies of every type ; there are arguments, on merits, for making sick visiting a unified national service, as it is in effect in Northern Ireland, and in associating it with nursing service. The suggestion made for arrangements with Friendly Societies and Trade Unions giving sickness benefit to replace the present system of Approved Societies, and to continue in substance under a slightly different form, the association of these organisations with State insurance, is eminently desirable. But it is not essential in the Plan for Social Security, and if for any reason it does not commend itself it can be omitted, in favour of national administration throughout of a national service. It is included, therefore, as one of the bracketed proposals of the Report.

73. In any case there is no reason for the State to enter directly or indirectly the field of voluntary insurance against sickness. Voluntary insurance to supplement compulsory insurance is an integral feature of the Plan for Social Security, and there are other fields in which direct State action may be needed for control or development of such insurance, but this particular field of voluntary insurance against sickness is covered adequately and on right principles by the Friendly Societies, with their long traditions of disinterested service and brotherly co-operation. It can be left safely in their hands.

B

VIEWS OF ORGANISATIONS GIVING EVIDENCE

74. Abolition of the present system of Approved Societies with separate finance and giving unequal benefits for compulsory uniform contributions was recommended by the great majority of the bodies that expressed views on the system to the present Committee. These bodies included the Trades Union Congress General Council, and the Scottish Trades Union Congress ; all other organisations of employees which submitted memoranda or gave evidence, such as the National Union of Railwaymen and the National Association of Local Government Officers ; the only employers' organisation which made definite recommendations on the general problems before the Committee, namely the Shipping Federation ; and the National Council of Women. The various associations of Local Authorities, including the Association of Municipal Corporations, the County Councils Association and the Association of County Councils in Scotland, recommended a comprehensive and unified scheme of social insurance and assistance and either by inference or specific reference envisaged the supersession of Approved Societies as separate financial and administrative units. Similar views were expressed by the bodies devoting themselves to the study of social problems, such as Political and Economic Planning (P.E.P.) and the Fabian Society ; the former of these argued that public administration could provide a much simpler, cheaper and more constructive type of service ; they said that for the great majority of insured workers an Approved Society is not a society at all ; it is not an association of members for mutual aid with any kind of corporate spirit or social life, but merely a complicated system of book-keeping and of officers who pay out or withhold benefits.

75. Abolition of the approved society system was accepted as necessary to a national scheme of unified insurance by two of the smaller groups of Approved Societies—namely the Association of Approved Societies and the Trades Union Approved Societies. It was opposed only by the remaining groups of societies concerned with the administration of health insurance ; these include the National Conference of Friendly Societies, the National Conference of Industrial Assurance Approved Societies, the societies associated with the Prudential Assurance Company, and the National Federation of Employees' Approved Societies. The first three of these, as stated, recommended standardisation of all the principal benefits, whether of cash or of treatment, given hitherto. On the view taken in this Report, this involves seeking some other basis than the present one—of financial autonomy and separate valuation of Approved Societies—for continuing the association of these organisations with the administration of national insurance. This basis can be found by arrangements on the lines suggested above for the Friendly Societies and Trade Unions giving sickness benefit. It can be found for the Industrial Life Offices by converting them into a public service.

76. At the introduction of national health insurance, recourse to the device of Approved Societies was natural. It made possible full utilisation in this field of the magnificent pioneer work of the Friendly Societies. By enlisting the business motive, energy and organisation of the Industrial Life Offices, it ensured that the machinery for dealing with the new masses brought into insurance for the first time, was available at once wherever there was need. But it did so at the price of including now nearly half of the insured population in Approved Societies which cannot by any stretch of the imagination be described as under the absolute control of their members and which, though making no profit—perhaps even a loss—themselves, are in effect governed by the profit motive either of the offices with which they are associated or of their agents. The advantages of direct self-government in social insurance can indeed be bought too dear ; the smaller the unit, the greater the reality

of self-government, but the greater also the disadvantages of any change of residence or employment, such as may be forced on insured persons by economic circumstances. The history of the first thirty years of national health insurance, while it preserves many instances of lively democratic self-help in small societies connected with particular places or trades, shows also an unmistakable general tendency towards larger units of administration. The evidence given to the present Committee presents an overwhelming consensus of public opinion that equal contributions to a national scheme of insurance should lead to equal rates of adequate benefit. Experience and evidence together point the way to making a single Approved Society for the nation. Examination shows that this can be done without losing any of the main advantages of the system of today or breaking the fruitful association between the State and the Friendly Societies that began in 1912.

Change 4. Supersession of the present scheme of workmen's compensation and inclusion of provision for industrial accident or disease within the unified social insurance scheme, subject to (a) a special method of meeting the cost of this provision, and (b) special pensions for prolonged disability and grants to dependants in cases of death due to such causes.

77. The system of workmen's compensation, introduced in a limited form in 1897 and generalised in 1906, is the oldest of the varied schemes which have come under review by the Committee and differs in principle from the methods adopted for dealing with all other forms of interruption of earnings. It places upon each employer a legal liability to compensate any employee for loss of earning capacity due to accident or industrial disease arising out of and in the course of his employment, and, breaking away from the general principles of the common law, provides compensation irrespective of any direct or indirect negligence of the employer and in spite of negligence by the employee. It fixes the compensation accordingly, not on the indemnity basis applicable under the common law to cases of injury due to the fault of another, but on the principle of a division of loss between the employer and the employee, and relates the amount of the compensation, subject to a maximum, to the average earnings of the employee. The employer's liability to pay compensation is excluded only where the injury was caused by serious and wilful misconduct of the employee himself and did not result in death or serious and permanent disablement ; for everything else, including accidents over which the employer had no control, even accidents caused by the wilful misconduct of the employee himself if they result in death or serious and permanent disablement, compensation must be paid. The employer may insure himself against his liability in any way he pleases, or, except in coal mining (where compulsory insurance has been in force since 1934), he may not insure at all.

78. This system has conferred great benefits in the past. It may be claimed for it that it has enabled employees in the great majority of cases to obtain the compensation provided for them without serious difficulty and without unreasonable delay and that by preserving the connection between the employer and the injured employee, it has facilitated the return of the employee, on recovery, to his former employment. At the same time it has given employers freedom in their arrangements for insuring against their liabilities and so has enabled the large employers and employers in organised industries to cover these liabilities on economical lines ; it has enabled all employers to cover, by one and the same policy, their workmen's compensation liability and their liabilities at Common Law. By making it possible for the premiums or levies to be adjusted to ascertained risks, it has given a financial

incentive towards prevention of accidents, to the benefit of employers and employees alike. The existing scheme of workmen's compensation has conferred benefits and has certain merits. If the conclusion is reached now that that system should be superseded in a unified Plan for Social Security, this conclusion rests not on a denial of any good in the present system, but on the possibility of replacing it by a better system. Neither in this, nor in any other field should the good be allowed to be the enemy of the better.

DISADVANTAGES OF WORKMEN'S COMPENSATION SYSTEM

79. There are disadvantages in the present system of providing for the results of industrial accident and disease which could and should be eliminated by change to a new system. The disadvantages include the following :—

(i) The present system rests in the last resort upon the threat or the practice of l tigation : a misfortune which is often not in any sense the fault of the employer and which he could not have prevented, is treated by methods applicable to fault. This method imports the risk of contention between employer and employee and of legal expenses on a scale exceeding that of the other forms of social security in this country or of compensation for industrial accident or disease in other countries. The authors of the original Act contemplated that disputes would be settled by friendly and informal arbitration, but this hope has not been realised and disputes are now generally settled by formal proceedings in the Courts. In a few mining areas joint committees of employers and employees have been established for settlement of claims, but even these do not always prevent formal legal proceedings in cases where agreement is not reached.

(ii) No machinery is provided for assisting the employee in presenting his claim and, except where he has effective backing from a Trade Union, Approved Society or other association, he is apt to feel that it depends upon his own strength and vigour in pressing demands to secure a fair deal. He suspects injustice often when there is no ground for the suspicion. He feels often, rightly or wrongly, that he is being subjected to improper pressure to reduce his claim, to accept an unfair lump sum settlement, to go back to light work which is not really beneficial or for which he is not ready.

(iii) No complete security is afforded for the payment of compensation. Insurance of the employer against his liability is not compulsory except in the mining industry. No doubt, in the vast majority of cases employers are adequately insured and failure to obtain compensation either in whole or in part is a comparatively rare occurrence. But the security is less absolute than that for benefit either under health insurance or under unemployment insurance.

(iv) The system fails to secure maintenance of necessary income. The Act, subject to certain safeguards, recognises the right of employer and workman in all cases to agree to settle a claim by payment of a lump sum, and this right—which finds no counterpart in systems of most other countries—is extensively exercised, particularly in cases of permanent or prolonged disability. Divergent views have been expressed as to the advantages or otherwise of this practice, but from the point of view of social security it is impossible to justify. It is certain that in many cases, whether because the sum agreed proves insufficient for the purpose or because it is injudiciously expended by the workman or used by him to meet pressing, but temporary, needs, the lump sum fails to provide any permanent source of income. It should be added that, in the process of bargaining about a lump sum, the injured workman is discouraged from recovery or from taking any kind of work lest he should prejudice his bargain.

(v) Demarcation disputes are inevitable, if compensation for disabilities has to be provided from different funds by different authorities, according to what may often be a difficult decision as to causation.

(vi) There are differences of principle in defining dependants under workmen's compensation from that adopted for unemployment insurance or for contributory pensions.

(vii) The costs of administration are higher in relation to workmen's compensation than they need be or than they are in compulsory social insurance. The relatively high percentages of administrative costs recorded in the case of some insurance companies are not, in fact, typical of workmen's compensation as a whole, since the greater part of insurance is undertaken by mutual indemnity associations and mutual insurance companies. The information collected in Appendix E shows costs of administration for employer's liability insurance, ranging from 45 per cent. of the premiums paid to insurance companies such as those represented by the Accident Offices Association down to 7 per cent. of the premiums paid to some of the mutual indemnity associations in coal mining ; insurance through mutual companies generally appears to cost about 20 per cent. of the premiums. Even this figure is substantially higher than the administrative costs of any form of compulsory State insurance. Procedure by negotiation between the parties, followed, if no agreement is reached, by litigation is inevitably and needlessly expensive as compared with procedure for determining claims by an administrative authority subject to appeal to special tribunals. * The costs incurred by or on behalf of workmen in presenting claims are not included in the figures cited above, and are sometimes considerable.

(viii) The inclusion of certain industrial diseases, as well as accident, for purposes of compensation, while necessary in principle, makes the fixing of liability on individual employers particularly inappropriate. The onset of disease is often gradual. If a workman has been engaged by a number of employers in succession, it may be difficult or impossible to decide with any certainty in which particular employment his disease began. There is risk, moreover, that an employee showing symptoms of an industrial disease may be discharged. Difficulties are experienced also, when an employee affected by disease of a recurrent nature changes or seeks to change his employment between successive attacks.

(ix) In the 45 years of its existence, the present system of dealing with the results of industrial accident and disease has contributed little or nothing to the most important purpose of all, which should have come first, namely, restoration of the injured employee to the greatest possible degree of production and earning as soon as possible. This failure was a natural, perhaps an inevitable, consequence of the principle adopted, of fixing liability for compensation on the individual employer. The Holman Gregory Committee, who more than 20 years ago recommended that the cost of any medical and surgical aid required by injured workmen over and above the medical treatment already available under national health insurance should be provided at the cost of the employer, recognised that this could not be done with advantage, either by increasing the monetary compensation of the workmen or by placing the onus of providing treatment upon the individual employer. They held that the solution lay in an extension of medical services already available under the National Health Insurance Acts, with the proviso that the expense of the additional services should be provided by the employers. No action in the direction suggested by the Holman Gregory Committee has yet been taken and the Accident Offices Association in giving evidence to the Royal Commission on Workmen's Compensation in 1940, described rehabilitation as not being their concern, though they modified this attitude somewhat in evidence to the present Committee. A few of the indemnity associations and mutual insurance companies have recently taken systematic steps to provide medical treatment or post-medical rehabilitation, but such action is a rare exception. Failure to provide adequately for the restorative treatment of persons injured in the course of their employment is a special case of the general inadequacy of treatment in the British social services. Industrial accidents, more commonly than not, call for hospital treatment at the medical stage and after that they require, in many cases, post-medical rehabilitation. Hospital treatment is just that for which no provision worth mentioning was made under national health insurance. Post medical rehabilitation has only just begun to receive practical attention. Failure to make provision for restoration of persons injured in employment is an illustration also of the objection to splitting social insurance into separate sections. The industrially disabled are a proportion only of all casualties by accident. An investigation made for the Departmental Committee under the Chairmanship of Sir Malcolm Delevingne in 1936–39 showed that in a large sample of fractures treated in hospitals only 30 per cent. arose through industrial accidents, while 15 per cent. came through road accidents and the remaining 55 per cent. were of a miscellaneous character arising through sport, accidents in the house and in other ways. What is needed is not a special arrangement for the industrially disabled, but rather a comprehensive scheme covering all casualties, however caused. Such a proposal, however, could not arise out of the scheme of workmen's compensation as it stands today.

80. The pioneer system of social security in Britain was based on a wrong principle and has been dominated by a wrong outlook. It allows claims to be settled by bargaining between unequal parties, permits payment of socially wasteful lump sums instead of pensions in cases of serious incapacity, places the cost of medical care on the workman or charity or poor relief, and over part of the field, large in the numbers covered, though not in the proportion of the total compensation paid, it relies on expensive private insurance. There should be no hesitation in making provision for the results of industrial accident and disease in future, not by a continuance of the present system of individual employer's liability, but as one branch of a unified Plan for Social Security. If the matter were now being considered in a clear field, it might well be argued that the general principle of a flat rate of compensation for interruption of earnings adopted for all other forms of interruption, should be applied also without reserve or qualification to the results of industrial accident and disease, leaving those who felt the need for greater security, by voluntary insurance, to provide an addition to the flat subsistence guaranteed by the State. If a workman loses his leg in an accident, his needs are the same whether the accident occurred in a factory or in the street ; if he is killed, the needs of his widow and other dependants are the same, however the death occurred. Acceptance of this argument and adoption of a flat rate of compensation for disability, however caused, would avoid the anomaly of treating equal needs differently and the

administrative and legal difficulties of defining just what injuries were to be treated as arising out of and in the course of employment. Interpretation of these words has been a fruitful cause of disputes in the past ; whatever words are chosen, difficulties and anomalies are bound to arise. A complete solution is to be found only in a completely unified scheme for disability without demarcation by the cause of disability.

The Case for Special Provision for Industrial Disability

81. Nevertheless, apart from the historical ground that compensation for industrial accident and disease has been established for more than forty years upon the different principle of being related to earnings, three arguments based on merits may be advanced for distinguishing between disability arising through industrial accident or disease and other forms of disability if it appears practicable to make such a distinction. First, many industries vital to the community are also specially dangerous. It is essential that men should enter them and desirable, therefore, that they should be able to do so with the assurance of special provision against their risks. Those who in taking such risks suffer prolonged or permanent disablement or death, should have a claim to compensation relating to their earnings, not to a subsistence minimum for themselves and their families. Second, a man disabled during the course of his employment has been disabled while working under orders. This is not true generally of other accidents or of sickness. Third, only if special provision is made for the results of industrial accident and disease, irrespective of negligence, would it appear possible—as on grounds of equity and for the avoidance of controversy it is desirable—to limit the employer's liability at Common Law to the results of actions for which he is responsible morally and in fact, not simply by virtue of some principle of legal liability.

82. The first of these arguments is a strong one. If an occupation is specially hazardous it should carry special remuneration—" danger money." But to give danger money only in the form of higher wages, that is to say, only so long as no accident has occurred, is of little value ; it does not ensure that more money is available when alone it is needed, i.e., when the danger has resulted in accident. This argument standing alone would justify provision of compensation on special terms in occupations with more than an average risk of accident or disease, while leaving accident or disease in other occupations to the general provision for disability however caused. If an occupation is such that the risk of accident in the place of employment is not materially greater than the ordinary risks of the streets or home, there may appear to be no strong reason for making special provision for the former, better than that which is made for the latter.

83. But the second and third of the arguments named above, though weaker than the first argument, are not easy to disregard. Moreover, to distinguish in the provision for disability, not only by the cause but also by the occupation or industry, or by occupation and industry in combination, is to multiply distinctions where there should be as few distinctions as possible. If compensation for disability due to industrial accident or disease is to be related to earnings at all, this had better be done, irrespective of the industry or occupation in which the disabled employee was engaged.

84. The question may be asked whether, before a final decision is taken on this point, any regard should be paid to the possible relation between compensation for industrial casualties and compensation for casualties due to enemy action. Such action may affect either persons serving in the Armed Forces of the Crown, or others such as members of the mercantile marine, or civil defence services, or civilians pursuing their normal avocations. Compensation for disability incurred during armed service is related to the

service rank of the injured person, but it is not related in any way to his previous earnings in civil life. It is possible, therefore, that of two men with equal civilian earnings of whom one undertakes military service and is totally disabled, while the other, remaining in civilian employment, is similarly disabled by an industrial accident, the latter will obtain more as industrial pension than the former as war service pension. But it is equally possible that a man will obtain more as war service pension than he would have obtained if he had remained in civilian life and had suffered an industrial accident. On general grounds the scheme for social security after the war should be framed with regard to permanent peace conditions, to suit those conditions as well as possible ; it should not be distorted from what will be best in itself by consideration of the special problems and exigencies of war. This applies both to war pensions for armed service and to the other cases of compensation for enemy action that are mentioned above.

85. On balance, the reasons for distinguishing between accident and industrial disease in any employment and other causes of injury, at least where death occurs or disability is prolonged, outweigh the reasons on the other side in favour of complete uniformity. The proposal made in Part V, accordingly, is that provision for industrial accident and disease in a unified Plan for Social Security can, and should be, combined with the advantages of making discriminating provision for the results of industrial accident and disease where these lead to death or prolonged disability. All forms of short-time disability up to 13 weeks will be dealt with by cash disability benefit, that is to say, by payments at the same flat rates irrespective of earnings. On the other hand, after 13 weeks of disability, compensation will be paid on a different principle, taking account of the earnings that have been lost ; there will be industrial pensions for prolonged incapacity due to accident or disease arising out of and in the course of employment. There will be industrial grants for dependants, in addition to the general widowhood provisions, where death results from such disease or accident. This proposal does not mean that there will be no need for Security Offices to determine, so far as they can, the causes where disability lasts for less than 13 weeks. It is essential, with a view to diagnosis and prevention, that the Ministry of Social Security should record and analyse all its experience. But there will, as a rule, be no need to make a decision as to cause before giving benefit ; attribution of a case of disability to industrial accident or disease will make a practical difference in the treatment of two cases only :—

(a) If death results or disability lasts more than 13 weeks. Less than 10 per cent. of all claims to workmen's compensation now last as long as that, though the cost of compensating such cases is a much larger proportion of the whole. On the scales suggested in para. 401, it is estimated that nearly three times as much in total will be paid as pension for disability due to industrial accident or disease after the first 13 weeks as will be paid in benefit for such disability during the first 13 weeks.

(b) If the disabled person has begun work so recently as not to have paid the minimum number of contributions required to qualify for disability benefit in general (para. 366). This will affect, as a rule, only juveniles at the beginning of their industrial careers, but it must be provided for. That is to say, there will be no contribution condition where disability arises through industrial accident or disease.

Retention of compensation adjusted to earnings in cases of prolonged disability will mean that there must be machinery for assessing compensation, but this can become administrative, subject to appeal to special tribunals, in place of being legal machinery.

The Case for a Special Method of Meeting Cost of Industrial Disability

86. Provision for industrial accident and disease by workmen's compensation in Britain differs from the provision made by social insurance for other interruptions of earning, not only in the basis upon which the compensation or benefit is calculated, but also in the method by which the necessary funds are obtained. The form in which provision for industrial accidents was made when workmen's compensation began in 1897, had two consequences. First, it threw the whole cost in the first instance upon the employers ; second, it adjusted the burden in each industry to the degree of risk in that industry. This method was justified in 1897 by the Home Secretary of that time, in introducing the Workmen's Compensation Bill on the ground that " when a person on his own responsibility and for his own profit sets in motion agencies which create risks for others he ought to be responsible for what he does." This principle, enunciated when the Workmen's Compensation Act was being applied to a limited class of industrial undertakings, is clearly appropriate only to a system of individual liability and is not even verbally applicable to workmen's compensation with its present extension to a large range of employments which are not conducted for profit, including both all employments under public authorities and those of domestic and institutional service. More important than this, the principle that each industry should bear its own risks of accident, conflicts with the principle which has found growing acceptance in other fields, of pooling of risks in social insurance. This view, now dominant in regard to unemployment insurance and asserted by an overwhelming majority of general opinion in regard to health insurance, has been advanced also in regard to workmen's compensation by the Mineworkers' Federation, representing the industry in which this issue is of primary importance. Under the wage system in mining, compensation for industrial accident and disease enters into the ascertainment of costs and, therefore, affects wages whenever these are above the minimum, so that the miners may claim that the cost of the exceptionally high risk of accidents in their industry is borne by themselves. The proposals of the Mineworkers' Federation as put to the Royal Commission on Workmen's Compensation were as follows :—

> " The contributions to the fund should be payable only by the employers. The cost of maintaining the Compensation Fund should be borne equally by all the industries in the country, and the contributions should be at a fixed flat rate calculated on a weekly basis in respect of each worker employed.

> " We consider that it would be inequitable to impose the heavy burden of unequal contributions upon the industries in which the incidence of accident and disease is inevitably high. The amount in respect of each workman should be assessed so as to cover the whole of the liabilities to be provided for."*

87. This argument for pooling of social risks is in accord with the general stream of public opinion and has force. It must be realised, however, that pooling of a risk between industries makes it difficult or impossible to maintain that the cost should be borne by employers only. In so far as industries depend upon one another, both employers and employees in each industry depend upon all other industries. There is no reason why the employer of a bank clerk or of a domestic servant, rather than the clerk or the domestic servant himself, should contribute to the cost of accidents in mines and in ships. In

---

*Memorandum of Evidence by Mineworkers' Federation to the Royal Commission on Workmen's Compensation, 1939, para. 173.

so far as there is community of interest between different industries, making it fair that all industries should share equally in providing for a risk which affects them unequally, this community of interest applies to the employees as well as to the employers. It is clear also that even if the risks of sickness and unemployment are pooled completely between all insured persons, as is proposed in this Report, there is a good social reason for taking a different line, in part at least, about the dangers of industrial accident and disease. Though a high risk of accidents is inevitable in mining, shipping and some other industries, it does not follow that all accidents are inevitable ; the number and severity of accidents can be diminished or increased by greater or less care on the part of those who manage industry. It is as just and socially desirable that part of the risk of industrial accident and disease should be borne separately by the employers in each industry, on the ground that part is within their control, as it is that part of the risk should be pooled, on the ground that some accidents are inevitable.

88. In meeting the costs of industrial disability, as in respect of the form of cash benefit for the persons disabled, the right course lies in a combination of methods. In part the risks should be pooled and met by the general insurance contribution. In part they should be kept separate and placed on employers, in order to give a definite financial incentive for prevention of accident and disease. It is not necessary for this purpose that employers in each industry should bear, as at present, the whole of its particular costs, provided that they bear some of it. Nor is it necessary to give a special financial incentive for prevention of danger in all employments ; in many employments the risk of industrial accidents is less than the risk of accident outside the place of work or is almost negligible. The special charge on employers designed to stimulate prevention of accidents and disease can in practice be confined to industries in which there is need for special precautions.

89. This is the proposal made here. One part of the funds required for benefits, pensions and grants in respect of industrial accident and disease will be obtained as part of the weekly contribution paid by an insurance stamp in respect of every employee, whatever the nature of his employment. Another part will be obtained by a levy on employers in industries scheduled as having materially more than the normal risk of accident or disease in industry as a whole. This levy will be based on the wages paid and on the degree of risk and can be raised or lowered, as the risk in any such industry or in any particular place of employment is found to be above or below expectation. The levy will cover not the whole of the excess cost in the scheduled industry above the normal, but only a prescribed proportion ; if it covered the whole there would be no pooling of risks between the hazardous and the non-hazardous industries ; the former would pay their costs up to the normal by insurance contributions and beyond the normal by levy. What proportion of the excess cost above the normal in the hazardous industries should be borne by levy and what part should be pooled is a matter for argument. Provisionally, it is suggested the levy should cover two-thirds only of the excess cost, leaving one-third to be borne by the general contributions of employers and insured persons and the State to the Social Insurance Fund. This plan introduces in a defined field of scheduled industries covering the most hazardous occupations, the principle of merit rating, with the object of giving to employers a financial incentive for diminution of accidents, and to the Ministry of Social Security a basis on which to press for preventive measures.

STATUTORY ASSOCIATIONS IN SCHEDULED INDUSTRIES

90. Exactly what industries should be scheduled as hazardous in whole or in part is a matter for further detailed enquiry. It may be assumed that

six of the seven groups for which compensation statistics are now collected by the Home Office, namely, mines, quarries, docks, shipping, constructional work and railways (apart from their clerical staff), would be scheduled. Some forms of factory work, such as woodwork, metal extraction and shipbuilding, would be scheduled, while others would not. It might be found desirable also to schedule certain sections of the building industry and also of agriculture. This is a matter in which trial and experience will be the best guide.

91. The proposal made in the preceding paragraphs for an industrial levy leads also to an important suggestion as to the machinery of administration. The risks dealt with by workmen's compensation are to a marked extent risks incidental to particular industries and occupations. In all these industries, as in many others that are less hazardous, employers have provided against their individual liabilities for compensation, by forming mutual indemnity companies specially associated with those industries. Within the framework of a general scheme of social security covering disability due to industrial accident and disease as well as all other forms of disability, there is advantage in recognising the specialised character of industrial accident and disease by setting up, at least in every industry scheduled as hazardous, and, therefore, liable to the special levy proposed, a statutory association of employers and employees to deal with this problem. Such a statutory association might have the following among other functions :—

(a) Promotion of safety in the industry, in co-operation with the department or departments responsible for safety regulations by research into the causes of accidents, by propaganda and instruction, and in other ways.

(b) Promotion of measures for rehabilitation and re-employment in that industry, in co-operation with the general national organs for that purpose covering all industries.

(c) Advice on the making of all regulations affecting safety in the industry, the scheduling of industrial disease, and methods of assessment of earnings.

(d) Collecting from individual employers their quotas of the total levy required in the industry as a whole, in accordance with a scheme to be prepared by the association and approved by the Ministry of Social Security.

(e) Establishment of schemes to supplement the benefits statutorily secured to all injured employees.

92. The statutory associations should be bilateral, combining the management and the labour in each industry. In so far as they dealt with matters that might be regarded as solely the concern of the employers (such as the method of fixing the employer's quotas in individual cases) it could be provided that decision should rest with the employers' side alone ; this power would make it possible for the employers in each scheduled industry as a body, subject to approval by the Ministry of Social Security, to adopt whatever system of levy, by individual merit rating or otherwise, they thought most conducive to the prevention of accidents or disease, and the consequent reduction of the levy. The distribution of the levy, however, though one of the necessary functions of a statutory association, is not its only or its main one. The main purpose of the proposal made here is, within the framework of general social security to utilise the knowledge, the initiative and the interest of those concerned in each industry, first, in making it as safe as possible, and, second, in mitigating as far as is humanly possible the consequences of those accidents and injuries that defy prevention.

VIEWS OF ORGANISATIONS GIVING EVIDENCE

93. The Trades Union Congress General Council urged to the Royal Commission on Workmen's Compensation that workmen's compensation should become a social service separate from all the other services, with compensation related to earnings in all cases and financed by a direct levy on all employers varying with the degree of risk. This involves complete duplication in the raising of funds, not from some industries only but from every one of hundreds of thousands of employers, many with a few employees or perhaps one or two only and with hardly any risk of accidents. It involves distinguishing the cause of disability and making an immediate wage assessment, sometimes for the purpose of giving little or no greater compensation for a few days or weeks in every case of apparent industrial accident or disease, in place of doing so at leisure in about 10 per cent. of the cases. As has been stated already, one of the most important sections of workmen in this connection—the Mineworkers' Federation—while agreeing in other respects with the Trades Union Congress, opposed the suggestion of making each industry contribute according to its risks ; they urged that the cost of all accidents wherever occurring should be borne by all employers equally.

94. On the side of the employers, as on that of the employees, there were differences of opinion. Several associations of employers—in mining, shipbuilding, cotton spinning, and the iron and steel trades—urged the retention of the present system ; in each of these industries there are strong mutual indemnity associations which take the burden of workmen's compensation off the individual employer at low administrative cost. Another association of employers—the Shipping Federation—urged the complete absorption of provision for industrial accident and disease in a unified scheme of social security, with flat rates of benefit in all cases and with funds raised for all purposes by equal contributions of employers and employees and at least as much from the National Exchequer. They argued (a) that there was no justification for removing administration of workmen's compensation from employers while requiring them still to pay the whole cost, and (b) that there was no justification for making the more dangerous industries pay higher premiums on account of their special risks. Compensation, in their view, covered innumerable cases where prevention was entirely beyond the control of the employer ; prevention of accidents was a matter for factory legislation which had been developed very largely since the first Workmen's Compensation Act of 1897. In view of the divergence of opinions between employers in the different industries on the question of amalgamating workmen's compensation with the other social services, the British Employers Confederation stated to the present Committee that they were not in a position to express a Confederation view on the question. They desired, however, to make it clear that " notwithstanding this divergence of opinion, the employers in all industries are unanimous on the principle that, so long as workmen's compensation is paid for entirely by employers, the administration of that service should continue to remain in the hands of the employers."

95. In addition to all the employees' organisations and the Shipping Federation among the employers' organisations, nearly all the bodies not directly concerned with the administration of workmen's compensation who expressed an opinion to the present Committee urged that the present system, based on individual liability and litigation, should be replaced by social insurance in one form or another. This view is accepted here and leads to the proposal for supersession of the present scheme. In framing a new scheme, the Report takes a middle line between the strongly conflicting views set out above. It accepts the argument of the Mineworkers' Federation for the pooling

of the cost of industrial accident and disease. It accepts, as limiting the application of this argument, the view of the Trades Union Congress General Council that these risks should remain, in part at least, a charge on particular industries or particular employments. It recognises the value of the work done by mutual indemnity associations in the main hazardous industries and provides for a substantial measure of industrial self-government and co-operation in adjusting the unified scheme to the different circumstances of different industries. It avoids the demarcation difficulties, delays and disputes which are inevitable if industrial accident and disease are dealt with separately from all other forms of interruption of earnings. Ninety per cent. of all cases of industrial accident and disease, those causing disability for less than thirteen weeks, will be dealt with in exactly the same way as other disability, by a flat rate of benefit. For most industries the cost will be met wholly and for the other industries to some extent as part of the single security contribution. Administration both on the side of contribution and on the side of benefits will be simplified, cheapened and, so far as possible, unified. Differentiation between disability due to industrial accident or disease and other cases of disability will be maintained only where it serves an important purpose ; in respect of benefits, by making special provision for cases where earning is stopped for a long period or completely ; in respect of contributions, in those industries in which it is just and desirable to emphasise the need for precautions, by making a special charge.

96. It may be claimed that whatever the form of the new scheme, employers should continue to bear the whole cost of industrial disability in future, as they have done in the past. To this there are three objections. First, as stated above, this claim is inconsistent with the argument for pooling costs in full or in part between different industries. Second, if employers are to bear the whole cost it is hard to justify taking the administration out of their hands ; it is hard, therefore, to give to the responsible organisations of workmen the chance of taking a part, not in litigation, but in co-operative treatment of industrial disability. Third, it is undesirable that, while most forms of interruption of earnings are met by benefit to which the insured persons, with others, have contributed and out of a fund in whose stability and economical administration they are directly interested, there should be one form of interruption for which the funds are provided wholly by someone else. Such an arrangement will lead to constant pressure to push up the compensation for that particular misfortune, though it needs in reality no more than other forms of misfortune. The actual contribution involved in this question is small. The employee's share of the insurance stamp that will be required to provide for industrial disability at the higher rates now proposed is less than 1½d. a week and, as is pointed out in para. 291, it would be easy to justify the same distribution of the total contribution, even if the employer was assumed to bear the whole of industrial disability. But the claim that he should do so is today no more than a claim of historical privilege and cannot in principle be admitted.

UNIFICATION OF RESPONSIBILITY WITH DIFFERENTIATION OF TREATMENT

97. The proposals made in regard to provision for industrial accident and disease are a leading illustration of the general principle underlying the Plan for Social Security, of unification of responsibility in order to avoid needless and harmful differences, combined with classification, that is to say, with giving to each need the treatment most appropriate for that need. It is important to notice that the two main differences proposed between provision for industrial accident and disease and provision for other forms of disability are not in themselves connected. The industrial levy is designed, not to meet

the cost of industrial pensions after thirteen weeks as distinct from disability benefit during the first thirteen weeks, but to meet a proportion of the additional cost both of disability benefit and of industrial pensions in industries which are specially hazardous, over and above the average cost in other employments. Industrial pensions will be paid to employees in all industries who are disabled by an accident arising out of, and in the course of, employment, if the disability lasts beyond thirteen weeks. The industrial levy will be imposed not on all employers, but only on employers in scheduled industries.

98. If the proposal made is accepted in principle—of including provision for industrial accident and disease within the general framework of social insurance but treating it in some ways differently — several important questions will remain for discussion and settlement. These include the treatment of partial incapacity and the relation between any payment made for this and other security benefits and pensions, such as those for unemployment, disability or retirement ; the rules by which earnings should be assessed ; the treatment of special schemes and contracting out ; the methods by which grants on death through industrial accident or disease should be assessed, distributed and administered ; the definition of industrial accident and disease ; the methods of transition from the existing system to the new system and the relation between claims for security benefit and claims against the employer for negligence. The last of these questions is considered briefly in paras. 258–264 as one aspect of the problem of alternative remedies. Retention of the employer's common law liability unchanged, in spite of the development of workmen's compensation, marks a departure in Britain from the practice of other countries, where the making of provision for the results of industrial accident and disease by way of social insurance has normally been accompanied by restriction of the employer's liability to cases of wilful or gross negligence. It is obviously desirable as a matter of social policy to remove provision for the consequence of industrial hazards from the arena of litigation and conflict between the parties to production, so far as this can be done without condoning reprehensible carelessness by the employer. One of the objects of the greatly improved provision for the results of industrial accident and disease that is now proposed is to secure this, and a review of the law of employers' liability is a natural corollary of making this provision. Some of the other questions named above are dealt with in Part V. It is clear, however, that to many of these questions no final answers can be given without further enquiry, and discussion with the organisations concerned. The fitting of workmen's compensation into the general Plan for Social Security should be accepted in principle : smooth fitting will require careful adjustments of detail.

NEW SCALE OF COMPENSATION FOR INDUSTRIAL ACCIDENT AND DISEASE

99. The foregoing discussion is concerned with the methods of maintaining income when earning has been interrupted by accident or industrial disease arising out of and in the course of employment. Detailed discussion of the amount to be paid must be reserved for another section. But it is appropriate here to take note of the fact that the existing system of workmen's compensation in Britain compares unfavourably with the systems of other countries, not only in methods, but in relation between the basic rate of compensation and the earnings which have been lost. The basic rate in Britain as fixed by the original Act of 1897 and continued in the Act of 1906 was a weekly payment not exceeding half the average earnings lost subject to a maximum of 20/-. In 1923 the maximum was raised to 30/- and special provisions were introduced to allow the lower paid workers, with average weekly earnings of less than 50/-, to receive a higher proportion on a scale ranging from one-

half to three-quarters.   In 1940 the compensation was further improved by a flat rate addition of 5/- to the weekly benefit and by the provision of allowances for children under 15 years of age at the scales in force for unemployment insurance—but subject to these special provisions and additions the rule of half earnings has remained unaltered.   A higher proportion of earnings has been adopted in nearly all other countries.   In a memorandum* submitted by the International Labour Office to the Royal Commission of Workmen's Compensation the practice of other countries is summarised as follows :—

> " According to the typical practice of the European and Canadian laws, pensions are granted at the rate of two-thirds of the wage loss for permanent incapacity whether total or partial.   In particular the percentages fixed by these laws are as follows, excluding the dependant's allowances :—
>
> 66⅔ per cent. : Belgium, British Columbia, Ontario, Germany, Italy, Sweden.
>
> 70 per cent. : Netherlands, Switzerland."

A percentage of 66⅔ is also common in the American States.

100.   In the Plan for Social Security it is proposed, accordingly, that the rate of industrial pension shall be two-thirds of the earnings that have been lost subject to a maximum fixed provisionally at £3 and to a minimum of being not less than would have been received as disability benefit.   In addition to this, the injured employee will receive children's allowances for all children.

101.   The question arises whether the new rates of industrial pension should apply to the existing cases of permanent disability due to accident occurring before the beginning of the scheme, and if so from what source and by what machinery the additional payments should be made.

102.   As regards the main question, it will undoubtedly be in accord with the sentiments of the British people that the benefit of the new rates should be given to existing cases and this principle has been adopted in the past. The temporary increase provided under the Workmen's Compensation (War Addition) Acts of the last war and the increase provided in this war by the Workmen's Compensation (Supplementary Allowances) Act, 1940, were both applied to existing cases in receipt of weekly payments, liability being placed in each case on the employers responsible for the weekly payment under the principal Act.   This increase, as stated, was confined to men still in receipt of weekly payments, that is to say, there was no revision of lump sum settlements.   In accord with this precedent it is proposed that the new rates of industrial pension should apply to existing cases of prolonged disability in respect of weekly payments.   There would be no re-opening of lump sum settlements.   For accidents occurring within thirteen weeks before the beginning of the new scheme compensation would be paid under the existing law for the first thirteen weeks of disability.

103.   The subsidiary questions of the source and machinery for providing the new rates of industrial pension in existing cases of disability present several points for settlement.   In the last war and in the present war, the giving of the increases at the cost of the employer already responsible was made possible by general agreement with the employers' representatives and with the insurance companies, in view of the continuance of the existing scheme of insurance and of premiums to the companies.   If the existing scheme is being superseded, whether on the plan proposed here or on any other plan, the cost of bringing existing cases of disability up to the new

---

* Royal Commission on Workmen's Compensation, 1939: Memorandum of Evidence by the International Labour Office, paras. 114 and 117.

scales must be provided as an initial charge on the new scheme in some special way, either by the State or by a levy on employers.

104. As to machinery of payment there are two main alternatives. Liability for the present payments rests upon the employers and insurance companies or indemnity associations which have accumulated reserves of meeting their liabilities ; the alternatives are :—

(a) That the existing payment should continue to be provided as at present by the insurance companies, with the Social Insurance Fund giving the additions involved in the new scales. On this plan the Security Offices would presumably have to accept without question the assessment of the employee's earnings and the amount of compensation agreed upon between employer and the employee or determined by any legal proceedings and would have to make its supplementary payments accordingly ;

(b) That the Social Insurance Fund should take over the whole responsibility for the existing cases, making a single payment at the new scales to the employee. This would be advantageous for the employee, but would involve considerable financial and other difficulties. The Social Insurance Fund would have to take over such proportion of the reserves of insurance companies and mutual indemnity associations of the Refractories Industries and Sandstone Industry, Silicosis Compensation Funds, and of such reserves set aside by individual employers as have been earmarked for purposes of this liability. The Security Office would be required to have power to recover any deficit from the individual employer concerned.

105. The practical questions that will arise as to the treatment of existing cases of disability are difficult. They are raised here, not in order to suggest that there is no answer to them, but in order to ensure that all the problems involved in unifying social insurance and making it adequate are considered before they become actual problems, and that after examination of all aspects they receive whatever solution will yield the maximum of justice for the minimum of administrative complexity. It should be added that if there is any prospect that weekly payments will be raised to new levels and that the increase will apply to all payments in force when the scheme begins, but will not lead to revision of lump sums, the attitude of employees towards the acceptance of lump sums under the existing law is likely to be affected. The application of the new rates and conditions of benefit or pension to existing cases other than those due to industrial accident or disease, namely, unemployment, non-industrial disability, widowhood and so forth is considered in para. 353.

Change 5. Separation of medical treatment from the administration of cash benefits and setting up of a comprehensive medical service for every citizen, covering all treatment and every form of disability under the supervision of the Health Departments.

106. This is the first part of Assumption B of the Plan, namely that there will be comprehensive health and rehabilitation services for all citizens who need them. The assumption and some of the principal problems involved in realising it are discussed in Part VI, paras. 426–437.

Change 6. Recognition of housewives as a distinct insurance class of occupied persons with benefits adjusted to their special needs, including (a) in all cases marriage grant], maternity grant,

widowhood and separation provisions and retirement pensions; (b) if not gainfully occupied, benefit during husband's unemployment or disability ; (c) if gainfully occupied, special maternity benefit in addition to grant, and lower unemployment and disability benefits, accompanied by abolition of the Anomalies Regulations for Married Women.

107.   The census includes married women who do not work for money outside their homes among unoccupied persons.   The unemployment insurance scheme recognises such women as adult dependants on their husbands, in respect of whom the benefit of the husband is increased if he is unemployed. The health insurance scheme does not recognise such women at all, except at the moment of maternity.   None of these attitudes is defensible.   In any measure of social policy in which regard is had to facts, the great majority of married women must be regarded as occupied on work which is vital though unpaid, without which their husbands could not do their paid work and without which the nation could not continue.   In accord with facts, the Plan for Social Security treats married women as a special insurance class of occupied persons and treats man and wife as a team.   It makes the standard rate of benefit or pension that for a man and a wife, subject to reduction if there is no wife or if there is a wife who is also gainfully occupied.   It reserves the description of " adult dependant " for one who is dependent on an insured person but is not the wife of that person.   It treats a man's contributions as made on behalf of himself and his wife, as for a team, each of whose partners is equally essential, and it gives benefit as for the team.   It meets the costs of all the various benefits required by the special class of housewives, partly by contributions made by their husbands and partly by contributions made by men and women before and after marriage.   The nature of the benefits required depends upon consideration of the economic and social implications of marriage.

SPECIAL INSURANCE STATUS OF MARRIED WOMEN

108.   Most married women have worked at some gainful occupation before marriage ; most who have done so give up that occupation on marriage or soon after ;   all women by marriage acquire a new economic and social status, with risks and rights different from those of the unmarried.   On marriage a woman gains a legal right to maintenance by her husband as a first line of defence against risks which fall directly on the solitary woman ;   she undertakes at the same time to perform vital unpaid service and becomes exposed to new risks, including the risk that her married life may be ended prematurely by widowhood or separation.   At the last census in 1931, more than seven out of eight of all housewives, that is to say married women of working age, made marriage their sole occupation ;   less than one in eight of all housewives was also gainfully occupied.   There has been an increase in the gainful employment of married women since 1931, but the proportion so employed was probably little above one in seven just before the present war.   Moreover, even if a married woman, while living with her husband, undertakes gainful occupation, whether by employment or otherwise, she does so under conditions distinguishing her from the single woman in two ways.   First, her earning is liable to interruption by childbirth.   In the national interest it is important that the interruption by childbirth should be as complete as possible ;   the expectant mother should be under no economic pressure to continue at work as long as she can, and to return to it as soon as she can.   Second, to most married women earnings by a gainful occupation do not mean what such earnings mean to most solitary women.   Unless there are children, the housewife's earnings in general are a means, not of subsistence but of a standard of living above subsistence, like

the higher earnings of a skilled man as compared with a labourer ; the children's allowances proposed in paras. 410–425 will make this true in most cases in future, even where there are children. In sickness or unemployment the housewife does not need compensating benefits on the same scale as the solitary woman because, among other things, her home is provided for her either by her husband's earnings or benefit if his earning is interrupted. She has not as a rule as strong a motive as other earners for returning to paid work as rapidly as possible.

109. The treatment of married women under the existing insurance schemes has been unsatisfactory, largely because it has not recognised sufficiently the effect of marriage in giving a new economic status to all married women. In national health insurance, women are allowed to carry on into the first year of marriage claims in respect of contributions made before marriage, though their needs in this initial period are not substantially different from their needs later. They are given a lower rate of sickness benefit, uncompensated by anything else ; though maternity is the principal object of marriage, there is no adequate provision for it in any case, and little or none for any loss of earnings involved. In unemployment insurance women equally carry on into marriage claims in respect of earlier contributions with full rates of benefit, but the Married Women's Anomalies Regulations are then invoked to raise a special barrier against their claims. The provision made for widowhood is at once inadequate to real needs where there are children, and lavish to unreal needs where there are no children. Provision for end of marriage by separation or desertion is left to public assistance.

110. The principle adopted here is that on marriage every woman begins a new life in relation to social insurance. She acquires at once under a Housewife's Policy, endorsed on or attached to her previous insurance document, a right to the benefits and grants set out in the plan under Marriage Needs (marriage grant, maternity grant, widowhood and separation provision, benefit during her husband's unemployment or disability if not herself gainfully occupied). She does not carry on rights to unemployment or disability benefit in respect of contributions before marriage ; she must acquire those rights, if at all, by fresh contributions after marriage. To mark the transition it is proposed that she should receive a marriage grant which, besides giving money when there is likely to be a felt need for it, has administrative convenience in encouraging early notification of marriage to the Security Office. The marriage grant, however, is not an essential part of the insurance scheme, and is, therefore, shown in brackets. It could be omitted and would make possible a reduction of the insurance contributions proposed for women. But it is proposed as something that is desirable even though not essential.

111. During marriage most women will not be gainfully occupied. The small minority of women who undertake paid employment or other gainful occupation after marriage, as shown above, require special treatment differing from that of single women. Such paid work in many cases will be intermittent ; it should be open to any married woman to undertake it as an exempt person, paying no contributions of her own and acquiring no claim to benefit in unemployment or sickness. If she prefers to contribute and to re-qualify for unemployment and disability benefit she may do so, but will receive those benefits at a reduced rate. On the other hand, whether she claims exemption or decides to contribute, she will, on giving up earning for the period of childbirth, in addition to the maternity grant available for all married women, receive maternity benefit for 13 weeks at a rate above the normal rate of unemployment and disability benefit for men and single women.

Unemployment, Disability and Maternity Benefits

112. The proposal to pay less than the normal rate of unemployment and disability benefit to housewives who are also gainfully occupied is likely to be questioned, but the case for it is strong, both on practical grounds and in equity. It is undeniable that the needs of housewives in general are less than those of single women when unemployed or disabled, because their house is provided either by their husband's earnings or by his benefit. The rates of benefit proposed in the Report rest in the last resort on an analysis of subsistence needs, including the need for rent, which does not arise normally for housewives. If the proposal discussed in paras. 197–216 had been adopted, for giving as benefit in each individual case the actual rent for which the unemployed or disabled person was responsible, together with a fixed sum for the estimated cost of food, clothing and other necessaries, married women generally would automatically have received less than single women. Though, for the reasons given in that discussion, this particular proposal has not been adopted, the principle applies. Subsistence benefit for housewives who are also gainfully occupied need not cover their rent.

113. On grounds of equity a proposal to pay lower unemployment and disability benefit to married women is right in view both of the special maternity benefit proposed and of the general balance of contributions and benefits. The special maternity benefit is obviously the most important of all the benefits required by housewives gainfully occupied. The actual proposal is that, while in unemployment and disability housewives gainfully occupied should get two-thirds of the normal rate for those benefits, for maternity benefit they should get 50 per cent. above that rate, that is to say, more than double of what they would get in unemployment or disability. No one is likely to challenge this, but the special maternity benefit must be paid for by someone. It is a benefit additional to other benefits, which will be confined almost wholly to gainfully occupied married women and will reduce the contributions available for supporting their unemployment and disability benefits. Even if in the interests of the child, maternity grant and benefit are made as fully available to the small class of unmarried mothers as they are to married mothers (as probably most married women themselves would desire) this does not affect the equities on this point as between married women and other women. Apart from this particular point, in the unified scheme the balance of contributions and benefits must be looked at as a whole and not individually. In that scheme housewives cannot complain of inequity. This can be seen by comparing what is proposed here with the present treatment of married women in unemployment insurance under the Anomalies Regulations and in health insurance.

Anomalies Regulations for Married Women

114. Both the Anomalies Regulations and the present reduction of sickness benefit to married women are based on facts which it would be wrong to ignore. The attitude of the housewife to gainful employment outside the home is not and should not be the same as that of the single woman. She has other duties. As regards sickness, experience has shown that at all ages up to retirement, claims for sickness benefit among married women are higher than among single women. The rate of benefit for married women was reduced, because, as matters stood, single women whose needs during sickness were greater appeared to be paying more than their share. The Anomalies Act of 1931 was introduced to deal with what was undoubtedly a scandal in unemployment insurance : the drawing of unemployment benefit by women who were in no real sense in search of employment. In districts and industries where married women were never accustomed to work and did not expect to find work, the

Unemployment Fund, before the Anomalies Act, was tending to become a means of endowing young married life.

115. The Anomalies Regulations, however, as they stand are open to the objection that they penalise the woman who marries, as compared with a woman who lives as a wife, without giving any compensating advantage to the former. This is a well-founded objection, but does not apply to the comprehensive insurance scheme now proposed. Quite apart from maternity grant and benefit, the unified scheme attaches advantages to the condition of marriage amply compensating for any loss involved in the lower rate of unemployment and disability benefit for those married women who are gainfully occupied. The unmarried woman living as a wife will get no widowhood benefits. If she is gainfully occupied she will pay contributions for all purposes, including medical treatment, pension and funeral grant which she would get without contribution if married ; she will not have the married woman's option of exemption. If she is not gainfully occupied she will be in Class IV and will equally be required to make contributions for medical treatment, pension and funeral grant which she would get without contributions if she were married. Though it is proposed that medical treatment should be given without contribution conditions, the legal liability of the unmarried woman in Class IV will remain and will be enforced, if she is not exempted for poverty under para. 363. For pension she will have to contribute throughout her working life, and if she does not do so will not be qualified for a pension. The contributions of the man with whom she is living, if he is married to someone else, will go to secure pensions and other benefits for his legal wife ; if he is not married, his contributions as a single man will go to support the benefits of married women generally.

116. The proposed abolition of the Anomalies Regulations for Married Women does not mean that the harm which they were intended to cure was unreal. But the harm was not confined to married women. Unmarried women living as wives, spinsters living at home and combining household duties with gainful occupation when and to the extent that it suited them, men with alternative independent occupations, might all have the same attitude towards regular employment, because they were not dependent on it. The remedy in all these cases lies partly in enforcing genuine availability for work, partly in imposing contribution conditions for full benefit which will limit the claims of all persons alike—married women and others—who are not in fact wholly or mainly dependent on employment for a living (as proposed in paras. 367–368). Such conditions would in effect be Anomalies Regulations directed, not against married women, but against the anomaly of providing compensation for loss of earnings to people who are not in intention or in practice dependent upon earnings.

117. Taken as a whole, the Plan for Social Security puts a premium on marriage, in place of penalising it. The position of housewives is recognised in form and in substance. It is recognised by treating them, not as dependants of their husbands, but as partners sharing benefit and pension when there are no earnings to share. It is recognised in substance in the greatly improved provision made for the real needs of widowhood and separation, for maternity in grant and benefit, for children's allowances and for medical treatment both of the housewife and of the children for whose care she has special responsibility. Though it is proposed that children's allowances, both when the responsible parent is earning and when his earning has been interrupted, should be paid from the National Exchequer and not from the Social Insurance Fund, this proposal, as is explained in para. 415, is based, not on principle, but on financial and practical grounds. The allowances are part of social

security, and a form of expenditure whose advantage will be felt by married women more than by any other class in the community. In the next thirty years housewives as mothers have vital work to do in ensuring the adequate continuance of the British race and of British ideals in the world.

Change 7. Extension of insurance against prolonged disability to all persons gainfully occupied and of insurance for retirement pensions to all persons of working age, whether gainfully occupied or not.

118. Many independent workers—small shopkeepers, crofters, fishermen, hawkers, outworkers—are poorer than many of those employed under contract of service and are as much dependent on good health for their earnings. All persons, even if not gainfully occupied throughout their working years, should have certainty of a subsistence income when they are too old to work if their other income fails, and should secure that subsistence income by contributions made by or on behalf of them throughout their working life. Each of the two extensions proposed here raises different questions and needs separate examination.

119. As regards insurance against disability, this is proposed only for persons gainfully occupied and not for persons, who, since they have no earnings, do not lose income if sickness prevents them from earning. It is proposed also that the disability for which benefit should be provided in the case of persons gainfully occupied otherwise than under contract of service (Class II) should be limited to " prolonged disability." The actual proposition is that to such persons benefit should be paid only if, and to the extent that, the disability lasts more than 13 weeks. The main ground for this limitation lies in the importance of avoiding the difficult administrative questions that will arise in regard to the control of benefit for short illnesses in the case of people working on their own account. The secondary reason for this limitation is that it makes a substantial difference to the contribution. Many of the independent workers are people who have limited means ; the contribution required of them since they have no employer should be kept as low as possible. It is proposed in effect that persons in Class II should carry the risk of their minor illnesses, as far as cash benefit is concerned ; like all others they will be entitled to treatment. Certain classes of persons not under contract of service, such as outworkers, share fishermen and small contractors for service, are now included under health insurance. Under the new scheme they should probably be placed in Class II, which would mean that they would no longer be insured compulsorily against the first 13 weeks of sickness. On the other hand, for prolonged disability, they will get altogether better provision than at present and they will continue to be qualified for pensions.

120. As regards pensions, the need to extend them to persons gainfully occupied as independent workers (Class II) is obvious, but it is not possible in a full security scheme to stop there. The persons of working age not gainfully occupied include a few who, through infirmity, are permanently incapable of work, and a few who, by possession of private means, may never need to work. They include many more who will work for gain at a later stage in their lives—students over sixteen—and many who may alternate between paid work and rendering unpaid service otherwise than as housewives —daughters looking after parents or sisters looking after brothers. Such persons do not need disability benefit, because disability should not affect their income, but they cannot count on continuance of their support throughout life and during the years of retirement. If they lose their unpaid livelihood through a change of family circumstances, while they are of working age, they will be able to obtain training benefit as a means of passage to other

livelihoods. They need to be assured of pensions for their old age. Those who work in employment all their lives will pay contributions for retirement pensions throughout ; it is contrary to insurance principle that others who equally need pensions should contribute only in part of their lives, or should be able, as at present, to make factitious contracts of employment late in life with a view to securing pensions at minimum cost. The proposal here is in principle to require contributions for pensions from or on behalf of all citizens throughout their working years and to make receipt of full pension depend upon contribution (paras. 367–368). This raises problems of enforcement but none that should be insoluble.

121. There is no doubt as to the desirability of applying insurance for treatment, funerals and pensions to persons in Class IV, having regard to the fact that most of them will be in that class only temporarily. The main difficulty in making this extension of insurance lies in the fact that there may be no income under the control of the insured person to which liability to contribute can attach. Where such persons are in fact doing unpaid work for a relative, it will be reasonable to expect the relative to provide the contribution as part of the reward of their service. But having regard to the relatively high level of contributions required, it is necessary to make provision for exempting from liability to contribute on the ground of possessing less than a certain income. This provision for exemption is made applicable also to Class II. The practical implications are considered in para. 363.

Change 8. Provision of training benefit to facilitate change to new occupations of all persons who lose their former livelihood, whether paid or unpaid.

122. Routine unemployment benefit, that is to say, payment to persons capable of work on the simple test of offering themselves as available for work at an employment exchange, must for practical reasons be limited to people who, by contributions in Class I, prove that they are, in fact, dependent upon employment. Only in employment are earnings related closely to particular days of work. The income of a farmer, a shopkeeper or a business manager may come at any time ; how busy or how active he is on a particular day is largely within his own control. It is not practicable to have a general system of maintaining earnings of persons gainfully occupied otherwise than by way of employment, by benefits conditional upon not working or appearing to work on a particular day. But some general provision must be made, not only for persons gainfully occupied whose livelihood may fail, but also for persons whose unpaid livelihood may fail, as it may for housewives in Class III, or for daughters and sisters and others who have kept house for their relatives in Class IV, and find a change in their household circumstances. The general provision for this is training benefit—a payment for a limited period at unemployment benefit rates, given in accord with Regulation without means test, but subject to conditions of training.

Change 9. Assimilation of benefit and pension rates for unemployment, disability, other than prolonged disability due to industrial accident or disease, and retirement.

123. There is no difference between the subsistence needs of those affected by different forms of interruption of earnings which is large enough and clear enough to justify a differentiation of benefits. Uniformity has the advantage of giving no motive to the insured person to claim one form of benefit rather than another (say unemployment rather than disability) because it is higher

and not because it really fits his case. The following notes deal with particular comparisons.

(i) *Unemployment and disability.* The sick man needs as a rule more income than the fit unemployed man, for special food or for attention ; the unemployed man also has more chances of small subsidiary earnings. If there were to be any difference between the two benefits, disability ought to be higher than unemployment benefit, not lower as at present. On the other hand, voluntary provision to supplement State benefit is both easier to make and much more widely made, for sickness than for unemployment. Equality of benefit is the safest line.

(ii) *Short and long disability.* As is pointed out in relation to Changes **12** and **13** below, it can be argued that benefit should increase rather than decrease as disability becomes prolonged. It may be argued, on the other hand, that after being disabled for some time the insured person should have been able to adjust his expenditure and lower his standards. But in general it is clear that in a long illness the sick man needs at least as much as at the beginning of illness. There is no real argument for the present practice of making disablement benefit less than sickness benefit, except the argument of expense.

(iii) *Unemployment or disability and retirement.* As is shown in para. 224, the needs of a retired person are in some ways less and in other ways more than those of an unemployed or disabled person of working age. On balance, the strict subsistence needs of the retired person are probably slightly less. But the difference is not great and the advantage of avoiding any stepping down from unemployment or disability benefit to retirement pension is considerable. Uniformity of rates for long and short disability and for retirement avoids the awkward problem of the point at which a reduction could be made if they were not uniform. Serious difficulties arise whatever the point chosen for reduction ; whether it be proposed after disability has lasted six months or two years or ten years, or to apply when a disabled man reaches his sixty-fifth birthday. The full rate of contributory pensions is put accordingly at the same amount as the rate of working age benefits (para. 251). But this full rate under the transition arrangements proposed in paras. 241–243 will be reached only in 20 years. During the transition, stepping down from disability benefit to contributory pension will be inevitable.

(iv) *Men and Women.* As is shown in paras. 217–222 the subsistence needs of men and women do not differ except in food, where the needs of the latter may be put at about 1/– a week less. On the whole it appears not worth while to distinguish the rates of benefits for single women from those for men, on account of 1/– difference in food. Different rates are proposed for married women gainfully occupied for the reasons given in Change **6**.

Change 10. Assimilation of benefit conditions for unemployment and disability, including disability due to industrial accident or disease, in respect of waiting time.

124. In all three schemes of provision for interruption of earnings, by unemployment, by industrial accident or disease, and by sickness or other accident, as they stand at present, payment is withheld for the first three days of interruption which are usually described as " waiting time ". But while some form of waiting time is found in all three schemes, the form is now different in each of the cases. In workmen's compensation for industrial accident or disease, the waiting time is provisional, in the sense that if the

interruption of earnings lasts for as much as four weeks altogether, payment is made retrospectively for the three first days, for which it had been withheld till then. In health insurance and in unemployment insurance the waiting time is absolute, that is to say no payment is made for the first three days of a continuous period of sickness or of unemployment however long it lasts ; but the rules defining a continuous period of sickness and of unemployment respectively, are different. It may be added that payment for the waiting time can be given as an additional benefit under health insurance, though this power has not been widely used ; in 1939 it covered about 4 per cent. of the total insured membership.

125. The question of the waiting time for unemployment insurance was considered recently by the Unemployment Insurance Statutory Committee on a reference from the Minister of Labour and National Service and the Report made by the Statutory Committee has been sent to the present Committee. In preparing this Report the Statutory Committee made a study of the practice of Trade Unions in regard to the waiting time in their schemes of, out-of-work benefit. They found a considerable variety of practice, some Trade Unions having an absolute waiting time, others a provisional waiting time, and others no waiting time at all. The second of these groups, with provisional waiting time, was the largest both in total of members and in volume of benefit and the Statutory Committee concluded that if there were no question of saving money for more urgent needs, a provisional waiting time was the plan with most general advantage. They expressed the opinion accordingly " that as and when occasion offers steps should be taken to make the waiting time for unemployment insurance provisional as that for workmen's compensation is provisional." They added that " though some differences between the different insurances may be necessary and be justified by differences in the risks insured against, unnecessary differences are an obvious cause of injustice and discontent. If it proves possible to introduce for all forms of lost earnings in common the principle of provisional waiting time, a very desirable simplification of our social insurance will have been effected." The proposal now made is in accord with this recommendation of the Unemployment Insurance Statutory Committee. It adopts, for unemployment and for disability alike, both the principle of the workmen's compensation scheme and the period of four weeks, as that for which interruption of earnings should last before payment is made for the first three days.

126. There remains the further question of defining what is meant by a continuous period of unemployment or disability. This is a highly technical matter in regard to which it may be necessary to adopt different procedure for unemployment and disability respectively.

Change 11. Assimilation of contribution conditions for unemployment and disability benefit, except where disability is due to industrial accident or disease, and revision of contribution conditions for pension.

127. Some contribution conditions for receipt of the benefits, pensions, and grants of the social insurance scheme are essential in order :

(a) To maintain the insurance principle that people should pay for their security, though not in full ;

(b) To determine the social security class in which each person falls ;

(c) To facilitate enforcement of contributions by making it to the interest of individuals to contribute regularly.

The need for simplifying and co-ordinating the present conditions is as obvious as the need for having some conditions at all. In regard to the working age benefits—for unemployment and disability—the simplest method would be to make the question whether a person was in full benefit or not during a benefit year (say 12 months beginning 1st October) depend upon contributions made by him in the preceding contribution year (12 months ending in the preceding July). The administrative practicability of this particular method needs further examination, having regard to the probable numbers of persons to be dealt with at any one time. But that, either in this way, or in some other way, great simplification of contribution conditions can be achieved under a unified system of insurance, is clear. Contribution conditions will not apply to claims for disability benefit arising out of industrial accident or disease.

128. In regard to pensions, the position is changed by extension of the scope of insurance from those employed under contract of service to the whole population of working age. With the limitation of scope hitherto, it was felt necessary to allow persons to qualify for pensions by a relatively short period of contribution of five years as employees ; this gave temptation to the making of factitious contracts of employment with relatives for the last five years of working age. Extension in the scope of insurance makes it possible and desirable to insist on contributions covering the whole of working life as a condition of pensions.

Change 12. Making of unemployment benefit at full rate indefinite in duration, subject to requirement of attendance at a work or training centre after a limited period of unemployment.

Change 13. Making of disability benefit at full rate indefinite in duration, subject to imposition of special behaviour conditions.

129. Prolongation of interruption of earnings, whether through unemployment or through disability, has normally two consequences :—

(i) The income needs tend to increase rather than to decrease ; the other means at the disposal of the insured person become exhausted ; expenditures on clothing and equipment which he may have been able to postpone become unavoidable, since they cannot be postponed indefinitely.

(ii) Measures other than the provision of income become increasingly necessary, to prevent deterioration of morale and to encourage recovery.

In view of these considerations, the existing provisions for dealing with prolonged interruption of earnings are unsatisfactory. For disability the cash benefit is drastically reduced, though the needs have almost certainly increased ; for unemployment the insured person is referred from benefit to assistance, which may give him higher, or lower, or equal income, but will give it subject to a means test, and normally will do nothing but give an income. The needs of persons suffering from prolonged unemployment or disability are, on the one hand, for as much income at least as before, without any means test discouraging voluntary provision, and, on the other hand, for the taking of steps to prevent deterioration and encourage recovery. It is proposed, accordingly, that the rates both for unemployment and for disability should continue without diminution so long as unemployment or disability lasts ; this abolishes the present distinction between sickness and disablement benefits under health insurance.

130. To reduce the income of an unemployed or disabled person, either directly or by application of a means test, because the unemployment or disability has lasted for a certain period, is wrong in principle. But it is equally wrong to ignore the fact that to make unemployment or disability benefit, which is adequate for subsistence, also indefinite in duration involves a danger against which practical precautions must be taken. Most men who

have once gained the habit of work would rather work—in ways to which they are used—than be idle, and all men would rather be well than ill. But getting work or getting well may involve a change of habits, doing something that is unfamiliar or leaving one's friends or making a painful effort of some other kind. The danger of providing benefits, which are both adequate in amount and indefinite in duration, is that men, as creatures who adapt themselves to circumstances, may settle down to them. In the proposals of the present Report, not only are insurance benefits being made for the first time adequate for subsistence without other means, but the possibility of drawing them is being extended to new classes not hitherto accustomed to industrial discipline. The correlative of the State's undertaking to ensure adequate benefit for unavoidable interruption of earnings, however long, is enforcement of the citizen's obligation to seek and accept all reasonable opportunities of work, to co-operate in measures designed to save him from habituation to idleness, and to take all proper measures to be well. The higher the benefits provided out of a common fund for unmerited misfortune, the higher must be the citizen's sense of obligation not to draw upon that fund unnecessarily.

131. This general principle leads to the following practical conclusions :

(i) Men and women in receipt of unemployment benefit cannot be allowed to hold out indefinitely for work of the type to which they are used or in their present places of residence, if there is work which they could do available at the standard wage for that work.

(ii) Men and women who have been unemployed for a certain period should be required as a condition of continued benefit to attend a work or training centre, such attendance being designed both as a means of preventing habitation to idleness and as a means of improving capacity for earning. Incidentally, though this is an altogether minor reason for the proposal, such a condition is the most effective way of unmasking the relatively few persons who may be suspected of malingering, who have perhaps some concealed means of earning which they are combining with an appearance of unemployment. The period after which attendance should be required need not be the same at all times or for all persons. It might be extended in times of high unemployment and reduced in times of good employment ; six months for adults would perhaps be a reasonable average period of benefit without conditions. But for young persons who have not yet the habit of continuous work the period should be shorter ; for boys and girls there should ideally be no unconditional benefit at all ; their enforced abstention from work should be made an occasion of further training.

(iii) The measures for control of claims to disability benefit—both by certification and by sick visiting—will need to be strengthened, in view of the large increases proposed in the scale of compulsory insurance benefit and the possibility of adding to this substantially by voluntary insurance through Friendly Societies.

(iv) Special attention should be paid to the prevention of chronic disability, by intensified treatment, advice and supervision of cases in which it is threatened and by research into its causes.

(v) Conditions imposed on benefit must be enforced where necessary by suitable penalties.

132. The practicability of adopting the principle of special treatment for prolonged disability depends on adequate development of the medical service (Assumption B in paras. 426–437). Practicability of the same thing in regard

to unemployment depends on the satisfaction of Assumption C (paras. 440–443), that is to say, on maintenance of employment to keep within reasonable numbers the men who are likely to exhaust unconditional benefit.

Change 14. Making of pensions, other than industrial, conditional on retirement from work and rising in value with each year of continued contribution after the minimum age of retirement, that is to say, after 65 for men and 60 for women.

133. The grounds for this proposal are set out in the general discussion of the Problem of Age in Section 2 of Part III. Briefly, they are (1) that making retirement from work a condition of pension is a logical consequence of giving adequate pensions ; (2) that giving to each individual an incentive to continue at work so long as he can, in place of retiring, is a necessary attempt to lighten the burden that will otherwise fall on the British community, through the large and growing proportion of people at the higher ages ; (3) that the age to which men can go on working with satisfaction to themselves and advantage to the community varies with every individual and from one occupation to another. The proposal to make the age of retirement flexible meets human as well as economic realities. Adequate pensions with a flexible age of retirement will increase happiness and wealth in many ways. Early retirement of men on pension is not wanted or useful as a cure for unemployment. On the contrary, there should be as few idle mouths as possible, at any age after childhood is past. This general statement requires two glosses.

134. First, in any particular occupation there may be a reason for enforcing early retirement and pension. Some occupations—e.g. service in the Armed Forces or the police—are not suited for men past middle life. In other occupations, e.g. the public service, it may be desirable to retire senior men before they are past work, in order that younger men may be able to get responsibility early enough to make good use of it. But neither of these reasons applies with anything like the same force to the ordinary industrial and clerical occupations.

135. Second, to make the age of retirement flexible is one way of adjusting supply of labour to fluctuations in demand. In times of good trade the older men will find it easier to keep their work and postpone retirement. In times of bad trade they will tend to retire earlier and reduce the supply of labour ; it is an essential part of the proposal that the period for which unemployment and disability benefit can be drawn after the minimum age of retirement should be restricted.

136. Minor but not unimportant advantages of the proposal as put here are (a) that it will facilitate enforcement of a retirement condition ; (b) that it will simplify administration by abolishing all exemptions for age ; and (c) that it will strengthen the finance of the Social Insurance Fund.

(a) There is no difficulty in making retirement from the service of a particular employer a condition of drawing pension. To enforce abstention from any kind of work as condition of a social security pension is less easy ; but the proposal that an insured person should be able to get a larger pension if he postpones claiming it while working after pensionable age, should facilitate enforcement, since those who do postpone while they can work will get an advantage by doing so. The practical problems of enforcing a retirement condition are discussed in para. 248.

(b) Abolition of exemption on account of age will mean that persons continuing to work after 65 for men or 60 for women will contribute as before, on ordinary employment books or occupation cards (para. 354).

(c) The rate of increase of pension above the basic rate that is proposed for each year of postponement (para. 246), while it should be sufficient strongly to encourage postponement, is below the full actuarial value of postponement.   (Appendix A, para. 20.)

Change 15. Amalgamation of the special schemes of unemployment insurance, for agriculture, banking and finance and insurance, with the general scheme of social insurance.

137.   At the introduction of unemployment insurance in 1911 for a limited group of industries, importance was attached to adjusting the premiums as far as possible to the risks, by giving rebates to regular employers, by refund of their personal contributions at 60 to men who by then had drawn less in benefit than they had paid, and in other ways ; it was contemplated moreover that, after experience had been gained, different rates of contributions, involving separate insurance stamps, should be fixed for different industries, and the Act of 1911 contained a section providing for this.   On the generalisation of unemployment insurance in 1920, while the hope of having differential rates of compulsory contribution for different industries by means of distinctive insurance stamps was abandoned, the principle of differentiation was retained, through a provision authorising the Minister to approve special schemes of insurance, to be set up by agreement between employers and workpeople in particular industries.   These industries would thus contract out of the general provisions of the Act.   At one time it was contemplated that contracting out would be extensive ; the Actuarial Report of 1919 indicates an expectation that roughly one-third of the insured population would be segregated from the General Scheme.   The possibility of contracting out by establishing special schemes was considered by a number of industries, but the onset of the depression in 1921 put an end to all such projects, except in two cases : the industries of insurance and of banking and finance.   The former of these established a special scheme in 1921, the latter at about the same time formulated proposals for a scheme which materialised in 1924.

138.   In the summer of 1921 power to contract out by any fresh industries was suspended, until the Unemployment Fund should again be solvent.   By the time that the Committee under Lord Blanesburgh appointed in November, 1925, considered the matter, views as to the nature of unemployment insurance had undergone change.   The power of the Minister of Labour to approve special schemes and allow industries to contract out had been suspended in 1921 on grounds of expediency.   The Blanesburgh Committee in 1926 objected to this power on principle, and they found themselves supported in their objection by all the principal associations of employers and of workpeople.   "All industries are, in a sense, inter-related and the effects of the lessening of production in one are felt to a greater or less degree by the others."   "As soon as an industry or other unit is shown to be within the scope of compulsory State insurance, there is no justification for allowing that industry or unit to derive any advantage from its lower than average risk of unemployment."

139.   The Blanesburgh Committee recommended accordingly that power to approve special schemes contracting out of the general scheme should cease and this recommendation was adopted in the Unemployment Insurance Act of 1927.   The Committee recognised also that as a matter of principle " the special schemes for the insurance industry and the banking industry ought not to be allowed to continue." But they came at the same time to the conclusion that these schemes " should not now be interfered with.   The provision of the 1920 Act, under which they were sanctioned, was quite legitimately taken advantage of by those concerned, and it would not . . . at this distance of time, be fair to withdraw from them the privileged position so acquired."   The Royal Commission of 1932 also decided to leave the position unchanged.

140. The actual provisions of the two schemes as they are today may be summarised as follows : The Insurance Special Scheme covers about 150,000 persons, with rates of contribution of 7/7 a quarter for men and 6/6 a quarter for women, paid by the employers. There is no contribution by the employees or by the State. The standard rates and conditions for receipt of benefit are the same as in the general scheme. Special higher rates and benefits for periods after exhaustion of the ordinary benefit may be granted at the discretion of the Insurance Board ; in practice, higher rates are granted to those who prove that they are regularly employed in the insurance industry and that they are seeking to continue in it. The Banking and Finance Special Scheme covers about 60,000 persons. The rates of contribution are 2/2 per quarter for men and women alike, payable by the employers. There is no contribution either from the employee or from the State. Conditions for the receipt of benefit are the same, and the rates for adults are the same as under the general scheme, with higher rates for young persons and juveniles, and higher allowance for dependent children (5/- a week each in place of 4/- a week for each of the first two and 3/- for each additional child). There is also power, at the discretion of the Board, to pay allowances to persons who have exhausted their rates of benefit. Both schemes maintain an effective employment register.

141. The case for amalgamating them with the general scheme is that implied in the Report of the Blanesburgh Committee. Unemployment insurance by industry is a line of development on which progress has ended. For historical reasons banking and insurance today hold a privileged position, allowing them the benefit of their specially low rate of unemployment. This privilege is not accorded to any industry included in the general scheme of unemployment insurance, though there are other industries with rates of unemployment well below the average. Nor has it been accorded to any of the classes of employees, such as institutional domestic servants or non-manual employees above the old remuneration limit of £250 a year, to whom the scheme has recently been extended. Retention of this historical privilege by these two special industries can no longer be justified.

142. On the other hand, both schemes are undoubtedly administered with efficiency and satisfaction to the persons covered by them. It would be regrettable to lose unnecessarily the interest and the good will that they represent. The suggestion is made in para. 378 that these schemes might administer statutory benefit to their members and become means of developing voluntary insurance to supplement statutory benefit. This is an arrangement that it might prove possible to extend to other industries ; contracting out could not be extended.

AGRICULTURAL UNEMPLOYMENT INSURANCE SCHEME

143. The position in regard to agriculture is, in principle, the same, though in some important respects different. Agriculture was excluded from the general scheme of unemployment insurance in 1920. When unemployment insurance was extended to agriculture in 1936, this was done by special legislation, providing benefits and contributions different from those of the general scheme. This difference of treatment was based on three grounds :—

(a) That agriculture should not be called on to contribute towards the debt (then exceeding £100 million) of the general scheme ;

(b) That agriculture, owing to its low wages, could not afford the contributions of the general scheme ;

(c) That the rate of unemployment in agriculture was lower than that in industry as a whole and that agriculture should be given the benefit of this lower rate of unemployment.

144. The special scheme for agriculture differs from those of banking and insurance in respect of contributions. Employer and employee contribute by stamps, as in the general scheme, though at lower rates ; the State contributes the same proportion as in the general scheme. All contributions, general and agricultural, go to a single Unemployment Fund, but separate accounts are kept and agricultural contributions (from employer, employee and the State) are reserved for agricultural benefit. The rates of benefit in the agricultural scheme are a little less than those of the general scheme, while the rates of contribution are much less. The rules governing the period of benefit are different.

145. The question of the amalgamation of the agricultural with the general scheme has been considered recently by the Unemployment Insurance Statutory Committee on a reference from the Minister of Labour and National Service. 'The Report of that Committee has been communicated to the Inter-departmental Committee and is to the effect that no immediate change should be made, but that the question should be considered in its wider aspect by the Inter-departmental Committee on Social Insurance and Allied Services.

146. Of the three reasons named above for keeping agriculture separate, the first no longer applies, as the debt of the general scheme has been repaid. The second reason does not apply with anything like its former force, in view of the recent rise of agricultural wages, and it seems right to base social security for the future on the assumption that agriculture will have a status equal to that of other industries in respect of terms and conditions of service. The third reason is contrary to the general principle which has now become accepted for unemployment insurance, namely that all industries stand together ; that the contributions in one industry should not be increased on the grounds that it has an especially high rate of unemployment ; that no industry should keep the advantage of its low rate of unemployment. The principle underlying unemployment insurance today is that industries cannot to any substantial extent control their own volume of unemployment and that no industry, accordingly, should contribute less to unemployment insurance because its normal rate of unemployment is below the average. The Unemployment Insurance Statutory Committee stated that if they were now considering the extension of unemployment insurance to agriculture they would not, on the sole ground of the lower risk of unemployment in agriculture, propose that the contributions should be lower than in the general scheme.

147. Two of the three reasons given for a special scheme for agriculture are no longer valid. As to one of the three, namely the level of wages and by consequence the level of benefits and contributions appropriate to agriculture, there may be uncertainty, that is to say it can be argued that the wages and conditions in agriculture will be materially different from those in other industries. This, however, would be a reason, not for giving agriculture the privilegé of its lower rate of unemployment, but for giving it a lower scale both of benefits and of contributions. Sharing of risks between agriculture and other industries would be consistent with providing a lower rate of benefit in agriculture on the ground of lower cost of living ; there is still a substantial difference between the rents paid by agricultural households and by industrial households. In the discussion of benefit rates in Part III, the suggestion is made accordingly (paras. 214–215) that the question of having, either for particular occupations or for particular regions, rates of unemployment and disability benefit below the general level, with a proportionate reduction of contributions, should be the subject of a special enquiry in preparing the detailed insurance scheme. One of the problems to be considered in such an enquiry would be the treatment for disability benefit of independent rural

workers with low money incomes, such as small-holders, crofters and fishermen. No differentiation is suggested in the rate of pensions.

148. The case for the retention of the special scheme for agriculture by which it can obtain benefits approximating to those of the general scheme at one-third of the present cost is a claim of privilege. In this case the privilege is recent, dating from the Act of 1936, while the privilege of the insurance and banking schemes is older, dating from 1921 or 1924. The view taken in this Report is that no claim of privilege should stand against the unification of social insurance today.

Change 16. Abolition of the exceptions from insurance

(a) **of persons in particular occupations, such as the civil service, local government service, police, nursing, railways, and other pensionable employments, and in respect of unemployment insurance, private indoor domestic service ;**

(b) **of persons remunerated above £420 a year in non-manual occupations.**

149. The argument for the first of these changes is much the same as in regard to the preceding change. If those industries which have a small risk of unemployment are required to stand in, together with all others, those industries which claim to have no risks of unemployment may also be required to stand in with the others. Any distinctions within the scheme lead to difficult demarcation problems. Where, as with the central government and with railway companies, some of the employees contribute for unemployment insurance while the others are exempt, the additional objection may be made that the industry escapes contributing its full share to the Unemployment Fund. Where one section of domestic service, namely indoor servants in private houses alone are excluded, while other domestic servants, such as those in establishments and institutions are included, anomalies and passage into and out of insurance are unavoidable. The view taken here is that, as regards unemployment, all industries should stand together ; as regards pensions and sickness insurance, if there are any occupations which have already made provision for these circumstances, they should do so in future in the light of the basic provision being made for all, including their members, by the national Plan for Social Security. All that is needed is that they should be given time to re-adjust their own schemes.

150. The proposal made here will mean that employees in the excepted occupations and their employers will have their contributions for social security increased very substantially and more than employees and employers in other occupations. The greater part of the security contribution is required as provision for contributory pensions, which under the plan will be paid up to a subsistence minimum to all citizens. But the full rate of contributory pensions will not be reached till the end of a substantial transition period. Within that period there is time for readjustment of occupational schemes of superannuation to the fact of the national scheme and, if this is desired by the insured persons and their employers, for a reduction of any contributions made to the voluntary schemes. It will probably be desirable by legislation to simplify the necessary procedure for such readjustments, subject to suitable safeguards.

151. Of the pensionable employments which are excepted, other than the civil service, the two largest are the railway service and local government service. The railway companies and the principal organisations of railway employees asked that the existing exceptions should be continued. On the other hand, the largest group of employers in local government service, namely the Association of Municipal Corporations in England and Wales and the representatives of one of the most important organisations of employees,

namely the National Association of Local Government Officers, advocated the inclusion of all persons now excepted in the general insurance scheme on the same terms as all others. The same view was taken by the Association of County Councils in Scotland.

152. The second change proposed, that is to say, abolition of exception on account of remuneration above the rate of £420 a year in non-manual occupations, rests on four distinct reasons :—

    (i) Abolition of the remuneration limit follows from the argument for the abolition of exceptions in particular occupations, including the civil service and other pensionable employments. It would be unjust to require lower paid civil servants to contribute to a scheme of which they felt little or no personal need, while exempting higher paid persons in the same occupation on the ground that they were paid more.

    (ii) Abolition of the remuneration limit avoids all the difficulties which arise through persons passing out of the insurance field in middle life or afterwards as their remuneration increases. In place of the complicated and unsatisfactory devices for continuance of voluntary insurance, all such persons will remain permanently insured compulsorily.

    (iii) Abolition of the remuneration limit puts an end to the troublesome questions as to the rate of remuneration in fluctuating occupations and as to the definition of non-manual work, which were discussed by the Unemployment Insurance Statutory Committee in 1936 when they recommended the raising of the remuneration limit from its then figure of £250 to £420 a year.

    (iv) Any remuneration limit, since it cannot in practice take account of family responsibilities, is bound to produce anomalies. If, for instance, medical service free of charge on treatment, but in respect of compulsory contributions, is limited to people with an income below £420, this will mean that a bachelor with an income of £410 a year gets his treatment without charge, while a man with an income of £430 and a family to support is required to pay for his own treatment and that of all his family.

Change 17. Replacement of unconditional inadequate widows' pensions by provision suited to the varied needs of widows, including temporary widows' benefit at a special rate, in all cases, training benefit when required, and guardian benefit so long as there are dependent children.

153. Widowhood is now dealt with by the grant of a small unconditional pension taking no account of real needs, inadequate in many cases and superfluous in other cases, as is the unconditional pension for old age. There is no reason why a childless widow should get a pension for life ; if she is able to work, she should work. On the other hand, provision much better than at present should be made for those who, because they have the care of children, cannot work for gain or cannot work regularly. The proposals set out in Part V (para. 346) include accordingly the following :—

    (a) In all cases widow's benefit for thirteen weeks at a rate equivalent to maternity benefit, that is to say, 50 per cent higher than unemployment and disability benefit, to allow time for readjustment to new conditions.

    (b) So long as there are dependent children, guardian benefit adequate for subsistence subject to adjustment for actual earnings.

    (c) Training benefit with a view to resumption of gainful occupation.

154. They include, also, retention of differentiation between deaths of breadwinners due to industrial accident or disease and such deaths due to other causes, by providing industrial grant in the former case, subject to further consideration of the amount, allocation and method of payment of this grant in the light of the general insurance proposals. Where the death of the breadwinner is due to a cause other than industrial accident or disease, there may in many cases, if not most cases, be a need for a cash grant over and above the special widow's benefit. Payment made on a death where this involves not merely funeral expenses but loss of maintenance should be sufficient to cover not only funeral expenses, but to provide a lump sum. This, however, is probably in general a matter for voluntary rather than compulsory insurance and is to a large extent provided voluntarily through industrial assurance policies taken out by men on their own lives or by wives on the lives of their husbands. The treatment of this problem depends upon the decisions taken on Change 23 below.

155. The rate of guardian benefit proposed is designed to be sufficient, in combination with children's allowances, to meet subsistence needs, even if the widow does not undertake any gainful occupation while she is looking after the children. Some widows in such a position may nevertheless be able to work and earn and may desire to do so. The right principle appears to be to treat such earnings, as it is proposed to treat earnings made by persons in receipt of retirement pension, by making a reduction of the benefit which allows the widow to retain a proportion, but not the whole, of her earnings in addition to full benefit.

156. The proposal to abandon the present system, under which pensions for life or till re-marriage are paid to widows irrespective of their family responsibilities, was supported by nearly all witnesses who expressed an opinion to the Committee on this point. In many cases, if not most, these witnesses, while holding that the widows of working age without children should be expected to work and not to receive pensions, emphasised the difficulty in which those who became widowed late in life, though before pensionable age, or whose children ceased to be dependent when they were already advanced in age, would have in finding, or being trained for, new employment. They suggested, in effect, that some special provision should be made for those who became widowed or whose children ceased to be dependent when they were, say, 50 and upwards. On this difficult point, after full consideration, the view taken in the Report is that no benefit as of right should be provided. Having regard to the prospective age constitution of the population, the principle that any person physically fit for work should be entitled to retire from work upon pension before reaching the minimum pension age of 60 for women or 65 for men cannot without grave danger be admitted in any scheme for social insurance. Those whose widowhood is due to industrial accident or disease will be covered by the special provision made for such cases. Those who at the time of the husband's death are totally disabled will get disability benefit. All other widows who, for any other reason, after the ending of widow's benefit are unable to obtain paid work of any type within their powers can and will be provided for by assistance. Permanent provision for widowhood as such, irrespective of the care of children and of need, is a matter for voluntary insurance by the husband.

Change 18. Inclusion of universal funeral grant in compulsory insurance.

157. All people when they die need a funeral. This need is now met for most, though not quite all, people in Britain by voluntary industrial insurance, but at an excessive expense—certainly in administration, probably also in actual expenditure.

c

Substantial sums are distributed as death benefit by Friendly Societies other than collecting societies and Trade Unions, and some of these benefits are used for funeral expenses, but for the great majority of people provision for funeral expenses is undertaken through the Industrial Life Offices, whose work is described briefly in paras. 182–189 and more fully in Appendix D. The cost ratio of all the Industrial Life Offices taken together (including profits and tax) in 1937–40 was 37·2 per cent. of the premiums, nearly 7/6 in the £.

158. As compared with this, the cost of administering a funeral grant as part of social insurance would be negligible. On the contribution side, it would mean adding one or two pence to the value of the insurance stamp, which would have to be affixed in any case to the insurance document ; on the benefit side it would mean paying one claim only for each person in respect of a fact of which there could be no doubt and which must be formally recorded by the State for other purposes. With this simple administrative task may be compared the work involved in unemployment insurance, in which on an average for every 100 insured persons 30 claims may be expected in every year. In each case there must be reference to a central register of contribution records and previous payments ; a number of difficult questions as to the fact of unemployment, as to cause of unemployment, and as to the availability of the insured person for work, may have to be answered ; in each case payment is a weekly one, spread probably over many weeks. Yet the administrative cost of unemployment insurance in 1939 was less than 10 per cent. of the contribution income. The administrative cost of contributory pensions in the same year was only 2½ per cent. of the amount paid as pensions. (See Appendix E, paras. 27–30.) The administrative expenses of funeral grant in social insurance could not well be more than 2 or 3 per cent. of the contribution, that is to say, more than about 6d. in the £ of premiums in place of 7/6 in the £ under the present voluntary system. There can be no justification for requiring the public who need insurance for direct funeral expenses to pay the heavy tax involved in industrial assurance.

159. The amount suggested for the funeral grant, namely, £20 for an adult with less for younger persons, is based on the following considerations. The cost of a funeral, as put to the Departmental Committee under Sir Benjamin Cohen in 1932 by the representative of the Undertakers Association, was for an adult £15 in London and £13 in industrial centres, with amounts ranging from £6 to £9 for children. These estimates, from their source, are not likely to be too low ; they are about twice as much as the costs actually incurred by Local Authorities today in providing not " pauper funerals " but funerals as far as possible indistinguishable from those which relatives of the dead might provide. Taking these estimates, and adding a margin for cemetery fees, it seems reasonable to put the necessary expenses of decent funeral for an adult at the figure suggested, though if it appeared desirable there would be no difficulty in providing a larger grant, as the contribution required is small. The weekly contribution required to secure a funeral grant of this amount is put in the Memorandum of the Government Actuary at about 1·8d. per week for an adult man and 1·1d. per week for an adult woman during working years, to cover themselves and dependants.

160. Some Regulation will be required to determine to whom in doubtful cases funeral grant for meeting expenses on a death should be paid, but in most cases there would be no doubt ; the spouse, the parent, the child—would be the obvious recipient. It will be reasonable also to exclude from funeral grant persons who are above the age of 60 when the scheme begins, leaving them to be covered by existing policies. The grant will be a money grant, and will not involve standardisation of funerals, since individuals will be able to spend either more or less than the grant, according to their resources and desires,

with the undertaker of their choice. There are other problems of transition from the existing system, and there is the general problem, dealt with below in Change 23, of the treatment of industrial assurance as a whole, in the light of the proposal of this section and of Change 3 in regard to Approved Societies.

Change 19. Transfer to the Ministry of Social Security of the remaining functions of Local Authorities in respect of public assistance, other than treatment and services of an institutional character.

161. The Poor Law, founded originally on the obligation of every parish to prevent destitution, was, until comparatively recently, the basic service for meeting need. But during the past 40 years there has been a strong trend away from the Poor Law and in favour of contributory State insurance and assistance administered on a national basis. The proposals in this Report (extending State insurance to new classes and new needs, raising rates of benefit, and prolonging the period of benefit) will considerably reduce the scope both of public assistance and of the Assistance Board. There can be no case for maintaining two or more large organisations performing precisely the same functions (payment of assistance according to needs) in respect of a reduced and declining number of recipients. It is therefore proposed that there should be one authority administering assistance on the basis of a uniform means test.

162. It is essential to the logic and aims of the Plan of Social Security that this authority should be national and part of the Ministry of Social Security. This view was accepted or recommended by the Association of Municipal Corporations, the County Councils Association and the London County Council, that is to say, by all the public assistance authorities in England and Wales. Representatives of Local Authorities in Scotland, while in general they held that the cost of public assistance should be made a national charge, suggested that in the interests of preserving local knowledge, administration should remain with the Local Authorities and staffs employed by them. The same view was presented by the National Association of Local Government Officers.

163. It is clear that the administration of the Ministry of Social Security must be decentralised, so that its local officers are in intimate touch with the problems and circumstances in their localities. This can be secured without making these officials servants of, and subject to the control of, the Local Authority. The present important function of the Relieving Officer of giving relief in cases of sudden and urgent necessity will, in future, have to be performed by the equivalent local officer of the Ministry of Social Security. There is no difficulty in practice in arranging for local administration by local officials of a Central Department. But, to make such officials servants of the Local Authority means either that the Local Authority has discretion in spending money to which it does not contribute in any way and in which, therefore, it has no motive to economise, or that it has no discretion, in which case the Local Authority becomes an agent without responsibility. It is neither desirable for the strength of local democracy that Local Authorities should have to administer a service without discretion and according to detailed ules nor compatible with a national minimum and a national Plan of Social Security that people should be given assistance according to a scale and conditions which vary from place to place.

164. The abolition of the Poor Law will still leave in the hands of Local Authorities the important and growing task of organising and maintaining institutions of various kinds, for treatment and welfare. In view of the increasing number of old persons, there is probably considerable scope for experimentation with and development of services concerned with the recreation and welfare of the old, including special housing facilities. The domiciliary

Poor Law Medical Service will presumably be merged into the comprehensive health service which is Assumption B of the Report, and in which Local Authorities will continue to play a very important part. Local Authorities also will have a vital part to play in the other fields of social welfare, such as housing, education and the recreative and cultural services. But these services will not be provided as part of the Poor Law. The Poor Law Code will, it is proposed, be abolished. The many-sided activities of Local Authorities in relation to social security will be organised either as part of the different main social services under the appropriate Committees for Public Health, Education and so forth, or under a special Social Welfare Committee concerned with or co-ordinating such cash-aid functions as rent rebates, or cheap or free school meals, to which a single means test would be applied.

165. The proposal in the Report, in accord with the views expressed by the English Local Authorities, is that responsibility for assistance should be transferred to the Ministry of Social Security while provision for institutions will in general remain with the Local Authorities, who will be empowered to give cash payments which are incidental to institutional treatment. The precise dividing line and the details of the transfer, including the consequential financial adjustments, will have to be worked out in consultation with the Local Authorities. But one thing is clear : there will be need for continuous and friendly collaboration between the proposed Ministry of Social Security and the Local Authorities. Both Central and Local Government have in their different ways a contribution to make to the future security and welfare of the people of this country.

Change 20. Transfer to the Ministry of Social Security of responsibility for the maintenance of blind persons, and the framing of a new scheme for maintenance and welfare by co-operation between the Ministry, Local Authorities and voluntary agencies.

166. Under the Blind Persons Act, 1920, a complete register of blind persons is made. Help to them takes three main forms :

(a) Non-contributory pensions subject to a means test payable as from the age of 40, but otherwise on the same terms as non-contributory old age pensions at 70 and, like them, administered by the Customs and Excise Department.

(b) Assistance by Local Authorities under the Blind Persons Act, 1938, including both money grants subject to means test, and provision of workshops, training centres and home teaching.

(c) Help by voluntary agencies.

167. These arrangements are open to two main criticisms. The first is that a plan of treating blind persons as if they were prematurely aged is not in accord with realities. Blind persons, though they may need some allowance to compensate them for their infirmity, should not get it in a form which assumes that they are past work and discourages earning. Nor is there any virtue in the age 40 as that at which blind persons are assumed to become the equivalent of sighted persons of 70. Second, placing primary responsibility on Local Authorities and local rates for assistance supplementary to the pension leads both to unjustifiable inequalities in the amounts granted according to the different policies of different authorities, and to settlement difficulties, since authorities which could find places for blind persons from other districts in their workshops and training centres may suffer by doing so, through becoming permanently liable for such persons.

168. The future treatment of the problem of blindness is profoundly affected by the general proposals of this Report. From this point of view

the most important fact in regard to blindness is that it now occurs mainly late in life. At one time one of the most frequent causes of blindness was disease within a few days of birth. Fortunately, the successful campaign against ophthalmia neonatorum is steadily reducing blindness from this cause. The age distribution of the registered blind in Great Britain in 1941 was as follows :—

Age Group				Number		Percentage of total
Under 5 ...	...	...		215	...	0·3
5–15	...	...	...	1,551	...	1·9
16–39	...	...	...	10,389	...	12·5
40–49	...	...	...	8,514	...	10·2
50–69	...	...	...	32,320	...	38·8
70 and over	...	...		30,218	...	36·3
				83,207	...	100·0

The great majority of blind persons, therefore, will be contributors either in Class I or in Class II in the years between 16 and onset of blindness. If, therefore, their blindness renders them incapable of work within the general definition of disability, they will be entitled to the appropriate rates of disability benefit and in due course to the appropriate retirement pension.

169. This does not mean that blindness needs no special consideration apart from general disability. On the contrary, it is a special problem, to be dealt with within the general framework by methods appropriate to the special conditions of the blind. These conditions are :—

(i) Blindness is a handicap not only in earning but in all occupations, such as that of a housewife. Even if in most cases this produces no need for cash income, additional to the earnings of the husband, it may do so in some cases.

(ii) Blindness is a handicap not only in useful occupation, whether for pay or not, but also in other sides of life. The subsistence needs of a totally incapacitated blind person may be more than those attached to many other, though not to all other, forms of disability.

(iii) Blindness may not prevent earning wholly and should not be treated on the assumption that it means total loss of earning power. Some kind of provision for partial incapacity is required.

(iv) The special provision needed by the blind is not wholly or even in the main a cash provision. The care of the blind is largely a matter of treatment and welfare, and the provision of special institutions.

From this last feature flows, in accordance with the general principles of the Plan for Social Security, the consequence that the special responsibilities now given to Local Authorities in respect of blind persons should to a large extent continue. Some of the Local Authorities who advocated transfer of public assistance cash payments generally to a national authority took a different line in regard to blindness.

170. The practical conclusion is that set out at the head of this section, namely, that the Ministry of Social Security should assume general responsibility for the blind as for other disabled persons and should prepare a revised scheme for dealing with the problem in consultation with the Local Authorities and voluntary agencies.

Change 21. Transfer to the Ministry of Social Security of the functions of the Assistance Board, of the work of the Customs and Excise Department in respect of non-contributory pensions, and probably of the employment service of the Ministry of Labour and National Service, in addition to unemployment insurance, and the work of other Departments in connection with the administration of cash benefits of all kinds, including workmen's compensation.

171. The precise form of departmental organisation to be adopted for administration of social security cannot be determined finally without reference to the general organisation of the work of the Government. There will clearly, however, be a considerable transfer of functions from other departments to the proposed new Ministry of Social Security. The following notes deal with the principal changes which seem likely to be required.

172. *Assistance Board :* There are arguments, on the one side, for associating assistance as closely as possible with insurance in administration, and there are arguments, on the other side, for keeping it distinct. In favour of a close association are (i) the general advantage from the point of view of the citizen of being able to deal with a single agency in place of being sent from one Department to another ; (ii) the fact that, in the transition period, a large proportion of those in need of assistance will be in that position only because the date of their birth brings them to retiring age before contributory pensions have risen to subsistence level. There will be others whose need for assistance is equally independent of any kind of default of their own, either trivial or serious. In favour of maintaining a distinction between the administration of assistance and insurance two arguments also may be advanced : (i) that it is important to make insurance appear to be, as it is in fact, something different from assistance and better, and that this end will be defeated if the two systems are administered together ; (ii) that the work of administering assistance, which is necessarily to some extent discretionary and involves domiciliary visits, requires a staff different in qualifications and training from the staff for insurance. On balance, the arguments for making assistance definitely part of the responsibilities of the Ministry of Social Security outweigh the arguments on the other side, and suggest that a separate organisation like the Assistance Board will no longer be appropriate. In any case, a specialised staff will be needed for assistance. There must also be special provisions for dealing with those who are in need of assistance through deliberate failure to comply with the conditions of insurance, that is to say, there must be machinery for meeting their needs without condoning their breach of citizen obligations.

173. *Customs and Excise Department :* The present work of the Customs and Excise Department in the administration of non-contributory pensions must clearly be combined with the administration of assistance pensions, that is to say, on the proposals made above, it will be transferred to the Ministry of Social Security.

174. *Employment Service :* The administration of unemployment benefit depends on the test of availability for work which is the function of employment exchanges ; payment of unemployment benefit and placing in employment must in practice take place at the same local offices. The question arises whether this necessary combination can be secured best by transferring the registration and placing function of the Ministry of Labour and National Service to the new Ministry of Social Security, or by retaining these functions in the Ministry of Labour and National Service, but housing the staff at the local Security Offices. Probably the former plan will be the more convenient, though either alternative is possible. In any case the Ministry of Labour and

National Service will continue to deal with labour questions generally, including training for which it will provide institutions, post-medical rehabilitation, wages and conditions of employment, disputes, survey of the labour market and welfare in places of employment. The Ministry of Social Security must co-operate closely with the Ministry of Labour and National Service, particularly, in regard to training and must co-operate also with the department or departments responsible for administration of the Mines and Factory Acts and the prevention of accident and disease.

175. *Other Departmental Transfers:* In addition to the transfer of unemployment insurance from the Ministry of Labour and National Service, there will be transfer of health insurance from the Health Departments and of workmen's compensation from the Home Office. The position of the Registry of Friendly Societies, office of the Industrial Assurance Commissioner, will depend to some extent upon the decision on Change **23** below. It will probably be desirable in any case for the Minister of Social Security to answer for the work of the Registry in Parliament, though it should be noted that this work is concerned also with Trade Unions, and with other types of society not closely associated with problems of social security.

Change 22. Substitution for the Unemployment Insurance Statutory Committee of a Social Insurance Statutory Committee with similar but extended powers.

176. The Unemployment Insurance Statutory Committee has three main functions in relation to unemployment insurance :—

(*a*) Supervision of the finance of the Unemployment Fund, including power to recommend changes of benefit and contribution which can be carried out without legislation, in order to adjust the income and the expenditure of the Fund ;

(*b*) Reporting on all Draft Regulations, after giving an opportunity to interested parties to make representations ;

(*c*) Reporting on any other matters referred to it by the Minister, acting thus as a standing Royal Commission.

The Committee consists of seven members, each holding office for five years, within which he cannot be dismissed ; none of the members can belong to the House of Commons ; one member at least must be a woman ; two are appointed after consultation with organisations of employers and employees and one after consultation with the Government of Northern Ireland. The Committee is independent of the Minister, but has no executive powers. Its function is that of making reports upon which the Minister and Parliament decide.

177. There will clearly be need for a similar body to give considered, impartial attention to the problems of unified social insurance. Such a body might well be constructed on the same lines as the Unemployment Insurance Statutory Committee, with or without the special representation of Northern Ireland. It would give to employers and employees a regular opportunity of making representation as to branches of insurance, other than unemployment insurance, which they do not enjoy at present. But there will be important differences of detail between the functions of the Unemployment Insurance Statutory Committee and those of a similar body for social insurance as a whole.

178. One difference will be that the Social Insurance Statutory Committee, even if it makes a financial report each year, should not be expected each year to bring the income and expenditure of the Social Insurance Fund into adjustment, or to make some recommendation for change each year. The finance of pensions and sickness is an affair not of a year, but of a lifetime.

It is not, in fact, desirable that the unemployment account of the Social Insurance Fund should be kept in balance every year. On the contrary, the Fund, by accumulating reserves in periods of good trade, and spending them or even running into debt on its unemployment account in periods of declining activity, may help to stabilise employment (*see* para. 442).

179. Another difference is that the Social Insurance Statutory Committee will have to deal with two problems which do not arise in the narrower scope of unemployment insurance—namely that of keeping benefits and contributions in relation to changes in the value of money and that of keeping benefits for different purposes in the right relation to one another, subject to whatever statutory minima are prescribed.

180. A number of problems of a type suitable for investigation by such a body as the suggested Social Insurance Statutory Committee will arise in the framing of the unified insurance scheme and in adjusting its details. It may be found convenient to have the Committee established in advance of the coming into operation of the scheme, so as to get these problems dealt with in good time.

[Change 23. Conversion of the business of industrial assurance into a public service under an Industrial Assurance Board.]

181. The business of industrial assurance is life assurance conducted with the use of collectors, that is to say, it is life assurance in which the premiums are received by means of collectors who make house to house visits for that purpose at weekly or other short intervals. Life assurance in which the premiums are not collected or are collected at intervals of two months or more is described as " ordinary " life assurance. The offices undertaking industrial assurance are described as Industrial Life Offices. They are of two kinds known as industrial assurance companies and collecting societies respectively ; the companies themselves are divided into proprietary companies paying dividends to shareholders and mutual companies. Beginning as insurance for burial expenses, the business has developed to include insurance for a variety of expenses that may arise at death, and life and endowment assurance generally, among persons of limited means ; it is now very large. In 1939 there were 103,000,000 policies of industrial assurance in force, more than two-and-a-quarter policies for every man, woman and child in Britain. There were about 65,000 full-time collectors in addition to several thousand part-time and spare-time collectors. The premiums received were over £74,000,000, and the expenses of management were nearly £24,000,000 in addition to dividends to shareholders amounting to over £1,750,000 after payment of £1,600,000 income-tax. In addition to premiums, the Industrial Life Offices received in 1939 about £20,000,000 as interest, representing the return on accumulations of earlier premiums. The premium income was nearly two-and-a-half times the total contributions of employers and insured persons to national health insurance ; that is to say, it was equivalent to the amount that would be raised by a contribution in the case of national health contributors of 1/10 a week for a man and 1/9 a week for a woman.

182. Though the total number of Industrial Life Offices is 160, nearly 90 per cent. of the whole business is concentrated in eight large offices, the Prudential, Pearl, Liverpool Victoria, Refuge, Co-operative, Royal London Mutual, Royal Liver and Britannic, each with a premium income in 1939 of more than £4,000,000 a year. All the larger offices except (in England) the Co-operative, have associated with them Approved Societies engaged in administering health insurance through the collectors engaged on industrial assurance. Most of the large offices undertake also a growing volume of ordinary

life assurance. The premium income of their ordinary branches in 1939 was about £30,000,000 a year ; a considerable proportion of this business is done with people who hold industrial policies as well.

183. The main facts as to the business of industrial assurance, the criticisms which have been made on it in the past and the reasons leading to the proposal made here for converting it into a public service under an Industrial Assurance Board are set out fully in Appendix D, to which reference should be made. Here they are given briefly :

184. Two of the proposals made above as integral parts of a comprehensive scheme of social insurance, namely supersession of the approved society system in its present form of giving unequal benefits for equal compulsory contributions (Change 3) and provision of funeral grant for all deaths (Change 18) affect directly the work of the Industrial Life Offices. Though much of the business undertaken by these offices, particularly their large and growing endowment assurance and the work of their ordinary branches, would not be directly affected by these proposals, the whole of their work probably depends for its economical and effective administration so much upon association with health insurance or on provision for funerals, that it is doubtful if any satisfactory or just scheme dividing the work of the offices could be devised. Moreover, to divide the work would deprive the administration of health insurance, to some extent at least, of the service of the present skilled staff.

185. Industrial assurance as now conducted has an excessive cost of administration. Including expenses of management, dividends to shareholders and income-tax, all of which are costs from the point of view of the policy-holder, the cost ratio of all the Industrial Life Offices taken together in 1937-40 amounted to about 7/6 in the £, or 4½d. in the 1/- of premiums. That is to say, of every 1/– paid by the policy-holders only 7½d. goes to the assurance fund. While a relatively high administrative cost is inevitable, so long as collectors are used, the actual cost is higher than necessary even with collectors, as is shown by the success of some of the larger companies in reducing their expenses of management materially by rationalisation. The business of industrial assurance could not have been built up without collectors, but it cannot be admitted that weekly collection of premiums is a permanent, indispensable requirement for securing regular voluntary contributions from persons of limited means. The centralised Friendly Societies have an administrative cost of 10 per cent. or 2/- in the £ of contributions. (*See* Appendix E, para. 23.) The Hospital Contributory Associations and the War Savings Committee are able to obtain small regular savings in peace as in war at a very small fraction of the administrative cost involved in industrial assurance.

186. Industrial assurance as now conducted is pushed in the interests of the Industrial Life Offices and their agents as sellers of insurance to a point beyond the interests of the public as buyers of insurance. This is shown both by the high proportion of their total incomes that is devoted to industrial assurance by persons of insufficient means and by the high proportion of abortive insurance, that is to say, of policies failing to reach maturity. In each of the three years just before the war the number of policies in six of the largest offices which, after some premium had been paid on them, ended prematurely, by lapsing, surrender for cash, or being made free for a reduced sum, was about two-thirds of the total number of policies issued and taken up in the year ; more than half of this two-thirds were forfeited completely. From these returns for six large offices, it may be estimated that, taking all offices together, there were issued in each of the last years before the present war about 10 million policies and that each year about 6¾ million policies ended prematurely. Of these, ¾ million were policies not taken up ; about

3¼ million were forfeited outright after the policy had been taken up and premiums had been paid on it ; about 2¾ million were converted into free policies for reduced sums or surrendered for cash. All the premiums paid on these policies had borne their share of the high administrative cost of collection. A higher proportion of abortive policies is probably inevitable in industrial assurance than in ordinary life assurance in view of the limited means and economic insecurity of the policy-holders. This makes it all the more important to remove the pressure upon the public to insure which results from the financial interest of the offices and the terms of remuneration of their agents.

187. Every independent Committee which has investigated the business of industrial assurance in the past—the Select Committee of 1889, the Parmoor Committee of 1919–20 and the Cohen Committee of 1931-33—has made strong criticisms on the conduct and results of the business. The last of these Committees attributed the " principal defects " of the business to " excessive competition with its almost feverish pressure for ' increase.' " While ruling out nationalisation of industrial assurance " as it now exists " as not a practical proposition, they added as a final sentence to the main body of their Report the following words : " We are convinced that if the changes which the due protection of the assuring public demands cannot be effected by less drastic measures the difficulties in the transference of the business to a single organization to which we have referred at length will ultimately have to be faced." No effect has been given to the proposals of the Cohen Committee for changes in the law of industrial assurance. The Industrial Life Offices have taken steps to meet some of the criticisms of this and earlier Committees, by grant of surrender values and free policies in place of lapsing and in other ways. But on the main subjects of the Cohen Committee's criticism—high cost of administration and high proportion of abortive insurance—the position was not substantially different in 1937–39 than at the time of the Committee's Report. Though many changes and improvements have been made in the business, there is no sign of a radical change, and no prospect of any general large reduction of administrative costs. Since the date of the Parmoor Report the largest of the life offices, the Prudential, with a premium income in 1937-40 of nearly £24,000,000, has by rationalisation of its staff decreased its expenses of management by one-third. The two next largest proprietary companies, the Pearl and the Refuge, with annual premium incomes in 1937–40 of about £9,000,000 and £6,000,000 respectively, have decreased their expenses of management by about one-quarter. These are noteworthy achievements, but they leave the total cost ratio in 1937–40 of the proprietary companies as a whole at 36·3 per cent. of the premiums and they cover only a part of the whole field of industrial assurance. In the fifty years from 1887 to 1937–40 the four chief mutual offices (societies or companies) operating throughout that period have reduced their expenses of management only from being 44 per cent. of the premiums to being 40 per cent. of the premiums. During that period of fifty years, the premium income on which these percentages are charged has risen from under £1,000,000 in 1887 to nearly £18,000,000 in 1937–40 ; the business of this group of offices has been growing more rapidly than that of the Prudential. In this group of offices recognition of book interest, that is to say, of the right of each agent to nominate his successor and in effect to sell his book, practically excludes the prospect of any large change of terms of service or reduction of costs.

188. The proposal to transfer life assurance among persons of limited means from the sphere of commercial undertaking to that of public service rests upon two sets of facts which distinguish such life assurance both from ordinary life assurance and from most other forms of business. In the first place,

life assurance is a contract for life or for a long period of years. It is not an article in regard to which the buyer can, without loss, change his purchase or his seller, if he is dissatisfied. He cannot, having bought insurance from one company one day, buy less insurance or different insurance another day, as he can change his grocer or buy less of an article which he can no longer afford. Life assurance is also an article of whose value in relation to other things it is difficult for the buyer to judge. It is important, therefore, that in buying life assurance persons of limited means should be guided by advice from the seller which is wholly disinterested. This does not apply to life assurance by people who have larger means and in general can have recourse to skilled, disinterested advice. In the second place, industrial assurance is now so closely associated with other forms of insurance that are either already the business of the State (health insurance) or should, as a means of reducing costs to the public, be undertaken by the State (such as funeral insurance), that it will probably be less difficult and more advantageous to make the association still closer than to break it up. The difficulties seen by the Cohen Committee in transferring the business to a single organisation are probably now less than the difficulties of dividing the business, which is the only alternative.

189. In addition to these two features, as to which there should be general agreement, industrial assurance has a third distinguishing feature, in judging of which there may be differences of opinion, namely, that it is a business requiring little or no investment of capital. The Parmoor Committee pointed out that " the share capital of industrial assurance companies exercises much less important functions than that of commercial or manufacturing undertakings," and added that " in these circumstances the case for high dividends appears . . . to rest upon somewhat slender foundations." Since the date of the Parmoor Committee, the industrial assurance companies have increased the share of valuation surpluses going to policy-holders and in other ways have improved the terms offered by them. But largely increased sums continue to be paid as dividends on capital which either has not been increased or does not need to be increased. All the money to speak of in industrial assurance has come from the policy-holders. The large dividends to shareholders are only to a very limited extent payment for necessary services by capital.

190. Conversion of the business of industrial assurance into a public service would involve the creation of a statutory corporation, that is to say, the setting up of an Industrial Assurance Board which would naturally to a large extent be founded on the experience and abilities of those now engaged in the business. The Board would have a statutory monopoly of the use of collectors and would be authorised to undertake life assurance, whether through collectors or otherwise, up to a low maximum sum assured, say £300. It would take over all the existing policies and honour them, safeguarding the rights of every policy-holder. It would compensate the shareholders. It would employ or compensate the staff, including dealing fairly with book interest, that is to say, with the valuable right of agents in certain offices to nominate their successors and in effect to sell their books. There will naturally be many difficult problems to solve ; in particular that of the line which should be drawn between the business taken over and that not taken over. There will be difficult problems of transition, involved in the introduction of the State funeral grant. But transition will be more easy if industrial assurance is made a public service than if the alternative plan is adopted of leaving it to continue as a competitive business in a restricted field.

191. Once established, the Industrial Assurance Board would set out to encourage more economical methods of insurance and saving than are represented at present by industrial assurance ; would reduce the staff required for collection as rapidly as this could be done without hardship, and would at

the same time place the staff at the disposal of the Ministry of Social Security for other work in the field of social insurance, whether in connection with health insurance or with other forms of insurance. The collectors now visiting at short intervals most of the houses in Britain have become in thousands of cases the friends and advisers of the families with whom they deal. Many of them are in effect travelling Citizens' Advice Bureaux ; they regard themselves as servants of the public. They can find in a new relation a better opportunity and not a worse opportunity of living up to that ideal.

192. The proposal made here is bracketed ; that is to say, it is not essential to the whole of the rest of the Plan for Social Security. The alternative (assuming the acceptance of the changes which are necessary, in relation to Approved Societies and in relation to a State funeral grant) is to leave to the Industrial Life Offices as business concerns the great and growing sphere which would still remain—of insurance for indirect expenses connected with funerals, of life and endowment assurance for purposes other than funeral expenses, and of insurance against minor needs. That is a possible alternative, but presents almost as many administrative difficulties as that of the proposal made here. It does not yield as good results to the public. It makes more difficult the problem of doing justice to the existing staff. It means a greater not a smaller breach of continuity for all concerned than does the proposal for conversion to a public service.

PART III

THREE SPECIAL PROBLEMS

SECTION 1

BENEFIT RATES AND THE PROBLEM OF RENT

193. The rates of benefit or pension provided by social insurance should be such as to secure for all normal cases an income adequate for subsistence, on the assumptions :—

(a) that assistance will be available to meet abnormal subsistence needs ;
(b) that voluntary insurance and saving to provide for standards of life above subsistence minimum will be encouraged and made easy.

It is assumed, further, that there will be allowances for all dependent children, while the parent on whom they are dependent is on benefit or pension. The rates of allowance required for subsistence needs of children are considered in this section. The general question of children's allowances, both when the parent is earning and when he is not earning, is discussed in paras. 410–425.

194. Determination of the minimum income required for subsistence, though simplified by the foregoing assumptions, remains a difficult problem on two grounds :—

(a) No reasoned forecast can now be made of the cost of living at the time when the insurance scheme may be expected to come into force. All that can be done is to make estimates of subsistence income at pre-war prices (for convenience the year 1938 is taken) and to say how these estimates would be changed for any assumed increase in prices above the pre-war level.

(b) The cost of living is not the same for all families, or in all parts of the country. The main difference is in respect of rents, which differ markedly between London, the rest of England and Scotland, and between industrial and agricultural households.

195. The problem presented by inequality of rents is discussed in paras 197–206, as a preliminary to determining rates of benefit. Thereafter subsistence needs are considered separately for persons of working age, for retired persons, for young persons and boys and girls of working age, and for children below working age.

196. It will be seen, from the discussion which follows, that any estimate of subsistence income for the population as a whole during unemployment and disability even at known pre-war prices, is to some extent a matter of judgment. Nor can any single estimate, such as is necessary for the determination of a rate of insurance benefit, fit exactly the differing conditions of differing households; while the main differences in the cost of living arise through variation of rents, there are differences also in the cost of fuel and other articles. The calculations made have been prepared in consultation with a Sub-Committee including Professor A. L. Bowley, Mr. Seebohm Rowntree, Mr. R. F. George and Dr. H. E. Magee, and in respect of items other than rent, have been approved by the Sub-Committee as affording a reasonable basis for fixing rates of unemployment and disability benefits which at 1938 prices would provide a subsistence minimum in normal cases. In regard to rent, the Sub-Committee express the view that no single figure can be justified on scientific grounds as fitting the needs.

The Problem of Rent

197. Rent has three characteristics differentiating it from other forms of expenditure :—

(i) Rent varies markedly from one part of the country to another.

(ii) Rent varies markedly as between different families of the same size in the same part of the country.

(iii) Expenditure on rent cannot be reduced during a temporary interruption of earning as that on clothing, fuel or light can.

198. The first of these differences between rent and other necessaries is illustrated by Table IV giving, for industrial households in each division of Britain and for agricultural households, the weekly expenditures in 1937-38 on rent and on food, clothing, fuel and light respectively, as deduced from the Ministry of Labour Family Budgets.* In order to allow for the differing numbers of persons per household in different divisions of the country, the expenditures are shown in columns 4 and 5 for " standard households " of the same size in all cases; adjustment to standard households reduces the expenditure shown where the number of persons per household is above the average for the country as a whole and increases it where the number is below average. In columns 6 and 7 these standardised expenditures are shown for industrial households in each division as a percentage of the mean for all divisions.

199. It will be seen that, for food, clothing, fuel and light, the percentages for the separate divisions all lie in a narrow range, between 94·2 and 104·9, with agricultural households spending 76·6 per cent. of the industrial mean. For rent, the range is much greater, from 70·4 per cent. in Scotland to 148·1 per cent. in London in industrial households, with agricultural households spending only 43·5 per cent. of the industrial mean. The average of the actual rents runs from 16·0 shillings a week in London to 7·6 shillings in Scotland for standard industrial households, and is 4·7 shillings in agricultural households. The expenditures of agricultural households relate to a time before the recent raising of agricultural wages.

---

* The main results were published in the *Labour Gazettes* for December 1940 and January 1941.

TABLE IV
WEEKLY EXPENDITURE ON NECESSARIES, 1937-1938

	Persons per Household (1)	Per Household in shillings		Per Standard Industrial Household, in shillings		Per cent. of Mean for all Industrial Households	
		Food, Clothing, Fuel and Light (2)	Rent (3)	Food, Clothing, Fuel and Light (4)	Rent (5)	Food, Clothing, Fuel and Light (6)	Rent (7)
*Industrial Households by Divisions**							
London (1456)	3·66	50·1	15·7	51·1	16·0	104·9	148·1
South-East (839)	3·67	45·0	11·2	45·9	11·4	94·2	105·5
South-West (776)	3·66	46·4	10·3	47·4	10·5	97·3	97·2
Midland (1276)	3·77	50·5	10·3	50·0	10·2	102·7	94·4
North-East (1035)	3·68	46·6	10·1	47·4	10·3	97·3	95·4
North-West (1281)	3·73	47·8	10·7	47·8	10·7	98·1	99·1
North (572)	3·69	46·0	9·2	46·6	9·3	95·7	86·1
Wales (434)	3·71	47·1	9·1	47·4	9·1	97·3	84·3
Scotland (980)	4·02	53·7	8·2	50·0	7·6	102·7	70·4
All Industrial Households (8649)	3·73	48·7	10·8	48·7	10·8	100·0	100·0
Agricultural Households (1313)	3·79	37·9	4·8	37·3	4·7	76·6	43·5

Source : Ministry of Labour Family Budget Enquiry.

* The figures in brackets give the numbers of households in each division for which budgets were obtained. The divisions are those of the Ministry of Labour and National Service.

200. Table IV gives averages for large regions. It conceals the second characteristic of rent, that within any region there are great differences of expenditure by individual households. The cost of necessary food, clothing, fuel and light is much the same, or can be made much the same, for all households of the same size in the same region. This is not true of rent. The wide variation of the rents paid by individual households is sufficiently illustrated by the following table from the Report of the Unemployment Assistance Board for 1938.

TABLE V
DISTRIBUTION OF RENTS PAID BY APPLICANTS FOR UNEMPLOYMENT ASSISTANCE, 1938

Rent	Free to 2/5	2/6 to 4/11	5/- to 7/5	7/6 to 9/11	10/- to 12/5	12/6 to 14/11	15/- to 17/5	17/6 to 19/11	20/- and over
	%	%	%	%	%	%	%	%	%
England and Wales ...	1·5	8·0	27·5	29·6	17·8	7·3	4·6	1·7	2·0
Scotland	6·6	23·8	39·7	22·7	5·3	1·2	0·4	0·2	0·1
London	0·8	2·0	8·6	14·7	22·6	17·6	15·7	7·2	10·8

Source : Unemployment Assistance Board Report, 1938, p. 198.

201. The average weekly rent paid by all industrial households included in the Ministry of Labour Family Budget in 1937-38 was 10/9. If any single figure is to be taken as the pre-war requirement for rent in fixing rates of benefit, a figure of 10/- a week is the natural suggestion. The figure should be below rather than above the average shown in the budgets, since these cover families living well above the subsistence level ; the average rents of applicants for unemployment assistance deduced from the table given above for each of the three regions would be appreciably below those shown by the family budgets for those regions. Mr. Rowntree by independent enquiry reached 9/6 a week as the best single figure for rent requirement in 1936. The figure of 10/- is for a household. For solitary individuals a figure of 6/6 is taken.

202. But neither 10/-, nor any other single figure, can fit the true requirements even reasonably well. A glance at Table V shows that an allowance of 10/- a week for rent in 1938 would have been anything from 2/6 to 7/6 too much for more than two-thirds of the Scottish households and anything from 2/6 to 10/- and upwards too little for half the London households. In no part of the country would it have been within 2/6 of the actual rent for as many as half the households. It would have been at least twice as much as was needed for more than half the agricultural households. With the present variety of rents, it is not possible to fix any uniform rate of insurance benefit as meeting subsistence requirements with any accuracy. Even when differences in the size of the family have been provided for by allowances for dependants, any uniform rate must be many shillings a week too high for many cases and many shillings too low for many other cases.

203. These misfits are made more serious by the third characteristic of rent—that it is a form of expenditure in which adjustment or postponement, when earnings are interrupted, is difficult or impossible. A man who feels able to commit himself to a high rent because his earnings are high, remains liable for it when his earnings stop ; unless he can meet the rent, he has not enough for subsistence. This consideration is relevant particularly to unemployment, sickness or accident, whose onset cannot be foreseen ; for retirement, which can be foreseen, there is greater possibility of adjusting rent to prospective resources.

204. In the social surveys which have been made shortly before the present war of living conditions in various British towns, Mr. Rowntree and others, in judging of subsistence needs and estimating what proportions of the population are in poverty or in varying degrees above it, have invariably and unavoidably allowed for the actual rent paid by each family and have calculated the income required for the other necessaries—food, clothing, fuel and so on—according to the size and constitution of the family. The question arises whether the rate of insurance benefit ought to be determined on the same principle, securing to each insured person when his earnings are interrupted the actual rent paid by him and a fixed weekly sum on top of that for his other needs. The suggestion that benefit should be determined in this way was made by the Association of Municipal Corporations, speaking from their practical experience in dealing with need, and by the Fabian Society. It was strongly urged by some members of the sub-committee who were asked to advise on the rates of benefit that would ensure adequate subsistence.

205. There is no doubt that if insurance benefit could be made variable, so as to allow for actual rent and not for an assumed average rent, it would meet subsistence needs more closely. This is the main argument for the proposal put to the Committee by the Association of Municipal Corporations and the Fabian Society. The proposal has other advantages also. First, if the actual rent is covered in every case, children's allowances can safely

be made exclusive of rent. There will be no risk of benefit being inadequate because a large family has made a large rent necessary. Second, the differentiation suggested elsewhere (paras. 111–113) between the benefit rates for single and for married women would take place automatically. The former will have rent to pay ; the latter, apart from exceptional cases, will not be responsible for rent. Third, the future course of rents is, if possible, even more problematical than that of prices generally, and may be different in different parts of the country, according to the housing policy of the Local Authority. It will be anomalous that of two people in the same town getting the same benefit for subsistence, one should be comfortable on a low rent in a subsidised municipal house or with a rebate because he is unemployed, while the other is left in want because he is paying a rack rent.

206. If benefit is to be related to needs, the case for adjusting it, if possible, to the actual rent paid is strong. This adjustment can be made and is made in paying assistance. Should it be made in determining benefit ? Should men who pay the same contribution get different rates of benefit when they are unemployed or sick, according to the rent which they pay ? The suggestion raises questions of principle and of practice.

207. On the question of principle, it can be argued that, as men for the same contribution get different rates of benefit, according to the number of dependants they must maintain, there is nothing unjust in differentiating benefit by reference to the rent which men have to pay. When a man contributes, he does not know just how much rent he will be paying when he next falls out of work or is sick. He ought to be insured against that liability for rent, whatever it may be ; social security, as the representatives of the Fabian Society put it, should guarantee the home, and an income for other necessaries.

208. Against this, it can be argued that the analogy between providing for dependants and providing for rent is a false one, because the amount of rent which a man pays is not independent of his will or of his financial resources ; a high rent is to some extent at least the sign of a larger income ; it is paid not for subsistence but as part of a standard of living above the minimum. Men with larger incomes do not as such have more dependants, so that giving allowances for dependants does not mean that high wage workmen get on the whole more benefit than low wage workmen when unemployed. But to adjust benefit by rent would mean this : on the average the skilled men would be found paying higher rents than the unskilled ; for equal contributions they would get, on an average, higher rates of benefit when unemployed or sick. Granted that the man with greater liabilities for rent should be insured against them, it can be urged he ought to be so by voluntary insurance to supplement the compulsory subsistence benefit.

209. This argument raises the fundamental question of fact as to whether rents above the average represent the wishes or the necessities of those who pay them. It is a question to which a clear-cut answer cannot be given : the answer probably varies from time to time and from one town to another, according to the housing situation. Such direct evidence as is available about the relation of rent and income shows that while rents, on an average, increase with income, the increase is not rapid, so that the proportion of income devoted to rent falls as income rises. The following Table VI relates to a random sample of more than 6,000 applicants for War Service Grants in 1939–42. The facts as to voluntary insurance payments are referred to in para. 286 and in Appendix D on Industrial Assurance. Here the table is used only in relation to rents.

TABLE VI

RENTS AND VOLUNTARY INSURANCE PAYMENTS OF APPLICANTS FOR WAR SERVICE GRANTS
IN RELATION TO INCOME, 1939-42

Income (*) shillings per week	Average Rent per household		Average Voluntary Insurance Payments	
	Shillings	Per cent. of Income	Shillings	Per cent. of Income
Under 40 ...	10·2	33·5	2·29	7·5
40–60 ...	10·2	20·4	2·41	4·8
60–80 ...	11·2	16·0	2·49	3·6
80–100 ...	11·9	13·2	2·84	3·1
100–120 ...	12·4	11·3	3·16	2·9
120–140 ...	14·0	10·7	3·73	2·9
140 or over ...	15·3	8·4	4·55	2·5
All households ...	11·3	15·1	2·64	3·5

(*) Pre-service income.

There is no difference between the average rents paid by households with incomes below 40/– a week and between 40/– and 60/– ; thereafter the average rent rises slowly to 12·4s. in the group between 100/– and 120/– of income ; beyond that it rises more rapidly. The table suggests that rents behave in main as necessaries in households with incomes up to £6 a week. The percentage of total income spent on rent falls from a third in the poorest group to a twelfth in the group with incomes of more than 140/– a week. These results for the country as a whole in war-time are similar to those for York in 1936. Mr. Rowntree's investigation showed that the average rents paid by the income classes into which he divided the working-class population differed only by 1·3s. a week as between the poorest and the most prosperous. This appears from Table VII below.

TABLE VII

RENTS IN RELATION TO INCOME IN YORK, 1936

Net income after deducting rent and rates	Rent including rates Shillings	Income (incl. amount paid for rent) Shillings	Rent as per cent. of Income
Class A Under 33/6	8·57	40·87	20·9
Class B 33/6 and under 43/6 ...	8·47	45·74	18·5
Class C 43/6 and under 53/6 ...	9·62	58·26	16·5
Class D 53/6 and under 63/6 ...	9·65	70·47	13·7
Class E 63/6 and over	9·87	97·60	10·1

Source : Rowntree, *Poverty and Progress*, p. 262.

The net incomes shown are those left after allowing for rent so that a high rent in itself tends to put the household in a lower income class ; this accounts no doubt for the fact that the rents in Class A are higher than those in Class B. But subject to this caution, the table supports the view that the level of rents is largely a matter of necessity, not of choice. Undoubtedly, those whose work compels them to live in London cannot in general avoid paying rents materially higher than their fellows elsewhere ; those who in any region pay rents above the regional average often do so because they have no alternative. On the other hand, individuals can and do choose to some extent between expenditure on house-room and other forms of expenditure ; sometimes they pay high rents because they can afford it or because they value good accommodation more than other things ; sometimes they pay low rents at the cost of heavier expenses in travelling to work. The amount of rent that a man pays represents often both a necessity and a comfort or a luxury, but is not divisible between these purposes. On the question of principle raised by the proposal to adjust security benefit to the actual rent paid by the individual, reasonable men may take different views.

210. On the question of practice, it is clear that to make the benefit vary with the actual rent would involve additional administration. Every applicant for unemployment or disability benefit or retirement pension (if the plan applied there) would be required to state the rent for which he was responsible, and the benefit to be paid to each applicant would have to be calculated separately. This in itself is not a serious objection ; unemployment benefit payments have now to be adjusted individually, according to the number of dependants. The extra work involved in this question on the application form and in checking the rent paid, where necessary, would be relatively small. A much larger practical difficulty would arise in determining the amount of the rent for which the applicant was responsible, in cases in which he was not the only earner in the house—where for instance he was one of an earning group, or was a householder with independent lodgers or a lodger himself. It is clear that such questions would sometimes prove very difficult ; they would arise often enough to add appreciably to the task of administering benefit. All that can be said is that the administrative difficulties of adjusting benefit for rent cannot be regarded as insoluble. They should be faced, if the proposal is necessary and right in principle.

211. As a modification of the proposal to adjust benefit to rent which would simplify administration while preserving its principle, it has been suggested that a standard allowance for rent, say 8/– a week, should be included in the benefit, and that anyone paying more rent than this could apply to have his benefit increased accordingly, up to a maximum rent of, say, 16/–. This plan would reduce the number of cases in which the actual rent had to be taken into account and would thus reduce administrative labour. But it would not touch the main practical difficulty of determining for what rent any particular applicant in a composite household was responsible, and, unless the standard allowance was made low, it would increase appreciably the cost of benefit as compared with the proposal to allow for actual rent in every case. There would be no saving on the persons with low rent (including all the agricultural labourers) to set against the additional payments to persons with high rent ; if, to avoid this result, the standard allowance was put low, the saving on administration would be small. It can be urged, on the other hand, that unless some allowance is made, either in this way or in another, for the exceptionally high level of rents in London, substantial supplementation of benefit by assistance may prove unavoidable in London. Even if differentiation for rents in the manner now suggested increased expenditure on benefit, this might be less than the saving which it would bring about on assistance. If the principle of adjusting benefit to rent without any difference of contributions is admitted, the suggestion made in this paragraph is probably the most practical way of giving effect to that principle.

212. As a second modification, it has been suggested that allowance for actual rent should be confined to the working age benefits, for unemployment and disability, and that retirement pensions should be uniform. There is much to be said for this modification on grounds of principle and of practice. While men cannot foresee unemployment and disability, they can foresee the coming of old age and its date ; they have time to adjust expenditure to the means which they have been able to provide, through compulsory insurance and through voluntary additions to it. Pensions, moreover, will as a rule be drawn for much longer periods than unemployment or disability benefits. It will appear indefensible that those who just before retiring have been able to

secure good accommodation at a relatively high rent should thereby retain this advantage for the rest of their lives, in kind if not in cash, as compared with those who have been less fortunate or less foreseeing. On the other hand, if those who are already drawing pension on the basis of one rent are free to move to more expensive accommodation and have their pension increased accordingly, pensions will come to look like a subsidy to landlords. On all grounds of principle and of practice, the basic provision made by compulsory insurance for retirement pensions should be uniform for all citizens in all regions.

213. With these two modifications, the proposal to vary the benefit in individual cases so as to allow for the actual rent paid cannot be dismissed either as impracticable or as clearly wrong in principle. Nevertheless the balance of argument in the end appears to be against the proposal, even with these modifications. The principle that a flat rate of insurance contribution should lead to a flat rate of benefit has a strong popular appeal and is much easier to defend than any departure from it. Some at least of those who advocated variation of benefit according to individual rents objected to any application of " insurance principle " to social security ; they favoured the financing of social security not by insurance contributions, but by graduated income-tax. If insurance contributions are retained, as is proposed in this Report, it seems best also to keep a rate of benefit without adjustment for individual rents. This decision is supported by the hope that the launching of the Plan for Social Security will coincide with a determined and successful effort to deal with urban congestion and shortage of housing. If and so far as this hope is realised, inequalities of rent bearing no relation to the accommodation obtained will disappear ; a high rent will then represent a free choice by the householder and it will become indefensible to favour that form of expenditure over other forms of expenditure in fixing scales of benefit.

214. But while the difficulties of principle and of practice, in the way of adjusting benefits to individual rents are probably sufficient to justify rejection of this proposal, the difficulty of meeting the differing requirements of households by a uniform rate of benefit in all parts of the country remains. The difficulty presents itself in regard to benefits and contributions alike. A rate of benefit adequate for needs, where rents are high, will be more than adequate for regions of low rent, and will involve contributions that may appear excessive in relation to the wages earned. The preceding discussion of rents raises the question whether a rate of benefit and of contribution uniform in every part of Britain and in every occupation is right. On an average, the rent of an industrial household in London in 1937–38 was about 6/– a week above the average of industrial households in the rest of Britain, and the latter in turn was about 6/– a week above the rent paid by agricultural households. It would be inequitable to pay different rates of benefit in differing regions while charging a uniform contribution ; some people outside London pay higher rents than some people in London. But there would be nothing inequitable in making regional or occupational differences in the rates of benefit and of contribution alike. To increase unemployment and disability benefits in London by, say, 3/6 a week for a single person, with 2/6 a week more for wife or dependant, making 6/– for man and wife, would mean adding about 6d. to the joint contribution of employer and employee in the case of a man and 4d. in the case of a woman. To provide, either for agricultural households as such or for rural regions, benefits lower by the same amounts than the general standard for industrial households outside London, would make possible a corresponding reduction of joint contributions. Any regional or occupational differentiation of benefits and contributions would detract from the simplicity of the social insurance scheme and would raise some difficulties

in administration. But so long as differentiation applies to contributions as well as to benefit it is equitable, and so long as it is confined to working age benefits, the administrative difficulty, which is chiefly that of determining the rate to be paid to a man who has moved from one region or occupation to another region or occupation with different rates, cannot be regarded as insuperable or, indeed, as extremely serious. For pensions, it is right and necessary to maintain a uniform basic rate on retirement at the minimum pension age with a uniform contribution, and this is proposed in the following section. For unemployment and disability differentiation of insurance contribution and benefit may well appear preferable to a situation in which benefit in London had to be supplemented in a large proportion of cases in order to cover rent, and in which agricultural labourers and their employers found themselves paying unwillingly the high contributions which are needed for benefit to suit urban conditions.

215. The practical conclusions which emerge from this discussion are as follows :—

(1) For the purpose of determining standard rates of unemployment and disability benefit household rent at pre-war levels is taken as 10/- a week for a household and 6/6 a week for a solitary individual.

(2) The practicability and desirability of differentiation of both benefits and contributions, regionally or occupationally, in the way suggested in the last paragraph should be examined further in consultation with the persons and bodies affected. If some such body as the Social Insurance Statutory Committee proposed in Change 22 of Part II is established, this question might conveniently be referred statutorily to that Committee, as the question of applying unemployment insurance to agriculture was referred to the Unemployment Insurance Statutory Committee under the Unemployment Act of 1934.

(3) The proposal to adjust benefit according to the rent actually paid by individuals should, provisionally, be rejected.

In accord with the first of these conclusions and with the estimates of other needs made below, a scale of uniform benefits and of the contributions needed to provide them has been prepared. If the further examination suggested in the second conclusion leads to regional or occupational differentiation of working age benefits and of the corresponding contributions, this differentiation can be introduced without affecting in any important way either the structure of the social insurance scheme or its financial implications. If, contrary to the provisional view taken here, it should be decided that adjustment for individual rents is desirable and practicable, this change also could be made without affecting the main structure.

216. These practical conclusions are suggested to make the best of a difficult situation, not as a solution of the problem of finding a subsistence basis for rates of benefit. The extreme variation of rents, between regions and in the same region, for similar accommodation is evidence of failure to distribute industry and population and of failure to provide housing according to needs. No scale of social insurance benefits free from objection can be framed while the failure continues. In this, as in other respects, the framing of a completely satisfactory plan of social security depends on a solution of other social problems.

PERSONS OF WORKING AGE

217. In considering the minimum income needed by persons of working age for subsistence during interruption of earnings, it is sufficient to take into account food, clothing, fuel, light and household sundries, and rent,

though some margin must be allowed for inefficiency in spending. Persons not working will not have to spend money in travelling to work, and it is assumed that there will be provision for excusing insurance contributions, both compulsory and voluntary, during interruption of earning. In so far as these contributions are not excused, they must be covered by the margin. So also must be covered by the margin any diversion of expenditure from things which are necessary to things which, though not necessary, may appear preferable to the individual.

218. *Food.* For food it is possible to make estimates on the basis of dietaries. At 1938 prices, it would have been possible to provide an adequate dietary, either on the scale laid down in the 1936 and 1938 Reports of the Technical Commission on Nutrition by the League of Nations or on the scale laid down in 1933 by the Committee on Nutrition of the British Medical Association, for a man and woman together at a cost of about 13/– a week. Reference to these dietaries does not imply a view that they are themselves incapable of improvement or would be accepted today as final by all authorities. The science of nutrition, like other sciences, progresses and shows how health may be improved by different ways of feeding. But a better dietary is not necessarily a more expensive dietary. Although the constituents of the League of Nations and the British Medical Association diets differ, there is no marked difference in their total cost. The 13/– may reasonably be divided as 7/– for a single man and 6/– for a single woman. These figures exclude special needs, such as those of invalids and of expectant and nursing mothers. For the latter additional nourishment is necessary and the question may arise of providing it as part of a health service.

219. *Clothing.* In respect of clothing it is not possible to determine the necessary expenditure with anything like the same accuracy as with food. The expenditures of industrial households in 1937–38 may be estimated from Ministry of Labour Family Budgets as 2/4¼ a week for a man and 2/6¼ a week for a woman or for a man and woman together 4/10½ ; for agricultural households the figures are 1/8 for a man and 1/7½ for a woman, or 3/3½ together. These expenditures are above the subsistence requirement, since they relate to households which are living above the minimum. Moreover, clothing is an item of expenditure which can for a time be postponed. In none of the Social Surveys undertaken in various towns before the war was the weekly cost of clothing for men and women together put as high as 3/–, the actual figures assumed ranged from 1/1½ to 2/11, and most of the estimates were below 2/–. It is reasonable to put the allowance for clothing in unemployment or disability benefit as 1/6 each for a man and a woman, or 3/– together This is very little below the actual expenditure of agricultural households in 1937-38.

220. *Fuel, Light and Household sundries.* The average weekly expenditure of industrial households of two persons in 1937–38 on coal, gas and electricity as given in Table VIII varied from 4/1 in the Northern Division to 5/4 in the North-East, averaging 4/10 for the whole of Britain. For households of one person the divisional averages varied from 6d. in Wales (very few households) to 3/1 in the North-West, the average for Britain as a whole being about 2/8. Subsistence expenditure can clearly be put below these figures, which relate to households living on an average well above the minimum. In a sample tabulation of households in the lower quartiles for fuel consumption, taken as representative of the poorer households, the average expenditure (as given in the last column of Table VIII) was 3/7 for a two person family, as compared with 4/10 in all industrial households. There is also some possibility of reducing or postponing expenditure on fuel and light, though not as much as in the case of clothing. On the other hand, some provision

TABLE VIII

COAL, GAS AND ELECTRICITY

Weekly Expenditure of Industrial Households, 1937–38

Persons per Household	LONDON sh.	LONDON No. of Households	STH. EAST sh.	STH. EAST No. of Households	STH. WEST sh.	STH. WEST No. of Households	MIDLANDS sh.	MIDLANDS No. of Households	WALES sh.	WALES No. of Households	NTH. WEST sh.	NTH. WEST No. of Households	NTH. EAST sh.	NTH. EAST No. of Households	NORTH sh.	NORTH No. of Households	SCOTLAND sh.	SCOTLAND No. of Households	GREAT BRITAIN sh.	GREAT BRITAIN No. of Households	GREAT BRITAIN Poorer Households (*) sh.
1	2·84	40	2·88	8	1·65	16	2·77	13	0·53	6	3·08	27	2·62	25	2·07	7	2·98	24	2·63	166	—
2	4·94	298	4·80	175	4·41	171	5·24	267	4·23	82	5·23	240	5·30	215	4·11	120	4·35	163	4·86	1,731	3·55
3	5·63	400	4·98	261	4·58	218	5·75	336	5·35	135	5·67	321	5·44	257	4·30	162	4·98	235	5·29	2,325	4·07
4	6·24	283	5·66	194	5·59	162	5·91	277	5·04	105	5·86	267	5·65	253	4·55	136	5·14	222	5·63	1,899	4·47
5	6·22	208	5·95	93	5·27	112	6·18	147	5·67	60	6·18	150	5·55	121	4·65	85	5·73	158	5·81	1,134	4·49
6	6·85	82	5·93	46	5·39	42	6·00	84	5·72	20	6·25	66	5·69	55	4·42	31	5·81	91	5·94	517	—
7	7·08	43	5·47	25	5·37	16	6·38	43	5·61	14	6·24	39	6·51	34	4·86	16	6·35	35	6·21	265	—
8	7·86	15	6·30	17	5·11	6	6·76	22	4·76	8	7·13	20	5·65	12	4·89	6	5·99	16	6·38	122	—
9 and over	7·96	15	7·23	7	5·98	16	6·80	18	4·79	4	7·23	17	6·49	10	5·62	6	7·13	25	6·84	118	—

Source: Ministry of Labour Family Budget Enquiry.

(*) The figures for " Poorer Households " relate to those in the lower quartiles, in a sample tabulation covering up to 30 households of each size in each Division.

must be made for household necessaries other than fuel and light. It is suggested that 4/- for a man and woman together and 2/6 for a man or a woman separately to cover these other necessaries, as well as fuel and light, should be adequate.

221. *Margin.* The foregoing calculations, particularly that for food, assume complete efficiency in expenditure, i.e. that the unemployed or disabled person buys exactly the right food and cooks and uses it without waste. This assumption is clearly not likely to be realised. Some margin must be allowed for inefficiency in purchasing, and also for the certainty that people in receipt of the minimum income required for subsistence will in fact spend some of it on things not absolutely necessary. It is suggested that a margin of 2/- a week for a man and a woman together and 1/6 a week for a man or a woman separately should be allowed.

222. From these considerations there emerges as a basis for fixing the rate of subsistence benefit at 1938 prices the following table :—

TABLE IX

Requirements for Adults of Working Age at 1938 Prices

	Man and Wife	Man	Woman
Food	13/-	7/-	6/-
Clothing	3/-	1/6	1/6
Fuel, Light and Sundries ...	4/-	2/6	2/6
Margin	2/-	1/6	1/6
Rent	10/-	6/6	6/6
	32/-	19/-	18/-

223. Strictly the figures for clothing and one or two minor items relate only to short periods of unemployment and disability, during which expenditure on renewals can be postponed ; more will be needed in prolonged interruption of earnings. On the other hand, there should be room for re-adjustment in such matters as rent or of retrenchment in the margin. On the whole, it seems fair to balance these considerations against one another and make no change in the rate of benefit as between short and long interruption of earnings during working years.

Retired Persons

224. The subsistence needs of retired persons are in some ways less and in other respects greater than the needs of persons of working age during interruption of earnings. The differences in respect of the main heads of expenditure are as follows :—

Food.—The food requirements of old people are placed by all authorities at substantially less than those of persons of working age. In calories they need about 75 per cent. of what is needed by working age adults. Some writers in the past have reduced the money requirement for the food of old persons in something like the same proportion. But there is no adequate reason for putting the needs of old persons for constructive and protective foods more than slightly below those of working age adults, while on the other hand, the food of old people will be more expensive because of their failing mastication and digestion. It is suggested that the food requirements of retired persons, in place of being put at 75 per cent. of those of a working age adult, should be put at about 85 per cent., or for a man 6/- a week and for a woman 5/6 a week.

Clothing.—The requirements of old people for clothing are not more than two-thirds of those of adults of working age. On the other hand, in contrast to unemployment and disability benefit for assumed temporary interruption of earnings, the pension must allow for renewals of clothing. Mr. Rowntree put the long period requirement for clothing at 4/– for a man and woman of working age, as compared with 3/– during temporary interruption of earnings, making the long period amount for a single person 2/–. It is suggested that the allowance for a pension for a retired person should be put at two-thirds of this, that is to say, 1/4 per week.

Fuel, Lighting and Household Sundries.—The requirements of retired persons are higher than those of persons of working age. It is suggested that they should be put at 3/– for one person in place of 2/6, and 5/– for two persons.

Margin.—This should be left for retired persons as for others at 2/– for two and 1/6 for one.

Rent.—Retired persons should be able to adjust their rents. It is suggested that 6/– for a single person and 8/6 for a couple should be sufficient.

225. The requirements for retired persons at 1938 prices become accordingly :—

TABLE X
REQUIREMENTS FOR RETIRED PERSONS AT 1938 PRICES

	Man and Wife	Man	Woman
Food	11/6	6/–	5/6
Clothing	2/8	1/4	1/4
Fuel, Light and Sundries ...	5/–	3/–	3/–
Margin	2/–	1/6	1/6
Rent	8/6	6/–	6/–
	29/8	17/10	17/4

This suggests that at pre-war prices the subsistence pension on retirement for a man and wife would be about 2/4 a week below the rate of benefit for unemployment or disability.

YOUNG PERSONS AND BOYS AND GIRLS OF WORKING AGE

226. The food allowance for boys and girls of working age and of young persons up to 21 should be slightly more than that for adults, say 7/6 a week for males and 6/6 for females. The clothing allowance should be the same as for adults, say 1/6 with the same margin of 1/6. These items accordingly add up to 10/6 for a male and 9/6 for a female. Rent can be presumed to be covered for boys and girls by their parents, and the actual contribution which such earners will make to other common costs will vary with circumstances. Adding 1/6 for this, to the figures of 10/6 or 9/6 for food, clothing and margin, the benefit needed for boys might be put at 12/– with girls 1/– less. For young persons of 18 to 20, who will in some cases already have separate households, a larger addition, including something for rent is needed. The determination of benefit rates in these cases must to some extent be arbitrary. As a practical conclusion it is suggested that the benefit rate at 1938 prices might be 12/– a week for boys and girls alike, for young men 16/– and for young women either 15/– or the same as the rate for young men, according to the decision taken (in para. 230) as to equalising or differentiating benefits for men and women.

DEPENDENT CHILDREN

227. For children, 5/– a week has commonly been assumed in the past as a suitable allowance. It seems doubtful, however, whether a figure as low as this can be justified if it has to cover subsistence needs. On the League of

Nations dietary the weekly cost of food for a child at 1938 prices would be as follows :—

0–5 years	... ...	4/6	10–14 years	... ...	7/–
5–10 ,,	... ...	6/–	14–15 ,,	... ...	7/6

The actual expenditure on clothing in 1937–38 for each child under 14 may be estimated from the Ministry of Labour Family Budgets at 1/4¼ a week in industrial households and 9½d. a week in rural households. In the case of children the allowance must cover the cost of clothing over a long period ; that is to say, it cannot be reduced on the assumption that such expenditure would be postponed as in the case of an adult during unemployment or disability. The minimum weekly cost of clothing for a child can hardly be put at less than an average of 10d. a week. If it is assumed that clothing costs vary with age in much the same way as food costs, the weekly requirement for each age group may be put as follows :—

0–5 years	... ...	7d.	10–14 years	... ...	1/–
5–10 ,,	... ...	10d.	14–15 ,,	... ...	1/3

For fuel and light Table VIII, based on the Ministry of Labour Family Budgets, shows average weekly cost rising fairly steadily from 4·86 shillings for two person households to 6·38 shillings for eight person households, i.e. by just over 1/6 for 6 persons. This suggests an allowance of 3d. per week per child to cover fuel, light and household sundries.

228. Even without any margin for inefficiency in purchasing, this calculation yields at 1938 prices the following amounts as required for children's allowances to cover subsistence needs without rent :—

0–5 years	... ...	5/4	10–14 years	... ...	8/3
5–10 ,,	... ...	7/1	14–15 ,,	... ...	9/–

This makes the average subsistence allowance at 1938 prices for each child about 5/11 for food, 10d. for clothing and 3d. for fuel and light or 7/– a week altogether instead of the 5/– which it has been common to assume in discussing children's allowances in the past.

Conclusion

229. The foregoing discussion suggests that at 1938 prices and on the assumption of a uniform allowance of 10/– a week for rent of a household the subsistence benefit should be 19/– a week for men of working age and 18/– a week for women of working age, and 32/– for a man and wife together. The corresponding subsistence pensions for retired persons should be 17/6 single and 29/6 for a couple, assuming 6/– for rent in the former case and 8/6 for rent in the latter case. The subsistence needs of children should be put materially higher than has been customary hitherto in discussions of children's allowances.

230. On these estimates of subsistence needs, two practical decisions have to be taken. The first is whether differentiation by sex should be maintained. The strongest reason for giving women, as such, lower rates of benefit than men would be a desire to avoid imposing on women rates of contribution excessive for their wages. Women's contributions will in any case be substantially below those of men, which have to carry provision for housewives. To make any further substantial difference between the contributions of the sexes women's benefit rates would need to differ from men's rates by much more than the 1/– a week during unemployment and disability than can be justified by examination of subsistence needs. On balance it seems not worth while to maintain any difference between the rates of single men and of single women. The second question is whether the pensions on retirement should, in accordance with subsistence needs, be put below the

working age benefits. The final answer to this depends on the discussion of the problem of old age in the following section. For the reasons given in para. 251 it is suggested that the insurance scheme should provide retirement pensions at the level of working age benefits and above subsistence needs.

231. The rates named above are based on 1938 prices. At the date of this Report (November, 1942) the cost of living is about 30 per cent. above the level of 1938. The level at which prices will tend to settle after the war cannot be foretold; it is unlikely that they will return in any short period to the pre-war level; it is reasonable to hope that they may be kept near the present level. As a basis of discussion, in framing the Social Security Budget, it has been assumed that the cost of living after the war will settle at about 25 per cent. above 1938. This yields in round figures a provisional post-war rate of benefit for a man and wife together of 40/- a week, and for a man or woman alone of 24/- a week, neglecting any difference of sex and rounding the single person's rate up to the nearest 1/-. These provisional rates allow for a rise of 25 per cent. or a little more in the cost of all necessaries, including rent and including also the margin suggested in para. 221. If rents can be kept at their pre-war level, the provisional rates are sufficient for a rise of about 33 per cent. on the other necessaries, including the margin. If, in spite of a rise of materially more than 25 per cent. over all necessaries, including rent, the provisional rate of unemployment or disability benefit for a man and wife together is kept at 40/- a week, this means cutting into the margin; if the margin is left out altogether, 40/- a week covers a rise of 33 per cent. in the cost of living, including rent. If retirement pensions are put at the same provisional rate of 40/- joint and 24/- single there is a further margin, because the actual subsistence needs are lower. For young persons of both sexes 18–20 a provisional rate of 20/- a week is suggested and for boys and girls one of 15/- a week.

232. For children's allowances it seems reasonable to take a provisional post-war rate of 9/- a week, covering an increase of nearly 30 per cent. in cost of subsistence above the 7/- required at 1938 prices. This does not include anything for rent or allow any margin. On the other hand, substantial provision in kind is already being made for children through school meals and supply of free or cheap milk. Allowing for this, in framing the Social Security Budget in Part IV the average cost of allowances in addition to existing provision has been put at 8/- per head per week.

SECTION 2

THE PROBLEM OF AGE

233. The problem of the nature and extent of the provision to be made for old age is the most important, and in some ways the most difficult, of all the problems of social security. It is so for two main reasons.

234. First, age, as a cause of inability to earn after childhood is past, exceeds in importance all the other causes of such inability together. Just before the present war there were at any moment about twice as many people in Britain of pensionable age, that is to say, 65 and upwards for men and 60 and upwards for women, as there were men and women of working age dependent on their earnings who could not earn through unemployment or disability of all kinds. The cost of pensions relatively to the rest of social security will increase inevitably through increase in the proportion of people of pensionable age in the population. This is shown by Table XI based on the White Paper as to Current Trends of Population in Great Britain prepared

by the Registrar-General and on further information supplied by him. The persons of pensionable age (65 for men and 60 for women) at the beginning of the century were about 2¼ millions or 1 in 17 of the whole population ; in 1931 they were about 4¼ millions or 1 in 10 of the population ; in 1961, less than twenty years from now, they will be more than 8 millions or 1 in 6 of the population, and they will continue to increase proportionately to the rest. On the other side, the Table shows the continuous decline of the child population which, if not arrested, will after 1971 bring about a rapid diminution of the whole population. In 1901 there were more than five children under 15 for every person of pensionable age. In 1961, less than twenty years from now, there will be one child under 15 for every person of pensionable age, and in 1971 the children will be outnumbered by the possible pensioners. These figures depend upon the assumptions made as to the future of birth-rates and death-rates, and the results will be different if these assumptions are not realised. In particular a large increase in the birth-rate would increase the number of children relatively to others.

TABLE XI

ESTIMATED POPULATION OF GREAT BRITAIN BY AGE GROUPS 1901 TO 1971

Year	Total Popula-tion	Under 15	Per cent. of Total	Men 15–64 Women 15–59 (both inclusive)	Per cent. of Total	Men 65 and over Women 60 and over	Per cent. of Total
1901	36,999,946	12,040,841	32·5	22,674,624	61·3	2,284,481	6·2
1911	40,831,396†	12,587,504	30·8	25,495,097	62·4	2,748,416	6·7
1921	42,769,196†	11,940,167	27·9	27,479,043	64·2	3,349,222	7·8
1931	44,795,357†	10,825,072	24·2	29,674,695	66·2	4,295,430	9·6
1941*	46,565,000	9,573,000	20·6	31,421,000	67·5	5,571,000	12·0
1951*	47,501,000	9,054,000	19·1	31,548,000	66·4	6,899,000	14·5
1961*	47,192,000	8,433,000	17·9	30,710,000	65·1	8,049,000	17·1
1971*	45,980,000	7,600,000	16·5	28,804,000	62·6	9,576,000	20·8

* These estimates are based on the assumptions as to fertility and mortality given in the White Paper on " Current Trend of Population in Great Britain " and depend upon the validity of those assumptions.

† These figures include a few persons not classified by age and therefore not included in any of the three age groups.

235. Second, the economic and social consequences of old age in the individual case are not uniform. Old age may cause acute poverty and it may cause no poverty at all. Mr. Rowntree in 1936 found that in York the poverty due to old age was more acute than that due to any other single cause. That was before the institution of supplementary pensions in 1940. But even then a great many of the aged were not in want at all. Of all the old age pensioners in York in 1936, only one-third were living below Mr. Rowntree's standard of human needs. For the rest, their pension of 10/- a week, with other resources, of their own or of their families, was enough to keep them above that standard. This conclusion of Mr. Rowntree's accords well with the fact that at the end of 1941 only 37 per cent., just over one-third, of all persons having contributory or non-contributory pensions had claimed and qualified for supplementary pensions ; the rest, nearly two-thirds, had either felt able to manage without applying for supplementation or had been disqualified under the means test. Besides these pensioners on 10/- a week who either did not claim or did not qualify for supplement, there are many old people who have no pension at all, yet are not in such need as leads them to apply for public assistance. Of all persons over 65 in Britain just before the war, nearly a third, and of those over 70 about one-fifth, were not in receipt either of State pensions or of public assistance in any form. Of

course, this meant in some cases that they were in want, but would not apply for assistance. It meant in the majority of cases that they were maintained by relations, by their work or savings, by pensions provided otherwise than through the general State scheme, or by a combination of these methods. The first two of these methods are clearly the most important. Superannuation provision is made now for persons in particular occupations by the State, by local authorities and by many private employers, and it is made by some Trade Unions and Friendly Societies for their members, but it is doubtful if all these forms of superannuation provision, taken together, cover as much as one-tenth of the whole field.

236. The first of the features noted above, namely the scale of the problem of old age, has two implications. On the one hand, the provision made for age must be satisfactory ; otherwise great numbers may suffer. On the other hand, every shilling added to pension rates is extremely costly in total ; when the number of persons of pensionable age reaches 8 millions, as it will in less than twenty years, every weekly shilling on the pension will mean £20,000,000 a year on the cost of pensions for all ; 5/– will mean £100,000,000 a year. It is dangerous to be in any way lavish to old age, until adequate provision has been assured for all other vital needs, such as the prevention of disease and the adequate nutrition of the young.

237. Age at present is dealt with, so far as the State is concerned, by a threefold system of pensions : (a) contributory pensions of 10/– a week given to men at 65 or women at 60 without means test and irrespective of whether they are working or not, limited practically to persons who have been in employment ; (b) non-contributory pensions of 10/– or less at the age of 70 subject to a means test ; (c) supplementary pensions confined to persons in receipt of one or other of the two classes of pensions named above, designed to meet needs adequately, subject to a means test different from that applied for non-contributory pensions. These arrangements, in addition to division of authority and unjustifiable differences of means test policy, have two principal defects. First, pensions, both contributory and supplementary, before the age of 70 are limited practically to persons in Class I. They are not generally available to persons who have worked on their own account or the wives or widows of such persons, or to persons or the wives of persons who have not been gainfully occupied. Since 1937 such persons, with others, have been able to enter a special scheme of voluntary insurance for pension, but apart from this no public provision is made for them in old age, except public assistance ; recourse to public assistance means recourse to an independent authority applying its own test of means. Second, the contributory pensions given as of right are manifestly inadequate, if there are no other resources ; at the same time they are often superfluous, since they may be drawn by people still able to earn a full living.

238. The problem for the future is how persons who are past work can be given a guarantee against want, in a form which gives the maximum of encouragement to voluntary saving for maintenance of standards above the subsistence minimum, and at the same time avoids spending money which is urgently needed elsewhere or money on a scale throwing an intolerable financial burden on the community.

239. Any Plan of Social Security worthy of its name must ensure that every citizen, fulfilling during his working life the obligation of service according to his powers, can claim as of right when he is past work an income adequate to maintain him. This means providing, as an essential part of the plan, a pension on retirement from work which is enough for subsistence, even though the pensioner has no other resources whatever ; some pensioners will have no other resources. It means also providing a pension which is not reduced if the pensioner has resources. On the contrary, direct encouragement of

voluntary insurance or saving to meet abnormal needs or to maintain standards of comfort above subsistence level, is an essential part of the Plan for Social Security proposed in this Report. It follows that the plan must include provision of pensions up to subsistence level, given as of right to people who are past work, regardless of the other resources that they then possess, but in respect of service and contribution during working life.

240. This does not mean that, as from the beginning of the Plan for Social Security, pensions up to subsistence level must be paid to all citizens who are past work, without regard to their other resources. On the contrary, for several reasons, it is important that the coming into operation of a scheme of adequate pensions given as of right should be gradual. One of the characteristics of old age as a problem in social security is that the coming of old age is inevitable and can be and is to a large extent foreseen. Provision for old age, whether by contributions to a compulsory scheme or otherwise, must be made over a long period before old age is reached ; provision independent of the State is made in fact, to a greater or less extent, through occupational superannuation schemes, voluntary insurance, or personal saving, by a number of people, substantial in itself though small in proportion to the total number of persons of pensionable age. The existence of this independent provision is not a reason which should lead the State to avoid making comprehensive adequate provision of its own for everybody in old age. But it does affect the steps by which that comprehensive provision should be introduced. A substantial proportion of the persons of pensionable age in Britain, though without pensions, have other resources ; they will not be in need of income for subsistence at the outset of the Plan for Social Security. At the outset none of them will have made any contributions for adequate pensions from the State. Some will have paid contributions as for the present inadequate pensions for a substantial period. Others will have paid such contributions for a few years only ; the present arrangements give an incentive to persons outside the contributory classes, on approaching the pensionable age, to get within those classes by employment which is sometimes specifically created for that purpose. Others outside the contributory classes will have paid no contributions at all. In view of the vital need of conserving resources, in the immediate aftermath of war, it is impossible to justify giving, as from the first day of the Plan for Social Security, full subsistence pensions to people who have neither contributed for such pensions nor are in need of them, who may in fact have full pension provision made for them in other ways in virtue of their occupation. The Plan for Social Security is based on the contributory principle ; that principle, which is good in itself and in accord with popular sentiment in regard to provision against other forms of insecurity through unemployment, sickness, and the like, has special advantages in relation to the problem of pensions. It both justifies and requires postponement of payment of full subsistence pensions as of right and thus gives time—

    (a) for the national income of the community to be built up again after the disturbance of the war ;

    (b) for the great variety of superannuation schemes now in existence to be adjusted, if necessary, to the establishment of universal subsistence pensions for all citizens ;

    (c) for solution of the difficulty of determining the proper rate of subsistence benefits and pensions which is presented by variation of rents.

Transition Period of Rising Pension Rates

241. These considerations point to the need for a transition period, during which passage from the present combination of inadequate contributory pensions and means pensions to adequate contributory pensions for all can

be accomplished. They suggest introduction of contributory pensions not at full subsistence level from the outset, but rising gradually to that level over a period of years, with assistance pensions granted meanwhile, after examination of individual needs and means, to ensure that no old person is in want. In the scheme of social security recently established in New Zealand there is for pensions a transition period of 28 years; pensions without means test for all citizens over 65 beginning in 1940 at £10 a year rise to £78 a year in 1968; meanwhile an age benefit of 30/– a week subject to reduction for means is available forthwith. For Britain the transition period suggested is one of 20 years from 1945 taken as the first year of the new Plan for Social Security to 1965 as the first year in which contributory pensions will become payable as of right irrespective of means at the full provisional rate of 40/– joint for man and wife or 24/– single. The treatment in the transition period of persons standing in different relations to the present insurance schemes raises difficult questions of both equity and administration. The persons to be considered fall into three main groups : those who at the launching of the new scheme will have complete qualification for contributory pensions under the old scheme in the sense that if they were then of pensionable age they would receive pensions ; those who will have no contribution qualification at all for pensions under the old scheme ; and those who will have made some contributions for such pensions but not enough to complete their qualification.

242. The persons with complete qualification for contributory pensions under the old scheme are those who are already in receipt of contributory pensions and those who, at 1st July, 1944, have at least five years of continuous insurance for pensions. The proposal made here is that, subject to the retirement condition mentioned below, all these persons should receive contributory pensions at the basic rate of 25/– joint (i.e. for man and wife) or 14/– single in 1945, rising every two years by increments of 1/6 joint or 1/– single up to the full basic rate of 40/– joint or 24/– single in 1965. On this proposal, all persons in this group will at all times have the same rate of basic contributory pension, irrespective of the date on which they reach pensionable age and claim pension. Those who claim in 1945 will get 25/– joint, rising to 26/6 in 1947, to 28/– in 1949 and so on. Those who claim for the first time in 1949 will come in at 28/– joint ; they will not get more because they have contributed longer under the new scheme. The second group, i.e. persons with no qualifications for the present pensions, are in the main the new classes proposed to be brought into pension insurance, namely Class II (persons gainfully occupied otherwise than under contract of service), Class IV (persons of working age not occupied) and persons in Class I who hitherto have been excepted from insurance. All these persons will contribute for pensions for the first time under the new scheme. It is proposed that they should be required to contribute for 10 years before being qualified for any pension. Thereafter, i.e., from 1955 onwards, on reaching the minimum pensionable age and retiring, they will receive a basic pension of 25/– joint or 14/– single, rising by 1/6 joint or 1/– single for every further year of contribution thereafter, the full basic rate of 40/– joint, or 24/– single being reached in 1965 for those claiming pension then or thereafter. Since persons in this group who are already within 10 years of pensionable age, that is to say, are over 55 for men or 50 for women at 1st July, 1944, may not be able to qualify for any pension, all such persons will have the option of applying for exemption from contribution for pensions, that is to say, will pay only that part of the insurance contribution which is required for purposes other than pension. As is explained below, many such persons may in fact be able to qualify for full pension by continuing to work and contribute after pensionable age. The third group includes persons who have made some compulsory contributions for pensions under the old scheme before 1st July, 1944, but have not the full

qualification of five years' continuous insurance up till then. It includes also the special voluntary contributors for pensions under the Act of 1937 who have subscribed for pensions and under present conditions can obtain them after ten years of contribution. The precise arrangements in regard to these classes must be defined by Regulations giving them the appropriate intermediate position between the first and second groups in respect of their former contributions. These Regulations will presumably require insured persons to establish their claim to be in the intermediate group by some contributions made before the adoption of the scheme by the Government is announced.

243. The proposals in paragraph 242 make a distinction in the application of the rising scale of contributory pensions as between the first group of persons (with full qualifications under the old scheme) and those in the second group (with no qualifications under the old scheme). For the former group the rate of pensions rises by simple effluxion of time. All persons in this group at any one time will have the same rate of basic contributory pension ; they proceed together up the rising scale of pensions, irrespective of the point at which they entered it and irrespective, therefore, of the number of contributions paid under the new scheme. The rate of pension for each individual in the second group depends not merely on effluxion of time but on the date after 1954 at which he retires on pension, that is to say, on the number of contributions paid by him under the new scheme ; for he has made no contributions under the old scheme. A person in this group who claims pension as soon as he has contributed for ten years in 1955 will get 14/– as basic pension for the rest of his life. His pension will not go up in 1956, while a person who does not retire till 1956 will obtain not 14/– but 15/– a week. It is arguable that both classes should be treated alike, either in the direction of making pensions rise by simple effluxion of time in both cases or by fixing pension for each individual according to the date of his first claiming. The case for the procedure proposed in regard to the second group is that, on the whole, the people in this group have a relatively large number for whom pension provision is being made in other ways ; it is not unreasonable to enforce a strict contribution condition upon them. The difficulty of applying the same procedure to the first group lies partly in the very differing contribution records before 1945 of those who will be in this group, and partly in the fact that to apply this procedure will mean that all those who retire and claim pension during the transition period will permanently have less than the full basic rate of pension, and thus if they have no other resources may be permanently in need of assistance. As this group includes most of the pensioners, it is important to frame a scheme which, so far as possible, will bring them all to the full basic rate and above need for assistance by the end of the transition period. If on further consideration of the equities as between the two classes it appeared desirable to treat the second group in the same way as the first group, and place all on a general rising scale irrespective of the date of claiming pensions and of the number of contributions old or new, this would increase the expenditure on pensions in 1965 by about £15,000,000 a year. If, on the other hand, it appeared desirable and practicable to treat the first group on the lines proposed for the second group, and make the basic pensions of the first group vary with the date when they claimed pension and the number of contributions paid under the new scheme—this would decrease the expenditure on pensions in 1965 by about £30,000,000.

Pensions Conditional on Retirement

244. Pensions have been spoken of above as provision for people who are past work. Pensions adequate for subsistence without other means should be given only to people who, after reaching a minimum age for retirement, have in fact retired from work. To give a full subsistence income to every

citizen on his or her reaching the age of 65 or 60 would impose an unjustifiable and harmful burden on all citizens below that age. The practical problems of making pensions conditional upon retirement are considered below. They are certainly not insoluble, nor can imposition of a retirement condition for receipt of pension be described as a means test, any more than imposition of a condition that a man should be unable to obtain work, in order to obtain unemployment benefit, can be described as a means test. The pensions proposed in the Plan for Social Security are retirement pensions, not old age pensions. There is no fixed age for retirement, but only a minimum pension age, 65 for men and 60 for women, at or after which each individual has the option of retiring and claiming pension. Till he does so, contributions by or on behalf of him have to be paid in the same way as for all other persons.

245. Making receipt of pension conditional on retirement is not intended to encourage or hasten retirement. On the contrary, the conditions governing pension should be such as to encourage every person who can go on working after reaching pensionable age, to go on working and to postpone retirement and the claiming of pension. The large and growing proportion of the total population who will be above the pensionable ages of 65 for men and 60 for women, makes it essential to raise the average age of retirement, if possible, and in any case to avoid doing anything which may bring about earlier retirement than at present. It is neither politically feasible nor would it be right to raise the statutory minimum age for pensions. The capacity of different people for work late in life varies from individual to individual. To attempt to force people to retire before their powers and desire for work fail, and to compel them by a rise in the minimum age of pensions to struggle on after their powers have failed, are two errors and injustices which should be avoided by any system of social insurance designed to increase human happiness. The right way of encouraging postponement of retirement is to make it attractive for people who can remain at work after they have reached the minimum pension age to do so ; such people should be allowed, by continuing to contribute and postponing claim to pension, to qualify for an addition to the basic rate which is given if pension is claimed at the minimum age. The object of encouraging continuance of work in later life will not be attained by granting pensions without a retirement condition. If these pensions are adequate for subsistence they will obviously encourage retirement. Even inadequate unconditional pensions will encourage early retirement in many cases. There are other superannuation schemes for some of which pension can be drawn only on retirement which may be earlier or later according to the choice of the individual ; provision of universal unconditional pensions by the State will lead many people to take this with their other superannuation provision and retire.

246. The rates of pension named in the preceding paragraphs have been described accordingly as basic pensions ; they are the rates for those who retire and claim pension as soon as they reach the minimum pensionable age. Any person who on reaching this age postpones claiming pension will have his pension increased in respect of each year of postponement. It is suggested that this increase should be at the rate of 2/- a week on a joint pension or 1/- a week on a single pension for each year of postponement, added to whatever would have been the basic pension for that individual, if he had reached minimum pensionable age in the year in which he claims pension. The effect of this can be illustrated by considering particular cases of persons in the first and second groups respectively. A married man in the first group (i.e. qualified for contributory pension under the present scheme) who reaches the age of 65 in 1949, if he then retires will receive a basic pension of 28/- a week, which by 1953 will rise to 31/- ; if instead of retiring he goes on working to 1953

he will be able to retire in 1953 on a pension of 39/– and will always have 8/– more a week than he would have had by retiring at 65. A married man in the second group (i.e. one outside the present contributory class) who reaches the age of 65 in 1955 and retires then will have a pension of 25/– and will remain always at that figure ; if he postpones retirement for four years to 1959, his basic pension will be 31/– and he will have an additional 8/– in respect of continuing to work after the minimum pensionable age, making his pension 39/–. The increases for postponement after minimum pensionable age are designed to give to the individual some, though not all, of the saving in pension expenditure resulting through his postponement and are related, therefore, o the amount of the basic pension which is postponed. When the basic pension reaches its full rate in 1965 for both groups it would be appropriate to make the increase for each year of postponement greater. The question may also arise of imposing a maximum upon the amount of total pension.

247. Insured persons who postpone claiming pension on reaching the minimum pensionable age will continue to contribute in their respective insurance classes, I, II or IV, and to draw the working age benefits. It will be necessary to impose restrictions on the period for which unemployment or disability benefit can be drawn after the minimum pensionable age, and it may prove desirable to make the increased pension above the basic rate depend not simply on the length of postponement, but upon actual contributions paid. These are matters to be dealt with by Regulations. Such restrictions will be particularly necessary in the transition period, during which unemployment and disability benefit will be above the basic rate of pension.

248. The application of a retirement condition for pensions presents some administrative problems, but for the reasons given above a retirement condition is essential, nor can the administrative problems fairly be regarded as either insoluble or even exceptionally difficult.

First, the proposal to increase pensions if retirement is postponed and contributions continue to be made, will give all classes (I, II and IV) alike an economic motive not to claim pensions, while they are still able to work with any regularity. By these means they will be able to get the advantage of their capacity to continue at work after pensionable age honestly, without the subterfuges involved in pretending to retire and not really retiring.

Second, retirement means giving up regular earnings, not being idle 100 per cent. of one's time. Every person receiving pension will be required to sign a periodic declaration either that he has earned no more than, say, £3 in each of the preceding 3 months or how much he has earned if he has earned more. From one-half to two-thirds of the excess above £3 a month will be deducted from his pension for the ensuing quarter.

Third, enforcement and detection of fraud presents no difficulties in the case of earnings by way of employment. The retired person will not be able legally to obtain employment, except through the possession of an employment book for which he will have to make application. Persons who continue to work after pensionable age without retirement will, as stated elsewhere, pay contributions in the ordinary way. It is for consideration whether those who take occasional employment after retirement should be able to do so as exempt persons (paying no contributions themselves though their employer pays contributions normally) or should pay contributions normally. But in either case they will need an employment book, whether marked for exemption or not, and the amount of their employment can be controlled.

Fourth, enforcement and detection of fraud in the case of gainful occupation otherwise than by way of employment raises greater difficulties. But under the proposals made here, this problem will not arise in the case of most of the people concerned (generally Class II or IV) for ten years, so that there is ample

D

time to develop any necessary administrative machinery. Provisionally it is suggested that no person retired on pension would be permitted to hold an occupation card in respect of a shop, small holding, fishing boat, etc., that is to say, for every such means of earning, someone else would have to hold the licence ; that person might be the wife of the pensioner, but this would automatically have the effect of making the rate of pension single. The shop-keeper or small holder of advancing years will be able freely to do odd jobs and help in the shop, but he will not find it easy to carry on his business just as before and continue to draw pension as for himself and a dependant. It may not be possible, nor is it important, to control closely the earnings which a retired person makes by writing or personal service.

249. It may be argued that it is unreasonable to require retirement as a condition of pension, unless and until the pension is adequate for subsistence. This might be so if the object in view was to encourage retirement. That, however, is not the policy underlying these proposals. On the other hand, an individual who proposes to go on working and earning has no reasonable case for expecting an increase of pension or any pension for which he has not paid, just because he has reached a particular birthday. Those who already have unconditional pensions will be allowed to keep them unchanged till they choose to retire. But no fresh unconditional pensions should be granted after the day appointed for beginning the new scheme.

SAFEGUARDING OF EXISTING PENSIONERS

250. In the application of the new scheme the position of all persons who at the beginning of the scheme, taken as 1st July, 1944, have pensions under the old scheme will be safeguarded. Those already in receipt of contributory pensions of 10/- a week without retirement condition will be allowed to retain their present pensions so long as they like continuing to work and to contribute ; when they retire, will enter the scale at the appropriate point. The same principle of safeguarding existing pensioners will apply also to non-contributory means test pensions. If, as is possible, the means test for the larger assistance pensions proposed is in some way more stringent than that for the non-contributory pensions now given at the age of 70, existing pensioners will keep the benefit of their present means test. The same principle will safeguard other special cases, such as that of women who were widowed before the Act of 1926.

251. The final rate suggested for basic pension (40/- joint and 24/- single) is the same as that suggested for unemployment and disability benefit. On strict subsistence arguments, it is possible to justify putting the rate of basic pension below the rate of working age benefit, say 37/- joint and 22/6 single. But there is strong public opinion in favour of securing for the aged something more than bare subsistence, and apart from this there is convenience in keeping pensions at least equal to working age benefits in order to avoid stepping down from benefit to pension on reaching a particular birthday. To keep the ultimate rate of contributory pensions to 37/- joint and 22/6 single will effect a saving only in 1965 ; by that time it is reasonable to hope that such a saving will not appear necessary.

252. There is nothing sacred about the number of years suggested here for the transition period ; it is possible to argue for more or for less than 20 years. But the case for anything less than 20 years is not strong. A male employee who pays for 20 years from the age of 45 to 65 will have provided personally less than one-sixth of the value of his pension, having paid five-twelfths of the full actuarial contribution for the last 20 years of his working life in place of 49 years ; an independent worker paying both the employer's and the employee's share will have provided less than one-third. Employees who con-

tribute under the new scheme for the full **49 years**—people reaching the age of 16 after the appointed day in 1944—will provide 42% of their own pensions ; the compensation to them is that the State takes off them, largely by assistance pensions at once and wholly by contributory pensions in 20 years at latest, the burden of providing for their parents. From another point of view—that of giving time for re-adjustment of existing voluntary schemes of superannuation—a substantial transitional period is necessary. Given a sufficient provision of assistance pensions to those who need them the transition involves no hardship.

253. The joint rate of benefit and pension proposed, namely 40/-, assumes a rent of 10/-. The average rent in London is at least 6/- above that. Whatever be done to adjust unemployment and disability benefits to rent (either individually or by higher rates of contribution and benefit in London, as suggested in para. 214 above), retirement pensions must be uniform throughout the country ; they cannot fit the needs even tolerably unless rents are made more uniform. In effect the transition proposals made here allow twenty years for dealing with the rent problem, that is to say for reducing both the anomalous rent level of London and the acute individual inequalities which exist throughout the country. Meanwhile, during the transition period, abnormally high rents will be dealt with by supplementation or assistance pensions.

CONCLUSION

254. There is no valid objection, either on the ground of equity or on the ground that a means test may discourage thrift, to postponing introduction of adequate contributory pensions for a substantial period of transition, during which needs are met by pensions subject to means test. As regards equity, the people who reach pensionable age during the transition period will not have paid contributions at the new rates for any substantial time. As regards thrift, only those who are now so old that they may expect to require pensions before the transition period ends can be affected at all, and of these only a small proportion can be affected substantially. The rising scale of contributory pensions will make it possible for everyone except people who are already close to pension age, by a very moderate additional provision of their own, to secure income adequate for subsistence and have no need for any means pension. There is all the difference in the world between a permanent system of pensions subject to means test and a transitional system of supplementation of rising contributory pensions, such as is suggested here. The first must be rejected ; the second is not open to serious objection.

255. There is no reason also to doubt the power of large numbers of people to go on working with advantage to the community and happiness to themselves after reaching the minimum pensionable age of 65 for men or 60 for women. The numbers of people past the pensionable age who, at each census, described themselves as still occupied rather than retired is very great. So is the number of those working as exempt persons after this age under the present schemes of health and unemployment insurance. There is no statistical evidence that industrial development is making it harder for people to continue at work later in life than it used to be ; such evidence as there is points in the opposite direction. The natural presumption from the increasing length of total life is that the length of years during which working capacity lasts will also rise, as health improves, as by freedom from want in childhood and by freedom from want and idleness in working years the physique and the courage of the citizens are maintained. A people ageing in years need not be old in spirit, and British youth will rise again.

256. The main proposals in regard to pensions in old age may be summed up as follows :—

(1) The Plan for Social Security includes the provision of pensions at basic rates equivalent to those for unemployment and disability benefit, that is to say, 40/- a week joint for man and wife and 24/- for a single pensioner, for all citizens without means test in virtue of contributions.

(2) These contributory pensions will be introduced gradually over a transition period of a suggested length of twenty years, during which the rate of basic pension will rise from 25/- for man and wife and 14/- for a single pensioner to the full rate.

(3) Assistance pensions will be available for all persons of pensionable age (65 for men and 60 for women) requiring them, on a uniform means test based on the Determination of Needs Act, both in supplementation of contributory pensions and for persons not qualified for any contributory pension.

(4) All contributory pensions under the plan will be retirement pensions, that is to say will be given only to people who have retired from work and will be subject to reduction of part of any earnings made after retirement.

(5) The basic rate of pension is that which can be obtained by people retiring at the minimum pensionable age of 65 for men or 60 for women. Any individual postponing retirement after reaching the pensionable age will be able to qualify for additions to the basic pension according to the length of the postponement.

(6) The position of all persons now in receipt of pensions will be safeguarded, that is to say such persons will be able to draw contributory pensions at the present rate without retirement until they decide to retire from work and take pensions at the larger new rate.

(7) The application of the rising scale of contributory pensions may differ as between persons within the scope of the present contributory pensions and persons outside their scope (mainly Classes II and IV and persons in Class I now excepted from insurance), in view of the fact that the former will and the latter will not have paid contributions under the present scheme.

257. The transition period of twenty years will not affect any man under the age of 45 at the beginning of the scheme. Every such man, whether working under contract of service or on his own account or as an employer, whatever his occupation, will be able to qualify for pension for himself and for his wife at the full basic rate, equivalent to unemployment or disability benefit, and to add to this by postponing his retirement. Every single woman under 40 will be equally unaffected by the transition period ; whether working under contract of service or independently or living at home and giving unpaid help to her family, she will be able to qualify for full basic pension and to add to it. A married woman who also undertakes gainful occupation will be able to qualify for full pension in respect of her own contributions and to draw pension when she reaches 60 irrespective of her husband's age. The proportion of the population affected by the transition period in any way will be small. Most of them will be able to get substantial contributory pensions, if not up to the full basic rate. Whether they do so or not, all of them will have security against want in a system of transitional assistance pensions. Nor does the proposal for a transition period mean that there will be no change in regard to pensions at once or during the transition. On the contrary, there will be five immediate changes of great importance followed by continual change during the transition as the rate of contributory pensions rises. The five immediate changes are :—

(1) The administration of all provision for old age will be unified in place

of being divided as at present between five separate bodies : Ministry of Health ; Department of Health for Scotland ; Customs and Excise ; Assistance Board ; and Local Authorities (for Public Assistance).

(2) Pension rates for persons now within the scope of contributory pension insurance will be raised forthwith by 25 per cent. joint or 40 per cent. single, subject to the retirement condition.

(3) All persons of working age not now within the scope of contributory pension insurance will be brought in forthwith for contribution with a view to qualifying for substantial contributory pensions after ten years and full contributory pensions after twenty years.

(4) Persons not now eligible for non-contributory pensions will be able, on proof of need, to obtain assistance pensions.

(5) In so far as any pensions continue to be granted, not as of right in respect of contributions, but subject to proof of need, needs and means will be judged on uniform principles in all cases. There will be a single test in place of several different tests as at present.

SECTION 3
THE PROBLEM OF ALTERNATIVE REMEDIES

258.　Some of the needs for which maintenance of income under a plan for social security is required, may arise through causes which give to the person in need a legal claim against another person. These cases are of three main types :—

(i) Industrial accidents, in respect of which an injured employee, apart from the Workmen's Compensation Acts, may have a claim against the employer at common law.

(ii) Other accidents, in respect of which the person injured may have a claim against another person as having caused the accident by negligence. Such cases arise mainly, though not solely, out of traffic by road ; in relation to one form of road traffic, by use of motor vehicles, there are special statutory provisions to secure insurance against such liabilities.

(iii) Breaking of marriage otherwise than by death, under conditions giving the wife a continuing claim to maintenance—after divorce, separation or desertion—against the husband.

Each of these types presents special features and involves varied questions of law and policy, too technical for exhaustive discussion here. In regard to each of them questions arise, under two distinct heads, as to which something should be said in general terms. How far should the possible existence of these other rights of the person in need of income affect his claim under the social insurance scheme ? Should the developments now proposed in social insurance be accompanied by any change of these other rights ?

259.　Under the first head, one general principle seems clear : The possible existence of an alternative remedy should not prevent an insured person from getting forthwith whatever social security benefits he would be entitled to claim if he had no such remedy. The testing of any alternative remedy is bound to take some time ; the needs of the injured person should be met at once. Prompt maintenance of income is of the essence of social security. The present arrangements under which the possible existence of a claim against an employer is ground for refusing sickness benefit to a disabled workman, should be ended. So also should the requirement that an employee must elect between claiming under the Workmen's Compensation Acts and claiming at common law.

260.　Another general principle also is clear. An injured person should not have the same need met twice over. He should get benefit at once without prejudice to any alternative remedy, but if the alternative remedy proves in fact to be available, he should not in the end get more from the two sources together than he would have got from one alone. This may mean one of two things :—

(a) that the third party remains liable to pay whatever is due from him as if there were no benefit, but that the injured person when he receives his damages refunds to the Social Insurance Fund what he has received as benefit.

(b) that the amount of the injured person's claim against a third party is reduced by whatever he can claim as benefit.

Arguments can be advanced for each of these methods. On the one hand, it may be said in favour of the first method that there is no reason why a person guilty of negligence should pay less than he would otherwise, because the person injured by negligence is insured against injury. On the other hand, it may be said in favour of the second method, that if comprehensive provision is made by the State for injury, however caused, the damage done to the injured person by the negligence of the third party is only any excess of his actual loss over the amount of the State's provision. There may even, as is suggested below, be a reason for saying that insurance provision should exclude altogether actions for damages in cases in which they could be brought now. This is a matter on which a different line can justifiably be taken in different types of case. The same rule, for instance, need not apply to industrial accidents as to other accidents, if the insurance provision made for them is different.

261. There arises yet another practical question—as to whether it should be left to the injured person to pursue his alternative remedy, or whether the Ministry of Social Security should be entitled to take proceedings, either with his consent or without it. This also is a matter on which different rules may well apply to different types of case. In the third of the types named above, arising out of cessation of the maintenance due in marriage, the Ministry if, on a claim made on it by the deserted or separated wife, it pays separation benefit, should be entitled, without requiring consent of the wife, to proceed against the husband for recoupment of its expenditure. In the other types of case it is doubtful whether the taking of proceedings need become a function of the Ministry.

262. Under the second head, a number of questions, some raising issues of general principle, some of them highly technical, call for examination. There are respects in which it may be right, as an accompaniment to extension of social security, to change the general law of liability for civil wrongs. It can be argued for instance that if comprehensive medical treatment is available for every citizen without charge quite irrespective of the cause of his requiring it, he ought not to be allowed, if he incurs special expenses for medical treatment beyond the treatment generally available, to recover such expenses in the action for damages. It can be argued again, that if what is judged to be adequate compensation is provided from a Social Insurance Fund for industrial accidents, irrespective of any negligence causing them, there is no reason why this compensation should be greater because the employer has in fact been negligent. The needs of the injured person are not greater. With the inevitable uncertainties of legal proceedings, suits for heavy damages on the ground of negligence cannot escape having something of the character of a lottery. In so far as danger of such proceedings is a penalty for negligence, it is more effective to make the penalty a direct one—of criminal proceedings undertaken by the public department responsible for securing industrial safety. Employers can and normally will insure against civil liabilities; they cannot insure against criminal proceedings.

263. In addition to the three principal types of case in which there may be alternative remedies a fourth type calls for mention, namely that of affiliation

claims by unmarried mothers. This may affect and be affected by the proposals in regard both to maternity benefit and children's allowances. The existing law and the practice of public authorities in regard to this matter may call for review in the light of the new position that will be created if the proposals of this Report are effected.

264. It is not possible in this Report to do more than to raise these questions. Considered answers can be given only after enquiry by some committee with technical and practical qualifications and with time to examine all the detailed issues involved.

PART IV

THE SOCIAL SECURITY BUDGET

265. The Plan for Social Security proposed in this Report is first and foremost a plan of how social insurance should be organised, with national assistance and voluntary insurance as subsidiary methods, for maintenance of income. The method of organisation is independent of the precise amounts to be given each week as benefit or pension. It might be difficult today to take definite decisions on questions of amount, because the future level of prices is uncertain ; the final figures must be written into the plan when the time and conditions of its coming into operation are known. But, for several reasons, it is necessary to suggest the rates of benefit or pension that would be suitable, on some reasonable assumption as to price levels. Only by giving figures can the relation of different scales of benefit to one another and to the cost of living be shown. Only in this way can the scale of contributions required for any given scale of benefits, and the suggested distribution of the total cost between the different parties to the scheme, be set forth in simple terms. For this purpose, the provisional scale of benefits set out in paras. 401–402 has been adopted. Subject to the difficulty of finding any single rate of benefit to cover the differing rents paid by different households, this scale is suggested as providing subsistence for normal cases, on the assumption of a cost of living after the war, including rent, about 25 per cent. above that of 1938. The point at which, and the extent to which it would be desirable to change this scale to suit a different cost of living are matters of judgment. In this scale, the standard rate of joint benefit for a man and wife together is put at 40/- a week, applying to unemployment, disability and retirement alike. The rates of benefit corresponding to this joint standard, for single men or women, for men or women whose spouses are gainfully occupied, for young persons and boys and girls, and for special risks, such as maternity and widowhood, are set out in para. 401.

266. The actuarial and financial problems involved in the Plan for Social Security, on the assumption of this scale of security benefits, are examined in detail in the Memorandum by the Government Actuary which forms Appendix A to the Report. Here the financial problem is considered in general terms, and the principles to be followed in obtaining the money required to meet the expenditure involved in the plan are explained and discussed. In this discussion and in the Memorandum of the Government Actuary, it is necessary to assume a date for the beginning of the scheme, so that the calculations may be related to the expected numbers and age constitution of the population. The date taken for this purpose is 1st July, 1944 ; estimates are given for 1945 as the first year of benefit and for 1965 as the first year of contributory pensions at the full rate. This assumes twenty years for the length of the transition period during which the rate of contributory pensions will rise by stages. As is stated in paragraph 252 there is nothing sacred about this number of years. If it became necessary to lengthen the transition period and postpone the coming of the full rate of contributory pensions, this could

be done without breach of contract with the contributors, who would have paid at the new contribution rates only for twenty years of their working lives in place of the forty or fifty years for which their successors will pay. If, on the other hand, it appeared possible and desirable to shorten the transition period and make the rate of contributory pensions rise more rapidly, this would not affect the principles of the scheme.

267. In addition to social insurance, the Plan for Social Security involves provision of other services which must be taken into account in framing a Social Security Budget. One of these services is national assistance, which will be administered by the Ministry of Social Security, but will be financed separately from the insurance scheme. Under the arrangements for transition the scope of national assistance, though smaller than that of assistance by the State and by Local Authorities at present, will be substantial at the outset of the scheme. It will diminish continuously, as the rate of contributory pension rises and fresh classes of contributors qualify for pensions. More important than national assistance as permanent elements in the Security Budget are the assumptions A and B of the plan. The plan assumes, first, a general system of children's allowances, sufficient to meet the subsistence needs of all dependent children when the responsible parent is in receipt of any insurance benefit or pension, and of all such children except one in other cases ; the allowance required for this purpose in addition to existing provision in kind, is taken as 8/- a week on an average of children of all ages. The plan assumes, second, the establishment of comprehensive health and rehabilitation services providing treatment for all citizens without a charge on treatment. Expenditure in realising these two assumptions falls appropriately in the Security Budget. Assumption C of the plan, namely maintenance of employment, is a matter not so much of expenditure as of organisation. In any case any expenditure involved in it does not fall into the Security Budget.

EXPENDITURE IN 1945 AND 1965

268. On the basis of the provisional rates of benefit and pension suggested in para. 401, the estimated total expenditure to be included in the Security Budget is set out in Table XII as for the first full year of the scheme, assumed to be 1945, and twenty years thereafter, that is to say, 1965. The

TABLE XII
ESTIMATED SOCIAL SECURITY EXPENDITURE 1945 AND 1965

	1945 £ millions	1965 £ millions
Social Insurance :—		
Unemployment Benefit (including training benefit)	110	107
Disability Benefit other than industrial	57	71
Industrial Disability Benefit, Pensions and Grant	15	15
Retirement Pensions	126	300
Widows' and Guardian Benefit	29	21
Maternity Grant and Benefit	7	6
Marriage Grant	1	3
Funeral Grant	4	12
Cost of Administration	18	18
Total Social Insurance	367	553
National Assistance :—		
Assistance Pensions	39	25
Other Assistance	5	5
Cost of Administration	3	2
Children's Allowances	110	100
Cost of Administration	3	3
Health and Rehabilitation Services	170	170
TOTAL	697	858

basis of the estimates is explained briefly in paras. 269–70 and more fully in the Memorandum by the Government Actuary. It will be seen that the total Security Budget both on purposes covered by the present schemes and on new purposes is put at £697 million in 1945, and £858 million in 1965. Of these totals £367 million in 1945 and £553 million in 1965 are in respect of social insurance, and will be met from the Social Insurance Fund, with self-contained finance subject to review by the Social Insurance Statutory Committee proposed in Change **22**.

269. The whole increase of social security expenditure between 1945 and 1965 is in respect of retirement pensions, reflecting both the growing proportion of pensioners in the population and the transition to full contributory pensions. The total of £300 million for retirement pensions in 1965 is based on the assumption that for all the persons within the present contributory classes single pensions rise by 1/– and joint pensions by 1/6 every two years from 1945 to 1965, irrespective of the date at which they retire, but that for the new pension classes (Classes II and IV and those now excepted from contribution in Class I) the contributory principle is applied strictly, so that, once such a man has retired, his pension does not change thereafter. This is in accord with the proposal in paras. 242–243 to treat these two groups of insured persons on different lines. The financial consequences of assimilating the treatment of the two groups are given in the last two sentences of para. 243.

270. The following notes deal with some of the principal points in the table :—

(1) The cost shown in 1945 for industrial disability includes the whole cost of existing cases of prolonged disability ; all the present weekly payments will be raised to the new rates. In respect of these cases there will be an offset against the amount shown, in the reserves held by the insurance companies and associations, against their liabilities at the present rates.

(2) Expenditure on funeral grant in 1945 is lower than in 1965 by reason of the proposed exclusion from this grant of persons over 60 at the beginning of the scheme, on the assumption that they will already have made provision for this need.

(3) The figure given for the cost of the health and rehabilitation services is a very rough estimate requiring further examination. No change is made in this figure as from 1945 to 1965, it being assumed that there will actually be some development of the service, and as a consequence of this development a reduction in the number of cases requiring it. The estimate assumes that hospital treatment with all other treatment is included in the health service in virtue of the compulsory social insurance contribution, that is, without further voluntary contributions or charge on treatment ; this proposal is subject to the further enquiry suggested in para. 437.

(4) In estimating the cost of disability benefit other than industrial the Government Actuary for reasons given in para. 22 of his Memorandum has assumed a sickness rate 12½ per cent. above that which now forms the basis of national health insurance finance. It is reasonable to hope that by the development of preventive and curative treatment the actual rate of claims will be kept materially below this assumption.

(5) The figure of £25,000,000 entered as the cost of assistance pensions in 1965 covers several different groups, of which the most important are the following :—

    (a) Women between 60 and 70 not entitled to present contributory pensions, in so far as they are in need, are now dealt with by public assistance. It may be assumed that with assistance pensions available the number of claimants will increase materially.

(b) Persons now outside the present scope of contributory pensions who are so old that they either obtain exemption from contributions altogether or reach the retiring age long before 1965 so that their pensions are inadequate and they are in need.

(c) Persons in Classes II and IV who obtain exemption from contribution on the ground of having less than £75 a year of income (para. 363 (iii)) and so do not qualify for contributory pensions.

The first two groups represent the survivors from the present system. The numbers and expenditure in respect of each of them is likely to decline very rapidly soon after 1965. In the third group the Government Actuary (Appendix A, para. 59) has allowed continuing expenditure on assistance pensions at the rate of £15 million a year, representing 240,000 full assistance pensions. It is reasonable to hope that the number of persons in Classes II and IV who, on grounds of poverty, will need exemption from contributions will be much less than this.

(6) The estimate of the cost of administration as £18 million in respect of social insurance and £3 million in respect of national assistance in 1945 is based on the following considerations. The actual administrative expenditure in 1938–39 was £14 million in respect of insurance services (excluding workmen's compensation) and about £6·9 million in respect of assistance both central and local. The scope of assistance in which the administrative costs are relatively high will be greatly decreased and should certainly not exceed the £3 million shown. The cost of administering industrial disability benefit and pensions should not be more than 10 per cent. of the much higher benefits provided (as is shown in Appendix E, the present mutual companies in mining work well below this percentage), i.e., should not exceed £1·5 million leaving £16·5 million for the rest of social insurance as compared with £14 million spent in 1938–9. Setting the increase of prices and in the total scope of insurance against the economies that will follow from co-ordination this appears reasonable.

(7) The sum of £57 million entered for disability other than industrial in 1945 allows for putting all persons on present disablement benefit at the beginning of the scheme up to the new rate of disability benefit. If, as is suggested in para. 353 (5), permanent invalids among these people are treated as pensioners on the rising pension scale, the cost of disability benefit in 1945 will be reduced by about £10 million (Appendix A, para. 56).

271. Table XII shows the total expenditure involved in the Plan for Social Security. This is not, of course, new expenditure; a great deal of it is already being incurred. The extent to which additional charges will be imposed on the various parties to social insurance can be considered best after examining the method proposed for distributing the total cost. How are the sums shown in Table XII to be provided? Three main sources have to be considered :—

(a) the National Exchequer, that is to say, the citizens in their capacity as tax-payers ;

(b) the prospective recipients of payments under the scheme, that is to say, the citizens in their capacity as insured persons ;

(c) the employers of insured persons where these are employed under contract of service.

Local Authorities will also have important functions, in relation to security, mainly though not wholly in the provision of institutions, bringing in a fourth possible source—the citizens in their capacity as rate-payers. In framing the Security Budget, expenditure from local rates has been brought into account only in so far as it is concerned either with medical treatment in institutions or with public or blind assistance. This expenditure is shown in Table XIII (p. 112) combined with that falling directly on the National Exchequer, since the ultimate division of these costs between national taxation and local rates cannot yet be finally determined. The many other expenditures of local authorities on allied social services, including housing, education, and welfare of mothers and children, though closely related to social security, have not been covered by the previous discussion and are not reckoned in the Social Security Budget.

TAXATION AND CONTRIBUTIONS

272. Before considering these sources, it will be convenient to state briefly the meaning attached here to the terms used in describing them. The distinction between taxation and insurance contribution is that taxation is or should be related to assumed capacity to pay rather than to the value of what the payer may expect to receive, while insurance contributions are or should be related to the value of the benefits and not to capacity to pay. Within insurance a further distinction may be drawn between voluntary and compulsory insurance. In voluntary insurance, the contribution is a premium which must be adjusted to some extent to the degree of risk ; persons with low risks must be allowed to pay less for the same rate of benefit than those with high risks ; otherwise they will not insure. In compulsory insurance, the contribution may vary with the risk but need not do so ; the considerations relevant to this question are discussed in paras. 86–87. For the present purpose, of considering the three possible sources of security finance, the question of adjustment of contributions to risk in compulsory insurance is secondary. The main issue lies between taxation and insurance contribution. Taxation implies regard to means ; an insurance contribution for the same benefit, whether or not it varies with the risk, should not vary with the means of the person who pays it.

273. Whatever mónies are obtained under the second and third heads, from insured persons as contributors and from their employers as employers, it is certain that the National Exchequer, that is to say the citizen as tax-payer, must continue to meet a substantial part of the total expenditure shown in Table XII. Indeed, the suggestion is made sometimes that social security should be financed only by taxation. The suggestion is put, or can be put, in two alternative forms. One is that social security should be financed wholly from general taxation, that is, should become completely and formally non-contributory. The other is that social security should be financed by particular taxes assigned to this purpose. This suggestion, in either of its forms, breaks with the contributory principle and logically, as is seen by some of its advocates involves dropping the term " insurance." The advantages that can be claimed for the second form of this suggestion over the first form is that it maintains some connection between paying and receiving, and may make it possible to widen the basis of taxation. It might, for instance, appear easier to reconcile wage-earners to income-tax, if the proceeds were earmarked for some purpose in which wage-earners had a personal interest, just as at one time a tax on petrol was introduced specifically to improve roads for the users of vehicles driven by petrol. But the arguments against assignment of taxes to particular purposes are strong ; assignment is a method rightly unpopular with those who have responsibility for framing the general budget and it is difficult to believe that it could prudently be applied to any part of a tax so fundamental as income-tax. Moreover, as the experience of the Road Fund shows, there is no assurance that the earmarking of a tax to its original purposes will be

respected. But it is unnecessary here to discuss the relative advantages or disadvantages of the two forms of the suggestion to abandon insurance contribution entirely in favour of taxation according to capacity. From the point of view adopted in this Report and advocated by the great majority of the organisations and persons who gave evidence to the Committee, the suggestion involves a departure from existing practice, for which there is neither need nor justification and which conflicts with the wishes and feelings of the British democracy. The scheme of social insurance which forms the centre of the Plan for Social Security is based on maintenance of the contributory principle, that is to say, of the principle that a material part of the total cost of maintaining income under the plan shall be met from monies contributed by citizens as insured persons, on the basis of each individual paying the same contribution for the same rate of benefit. Contribution means that in their capacity as possible recipients of benefit the poorer man and the richer man are treated alike. Taxation means that the richer man, because of his capacity to pay, pays more for the general purposes of the community. These general purposes may, and in practice they must, include bearing a part of the cost of social security ; if security is to be based on the contributory principle, they cannot include bearing the whole cost.

274. The contributory principle was emphasised or accepted by all the organisations most widely representative of insured persons in Britain— notably the National Conference of Friendly Societies and the Trades Union Congress General Council. It is maintained as a central feature of the Plan for Social Security on grounds according with this expression of views. These grounds may be summarised under three heads :—

(i) The insured persons themselves can pay and like to pay, and would rather pay than not do so. It is felt and rightly felt that contribution irrespective of means is the strongest ground for repudiating a means test.

(ii) It is desirable to keep the Social Insurance Fund self-contained with defined responsibilities and defined sources of income. The citizens as insured persons should realise that they cannot get more than certain benefits for certain contributions, should have a motive to support measures for economic administration, should not be taught to regard the State as the dispenser of gifts for which no one needs to pay.

(iii) To require contribution on an insurance document for each individual has administrative convenience, particularly for a scheme which, while it covers all citizens, takes account of their different ways of livelihood, and classifies them, giving different benefits according to their needs. Contribution provides automatically the record by which the insured person's claim to be qualified for any particular benefit can be tested.

275. There remains the question as to whether, in addition to the National Exchequer (that is to say the citizen paying as tax-payer according to capacity) and the insured person (that is to say the citizen paying at a flat rate for flat benefits irrespective of earnings and capacity), money should be obtained also from a third source, namely the employer, where the insured person is employed under a contract of service. In regard to one particular risk, that of accident and disease arising in the course of employment in hazardous industries, there is a special reason for an employer's contribution, adjusted to the degree of risk ; this reason lies in the desirability of giving a stimulus to prevention of accident and disease. Apart from this special case, the argument for keeping employers' contributions in social insurance is not as strong as is the argument for keeping contributions from the insured persons. The present form of employers' contribution, as a share of the cost of an insurance stamp affixed to an insurance document for each week of employment, is a tax on the giving

of employment ; it is not related to the employer's profits or capacity to pay ; it varies from one employer to another in proportion to his total expenses, according as he uses much or little labour ; it does not vary according to the extent to which the employer, in the management of his business, endeavours to avoid unemployment or sickness. It can be argued that, even if some form of contribution by employers as such is retained, it would be desirable to explore forms alternative to the present one, in particular the suggestion made many years ago by the Royal Commission on the Poor Laws and Relief of Distress of a tax on dismissals. But neither this suggestion nor any other alternative proposed hitherto to the present tax on employment is free from difficulties and objections.

276. If a contribution by employers as such, and not as tax-payers according to capacity to pay, is to be retained, it is hard to find a practical alternative to the present system of a charge for each week of employment given. Though such a contribution can be described as a direct tax on employment, it can equally be described as an addition to wages ; it does not enter into the cost of production any more or less than do wages or the contribution of the employee that is taken out of his wages ; it can and should be regarded as a proper part of the cost of production, maintaining the labour force that is necessary both when it is actually working and when it is standing by. In proportion to the total cost of production, any reasonable employer's contribution to social security is bound to be small and may be well worth making for the sake of the advantages that it brings. It is to the interest of employers as such that the employees should have security, should be properly maintained during the inevitable intervals of unemployment or of sickness, should have the content which helps to make them efficient producers. It is equally desirable, that employers should feel concerned for the lives of those who work under their control, should think of them not as instruments in production, but as human beings ; most of them do feel this concern and accept and welcome the social insurance contribution as a mark of it. It is desirable finally to give to employers a definite status, based on contribution, for making representations as to the administration of social insurance and its possible improvement. On balance the arguments for maintaining a direct contribution by employers towards the costs of social security, if less strong than those for maintaining contributions by insured persons, outweigh any arguments on the other side. In the plan of this Report a substantial employer's contribution is retained, as something to be paid irrespective of profits, in respect of each week of employment of an insured person.

TRIPARTITE SCHEME OF CONTRIBUTION

277. The finance of the Plan for Social Security is based accordingly on a continuance of the tripartite scheme of contributions established in 1911. That scheme has been in force for thirty years and has won general acceptance. The plan includes the setting up of a Social Insurance Fund from which all the benefits secured in virtue of contribution will be paid and into which money will flow in two main streams : one springing from the sale of insurance stamps, and representing the joint contributions of insured persons and their employers in Class I or of insured persons alone in Classes II and IV ; the other coming as a contribution from the National Exchequer out of monies raised by general taxation. The industrial levy in hazardous industries (para. 89) will provide a third lesser stream. Most, if not all, citizens of working age will pay in two ways ; an insurance contribution which for equal rates of benefit will be the same for all regardless of means, and a share of national taxation, direct or indirect, adjusted to their means. Those who are employers will

pay in a third capacity as well. The Social Insurance Fund will be one, but will have separate accounts for different purposes as explained in para. 42.

278. Assuming the scale of benefits set out in para. 401 the rates of contribution to be required from insured persons and employers are suggested in para. 403. The principal rates are for an adult man in Class I, 7/6 a week and for an adult woman in Class I, 6/- a week, as joint contribution from the insured person and from the employer together. The corresponding rates for other classes and for boys and girls, the possible adjustments for special cases, and the division of the joint contribution between the insured person and the employer are dealt with in paras. 403-408.

279. The considerations leading to the contributions suggested for various classes of persons are explained in the Memorandum by the Government Actuary. The main points may be summarised as follows :—

(i) The joint contributions of employers and insured persons in Class I are designed to provide two-thirds of the cost of unemployment and five-sixths of the cost of retirement pensions, of maternity and of disability (other than that covered by the industrial disability levy) in the case of new entrants to the scheme at sixteen ; the whole cost of marriage and funeral grant ; five-sixths of the cost of other benefits, including widows' and guardian benefit ; and a payment towards the cost of health and rehabilitation services. The division of the joint contribution in Class I, between insured persons and their employers, is explained in para. 280 ; reference should be made also to paras. 96 and 291.

(ii) The contributions of insured persons in Classes II and IV, where there is no employer, are designed to provide for the benefits given in Classes II and IV respectively the same share of the total cost as is covered in Class I by the insured person and his employer together.

(iii) Employers in industries scheduled as hazardous, in addition to their share of the joint contribution, pay an industrial levy. The levy is designed to cover two-thirds of the cost of accident and disease in such industries above the average for all other industries, the remaining third being shared between the employees and employers in all industries and the Exchequer.

(iv) Of the joint contribution in Class I named in para. 278, 10d. a week in the case of an adult man and 8d. a week in the case of an adult woman is assigned for the health and rehabilitation services, including free hospital treatment, with appropriate lower contributions for non-adults. Insured persons in Classes II and IV will contribute for these services the amount of the joint contribution in Class I.

(v) The National Exchequer provides one-third of the total cost of unemployment benefit, one-sixth of the cost of pensions and of disability and maternity benefits for new entrants at age 16, together with the cost of bringing in the existing population of all ages for the ordinary benefits at the flat rate of contribution, one-sixth of the cost of industrial disability not covered by industrial levy and the whole cost of children's allowances and national assistance.

(vi) The National Exchequer and the local rates meet the cost of the health and rehabilitation services with the help of a grant from the Social Insurance Fund representing the receipts from the contributions assigned to these services. Division of costs between the National Exchequer and the local rates depends upon the further investigation of the finance and organisation of these services, suggested in para. 437.

(vii) The accumulated reserves in hand from the existing pensions, health and unemployment schemes are assumed to be transferred to the Social Insurance Fund and invested.

280. As regards division of the joint contribution in Class I, between insured persons and their employers, the view taken here is that it is reasonable for the cost of unemployment, of disability other than that covered by industrial levy in industries scheduled as hazardous, and of retirement pensions and widowhood to be divided equally between the two parties, for employers to continue to make a contribution towards the cost of medical treatment for their employees, for the insured persons to be charged with funeral, marriage and maternity grant and the bulk of the insurance contributions for medical treatment.

SHARES OF THE THREE PARTIES

281. On the basis of the contributions suggested for different parties to the tripartite scheme of social insurance, the actual or estimated cost of the Plan for Social Security to each of the three parties at various dates is shown in Table XIII. The first column of this table gives the actual expenditure incurred on the relevant social services in 1938–39 ; it does not include the expenditure of individuals on medical treatment and on various forms of voluntary insurance which are included in the plan for the future. The actual expenditure today is materially above the figure for 1938–39 through granting of supplementary pensions, raising of rates of contribution and benefit, raising the remuneration limit for non-manual workers in health, pensions and unemployment insurance, lowering the pension age for women, and in other ways. The second column of the table represents an attempt to estimate the prospective cost to each party in 1945 if the existing schemes were continued at their present scales. The figures in this column are necessarily to some extent speculative. They suggest that the expenditure included in the Security Budget in 1945 as the result of the proposals made here will be in total about £265 million more than would have been so included under the existing schemes and that of this increase the amount falling on the National Exchequer and local rates will be £86 million, which may be reduced by £10 million if the suggestion made in para. 353 (5) and 270 (7) is adopted.

282. As regards the shares of the various parties the difference of £86 million to the Exchequer and local rates between the estimated costs of the present scheme and of the proposals is less than the cost of children's allowances. The increase in the total receipts from insured persons is due only in part to the raising of the rates of contribution. Other parts represent contributions from classes not at present insured and transferred to social security, and expenditure previously met in other ways, e.g. cost of funerals and a large part of medical treatment. The increase of the employers' contributions from £66 million in 1938–39 to £137 million in 1945 corresponds to the proposed increase in their rate of contribution. The proposals increase the total receipts from insured persons and their employers very much at the outset of the scheme, while limiting the additional cost to the Exchequer to that of children's allowances. Thereafter the receipts from insured persons and employers remain stationary and the National Exchequer takes up the growing burden of pensions. This as explained in para. 292 accords with the requirements of financial policy. Of the estimated receipts from insured persons of £194 millions in 1945 about £34 millions will be assigned for health and rehabilitation services in accordance with para. 279 (iv) above, and the remainder will be available for cash benefits. Of the £137 millions estimated to be received from employers in 1945, £6 million will be assigned for health and rehabilitation services and the remainder will be available for cash benefits.

TABLE XIII

ESTIMATED COST OF SOCIAL SECURITY TO EXCHEQUER, INSURED PERSONS AND EMPLOYERS
AT VARIOUS DATES

| | 1938–39 | £ millions 1945 | | 1965 |
| | | Present Schemes | Proposed | Proposed |
	(1)	(2)	(3)	(4)
National Exchequer (and Local Rates for hospitals and public assistance)	212	265	351	519
Insured Persons...	55	69	194	192
Employers	66	83	137	132
Other (mainly interest)	9	15	15	15
Total	342	432	697	858

NOTE.—The total of £212 millions shown as the national expenditure and certain
local authority expenditure in 1938–39 is based on Table XXIII in Appendix B and is
made up of £135·3 millions as Exchequer contribution for social insurance and assistance,
£26·3 millions from the local rates on public assistance and blind assistance and £50 millions
as estimated expenditure from taxation and rates on institutional medical services. The
contribution from insured persons is that shown in Table XXIII. The contribution from
employers is that shown in Table XXIII with an addition of £13 millions for the assumed
cost of workmen's compensation including cost of administration. The £137 million
shown as receipts from employers in 1945 includes £5 million from reserves held by
employers or their insurers against existing compensation claims.

CONTRIBUTIONS IN RELATION TO BENEFIT AND CAPACITY

283. The rate of contribution from an adult man in Class I that emerges
from the Memorandum of the Government Actuary on the assumptions made
there is 4/3 a week. Is that a reasonable sum to ask the individual to pay
for security irrespective of his means ? Is it likely to be within his capacity ?
An answer to these questions can be given from three standpoints : first, of
looking at what the individual will get in virtue of his payment ; second, of
looking at what he has shown himself capable of paying and willing to pay
in the past ; third, by comparing his share of the total with that of the other
parties.

284. For an answer from the first standpoint material is provided by
Table XIV, comparing in summary the benefits to which a contributor with
family responsibilities, within the present unemployment insurance scheme,
would have been entitled before the war and would be entitled under the plan
of the Report in virtue of contributions and without enquiry as to his means.
It does not mean, of course, that no provision of any kind, other than that
shown in the Table, was made for any of the various needs before the war ;
both public and private hospitals, for instance, were available, subject to
examination of means or by voluntary contribution. Nor does it mean that
the whole of the provision shown as proposed will be paid for out of the Social
Insurance Fund, built up by insurance contributions ; children's allowances,
for instance, included in the weekly amounts of benefit will be paid for wholly
and medical treatment will be paid for mainly out of general taxation, national
or local, and not from the Fund. But children's allowances and treatment
are part of the Plan for Social Security and will be received by every citizen
requiring them without further payment or enquiry as to means. The comparison is between what a contributor of 1/7 a week could obtain as of right
before the war and what a contributor of 4/3 a week will obtain as of right

	Pre-War*		Proposed in Plan for Social Security	
	Amount	Period and Conditions	Amount	Period and Conditions
Unemployment	33/- per week.	26 weeks (followed by assistance on means test).	56/- per week.	Unlimited in time without means test at any time. Subject to attendance at a training centre if unemployment is prolonged.
Disability other than industrial	15/- per week.	26 weeks, followed by 7/6 per week in disablement. Additional benefit in some cases.	56/- per week.	Unlimited in time without means test at any time.
Old Age	20/- per week.	—	40/- per week.	On retirement. 2/- a week increase for each year of postponement of retirement. (Full rate only after 'transition period. Assistance pensions on means test meanwhile.)
Widowhood	18/- per week.	—	40/- per week.	Reduced by part of any earnings. 52/- per week for first 13 weeks without reduction.
Maternity	£2.	—	£4.	
Maternity if wife gainfully occupied ...	£2 additional.	—	36/- per week for 13 weeks additional.	
Funeral	Nil.	—	£20.	With smaller sums for children.
Industrial Disability	Half earnings up to maximum of 30/- per week.	Subject to compounding for lump sums.	56/- p.w. for 13 weeks followed by pension of two-thirds earnings up to maximum of 76/- p.w. but not less than 56/- p.w. No compounding for total disability.	
Medical Treatment	General Practitioner for man, with additional treatment benefits in some cases.	—	Comprehensive medical treatment, including hospital, dental and ophthalmic, nursing and convalescent homes for whole family. Post-medical rehabilitation.	

* Some of the pre-war rates of benefit shown above have been revised in the course of the present war. At the date of the Report the benefit in unemployment was 5/- higher than that shown, and that for disability was 3/- higher. For industrial disability, the pre-war maximum of 30/- has been raised to 35/- and children's allowances of 4/- for each of the first two children and 3/- for subsequent children have been added. For pensions the pensionable age in the case of women has been lowered from 65 to 60. With these changes the contributions for unemployment, health and pensions were raised, so that the total contribution by an adult man in 1942 was 1/10 a week in place of 1/7 in 1938.

under the plan. The rates of benefit per week in most cases are doubled (as with pensions) or more than doubled (widowhood, maternity, disability, both industrial and other). But the difference is not only or mainly in the rates per week, it is also in the duration of benefit, and its extension of scope. Needs hitherto uncovered by compulsory insurance like funerals are included, as well as an immense extension of medical treatment.

285. For an answer from the second standpoint, reference can be made to the family budgets collected by the Ministry of Labour in 1937-38. These show the average actual expenditure of industrial households on purposes falling wholly or partly within the Plan for Social Security to have been more than 6/- a week, exclusive of trade union subscriptions of about 1s. 4d. a week ; the details of this expenditure amounting to 73·25d. a week are shown in column 2 of Table XV below. In comparing these figures with the contribution now proposed, two adjustments must be made. In the first place the expenditure shown in the industrial household represents more than one wage-earner. On an average each such household contained 1·75 wage-earners, but of these only 1·22 were males of 18 years and over. As will be seen, the household expenditure of compulsory insurance contributions is given as 24·75d., while the actual contribution at the date of the budgets for an adult man was 19d. If the household expenditures on insurance premiums, payments to pension funds, etc., and on various forms of medical treatment and appliances are reduced in the same proportion, the figures given in column 3 of Table XV are reached, as representing the expenditure which may fairly be regarded as coming out of the wages of one adult man in 1937–38. In the second place, the contribution proposed is related not to 1937–38 prices, but to those prices with an addition of 25 per cent. The addition to wages will certainly not be less than that. For comparison accordingly with the contribution of 4/3 proposed, the figures in column 3 must be increased by 25 per cent., as is done in column 4 of the Table. This yields a total expenditure out of the wages of an adult man for purposes covered in whole or in part by a security contribution of 70·30d., say 5/10, as compared with the 4/3 proposed. It is not contemplated, of course, that on the introduction of compulsory social insurance voluntary insurance should cease or even diminish. It is certain that a very large amount of it will continue ; ultimately it should increase, as the standard of living rises. But if only half of what is now devoted to insurance premiums, and only three-quarters of what is now devoted to medical treatment, were regarded as available as contribution to the compulsory insurance scheme the proposed contribution of 4/3 could be met without any difficulty.

286. In making this comparison of present expenditures and proposed social insurance contributions the following points must be borne in mind :—

(1) The expenditures shown in Table XV for industrial households are an average ; they are not the amounts paid by the poorest households. But as has been shown in Table VI in para. 209, one of the characteristics of voluntary insurance payments (which are largely payments for industrial assurance) is that people with the smallest incomes contribute generally a larger proportion of these incomes for this purpose than do those who are better off, so that the difference of expenditure per week between the poorer households and the richer households is not great. The amounts paid as shown in that table averaged 2/3 per week for persons with incomes of less than £2 a week and 2/10 per week where the income was between £4 and £5 a week.

(2) The capacity of the lower-paid workers to pay insurance contributions without trenching on resources needed for subsistence will be increased materially by children's allowances.

TABLE XV

EXPENDITURE ON SECURITY IN INDUSTRIAL HOUSEHOLDS
(Pence per week)

	1937-38 PRICES		
(1)	Per Household	Per Adult Man	Per Adult Man at 25% increase
	(2)	(3)	(4)
Insurance premiums, payments to pension funds, etc.	28·50	21·88	27·35
Medical treatment, including hospital, doctor, dentist, optician, midwife, nursing, drugs and appliances ...	20·00	15·36	19·20
Compulsory insurance	24·75	19·00	23·75
TOTAL	73·25	56·24	70·30

(3) Contributions for voluntary insurance must in general be paid whether the contributor is earning or not, that is to say, in unemployment, sickness and often in old age. To some extent Friendly Societies and similar organisations provide for remitting such contributions, but they cannot do so indefinitely, and the general rule of voluntary insurance is that contributions must ultimately be paid for every week, whether there are earnings or not. In social insurance on the other hand, contributions are required of employees only when wages are being earned. Social insurance, unlike voluntary insurance, gives to these contributors an additional benefit of remission of substantial contributions when, for any reason, they are not in receipt of earnings.

It is difficult, in the light of these considerations, to believe that a contribution on the scale imposed would be beyond the powers of any appreciable number of insured persons.

THE CONTRIBUTION OF INSURED PERSONS

287. There remains the third question of the division of financial burdens between the three parties to security. There is nothing sacred about the division suggested in this Report ; it is no more than a basis for discussion and argument. It is possible to argue that the contribution of employers should be reduced, at the cost either of the insured persons or of the National Exchequer. On behalf of insured persons it can be argued that even if the contribution proposed is within the capacity of most adult men, it is not within that of persons with low wages, and that these should be relieved at the cost of the tax-payer or the employer ; the possibility of adjusting rates of benefit or contribution or both for particular sections of the insured population, after enquiry, is provided for in para. 408. On behalf of the Exchequer it may be pointed out that some of the expenditures proposed to be borne wholly or mainly by the Exchequer are for purposes which have hitherto been the accepted responsibilities of individuals, such as the maintenance of children or the securing of medical treatment. It may be argued that it is dangerous to shift too many financial burdens from the citizen as consumer on to the citizen as tax-payer because that may lead to extravagances. All men know of themselves as consumers but do not always realise themselves as tax-payers. All these and many other matters are open to argument. The rates of benefit

proposed in the Report are provisional in so far as they depend on assumptions as to the level of prices ; the rates of contribution proposed are even more provisional, for they depend on views of financial policy and social equity as to which reasonable men may differ. All that is claimed is that the proposals made here are a fair basis for discussion, and that if the Security Budget is looked at as a whole the division proposed between the three parties is not on the face of it unreasonable. As appears from Table XII, at the end of the transition period, the total expenditure on insurance and assistance and children's allowances and on the comprehensive health and rehabilitation services will be in the neighbourhood of £858 million a year, of which £553 million will represent cash insurance benefits and their administration. As appears from Table XIII, the total contribution by insured persons will amount to about £192 million, of which about £33 million is assigned as payment for medical treatment. If the total contribution by insured persons of all classes is compared with the total Security Budget, it represents about 22 per cent. If their contribution for cash insurance benefits is compared with the total of these benefits it amounts to 29 per cent. If their contribution for medical treatment and rehabilitation is compared with the estimated total cost of these services it amounts to about 19 per cent. These proportions include the contributions made by independent workers, employers and others in Classes II and IV. The contribution of the employees themselves will be about one-quarter of the cash benefits which they receive exclusive of children's allowances and assistance. In terms of the debate which introduced national health insurance, the Plan for Social Security for the employee represents not 9d. for 4d., but 1/– for 3d. But this only means that citizens paying these contributions, irrespective of their earnings, will have to pay in addition as tax-payers according to capacity.

288. In the division of the joint contribution in Class I (employees under contract of service) a larger proportion is assigned to the employee than to the employer. This follows from the extension of insurance to social needs, such as the provision of medical treatment for dependants or of funerals, with which the employer has no obvious concern. In the Security Budget, the total appearing as employers' contributions is materially less than the total of contributions from insured persons. This follows not only or mainly from the unequal division of contributions in Class I ; it is due in large part to the fact that the insured persons include substantial numbers of independent workers, among them many employers, in Class II and others in Class IV. The figures in Table XIII do not mean, of course, that employers on the whole will pay less than insured persons pay. The sum shown as employers' contributions in the Security Budget is only the sum which will be paid by employers either as share of the insurance stamp for each week of employment given by them or as industrial levy in the hazardous industries. Employers will pay also in two other ways, as themselves insured persons and if they make any profit, as tax-payers. In this last capacity as tax-payers, employers will find themselves paying a considerably larger proportion of the whole than before ; the general effect of the financial proposals is to place a larger proportion of the ultimate burden upon the tax-payer than is at present the case, because he can be charged according to capacity to pay. The amount that the insured person contributes should not be governed by the amount which can safely be placed upon the employer in the form of a charge on employment. It should be high enough to give the insured person, because he has contributed substantially without reference to means, a justifiable claim to receive benefit without reference to means.

FINANCE OF INDUSTRIAL DISABILITY

289. Employers will contribute not only by a share of the insurance stamp in all cases, but if they are engaged in hazardous industries will pay also through

industrial levy a proportion of the special cost of accident and disease in those industries above the average for other industries. The general principle adopted in this Report is that in social insurance the individual has no claim to get better terms for himself because his risk is less and that in general all industries as well as all individuals, being inter-dependent on one another, should stand in together on the same conditions. This principle, explained in paras. 24–26, underlies the proposals to supersede the present system of approved societies (Change **3**) to amalgamate the various schemes of unemployment insurance (Change **15**) and to abolish exceptions from insurance (Change **16**). But, as is shown in paras. 86–89, there is a definite social reason for keeping separate part, though not the whole, of the cost of industrial accident and disease and making a special levy on hazardous industries to meet it, in order to give to those who manage these industries a financial motive for avoidance of dangers.

290. The financial bearings of this proposal upon industries generally and upon particular industries depends both on the line taken for dividing hazardous industries from those which are not scheduled as hazardous and on the proportion of the additional cost in the hazardous industries which is borne by them as compared with the proportion that is pooled. In the Memorandum of the Government Actuary, the risk of accidents in the industries which it is not proposed to schedule is estimated to be such that if all industries had this standard risk the total cost of industrial disability would only be about £7½ million a year. The hazardous industries in addition to this have risks which are estimated to involve expenditure of a further £7½ million a year. Assuming that the industrial levy in the hazardous industries is fixed so as to meet two-thirds of this additional cost, that is to say £5 million, the remaining one-third or £2½ million will be pooled, that is to say, will be borne by employees and employers in all industries and the State under the general system for a collection of insurance contributions. A very considerable proportion of the £7½ million on expenditure above the standard occurs in coalmining. It is estimated by the Government Actuary that the proposals made in this Report will mean that accident and disease in mining will be borne by the Social Insurance Fund in relief of the mining industry to the extent of about £1¼ million a year. Similar though smaller subsidies in relief of their exceptional cost of accident and disease will be received by other hazardous industries such as shipping, quarries or constructional work.

291. Of the total cost of industrial accident and disease estimated at £15 million in 1945 apart from administration, £5 million, as stated, will be borne by levy and £10 million will be borne by contributions paid through insurance stamps and by proportionate grant from the National Exchequer. This £10 million represents about 3·3d. per week per adult man from employee, employer and the State. The employee's share represents 1·4d. per week. For the reasons given in para. 96 it is desirable as a matter of principle that the employee should pay this share. But, if he did not do so, it might well be argued that the total contribution should still be divided much as at present. There is no strong reason for placing on the employer any share of the ordinary widow's benefit and still less of the guardian benefit which is concerned with the care of employees' children. In fact it is proposed that the employer should contribute to these benefits 1·7d. per week.

Changing Proportions

292. The proportions named in para. 287 relate to a period twenty years hence when the scheme for contributory pensions will be in full operation. When the scheme begins, the share of the insured persons will be greater and will decline gradually. The receipts from insured persons of all classes

(including those working as employers or independent workers and those not gainfully occupied) will represent about 28 per cent. of the total Security Budget in 1945, as compared with 22 per cent. in 1965. For cash benefits alone, the share of these insured persons in 1945 will be about 44 per cent., as compared with 29 per cent. in 1965. This change of proportions follows from the fact that most insured persons must contribute for retirement pensions at subsistence level for many years before reaching the pensionable age and that the State, in place of funding these contributions, uses them to meet expenditure in providing pensions on a rising scale for the older part of the population who cannot contribute so long. To make the burden on the National Exchequer as light as possible at the outset of the scheme is in accord with the probable economic and political requirements. When hostilities end, the need for heavy expenditure from the National Exchequer will not end ; it can decline only gradually as war commitments are liquidated and the permanence of peace becomes assured. Undertaking the future responsibilities of the plan for pensions is an act of faith in the building up of the national income and of the resources from which national taxation must be drawn. There is no reason to lack that faith for the future, but in the immediate aftermath of war there are strong reasons for keeping the hands of the State, as far as possible, free for expenditures which are as vital as social security, and cannot be undertaken by anyone except the State.

293. The question may be raised whether, if necessary, the contributions of insured persons could after the beginning of the scheme be increased with a view to meeting a larger proportion of the cost of pensions. If the proposals for converting industrial assurance into a public service are accepted, there will in due course be a large saving to insured persons, both in respect of the extent of funeral insurance and in costs of administration. But this saving can only be realised gradually. And even when it is realised it may appear better to leave it as a margin for further voluntary insurance and saving than to use it to increase the compulsory contribution in relief of the tax-payer.

294. The scale of benefits that should ultimately be written into the Plan for Social Security cannot be settled now, for it depends on the future level of prices. No particular scale is an essential part of the plan itself. But there are reasons for saying that on a reasonable assumption as to the probable level of prices after the war the scale of benefit proposed or something like it is the most appropriate ; there are reasons against departing materially from that scale either by way of deficiency or by way of excess. The scale of benefits is based on subsistence needs. To give less, if the individual has no other resources, means paying for unemployment or disability in lower physical efficiency ; this is more costly to the community than paying in money. To give less, because an individual has other resources, means applying a means test. It is not possible to avoid making help in some cases depend on proof of need and absence of other resources ; a substantial measure of supplementation according to needs and means is necessary in the transition period of pensions, in order to avoid giving pensions in that period, at the cost often of poorer contributors, to people who do not need them and have not contributed for them. But a permanent scale of benefit below subsistence, assuming supplementation on a means test as a normal feature, cannot be defended. On the other hand, to give by compulsory insurance more than is needed for subsistence is an unnecessary interference with individual responsibilities. More can be given only by taking more in contributions or taxation. That means departing from the principle of a national minimum, above which citizens shall spend their money freely, and adopting instead the principle of regulating the lives of individuals by law. The scale of benefit

suggested in this Report is a basis for discussion only. But it is based on reasons and should be changed only for better reasons.

295. Whether or not the scale of benefits suggested here as a basis of discussion be adopted, the relation between benefits and contributions remains. To give benefits at rates 25 per cent. or 50 per cent. above those suggested here means increasing the contributions of each of the three parties of the scheme in the same proportions, or increasing the share of one party to the contribution by less and of another party or parties by more. In so far as an increase of the rates of benefit and contribution suggested here was made necessary by change in the value of money, that is by a level of prices after the war materially more than 25 per cent. above the level of 1938, that would be a difference only in money terms. Wages and other incomes will presumably rise roughly in proportion to prices; and contributions in terms of money can be raised without representing a larger proportion of wages. In so far as increase of the rates of benefit and contribution above the scales proposed was dictated by social policy and not by change in the value of money, that would represent a decision to put the national minimum higher than bare subsistence.

Social Security Worth Its Money Price

296. In this part of the Report the price of social security has been shown, so far as it can now be shown, in terms of money. Is it worth the price to each of the three parties concerned in paying—insured person, employer and the State? For the insured person the answer is clear. The capacity and the desire of British people to contribute for security are among the most certain and most impressive social facts of today. They are shown in the phenomenal growth both of industrial assurance and of hospital contributory schemes. They have been shown in the work of the Unemployment Insurance Statutory Committee on every occasion when a question was raised either of extending insurance or of adjusting benefits or contributions; on every occasion the pressure has been to come into insurance rather than to keep out, and to get higher benefits rather than to pay lower contributions. There is no reason for fearing that for the ordinary industrial wage-earner a contribution on the scale suggested in this Report would be either beyond his capacity or beyond his desires. The popularity of compulsory social insurance today is established, and for good reason; by compulsory insurance, so long as it is confined to meeting essential needs, the individual can feel assured that those needs will be met with the minimum of administrative cost; by paying, not, indeed, the whole cost, but a substantial part of it as a contribution, he can feel that he is getting security not as a charity but as a right.

297. For the employer, the answer should also be clear. What he pays as insurance contribution is part of the cost of his labour—from his point of view an addition to wages. At whatever reasonable point the employer's insurance contribution is fixed, it is a small part of his total bill for labour and of his costs of production; it is the sign of an interest which he should feel and does feel in the men whose work comes under his control.

298. For the State, the initial burden of the Social Security Budget is at most £86 million a year above that involved in the existing schemes. The main burden on the State comes not now, but twenty years later, through provision for the large and growing part of the population that will be past the normal age of productive service. That is a burden which cannot be escaped; the facts are inexorable; the older people will be here and will be maintained—if not by pensions in their own right, then at the cost of their individual families, by charity, or by pensions subject to a means test. The plan of this Report ensures that this inevitable burden shall be

foreseen and shall be made as light as possible, by encouraging those who can work to go on working, and shall be borne fairly by the community as a whole.

299. The Social Security Budget presents figures large in relation to budgets of former time. They are not large in relation to the total national income and the Plan for Social Security is only a means of redistributing national income, so as to meet openly needs which must be met in one way or another. For reasons given in paras. 445-447 it does not seem open to question that just before the war, the British community was rich enough in real things to have avoided real want. It would be wrong not to hope that the British community can so organise itself as to be as rich again. The Social Security Budget is merely a way of translating this fact and this hope into money terms.

PART V

PLAN FOR SOCIAL SECURITY

Assumptions, Methods and Principles

300. *Scope of Social Security :* The term " social security " is used here to denote the securing of an income to take the place of earnings when they are interrupted by unemployment, sickness or accident, to provide for retirement through age, to provide against loss of support by the death of another person and to meet exceptional expenditures, such as those connected with birth, death and marriage. Primarily social security means security of income up to a minimum, but the provision of an income should be associated with treatment designed to bring the interruption of earnings to an end as soon as possible.

301. *Three Assumptions :* No satisfactory scheme of social security can be devised except on the following assumptions :—

(A) Children's allowances for children up to the age of 15 or if in full-time education up to the age of 16 ;

(B) Comprehensive health and rehabilitation services for prevention and cure of disease and restoration of capacity for work, available to all members of the community ;

(C) Maintenance of employment, that is to say avoidance of mass unemployment.

The grounds for making these three assumptions, the methods of satisfying them and their relation to the social security scheme are discussed in Part VI. Children's allowances will be added to all the insurance benefits and pensions described below in paras. 320-349.

302. *Three Methods of Security :* On these three assumptions, a Plan for Social Security is outlined below, combining three distinct methods : social insurance for basic needs ; national assistance for special cases ; voluntary insurance for additions to the basic provision. Social insurance means the providing of cash payments conditional upon compulsory contributions previously made by, or on behalf of, the insured persons, irrespective of the resources of the individual at the time of the claim. Social insurance is much the most important of the three methods and is proposed here in a form as comprehensive as possible. But while social insurance can, and should, be the main instrument for guaranteeing income security, it cannot be the only one. It needs to be supplemented both by national assistance and by

voluntary insurance. National assistance means the giving of cash payments conditional upon proved need at the time of the claim, irrespective of previous contributions but adjusted by consideration of individual circumstances and paid from the national exchequer. Assistance is an indispensable supplement to social insurance, however the scope of the latter may be widened. In addition to both of these there is place for voluntary insurance. Social insurance and national assistance organised by the State are designed to guarantee, on condition of service, a basic income for subsistence. The actual incomes and by consequence the normal standards of expenditure of different sections of the population differ greatly. Making provision for these higher standards is primarily the function of the individual, that is to say, it is a matter for free choice and voluntary insurance. But the State should make sure that its measures leave room and encouragement for such voluntary insurance. The social insurance scheme is the greater part of the Plan for Social Security and its description occupies most of this Part of the Report. But the plan includes national assistance and voluntary insurance as well.

303. *Six Principles of Social Insurance :* The social insurance scheme set out below as the chief method of social security embodies six fundamental principles :

Flat rate of subsistence benefit

Flat rate of contribution

Unification of administrative responsibility

Adequacy of benefit

Comprehensiveness

Classification

304. *Flat Rate of Subsistence Benefit :* The first fundamental principle of the social insurance scheme is provision of a flat rate of insurance benefit, irrespective of the amount of the earnings which have been interrupted by unemployment or disability or ended by retirement ; exception is made only where prolonged disability has resulted from an industrial accident or disease. This principle follows from the recognition of the place and importance of voluntary insurance in social security and distinguishes the scheme proposed for Britain from the security schemes of Germany, the Soviet Union, the United States and most other countries with the exception of New Zealand. The flat rate is the same for all the principal forms of cessation of earning— unemployment, disability, retirement ; for maternity and for widowhood there is a temporary benefit at a higher rate.

305. *Flat Rate of Contribution :* The second fundamental principle of the scheme is that the compulsory contribution required of each insured person or his employer is at a flat rate, irrespective of his means. All insured persons, rich or poor, will pay the same contributions for the same security ; those with larger means will pay more only to the extent that as tax-payers they pay more to the National Exchequer and so to the State share of the Social Insurance Fund. This feature distinguishes the scheme proposed for Britain from the scheme recently established in New Zealand under which the contributions are graduated by income, and are in effect an income-tax assigned to a particular service. Subject moreover to one exception, the contribution will be the same irrespective of the assumed degree of risk affecting particular individuals or forms of employment. The exception is the raising of a pro-portion of the special cost of benefits and pensions for industrial disability in occupations of high risk by a levy on employers proportionate to risk and pay-roll (paras. 86–90 and 360).

306. *Unification of Administrative Responsibility :* The third fundamental

principle is unification of administrative responsibility in the interests of efficiency and economy. For each insured person there will be a single weekly contribution, in respect of all his benefits. There will be in each locality a Security Office able to deal with claims of every kind and all sides of security. The methods of paying different kinds of cash benefit will be different and will take account of the circumstances of insured persons, providing for payment at the home or elsewhere, as is necessary. All contributions will be paid into a single Social Insurance Fund and all benefits and other insurance payments will be paid from that fund.

307. *Adequacy of Benefit :* The fourth fundamental principle is adequacy of benefit in amount and in time. The flat rate of benefit proposed is intended in itself to be sufficient without further resources to provide the minimum income needed for subsistence in all normal cases. It gives room and a basis for additional voluntary provision, but does not assume that in any case. The benefits are adequate also in time, that is to say except for contingencies of a temporary nature, they will continue indefinitely without means test, so long as the need continues, though subject to any change of conditions and treatment required by prolongation of the interruption in earning and occupation.

308. *Comprehensiveness :* The fifth fundamental principle is that social insurance should be comprehensive, in respect both of the persons covered and of their needs. It should not leave either to national assistance or to voluntary insurance any risk so general or so uniform that social insurance can be justified. For national assistance involves a means test which may discourage voluntary insurance or personal saving. And voluntary insurance can never be sure of covering the ground. For any need moreover which, like direct funeral expenses, is so general and so uniform as to be a fit subject for insurance by compulsion, social insurance is much cheaper to administer than voluntary insurance.

309. *Classification :* The sixth fundamental principle is that social insurance, while unified and comprehensive, must take account of the different ways of life of different sections of the community ; of those dependent on earnings by employment under contract of service, of those earning in other ways, of those rendering vital unpaid service as housewives, of those not yet of age to earn and of those past earning. The term " classification " is used here to denote adjustment of insurance to the differing circumstances of each of these classes and to many varieties of need and circumstance within each insurance class. But the insurance classes are not economic or social classes in the ordinary sense ; the insurance scheme is one for all citizens irrespective of their means.

THE PEOPLE AND THEIR NEEDS

310. *Six Population Classes :* The Plan for Social Security starts with consideration of the people and of their needs. From the point of view of social security the people of Britain fall into six main classes described briefly as I—Employees ; II—Others gainfully occupied ; III—Housewives ; IV—Others of working age ; V—Below working age ; VI—Retired above working age. The precise definitions of each of these classes, the boundaries between them and the provision for passage from one to another are discussed in detail in paragraphs 314–319. The approximate numbers in each class and their relation to security needs, as listed in the following paragraph, are given in Table XVI. Some needs, for medical treatment and for burial, are common to all classes. In addition to this, those in Class V (Below working age) need children's allowances, and those in Class VI (Retired above working age) need pensions ; neither of

TABLE XVI

Population by Security Classes

Approximate Numbers in Great Britain, July 1939

Class	Number Million	Contribution Provisions	Relation to Security Scheme — Security Provisions							Other Provisions
			Medical Treatment	Funeral grant	Retirement pension	Disability benefit	Unemployment benefit	Training benefit (f)	Industrial pension	
I. Employees ...	18·4	Insured by weekly contribution on Employment Book	x	x	x	x	x	—	x	Removal and lodging grant: Industrial grant.
II. Others gainfully occupied	2·5	Insured by contributions on Occupation Card	x	x	x	x (b)	—	x	—	
III. Housewives ...	9·3 (a)	Insured on marriage through Housewife's Policy	x	x	x	—(c)	—(c)	x	—(c)	Marriage grant, maternity benefit (d) and grant, widows' benefit, guardian benefit, separation benefit.
IV. Others of working age	2·4	Insured by contributions on Security Card	x	x	x	—	—	x	—	
V. Below working age	9·6 (h)	None	x	x	—	—	—	—	—	
VI. Retired above working age	4·3	Insured by contributions made during working age	x	x	x	—	—	—	x (e)	
	46·5									

(a) Married women gainfully occupied estimated at 1·4 million are included in the numbers shown for Class III and excluded from the numbers shown for Classes I and II.

(b) After 13 weeks of sickness.

(c) If gainfully occupied and not exempt.

(d) If gainfully occupied even though exempt.

(e) If granted before reaching the age of retirement and if higher than the retirement pension.

(f) Includes removal and lodging grant where needed.

(g) The numbers shown in Class V are on the basis of the present minimum school leaving age, viz. 14. In the Report it is assumed for the purpose of children's allowances that the minimum school leaving age is 15.

these classes can be called on to contribute for social insurance. The other four classes all have different needs for which they will be insured by contributions made by or in respect of them. Class I (Employees), in addition to medical treatment, funeral expenses and pension, need security against interruption of earnings by unemployment and disability, however caused. Class II, i.e., persons gainfully occupied otherwise than as employees, cannot be insured against loss of employment, but in addition to medical treatment, funeral expenses and pension they need provision for loss of earnings through disability and they need some provision for loss of livelihood. Class III (Housewives) not being gainfully occupied do not need compensation for loss of earnings through disability or otherwise, but, in addition to the common needs of treatment, funeral expenses and pension, they have a variety of special needs arising out of marriage. Class IV (Others of working age) is a heterogeneous class in which relatively few people remain for any large part of their lives : they all need provision for medical treatment, funeral expenses and retirement, and also for the risk of having to find a new means of livelihood.

311. *Eight Primary Causes of Need :* The primary needs for social security are of eight kinds, reckoning the composite needs of a married woman as one and including also the needs of childhood (Assumption A) and the need for universal comprehensive medical treatment and rehabilitation (Assumption B). These needs are set out below ; to each there is attached in the security scheme a distinct insurance benefit or benefits. Assistance may enter to deal with any kind of need, where insurance benefit for any reason is inadequate or absent.

Unemployment : that is to say, inability to obtain employment by a person dependent on it and physically fit for it, met by unemployment benefit with removal and lodging grants.

Disability : that is to say, inability of a person of working age, through illness or accident, to pursue a gainful occupation, met by disability benefit and industrial pension.

Loss of Livelihood by person not dependent on paid employment, met by training benefit.

Retirement from occupation, paid or unpaid, through age, met by retirement pension.

Marriage needs of a woman, met by Housewife's Policy including provision for :—

(1) Marriage, met by marriage grant.
(2) Maternity, met by maternity grant in all cases, and, in the case of a married woman in gainful occupation, also by maternity benefit for a period before and after confinement.
(3) Interruption or cessation of husband's earnings by his unemployment, disability or retirement, met by share of benefit or pension with husband.
(4) Widowhood, met by provision varying according to circumstances including temporary widow's benefit for readjustment, guardian benefit while caring for children and training benefit if and when there are no children in need of care.
(5) Separation, i.e. end of husband's maintenance by legal separation, or established desertion, met by adaptation of widowhood provisions, including separation benefit, guardian benefit and training benefit.
(6) Incapacity for household duties, met by provision of paid help in illness as part of treatment.

Funeral Expenses of self or any person for whom responsible, met by funeral grant.

Childhood, provided for by children's allowances if in full-time education, till sixteen.

Physical Disease or *Incapacity*, met by medical treatment, domiciliary and institutional, for self and dependants in comprehensive health service and by post-medical rehabilitation.

312. *Other Needs :* The needs listed in para. 311 are the only ones so general and so uniform as to be clearly fit subjects for compulsory insurance. There is, partly for historical reasons, a problem as to the provision to be made for fatal accidents and diseases arising out of employment, by means of an industrial grant. There are many other needs and risks which are sufficiently common to be suited for voluntary insurance, and to a varying extent are already covered by that method. They include a great variety of contingencies for which provision is made by life and endowment insurance ; there are risks of fire, theft, or accident ; there are exceptional expenditures such as those on holidays and education.

313. *Explanation of Terms :* Before defining more closely the classes into which the people must be divided for purposes of social security, it is necessary to explain three terms. " Exception " means that certain types of persons are not within a particular class, though apart from the exception they would be ; exception is general, not individual, altering the definition of a class. " Exemption " means that a person though within a particular class is exempted individually from paying the contributions of that class ; his employer, if he has one, remains liable for contributions, but these contributions are not counted in judging of the insured person's claim to benefit. " Excusal " means that contributions for which an insured person and his employer, if he has one, would otherwise be liable, are not required, but for the purpose of satisfying contribution conditions for benefit are deemed to have been paid ; excusal is normally conditional on the insured person proving that he is unemployed or incapable of work. Exemption and excusal are dealt with more fully in paras. 363-364.

314. *Employees (Class I) :* These are, in general, persons depending for their maintenance upon remuneration received under a contract of service, including apprenticeship. The exact boundaries of this class will be adjusted by certain exceptions and inclusions. There will also be provision for exemption, that is to say, for allowing persons who take work falling within Class I to escape payment of their contributions while still requiring contributions by the employer. Insured persons in this class will hold an employment book which they will present to the employer for stamping.

The principal exception suggested is for family employment, that is to say, employment of one member of a family by another forming part of the same household. This is a development of the existing exception of fathers, sons, daughters etc., under Agricultural Unemployment Insurance, and is designed to prevent fictitious claims for benefit. Persons excluded from Class I by this exception will fall into Class II.

Persons in Class II or IV taking work temporarily under a contract of service will be allowed to claim exemption from their own contributions, and persons in Class III undertaking such work will be allowed to obtain exemption so long as they desire it. Exempt persons will present to the employer a special card to be stamped by him with the employer's contribution.

On the other hand, certain exceptions and exemptions under the present scheme will no longer apply. In particular :—

(i) There will be no exception of employees on the ground of the regularity of their employment or that it entitles them to pension. The basis of the security scheme is that all should contribute compulsorily irrespective of their personal risk. For men in the Armed Forces special arrangements for contribution will secure their rights to the benefits of the scheme when they return to civil life. For men in the merchant service there will be special arrangements for contribution adjusted to the conditions of their employment.

(ii) There will be no exception of any employees by a remuneration limit.

(iii) The right of persons above normal working age to claim exemption will cease on the introduction of the principle that pension is payable only on retirement from work and that men and women reaching the ages of 65 and 60 respectively, will have the option either of continuing to work and contribute or of retiring on pension at any time thereafter.

The possibility of either including in Class I and so insuring against unemployment certain classes of persons who are not technically under a contract of service but work in effect for employers (e.g. manual labour contractors, out-workers and private nurses) or of insuring such classes by special schemes, taking account of their special circumstances, needs further exploration. In one of these classes for instance, namely nurses, in addition to the fact that nurses work sometimes under contract of service and sometimes not, there are special needs arising out of their exposure to infection and out of the urgency of their duties, rendering necessary the possibility of intervals for rest and recuperation. The problem of giving some income security under a special scheme to share fishermen should also be explored. As stated above, apprentices generally will be included in Class I, but special arrangements may be made in regard to their rate of contribution (*see* para. 408).

315. *Others Gainfully Occupied (Class II)* : These are, in general, all persons working for gain who are not in Class I. Most of these will be persons working on their own account as employers or by themselves, including shopkeepers and hawkers, farmers, small holders and crofters, share fishermen, entertainers and renderers of professional and personal service and out-workers. They will include also persons who, though technically under contract of service, are excepted from Class I on the ground of family employment. Apart from the possibilities whose exploration is proposed above, persons gainfully occupied otherwise than under contract of service will not be insured against unemployment. Persons in Class II will pay contributions upon an occupation card. If a person in Class II gives up his independent occupation and takes insurable employment he will pass into Class I and will in due course acquire a claim to unemployment benefit in addition to the other benefits of Class II. If he takes insurable employment temporarily he will be allowed to work as an exempt person, i.e. only the employer's contribution will be paid and he will neither contribute for unemployment nor acquire a right to unemployment benefit. Conversely, a person whose main occupation is employment under a contract of service but who also works regularly or occasionally at some other gainful occupation, will be able to obtain exemption from Class II contributions. Persons in Class II will be able to apply for exemption on the ground that their income is below a certain minimum, say £75 a year (para. 363).

316. *Housewives (Class III)* : These are married women of working age living with their husbands. Any housewife who undertakes paid work as well, either under a contract of service or otherwise, will have the choice either of contributing in the ordinary way in Class I or Class II as the case may be, or of working as an exempt person, paying no contributions of her own.

317. *Others of Working Age (Class IV)* : These are in the main students above 16, unmarried women engaged in domestic duties not for pay, persons of private means, and persons incapacitated by blindness or other physical infirmity without being qualified for benefits under the social insurance scheme. The last of these groups will be a diminishing one. Blindness and other physical infirmities will occur in most cases after people have had a chance of contributing under the scheme and qualifying for disability benefit. At the outset there will be a number of people who became incapacitated before the scheme began. After the scheme has been established, persons in receipt of any benefit or pension in respect of contributions in other classes will be treated as still belonging to those classes and not as in Class IV. Those incapacitated or in institutions will be subject to the special arrangements appropriate in each case. All the others in Class IV will be required to hold security cards and to pay contributions thereon unless and until they pass into another class. This security card must be produced to obtain an employment book or occupation card. Persons in Class IV will be able to apply for exemption from contributions on the ground that their total income is below a certain minimum, say £75 a year (para. 363).

318. *Below Working Age (Class V)* : This class will include all persons below 16 who are in full-time education, whether compulsorily or voluntarily.

319. *Retired Above Working Age (Class VI)* : The minimum pensionable age for retirement on social insurance pension will be 65 for men and 60 for women, but persons who continue to work after these ages will pay contributions in the ordinary way and will be treated as belonging to Class I or Class II.

BENEFITS AND OTHER INSURANCE PAYMENTS

320. *Benefit, Pension, Grant and Allowance* : The term " benefit " denotes a weekly payment continued as a rule so long as the need lasts, as with unemployment, disability and guardian benefit, but sometimes given for a limited time only as with training, maternity, and widow's benefit. The term "pension" denotes a weekly payment presuming permanent or prolonged loss of earning power through age (retirement pension), or through industrial accident or disease (industrial pension). The term " grant " means a single payment for a specific purpose such as marriage, maternity, removal, or funeral, or in respect of fatal industrial accident or disease. The term " allowance " means a weekly payment in respect of a dependant, such as the allowance given to dependent children or the dependant allowance added to unemployment and disability benefit in respect of a person above the age of childhood.

321. *No overlapping of Benefit or Pension* : Subject to the exception suggested in para. 333 for partial incapacity pension arising from industrial accident or disease, only one benefit or pension can be drawn at the same time from the Social Insurance Fund. Receipt of benefit or pension can be combined with receipt of a grant or allowance.

322. *Contribution Conditions for Full Benefit* : The rates and periods of benefit or other insurance payment suggested below are for people in full benefit. The contribution conditions required for full benefit and the consequences of not being in full benefit are set out in paras. 367–368 below. In general, no person need fail to be in full benefit merely by reason of being unemployed, so long as he is available for work, or by reason of being disabled.

323. *Waiting Time* : For unemployment and disability of all kinds there will be a provisional waiting time of three days, that is to say, benefit will not be paid for the first three days of a period of unemployment or disability unless and until it lasts in all for four weeks.

324. *Joint and Single Benefit and Retirement Pension :* Benefit for unemployment or disability and pension for retirement will be at two rates—as for a man and wife (joint benefit or pension) and as for one person (single benefit or pension). Though paid normally to one of the couple, a joint benefit or pension will be regarded as shared between them ; if a man and wife in receipt of a joint retirement pension separate, it will be divided equally between them. The wife of an unemployed or disabled man will be regarded as sharing the joint benefit paid in his case (if she is not gainfully occupied) and not as a dependant in respect of whom he receives an increase of benefit or an allowance.

325. *Dependant Allowance :* If a single person entitled to unemployment, disability or training benefit has living with him or her a person above the age for children's allowance, not gainfully occupied and dependent upon him or her, an allowance in respect of that dependant will be added to the benefit, subject to Regulations which may require previous registration of the dependant and will define dependancy.

NOTE.—(i) The dependant allowance is not confined to adults, and may, therefore, cover both adults and people between 16 and 21. The examination of subsistence requirements in paras. 217-226 suggests that there is no substantial difference between the physical requirements of persons 16 to 21, and above that age.

(ii) The term "gainfully occupied" is used here subject to further definition as to how much occupation should exclude a person from the category of being a dependant. In the application of dependant allowances under unemployment insurance at present the rule is that a person is not dependent if he or she earns as much as the dependant allowance. It is for consideration whether this rule will suit the new scheme or whether a different rule, involving consideration of whether a person seeks exemption from contribution or not, should be applied.

(iii) Under the present unemployment insurance scheme, complicated provisions and rulings exist to determine the question of dependancy. If this question is left for decision until after a claim to benefit has arisen, those complications are probably unavoidable, and the suggestion is made accordingly of requiring registration previous to the claim in the case of any dependant. This suggestion raises a number of administrative questions requiring further consideration.

326. *Unemployment Benefit :* This will be a weekly payment continued without means or needs test throughout working age, so long as the insured person remains unemployed and available for work, but subject to the proviso that after he has drawn unconditional benefit for a limited period, the insured person, as a condition of remaining on benefit, will be required to attend a work or training centre. Receipt of indefinite unemployment benefit will be subject to being in full benefit, i.e. having paid contributions as required in paras. 366-367. Disqualifications, as at present, will apply to men refusing suitable employment, dismissed for misconduct or leaving their work voluntarily without just cause. Employees continuing to work after reaching the minimum pensionable age will be able to obtain unemployment benefit, but the period for which they can draw such benefit will be limited.

327. *Limited Unconditional Period :* The normal period of unconditional unemployment benefit will be six months, subject to the following adjustments :—

(*a*) The period may be increased generally by Order of the Minister for Social Security on the ground of a general depression of trade ;

(*b*) A shorter period may be prescribed by Regulations for persons below adult age ;

(*c*) Men of good contribution record who have made small claims may be entitled to additional days of unconditional unemployment benefit.

Unconditional benefit will be paid only to persons producing proof of unemployment by signature of a register or otherwise and of readiness to accept suitable employment.

> NOTE.—The suggestion in para. (*c*) for carrying on the present arrangements for additional days of benefit under the general unemployment insurance scheme is provisional, subject to further enquiry as to its desirability under new conditions.

328. *Unlimited Conditional Benefit :* Any person exhausting his claim to unconditional benefit, but otherwise in full benefit, will be able to continue to draw unemployment benefit without means test, subject to attendance, as required, at a work or training centre.

329. *Removal and Lodgings Grant :* Subject to Regulations, provision will be made for grants, by way of loan or otherwise, to meet in whole or in part expenses of removal and temporary lodging, to persons taking work or training at a distance from their present homes.

330. *Disability Benefit :* This will be a weekly payment available to persons in Classes I and II continued, subject to being in full benefit (para. 367), so long as they are physically incapacitated from work from any cause, throughout working age or till replaced by industrial pension. It will be paid to any person in Class I for the whole period of disability subject to the waiting time of three days provided by para. 323. In Class II it will be paid only for prolonged disability, that is to say only after disability has lasted thirteen weeks. During the first thirteen weeks of any illness, persons in Class II though receiving treatment will not receive cash benefit or be excused from contribution.

331. *Industrial Accident and Disease :* Provision for disability or death through accident or disease arising out of and in the course of employment will be included in the social insurance scheme, like disability or death due to any other cause. Medical treatment of employees affected by industrial accident or disease will be provided as part of the national medical service. Post-medical rehabilitation will be provided as part of a general service, to be organised by the Ministry of Labour and National Service, for all persons capable of profiting by it, irrespective of the cause of their disability. Administration of cash benefits will be undertaken by the Ministry of Social Security. The separate system of workmen's compensation will be superseded. But a number of important differences will continue to be made between the results of industrial accident or disease and disability or death due to other causes. These differences are set out in paras. 332–335 relating to industrial pension, partial disability, industrial grant, conditions of benefit and pension. There will also be an industrial levy on employers in scheduled industries to meet a proportion of the special cost of accidents and disease occurring in them (para. 360). Amendment or review of some of the present provisions— as to remuneration limit, common law liability, lump sum compensation, definition of dependants, and principles and machinery for assessment of earnings and distribution of death grants—is proposed (para. 336).

332. *Industrial Pension :* If disability due to industrial accident or disease lasts for more than thirteen weeks, disability benefit at a flat rate will be replaced by industrial pension related to average earnings so long as disability continues. The industrial pension for total disablement will be at the rate of two-thirds of the earnings of the employee when in full employment, subject to a minimum of being not less than the benefit which he would have

E

received for ordinary disability, that is, joint or single benefit according to whether he is married or single, with dependant allowance where that would be payable, and subject to a maximum of £3 a week. Industrial pensions will not be awarded in respect of disablement arising after the minimum pensionable age, but a pension granted before that age has been reached will, if greater than the retirement pension, continue to the end of life in place of retirement pension. Since industrial pension is related to the earnings, it will be the same for single as for married men, except that the minimum for the married man will be higher, being the rate of joint disability benefit and not of single disability benefit.

333. *Partial Disablement :* A proportion of the industrial pension will be granted for partial disablement, in accord with the loss of earning capacity. Since a person in receipt of a partial industrial pension may be able to work and therefore may become unemployed or fall sick, he may qualify for unemployment or disability benefit. Since the partial industrial pension is in respect of his lowered earning capacity, he will be able to an extent to be defined by Regulations to combine partial industrial pension with unemployment or disability benefit simultaneously. This is an exception for special reasons to the general rule in para. 321 against overlapping of benefits.

334. *Industrial Grant :* If death results from industrial accident or disease, a grant will be paid in respect of the widow, if any, and of persons wholly or mainly dependent on the deceased, in addition to funeral grant and widow's and guardian benefit, but taking account of this provision. The amount of the industrial grant, the dependants to be taken into account, and the form and allocation of the grant will be determined in accord with the Regulations of the Minister of Social Security to be made after further investigation and consultation with the interested parties. No industrial grant will be paid in respect of deaths occurring after the minimum age of retirement.

335. *No Contribution Conditions on Industrial Claims :* No contribution conditions will be imposed for payment of benefit, pension or grant in respect of disability or death due to industrial accident or disease: that is to say, the right to such payments will depend on whether or not disability or death is due to accident or disease arising out of and in the course of employment under a contract of service.

336. *Changes in Present Compensation Provisions :* The present provisions in regard to compensation for industrial accident and disease will be affected in the following among other ways :—

(a) Abolition of the remuneration limit for non-manual workers. No persons otherwise entitled will be excluded on the ground that his remuneration exceeds a given figure.

(b) Restriction of lump sum payments for disability to cases in which the Security Office is satisfied that such a payment is in the employee's interest either because the disability does not make him incapable of earning a wage sufficient for subsistence or because of some other special reason.

(c) Dealing with claims by administrative rather than legal procedure. Assessment of industrial pensions and grants will be undertaken by officers specialising in that work, subject to the right of appeal by employee or employer or associations of employees or employers to special local tribunals consisting of three regular members (in place of a Chairman and assessors from a panel as with Courts of Referees).

(d) Review of the law of employers' liability in view of the improved provision for the results of industrial accident or disease.

(e) The setting up of statutory associations of employers and employees in industries scheduled as hazardous, with various functions of administration and advice as indicated in paras. 91–92.

337. *Contributory Retirement Pension :* Any person in Classes I, II or IV, on reaching the minimum pensionable age of 65 for a man or 60 for a woman, will be able to retire upon a contributory pension which will be at the same basic rate for single men and single women. There will be a joint retirement pension for a man and wife, payable when both are of pensionable age, and also when the husband alone is of pensionable age, if the wife is not gainfully occupied. A married woman who has been gainfully occupied and has paid the required contributions will be able to retire on pension on reaching the minimum pensionable age and ceasing from gainful occupation, irrespective of her husband's age. A married woman who has not been gainfully occupied or who has obtained exemption from contributions in respect of gainful occupation, will not be able to obtain pension so long as her husband is working, but on his retirement will share the joint pension.

> NOTE.—In accordance with paras. 233–257, to which reference should be made for a full account of the proposals in regard to old age, contributory pensions will rise to the full rate gradually during a transition period of about twenty years. During this period assistance pensions taking account of subsistence needs, as determined for the purpose of contributory pensions, will be given subject to consideration of means, either in supplementation of contributory pensions or in place of them, as may be required. During this period the rate of unemployment or disability benefit will be materially higher than the rate of contributory pensions and the right of persons who continue at work after reaching the minimum pensionable age to draw unemployment or disability benefit in place of going on pension will be restricted by Regulations.

338. *Increase of Pension above basic rate :* A person continuing gainful occupation in Class I or Class II after reaching minimum pensionable age will continue to contribute, and in respect of each year of postponement, subject to making the prescribed number of contributions, will have his rate of pension on retirement increased. Such a person, until he retires, will be able to obtain benefit in unemployment or disability, but not for more than (say) 20 weeks in any benefit year. If a person who has retired on pension thereafter undertakes paid work, either in employment or otherwise, the amount of his pension in any three months will be reduced by a proportion of his earnings in a previous three months. Though in Class IV there will be no retirement from work, a person in this class on reaching the minimum pensionable age will be able to decide either to go on pension at once or, by postponing application for pension and continuing to contribute, to obtain later a pension increased above the basic rate.

339. *Marriage needs :* For the purpose of the Social Insurance scheme housewives form a special Class (III). Every woman on marriage will become a new person, acquiring new rights and not carrying on into marriage claims to unemployment or disability benefit in respect of contributions made before marriage. Some new rights, as for marriage grant and maternity grant, apply to all married women ; all women also during marriage will continue to acquire qualifications for pensions in old age through contributions made by their husbands. Some of the new rights, as for share of benefit due to husband's unemployment or disability, apply only to married women who are not gainfully occupied. Some, as for maternity benefit in addition to maternity grant, apply only to married women who are gainfully occupied. Some of the claims arise only on the end of marriage—either by widowhood

or by divorce or other forms of separation. There has to be considered, finally, in connection with provision for marriage, the problem of the unmarried person living as a wife.

340. *[Marriage Grant]* : Every woman on marriage will be entitled to a grant at the rate of £1 for every 40 actual contributions prior to marriage in Classes I or II up to a maximum of £10. This grant is desirable both as compensation for giving up previous qualifications for benefit and having to requalify if she continues in gainful occupation, and also in order to obtain prompt notification of marriage. It is bracketed, however, as something not essential to the rest of the Scheme and something that might be omitted if it were thought necessary to reduce contributions (see para. 403).

341. *Maternity Grant and Maternity Benefit* : All married women, whether themselves gainfully occupied or not, will be entitled to a maternity grant, and also to medical attention and midwifery and nursing services as part of the comprehensive health service. Married women who are also gainfully occupied will be entitled to maternity benefit, in addition to maternity grant, for a period of 13 weeks including the date of the birth, on condition of giving up for the time their gainful occupation. The maternity grant is not intended to cover the whole cost of maternity, which has a reasonable and natural claim upon the husband's earnings. But it should be raised materially above its present figure. The maternity benefit is intended to make it easy and attractive for women to give up gainful occupation at the time of maternity, and will be at a rate materially higher than ordinary unemployment or disability benefit.

342. *Benefit in Husband's Unemployment and Disability* : If a man insured against unemployment or disability has a wife who is not herself gainfully occupied, joint benefit will be paid, sufficient for the subsistence of both. The extent of gainful occupation by the wife which should be ground for giving single benefit only will need definition. One plan would be to adopt the present practice in unemployment insurance of giving dependant allowance unless the wife is earning as much as the allowance. An alternative plan would be to allow the joint rate of benefit in the husband's unemployment or disability, wherever the wife had applied for and obtained exemption from contributions ; that is to say, the wife could choose either to qualify for benefit in her own unemployment or disability or to share in joint benefit when the husband was unemployed or disabled.

343. *Retirement Pension on Husband's Contributions* : When a husband and wife are both of pensionable age they will be able on his retirement to obtain a joint retirement pension which, though normally paid to one of the two, will be regarded as belonging to both and will be divided equally if they separate. Contributions paid by a man so long as legal marriage lasts will be reckoned as contributions on behalf of his wife for her pension whether or not he is living with her. A wife will not be entitled to pension in respect of her husband's contributions merely on the ground that she is of pensionable age, if he has not yet retired. If the husband is of pensionable age and retired but the wife is below pensionable age, joint pension will be paid if she is living with him and is not gainfully occupied. This will be subject to Regulations requiring a minimum duration of the marriage before joint pension is claimed.

344. *Household Help in Sickness* : The housewife who has no gainful occupation or who has so little that she prefers to be exempt from contributions will get no disability benefit in sickness ; she will not have lost earnings on which she depended. But it may well happen in sickness that she feels unable to take the necessary hospital treatment because she cannot leave her household duties. The comprehensive health service should include means of giving household help to housewives, where this appears to be necessary to make

possible their most effective medical treatment. This should be organised as part of the welfare service of hospitals and given on the recommendation of the doctor who sends her to the hospital. This service could, if necessary, be extended to giving necessary household help when the housewife is ill at home. But this hardly seems likely to be needed ; neighbourly and family help should meet such cases. The case is different when it is important to overcome difficulties in getting a patient to hospital as soon as her health requires it.

345. *Married Woman Gainfully Occupied* : A woman who after marriage undertakes gainful occupation, under contract of service in Class I, will always have the right to claim exemption, that is to say, to pay no contributions of her own, though her employer will pay contributions. Whether or not she claims exemption, she will receive maternity benefit. If she claims exemption, she will not qualify for unemployment or disability benefits during marriage or for retirement pension except as one of the married team, that is to say, except for her share of the joint retirement pension mentioned in para. 343. If, on the other hand, in place of claiming exemption, she prefers to contribute, she will, subject to the normal contribution and benefit conditions, be able to obtain :

(*a*) Unemployment or disability benefit at a reduced rate but subject to the same conditions as other insured persons, i.e. without any Anomalies Regulations for Married Women.

(*b*) Pension on her own retirement from gainful occupation after 60, irrespective of her husband's age and occupation.

A married woman will equally be able to obtain exemption if she takes gainful occupation in Class II.

346. *End of Marriage by Widowhood* : The provision to be made for widowhood depends upon the circumstances of the widow, including her age, the existence or not of dependent children and the question whether the death of the husband was due to industrial accident or disease or to some other cause.

If the widow is of pensionable age, that is to say above 60, she, subject to the husband being in full benefit by contributions, will receive retirement pension at the single pensioner's rate. For widows of working age no permanent pension will be provided, but every such widow will receive a widow's benefit at the same rate as maternity benefit for 13 weeks. At the end of that time, if and so long as she has the care of dependent children, she will be entitled to guardian benefit. This with children's allowances will be designed to be enough for subsistence even if the widow earns nothing by work. If she does go out to work, a reduction of the full guardian benefit will be made, of a proportion of her earnings. Guardian benefit will cease so soon as the last child ceases to be dependent, if the widow re-marries, and if and when she retires on pension (a rare case). A widow in receipt of widow's or guardian benefit, if she takes employment or is otherwise gainfully occupied, will have the option of doing so as an exempt person.

Every widow of working age and capacity will be able to apply for training benefit. After training, a widow of working age without dependent children, will become liable to work and contribute as a single woman.

The widow will be entitled to funeral grant in respect of herself and of any dependent child.

If the death of the husband has taken place through industrial accident or disease, an industrial grant, that is to say, compensation in the form of a lump sum related to the husband's earnings will be paid in addition to any of the other benefits, but taking account of them, and subject to the power of the Ministry of Social Security to control the disposition of the grant.

If at the time of the death of the husband the widow, though childless, is totally disabled she will, subject to her husband's contributions, be able to obtain disability benefit so long as the disability lasts, after widow's benefit.

347. *End of Marriage otherwise than by Widowhood :* Divorce, legal separation, desertion and voluntary separation may cause needs similar to those caused by widowhood. They differ from widowhood in two respects : that they may occur through the fault or with the consent of the wife, and that except where they occur through the fault of the wife they leave the husband's liability for maintenance unchanged. If they are regarded from the point of view of the husband, they may not appear to be insurable risks ; a man cannot insure against events which occur only through his fault or with his consent, and if they occur through the fault or with the consent of the wife she should not have a claim to benefit. But from the point of view of the woman, loss of her maintenance as housewife without her consent and not through her fault, is one of the risks of marriage against which she should be insured ; she should not depend on assistance. Recognition of housewives as a distinct insurance class, performing necessary service not for pay, implies that, if the marriage ends otherwise than by widowhood, she is entitled to the same provision as for widowhood, unless the marriage maintenance has ended through her fault or voluntary action without just cause. That is to say, subject to the practical considerations mentioned in the note below she should get temporary separation benefit (on the same lines as widow's benefit), and guardian or training benefit where appropriate.

NOTE.—The principle that a married woman who without fault of her own loses the maintenance to which she is entitled from her husband should get benefit is clear. It is obvious, however, that except where the maintenance has ended through divorce or other form of legal separation establishing that the default is not that of the wife, considerable practical difficulties may arise in determining whether a claim to benefit, as distinct from assistance, has arisen. There will often be difficulty in determining responsibility for the break-up of the marriage. There will in cases of desertion be difficulty in establishing the fact or the permanence of desertion. There will in all cases be the problem of alternative remedies open to the wife. The point to which the principle of compensating a housewife for the loss of her maintenance otherwise than by widowhood can be carried in practice calls for further examination. It may for practical reasons be found necessary to limit the widow's insurance benefit to cases of formal separation, while making it clear that she can in all cases at need get assistance and that the Ministry of Social Security will then proceed against the husband for recoupment of its expenditure.

348. *Unmarried Person Living as a Wife :* Treatment of this problem, complicated by the possibility that either or both parties in this extra-legal relation may have a legal spouse, is necessarily difficult. The main principles on which it should be approached are as follows :—

(i) A man who is himself unmarried but has living with him as his wife a woman who is not herself gainfully occupied should be able during unemployment and disability to obtain a dependant allowance as he could for any other dependant, bringing benefit up to the joint rate for two persons. On principle it seems right to exclude dependant allowance in such cases where the man already has a legal wife, though the practical problems involved in this need further examination.

(ii) Widow's and guardian benefits should not be paid except to a woman who was the legal wife of the dead man. Retirement pension should not be paid in respect of contributions other than the woman's own contributions, except to the legal wife of the retired man.

(iii) Maternity grant and maternity benefit raise the most difficult of all questions in this connection. On the one hand, it may be said that, in the interests of the child, grant and benefit should be paid where appropriate, irrespective of the marital relation of the parents. Against this it may be said that the interest of the State is not in getting children born, but in getting them born in conditions which secure to them the proper domestic environment and care. The decision in regard to maternity grant may depend on whether or not it is thought to be practicable and desirable administratively to require previous registration of an adult dependant. In that case a man who had an unmarried person living with him as his wife, on registering this, would be qualified to obtain dependant allowance for her during unemployment and disability and maternity grant also. In regard to maternity benefit, in spite of the fact that this is for married women to some extent a compensation for lower unemployment and disability benefits if gainfully occupied, it will probably be felt right, in the interests of the child, to make this benefit equally available to unmarried mothers, so that they may have the same opportunity of withdrawing from gainful occupation at the time of the confinement. An unmarried mother will have an affiliation claim against the father and it may be proper to give the Security Office the right of proceeding against him for recoupment of maternity benefit, but even if the Security Office has this right it should not in practice exercise that right in such a way as to discourage an application for maternity benefit from the woman.

349. *Training Benefit :* Subject to Regulations, the Security Office will be authorised to give a training benefit to persons capable of work and available for work, who are not entitled to unemployment benefit and need to find a new means of livelihood. The benefit will be at the same rate as unemployment benefit, including dependent allowance, and will be granted without means test up to a maximum period normally of 26 weeks, subject to satisfactory attendance at a training centre. The Regulations will provide for payment of removal and lodging grants where necessary and may provide for payments to cover additional expenditures incurred by persons under training. Training benefit will be available for the following cases :—

(i) Persons who have been gainfully occupied in Class II but lose their livelihood and are accepted for training for new work, in employment or otherwise.

(ii) Widows (or deserted or separated wives) of working age with or without dependent children.

(iii) Persons in Class IV whose circumstances change, so as to make it necessary for them to earn, e.g., spinsters who have been rendering unpaid service which is no longer needed, and persons who lose private means.

350. *Funeral Grant :* Subject to contribution conditions, a funeral grant varying with the age of the deceased person will be made in respect of every death. The person to receive the grant in each case will be defined by Regulations which may provide for nomination of a recipient by the person insured and will require the recipient to undertake responsibility for the funeral. The grant suggested on full benefit is £6 for a child under 3 years of age, £10 for a child between 3 and 10, £15 between 10 and 21, and £20 thereafter. The relevant contributions will be those of the deceased person if gainfully occupied, of the father or widowed mother in case of dependent children, of the husband in case of a housewife. Persons retired on pension will always be on full benefit for funeral grant, as will widows receiving guardian or training benefit. A funeral grant will not be paid in respect of persons aged 60 or more at the beginning of the scheme.

351. *Blind Persons :* Where blindness occurs, as in most cases it now occurs, late in life, those who are wholly incapacitated by it will be qualified by contributions for disability benefit, or industrial pension. The special needs of blind persons, including provision of partial incapacity allowance additional to disability benefit for special expenses, welfare and opportunities for useful work and occupation will be covered under a new scheme to be prepared by the Ministry of Social Security in consultation with the Local Authorities and other agencies concerned, on the general principle that the primary responsibility for cash payments falls upon the Ministry of Social Security and that provision of institutions and care associated with them falls on the Local Authorities.

352. *Other Infirm Persons :* Cripples, chronic bronchitics and other classes of permanent invalids will, like blind persons, normally have been contributors in either Class I or II and will receive disability benefit on becoming infirm. Where infirmity starting before working age prevents the person from entering a gainful occupation and therefore from qualifying for disability benefit provision will be made for national assistance in case of need.

353. *Application to Existing Cases :* The application of the new rates of insurance payment to existing cases of disability, unemployment and widowhood raises questions which may be answered differently for different forms of payment as follows :—

(1) In regard to industrial disability, it is proposed that all persons who, at the beginning of the scheme, are in receipt of weekly payments less than the industrial pension which they would have received under the scheme shall, if and when their disability has exceeded thirteen weeks in length, be granted the new rates (paras. 101–105). No contributions have been required for industrial disability benefit and pension in the past and no contribution conditions are proposed in future.

(2) In regard to pensions it is proposed that existing pensioners, if and when they retire and give up work, shall receive contributory pensions according to the rising scale (para. 242). These pensioners will get pension above the rate for which they have contributed but subject to a new condition.

(3) In regard to unemployment, which is assumed to be of a temporary character, the new rates will apply as from the beginning of the scheme to all persons who are unemployed thereafter. For persons whose unemployment is prolonged the benefit will be conditional on attendance at a training centre.

(4) In regard to widows, the temporary widow's benefit will apply only to deaths occurring after the beginning of the scheme. The guardian benefit will be available for persons widowed before the beginning of the scheme. Existing widows without children will retain their present pensions.

(5) The treatment of disability other than industrial raises questions which are both important and difficult. The numbers involved are large. In February 1942 there were about 425,000 persons in receipt of sickness benefit and 375,000 persons in receipt of disablement benefit under the present scheme. The right line for treating these people in relation to the rest of the Social Insurance Scheme is not clear. In the past, when contributions and benefits have been raised, the new rates have been applied automatically to all the existing cases, but the increases of benefit were small, whereas in regard to sickness and disablement the difference of levels between the present scheme and the proposed scheme is great. Moreover, new classes are being brought into insurance.

Finally the pension rates are being raised, not at once, but over a period of years. To apply the new rates or disability automatically to all existing cases of sickness and disablement at the beginning of the scheme would have two effects which might cause criticism : (a) the new rates could not well be limited to the present contributory classes, so that it might become necessary to give high disability benefits to permanent invalids who have hitherto been outside any insurance scheme ; (b) many of the prolonged disability cases would be persons advanced in years and nearing the pension age. Under the proposals for pension when they reach that age they will receive during the transition period not the full pension of 40/– joint or 24/– single, i.e. the same as disability benefit, but something which may be much less. Thus if a permanent invalid with a wife, now receiving 10/6 a week as disablement benefit were raised to 40/– in 1945 at the age of 63, he would come back to 26/6 in 1947. It would obviously cause great trouble to put permanent invalids up for one or two years to the new rates, only to take them down again as soon as they reached pensionable age. These considerations suggest that the new scales of disability benefit unlimited in time should apply only to people who pay the initial qualifying contributions under the new scheme, and that persons who fail to qualify through being permanent invalids should be treated as prematurely pensioned, their disability benefit at any time being kept to the level of what they would get as persons retired on pension. The question, however, is difficult and calls for further examination of the numbers and classes of persons concerned, and of the method of distinguishing between those who are to be treated as permanent invalids on pension and those who may qualify for disability benefit.

COMPULSORY INSURANCE CONTRIBUTIONS

354. *Single Contribution :* There will be a single weekly contribution for all purposes for each person, paid by affixing an insurance stamp to the appropriate insurance document, described as employment book for Class I, occupation card for Class II, security card for Class IV. This is subject to the following provisos :—

(a) In addition to the contribution paid by insurance stamps there will be an industrial levy on employers in scheduled industries (para. 360).

(b) Regulations may provide for payment of contributions in Classes II and IV at intervals longer than a week.

(c) Regulations may provide for a reduced contribution for periods of employment for less than a week (para. 408 (d)).

355. *Class I Contribution :* In Class I, the insurance stamp will be affixed to the employment book by the employer and will represent the joint contribution of employer and employee, the employee's share being deducted from his wages or salary.

356. *Class II Contribution :* Every person carrying on any occupation for gain, otherwise than by way of employment in Class I, will be required to hold an occupation card and to affix to this an insurance stamp representing his Class II contribution for each week that he holds the card unless he is exempted or excused under paras. 363–364.

357. *Class III Contribution :* Contributions in respect of housewives, that is married women of working age, will be paid as part of their husband's contributions, the contributions of all men being higher than those of women in order to provide part of the benefits of housewives. Housewives who also

undertake employment (Class I) or other gainful occupation (Class II) will have the choice of obtaining :

(i) Ordinary employment books or occupation cards paying the full contributions and getting unemployment or disability benefit at reduced rates with maternity benefit ;

or (ii) Exemption from their own contributions in the appropriate class, and getting only maternity benefit.

A housewife working as an exempt person in Class I who is disabled by an industrial accident or disease will get disability benefit in the first instance at the reduced flat rate, but after 13 weeks will get industrial pension, so long as she is disabled.

358. *Class IV Contribution* : Every person not holding an employment book, occupation card or housewife's policy will be required to hold a security card and to affix to this an insurance stamp representing his Class IV contribution for each week, unless he is exempted under para. 363.

359. *No Exception for Pensionability of Occupation or Rate of Remuneration.* There will be no exception from the obligation to contribute either for particular employments or occupations on the ground that they are regular or pensionable or for individuals on the ground that their remuneration or income exceeds a specified amount.

360. *Industrial Levy* : In addition to the contribution for industrial accident and disease included as part of the employer's share of the insurance stamp in every case in Class I, there will be a special levy on employers in industries scheduled as liable to materially more than the normal risks of industrial accident or disease, with a view to providing for two-thirds of the additional cost of disability in respect of those employments. The amount of the levy will depend upon the degree of risk in the particular employment and the employer's pay-roll.

361. *State Contribution* : In accordance with the proposals set out in Part IV, para. 279, the National Exchequer will make a contribution to the Social Insurance Fund, in addition to paying the whole cost of children's allowances and national assistance, and the cost of treatment and rehabilitation subject to a grant towards this cost made from the Social Insurance Fund.

362. *Demarcation of Classes* : Since no person will be expected or allowed to contribute in more than one insurance class at one time, provision must be made both for movement from one class to another and for persons who, while remaining in their present class, take work which in the normal way would bring them into another class. Movement from one class to another will mean obtaining the document appropriate to the new class by surrendering the insurance document already held. Where, without leaving his present class, a person takes work which would normally bring him into another class, he will be able to obtain exemption from the contribution of the other class. Many detailed points in regard to movement from class to class and demarcation of classes will be dealt with by Regulations. The general principle is that, except in so far as exempted or excused for any of the reasons stated in paras. 363-364 and subject to the option for housewives in para. 357, every person of working age will make a contribution on a single document and will not make a contribution in more than one class.

363. *Exemption from Contributions* : Exemption means that, on application being made by him, an individual is allowed to escape contributions for which he would otherwise be liable. Exemption may be either for a fixed period or indefinite during continuance of the grounds of exemption. Exemption involves possession of an insurance document marked as for exemption.

Except in the case of maternity benefit, contributions from which persons are exempted are not deemed to be paid by them for the purpose of satisfying contribution conditions for benefit. Exemption will be allowed

(i) From Class I on the ground that the principal occupation is Class II or Class III. In this case the insured person must present to the employer an employment book marked for exemption and the employer must affix stamps for his share of the joint contribution ;

(ii) From Class II on the ground that the principal occupation is Class I or Class III ;

(iii) From Class II or Class IV in any contribution year (or quarter) on the ground that total income in that year (or quarter) has been less than at the rate of £75 a year ;

(iv) From contributions for pensions by persons over the age of 55 for men or 50 for women at the beginning of the scheme (say 1st July, 1944) who are not within the present pension contributory classes.

NOTE.—The right to obtain exemption from Class II or Class IV contributions on the ground of total income below £75 a year is suggested in order to deal with the difficulty of enforcing contributions where there is no income obviously available to pay them. Some of those in Class II (street sellers and others) may be extremely poor ; some of those in Class IV may have no cash incomes of their own, but may merely receive support from a relative with whom they live. It is desirable nevertheless to secure Class IV contributions so far as possible in such cases, as the title to pension ; those who get unpaid domestic service from daughters or sisters who might otherwise be earning should pay the security contributions of these persons. Moreover, the bulk of persons in Class IV at any time (other than those permanently incapacitated) will have been or will be gainfully occupied at some other stage of their lives and will have made or will make contributions whose continuity should be maintained as a qualification for pension. It is probably necessary to give the possibility of exemption where there really is no income to meet the contributions. But the income to be considered is total income, not the earnings in a particular gainful occupation.

A further question in regard to exemption under this heading is whether the exemption should be total or from a part of the contribution only. All persons will receive medical treatment. It may be desirable to provide both for total exemption from contributions when the income is below a small minimum figure (or possibly for the National Exchequer in such cases to pay the contributions by way of assistance) and in other cases to provide for exemption only from that part of the contribution which is not required for medical treatment. The relatively small contribution for medical treatment would in effect become a registration fee.

The grounds for the fourth type of exemption (from pension contributions in case of persons over 55 or 50 in 1944) are given in para. 242.

In addition to the four types of exemption named above, provision must be made for exemption from contributions or other suitable treatment in respect of persons in prisons or similar institutions.

364. *Excusal of Contributions :* Excusal means that contributions to which a person would otherwise be liable are not required, and for the purpose of contribution conditions are deemed to have been made by him or on his behalf, although they have not in fact been made. Grounds of excusal are :—

(i) From Class I contributions : certified unemployment or disability, and maternity.

(ii) From Class II contributions : certified disability after 13 weeks and maternity.

(iii) From Class IV contributions : receipt of widow's or guardian benefit.

(iv) From all contributions : receipt of training benefit.

365. *Contribution Year and Benefit Year :* Each class of insurance document —employment book, occupation card or security card—will be current for a contribution year ending July, and will be exchanged at the end of that year for a new document current for the next contribution year. Subject to further examination of the administrative problems involved, the benefit year for all benefits will run for twelve months from the 1st October; and the claim of an insured person to be in full benefit for benefits, grants and allowances in that benefit year will depend upon the contributions made or excused in the preceding contribution year. For a housewife the relevant contributions are those of her husband.

366. *Initial Qualifying Contributions :* When the scheme is in full operation, no person will be able to obtain unemployment or disability benefit until he has paid 26 actual contributions, or to obtain disability benefit for more than 52 weeks unless he has paid 156 actual contributions ; these conditions do not apply to disability due to industrial accident or disease for which there are no contribution conditions. The qualifying contributions for pensions are explained in para. 242 dealing with the transition from the present pensions to the new scheme. No initial contribution conditions will be required for widows or guardian benefit. At the outset of the scheme, transitional Regulations will be required defining the extent to which contributions made under the present schemes shall be taken into account as qualification for the new benefits.

367. *Conditions for Full Benefit :* In order to be in full benefit during any benefit year for unemployment, disability, training, widow's or guardian benefit, or any of the grants or allowances other than industrial or funeral grants, 48 contributions must have been paid or excused in the preceding contribution year by or in respect of the insured person. In order to be in full benefit for pension there must have been paid, or been excused, by or in respect of the insured person, contributions averaging not less than 48 a year throughout his working life since the beginning of the scheme. In general any person dependent on earnings will remain in full benefit, by certifying unemployment or disability when not earning. Only those who do not depend on their earnings are likely to be out of full benefit, e.g., seasonal workers or others taking work occasionally only and not continuously available for work. There may also be persons in Class IV who obtain exemption under para. 363 or neglect contribution and persons coming to Britain late in life or leaving it for a time. The right to full maternity benefit will be governed by special conditions allowing contributions to count whether made by both parties or only by the employer, with the insured woman having exemption ; the number of contributions required for full benefit is a matter for further consideration. The contributions required for full benefit in respect of funeral grant will be prescribed by Regulations, in accord with the general principle that the contributions to be taken into account are those of or in respect of the deceased person if of working age, and those of the responsible parent if the deceased person was below working age. The Regulations should make it easy for persons to keep in benefit by taking account of contributions paid or excused either in the past contribution year or over an average of three

contribution years, and the number of contributions required should be materially less than to qualify for unemployment or disability benefit. Subject to the exclusion from funeral grant of all persons who are over 60 at the beginning of the scheme, persons retired on pension will automatically be on full benefit for funeral grant. The provisions of this paragraph, like those of the preceding paragraph will apply when the scheme is in full operation. Transitional Regulations will be required to define the extent to which contributions made under the present schemes shall be taken into account at the outset of the new scheme.

368. *Reduced Benefit:* The benefit to be accorded to persons who are not on full benefit will be determined by Regulations appropriate to each type of benefit. In the case of unemployment, disability and maternity benefit, these Regulations may provide either for reducing the weekly rate of benefit or for reducing the period in respect of which it can be drawn. In the case of pension the Regulations will provide either for postponing the date of retirement or reducing the rate of pension. In the case of funeral grant they will provide for reducing the amount of the grant, but for the reasons given in the preceding paragraph it will be rare for people not to be on full benefit.

NOTE.—The Regulations in regard to title to pension may be different according as failure to be in full benefit is due to the claimant having been exempted from payment of contributions under paragraph 363 (iii) or is due to some other cause. The Regulations should allow persons who have been exempted under paragraph 363 (iii) to pay the exempted contributions subsequently within a limited time, with a view to qualifying for pension.

NATIONAL ASSISTANCE

369. *Assistance as part of Security:* Assistance will be available to meet all needs which are not covered by insurance. It must meet those needs adequately up to subsistence level, but it must be felt to be something less desirable than insurance benefit; otherwise the insured persons get nothing for their contributions. Assistance therefore will be given always subject to proof of needs and examination of means; it will be subject also to any conditions as to behaviour which may seem likely to hasten restoration of earning capacity. The cost of assistance will be met directly by the National Exchequer. But though distinct from social insurance national assistance will be combined with it in administration, as a minor but integral part of the work of the Ministry of Social Security.

370. *Transitional Scope of Assistance:* In the transitional period for pensions before contributory pensions reach subsistence level, assistance pensions will be required in a considerable number of cases and will form a large part of the total work of assistance.

371. *Limited Permanent Scope of Assistance:* The proposals in this Report (extending State insurance to new Classes, raising rates of benefit and prolonging the period of benefit) will make the permanent scope of assistance much less than that of public assistance and of the Assistance Board at present. Nevertheless there will remain a real, if limited, continuing scope for assistance covering the following main classes.

(a) Persons failing to fulfil contribution conditions either because they have less than the qualifying minimum (para. 366) or because they never become fit for work, or because they are not in full benefit for unemployment, disability or pensions, or because being in Class II or Class IV they claim and obtain exemption on the ground of deficient total income (para. 363).

(b) Persons failing to fulfil conditions for benefit. The most important of these are likely to be (i) men disqualified for unconditional unemployment benefit through refusal of suitable employment, through leaving work without just cause, through dismissal for misconduct, and (ii) those who are disqualified for conditional unemployment benefit by failure to attend a work or training centre.

(c) Persons with abnormal needs in respect of diet, care and other matters.

(d) Persons in need through causes not suitable for insurance, e.g., some forms of desertion or separation.

372. *Unified Means Test :* The three differing tests of needs and means which are now applied by separate authorities for non-contributory pensions, supplementary pensions and public assistance, will be replaced by a test administered by a single authority on principles uniform in themselves, though taking account of the different problems which arise in relation to different classes of case. Giving of assistance involves consideration on the one hand of needs and on the other hand of the applicant's resources for meeting them. The needs of adult persons and of children should be based on estimates of what is necessary for subsistence on the principles discussed in paras. 193–232. For old persons it is reasonable to add a margin above the subsistence minimum, as is proposed in regard to contributory pensions by bringing them ultimately up to unemployment and disability benefit. Consideration of the applicant's resources raises two questions : of the ownership of the resources to be taken into account and of the treatment of resources of different kinds. As regards the ownership of the resources to be taken into account, there appears to be no reason for disturbing materially, if at all, the settlement reached under the Determination of Needs Act. As regards the treatment of resources of different kinds, this matter is now dealt with partly by Statute, partly by Regulations, and partly by administrative discretion. It is suggested that, in future, it should be wholly a matter for Regulations to be made subject to the approval of both Houses of Parliament. Regulations have the advantage over Statute both that they can be amended more easily in order to provide for changed circumstances, and that they can be more detailed than Statutes. On the other hand, they have the advantage, as compared with administrative discretion, that the making of a new Regulation calls attention of all parties concerned to any additional rights that may be granted to them. Regulations are available to all officers, members of Appeal Tribunals and the public. They set standards to which administration must conform and they ensure reasonable consistency of treatment between one place and another and between one time and another. Under the Regulations it will be possible to make suitable considered allowance for capital, for earnings, for war disability pensions, for social insurance benefits and pensions, and for other income.

373. *Cases of Special Difficulty :* At the basis of any system of social security covering all those who comply with reasonable just conditions for insurance and assistance, there must be provision for a limited class of men or women who through weakness or badness of character fail to comply. In the last resort the man who fails to comply with the conditions for obtaining benefit or assistance and leaves his family without resources must be subject to penal treatment.

374. *Some Assistance Problems :* On transfer of responsibility for assistance to a central authority it may be necessary to make some amendment of the present provisions as to (a) giving of assistance to persons on strike or locked-out ; (b) giving of assistance on loan with recovery thereafter ; (c) giving of assistance in kind.

Voluntary Insurance

375. *Scope for Voluntary Insurance :* Compulsory social insurance provides, up to subsistence level, for primary needs and general risks. The scope of voluntary insurance is two-fold :—

(*a*) To go beyond subsistence level in meeting general risks, by adding to the amount of compulsory benefits ;

(*b*) To deal with risks and needs which, while sufficiently common for insurance, are not so common or uniform as to call for compulsory insurance.

In so far as voluntary insurance meets real needs, it is an essential part of security ; scope and encouragement for it must be provided. The State can ensure this negatively, by avoiding so far as possible any test of means for its compulsory insurance benefits, and by limiting such benefits to subsistence and primary needs. The State can ensure this positively by regulation, by financial assistance or by itself undertaking the organisation of voluntary insurance. In considering the action of the State in regard to voluntary insurance, regard must be had to the extent to which voluntary insurance has already developed in various fields and the different circumstances under which it has developed.

376. *Encouragement of Thrift :* Development of voluntary insurance and saving among persons of limited means is desirable also from another point of view. Material progress depends upon technical progress which depends upon investment and ultimately upon savings. If the distribution of the product of industry in any community is very unequal, savings come naturally either from the surplus income of the wealthy or from profits which are not distributed. If and in so far as, after the war, incomes are distributed more equally than at present or the share of wages of the total product is increased, it is important that part of the additional resources going to wage-earners and others of limited means should be saved by them instead of being spent forthwith. Increase of means brings a corresponding increase of obligations, in this as in other respects. A continuation of the War Savings movement in one form or another after the war seems likely to be an essential measure of economic policy. The same purpose can, and should be, served by development of organs for voluntary insurance to supplement State insurance.

377. *Unemployment Insurance through Trade Unions :* Voluntary insurance against unemployment is practically limited to Trade Unions, which, alone of all organisations other than the State with its Employment Exchanges, can test the genuineness of unemployment and availability of the insured person for work. Even within the Trade Unions, the sphere of voluntary insurance against unemployment is limited and it has shown no signs of growing. The number of wage-earners who by voluntary insurance now add anything substantial to what the State provides probably does not exceed one million. In the main, unemployment insurance must be compulsory, if it is to be effective. But under the existing unemployment insurance scheme scope and encouragement are afforded for voluntary insurance by arrangements under which Trade Unions giving their own benefit may act as agents for administering the State benefit and receive a grant for administrative expenses on this account.

378. *Voluntary Insurance through Special Schemes :* The Trade Union Schemes of out-of-work pay enable a limited number of skilled wage-earners to supplement their statutory unemployment benefit ; most of the insured population make no such provision and have no easy means of doing so. Both on general grounds and in view of the extension of compulsory insurance to higher income ranges among non-manual workers, the possibility of extending the opportunities for supplementary insurance against unemployment should be explored. One obvious way lies in the development of special schemes for particular industries as a means not of contracting out of compulsory insurance but of adding to it. The two special schemes already established, in the Insurance industry and in Banking and Finance, cannot, under the proposals made here, continue as alternatives to the general scheme. But they might continue for the purpose of adding to statutory benefit and of administering it with their own benefit under an arrangement with the Social Insurance Fund. The principle of giving statutory sanction to special schemes for supplementary benefit is already admitted, under Section 72 of the Unemployment Insurance Act, 1935, though the powers given by that Section have not been used hitherto. In the actual special schemes for Insurance and for Banking it has been found possible to provide benefits exceeding those of the general scheme without any direct contribution from the employees or the State and a contribution from the employer of 2d. or 6d. a week. Half that sum would provide a very substantial supplementary benefit and justify the State in continuing to entrust insurance in these industries to the same agencies. If the organisation which has built up these two schemes could be directed successfully to such a new purpose, it might set a fruitful example to other industries.

379. *Friendly Benefits :* Provision for sickness is the classic ground of voluntary insurance efforts in Britain. The registered Friendly Societies, in 1939, had approved society membership of $5\frac{1}{2}$ million and expenditure on cash benefits for sickness in that year per head of this membership was practically equal to expenditure on sickness and disability per head of membership under the health insurance scheme ; that is to say, these $5\frac{1}{2}$ million members doubled by voluntary insurance the provision for sickness made for them by the State scheme. Sickness benefit given by Friendly Societies covers accidents also of all kinds ; other benefits—on death, on maternity, on old age and by way of deposit insurance—are provided on a substantial scale. The membership of the registered Friendly Societies has grown, since the introduction of national health insurance in 1911, but this growth has been steady rather than spectacular and these societies still cover not much more than a quarter of the total number for whom disability benefit is required. That proportion is too low to justify keeping compulsory disability benefit below subsistence level. It is large enough, however, to make it unnecessary for the State to take any action in regard to voluntary insurance against sickness, except to leave scope and encouragement for the Friendly Societies. One of the principal objects of the proposal to use Friendly Societies and Trade Unions giving friendly benefits as organs for the administration of State disability benefit is in order to encourage through these associations the greatest possible supplementation of State insurance by voluntary insurance in this field.

380. *Unregistered Friendly Societies :* In addition to the registered Friendly Societies mentioned in the last paragraph, there exist innumerable unregistered Societies of every degree of permanence and financial stability. Some are large and firmly established institutions with Approved Societies attached to them ; others are fleeting. Little definite information as to the scale and methods of these societies is available since they come now under no official scrutiny, but figures collected by Mr. Rowntree for York suggest that in numbers the membership of unregistered Friendly Societies is comparable to that of the registered societies. There appears to be good ground for requiring every society in whatever form which receives contributions with a view to providing payments in sickness or on death to be registered and to conform to statutory conditions.

381. *Superannuation Schemes :* Provision for retirement additional to or exclusive of old age pensions is now made in many occupations as a whole (civil service, local government service, teaching, railway service, public utilities) and by innumerable individual firms. No special action by the State is called for, except that of making its own development of compulsory insurance for retirement gradual, so as to give time for any necessary rearrangements of the occupational and voluntary schemes.

382. *[Life and Endowment Insurance :]* The development of insurance for funeral expenses, against death generally and for endowment through the agency of Industrial Assurance Companies and Collecting Societies is discussed in Appendix D and under Change **23** in Part II. For reasons set out there it is proposed that there should be established under the general supervision of the Minister for Social Security an Industrial Assurance Board working not for profit. This statutory corporation would have a monopoly of insurance with the use of collectors and would be authorised to undertake ordinary life assurance subject to a maximum of amount insured, say £300, in order to prevent its entry into the general field of life assurance. The Board would take over the bulk of the work of the existing Industrial Life Offices with their staffs and would bring about economies, first by eliminating competition, second by encouraging payment of premiums otherwise than through collectors, third by limiting voluntary insurance so far as possible to insurance likely to be within the permanent means of the policy-holder. This proposal is bracketed, as desirable, but not essential.

383. *Loss of Independent Earnings :* It appears impracticable to provide unemployment benefit generally, except where there is employment under contract of service. Independent earners of Class II will be able to obtain training benefit, if they need to change their occupation. For deficiency of earnings in their occupation, whether through seasonal fluctuations or through other causes, no general provision can be made, but the possibility of voluntary insurance, possibly with State aid, for particular sections of Class II needs full exploration. It might become a function of the Industrial Assurance Board.

384. *Voluntary Continuation of Compulsory Insurance :* Persons who pass out of compulsory insurance against sickness or for pensions, through change of occupation (from employment to independent earning or to no paid occupation) or through rising above the remuneration limit for non-manual workers, can now continue voluntarily in insurance will become unnecessary. These arrangements are used extensively, there being nearly 1 million voluntary contributors for health or pensions insurance. With the extension of compulsory insurance to Classes II and IV and the removal of the remuneration limit, they will become unnecessary, though there will be problems of transition from the old system to the new system. Health service, retirement pensions and funeral grant will be available for all at all times in return for compulsory contributions. It may be argued that those who after contributing for disability benefit in Class I or Class II give up gainful occupation late in life, but before retiring age, should be allowed to continue insurance for this benefit. The answer is that cash disability benefit, as distinct from medical treatment, is compensation for earnings lost through disability ; in the case considered there are no earnings at the time when disability occurs.

ADMINISTRATION

385. *Ministry of Social Security :* The administration of the Plan for Social Security as a whole, including social insurance, national assistance and voluntary insurance, will be undertaken by a Ministry of Social Security under a Cabinet Minister. The Ministry will establish a network of regional and local Security Offices for the administration of cash benefits and assistance, and for other work connected therewith. The Ministry of Social Security will not be responsible for medical treatment which will fall within the sphere of the Health Departments, but there will be a Joint Committee of the Ministry of Social Security and of all Departments concerned in Health and Welfare for promotion of measures designed tb prevent disease and reduce the burden on the Social Insurance Fund. In the organisation of the Ministry two points will be regarded as of outstanding importance :—

(a) Decentralisation and close contact with local agencies of all kinds in dealing with the varied needs of insured persons ;

(b) Selection and training of staff with special regard to their functions in serving the public and in understanding the human problems with which they will be concerned.

386. *Employment Service :* The employment service of the Ministry of Labour and National Service will either be transferred to the Ministry of Social Security together with the administration of unemployment insurance, or, if retained as part of the functions of the Ministry of Labour and National Service, will be conducted at the local Security Offices.

387. *War Pensions :* The relation of the proposed Ministry of Social Security to the Ministry of Pensions is a matter for further consideration. The Ministry of Pensions is essentially a Ministry of War Pensions concerned with providing compensation for disablement and death resulting from :—

(a) Service during the war with the Armed Forces and their auxiliary services.

(b) War injury sustained by members of the Mercantile Marine, Fishing Fleets and Light Vessel Services.

(c) War service injury suffered by members of Civil Defence Services.

(d) War injuries sustained by the civil population.

The Ministry of Pensions dates from the war of 1914–18 and the proposals made at various times since that war either to merge the administration of war pensions with some other department or to add to the Ministry of Pensions functions exercised by other departments, such as the administration of old age pensions by the Customs and Excise Department, have had no result. Importance is rightly attached by those interested in the fair treatment of men and women who have given war service to ensuring just and sympathetic consideration of claims based on war disabilities. This object has appeared in the past likely to be served best by having a separate Ministry. On the other hand, the clients of a Ministry of Pensions in the future will all be clients or potential clients of the Ministry of Social Security. Merger of the two Ministries would have the advantage to the individual that, whatever his casualty, he would have to deal with one Ministry only for cash payments and it would facilitate adjustments between war pension payments, disability benefit, guardian benefit or retirement pension. It would avoid duplication of staff and would make easy adjustment of staff to the prospective gradual diminution of war pensions. Whether or not these possible advantages outweigh the reasons for maintaining a separate Ministry of War Pensions is a matter requiring full examination. A similar problem arises as to treatment. Assuming a comprehensive health and rehabilitation service organised by the health departments and the Ministry of Labour and National Service, this service should presumably be available to and used for sufferers from war disability in preference to the setting up or maintenance of separate provision for them.

388. *Register of Insured Persons :* Social insurance involves keeping a register of each insured person and contributions and benefits. The total work involved will be much less than at present when such records are kept separately for unemployment insurance and for each of the Approved Societies in respect of health insurance, in addition to records kept for workmen's compensation and pensions. The question will arise whether this register should be kept centrally or should be decentralised into six or seven regional registers. There are advantages and disadvantages in each course.

389. *Social Insurance Fund :* All compulsory insurance contributions will be paid into a Social Insurance Fund and all the benefits and other insurance payments will be paid from that Fund. Assistance will be paid from money provided by the Exchequer. The Social Insurance Statutory Committee described in the next paragraph will report periodically on the financial condition of the Fund and will have the duty and power of recommending changes of contribution and benefit with a view to adjusting the income of the Fund to its liabilities under the various accounts into which the Fund will be divided.

390. *Social Insurance Statutory Committee :* A Statutory Committee will be established for Social Insurance, on the lines of the Unemployment Insurance Statutory Committee, with the following powers :

(a) Making of periodical reports on the financial condition of the Social Insurance Fund and each of its accounts and recommendations for changes of contribution and benefit in accord with such reports ;

(b) Reporting on all Regulations and Orders before they are made, subject to power of the Minister to bring Regulations and Orders into force provisionally for not more than six months pending the consideration by the Committee ;

(c) Reporting on any matter referred to them by the Minister ;

(d) Reporting on the adequacy of the benefits for subsistence needs and recommending changes of benefit and contribution required to adjust benefit rates to changes in the value of money.

NOTE.—The first three of these powers, (a), (b), and (c), are the same as those of the Unemployment Insurance Statutory Committee ; the last is additional.

391. *[Industrial Assurance Board] :* The work of voluntary insurance, in so far as it is transacted directly on behalf of the State, will be conducted by an Industrial Assurance Board with independent finance and statutory powers subject to the general responsibility of the Minister (*see* paras. 181–192 and Appendix D).

392. *[Arrangements with Friendly Societies] :* While financially independent Approved Societies as administrators of compulsory cash benefits for sickness will disappear, societies giving friendly benefits of a substantial amount will be able under arrangements with the Ministry of Social Security to act as agents for paying out together their voluntary benefits and the benefits of the compulsory scheme, thus retaining an integral part in the administration of disability benefits and the advantage to the individual of getting his total cash provision in the case of disability from a single source. These arrangements, as is explained in paras. 66–69, will apply both to Friendly Societies and to Trade Unions giving friendly benefits. The making of such arrangements depends on the consent of the societies concerned. The proposal to make them is bracketed, as desirable but not essential (*see* para. 72). Existing arrangements with Trade Unions with regard to unemployment benefits will continue on the same lines.

393. *Statutory Associations in Scheduled Industries :* In each of the industries scheduled as having materially more than the average industrial risk of accident or disease and in any other industries in which this appears desirable Statutory Associations of employers and employees will be established for the purposes set out in paras. 91–92.

394. *Appeal on Benefits :* All decisions by, or on behalf of, the Ministry of Social Security on claims for benefit, in respect alike of amount and of conditions or period, will be subject to appeal to independent local tribunals analogous to the existing Courts of Referees with further appeal to an Umpire appointed by the Crown, whose decision will be final. The machinery will be local and informal and will be uniform for all claims, except possibly those for industrial pension and industrial grant (*see* para. 336 (*c*)).

395. *Appeals on Contributions :* Determination by or on behalf of the Minister as to liability to contribution, including the class in which contribution shall be made, will similarly be subject to appeals to local tribunals consisting of Chairmen of the Courts of Referees with further appeal to the Umpire. The problem of the relation between decisions of the Umpire and the ordinary Courts of Law is a matter for further examination.

396. *Children's Allowances :* Some organisation will be needed for administering the proposed children's allowances, that is to say, both for authorising the payments and for making them. For the reasons given in para. 424, the most appropriate department for this purpose appears to be the Ministry of Social Security, but the Ministry should act in close co-operation with the authorities concerned for the welfare and the education of children.

397. *Advice to Citizens :* One of the serious disadvantages of the present division of security functions between so many different agencies is the difficulty experienced by insured persons in understanding their rights and duties and in finding their way through the system to the proper authority to deal with their case. This, apart from the direct loss and delay to insured persons, leads sometimes to unjustified resentment and sometimes to lack of interest. The social security system even when unified and simplified in the way proposed here must still be a machine with many parts and complications to deal with all the complexities of need and variety of persons. Citizens cannot be left to find out all about it by reading official pamphlets, however clearly they may be written. There should be in every local Security Office an Advice Bureau to which every person in doubt or difficulty can be referred and which will be able to tell him, not only about the official provision for social security, but about all the other organs—official, semi-official and voluntary, central or local—which may be able to help him in his difficulty.

398. *Statistics and Intelligence :* The Ministry of Social Security should have a Division of Statistics and Intelligence, under first-rate leadership and with adequate resources to make use not only of its own material but of the experiences of other countries in the same field. The Ministry should be able to make grants for the carrying out of research in all matters where further knowledge might reduce the burdens on the Fund.

399. *Loss of Office :* Provisions will be required to prevent hardship in the case of persons employed in the administration of the present insurance schemes or the allied services who are displaced as a result of the changes made and for whom suitable alternative employment is not available.

NOTE.—On balance, there is not likely to be any large immediate change in the total numbers of persons required to administer the unified

Plan for Social Security as compared with the numbers now employed in social insurance and allied services by the National Government, by Local Authorities or by other agencies, including Approved Societies, insurance companies, and indemnity associations. On the one hand, extension of the scope of social security, through bringing in new classes into insurance and new benefits, will increase the total amount of work to be done. On the other hand, unification of administration and substitution of insurance for assistance will reduce the staff required for the same amount of security. Ultimately the total numbers of staff needed will tend to fall rather than rise, but at first these two influences seem likely to offset one another. Social security under the new system, while it certainly involves no great increase in the number of officials, if any increase at all, is unlikely to involve making any large numbers of those now employed redundant at any early date. But some changes and transfers are inevitable and it is essential that in making these changes for the common good the community should do justice to those whose livelihoods are affected by them.

400. *Loss of Business :* Another problem is presented by the possible effects upon established businesses of certain of the proposals in the Report, in particular those relating to workmen's compensation and to funeral grant. Supersession of the present scheme of workmen's compensation, whether by the proposals of the Report (Change 4 in paras. 77–105) or by any other form of converting into a social service, will make superfluous part of the business of those insurance companies which have undertaken employers' liability. Acceptance of the proposal for a funeral grant (Change 18 in paras. 157–160) may affect the business of industrial assurance very considerably, whether the existing provisions of the Industrial Assurance Act of 1923 are left or are changed. Most of the offices undertaking industrial assurance will also be affected by the proposal to supersede the approved society system in its present form (Change 3 in paras. 48–76). This does not raise a case for compensation for loss of business, since the Approved Societies are independent bodies which cannot make a profit, but that, in practice, the change may affect the business of industrial assurance is clear. If the recommendation for conversion of industrial assurance into a public service (Change 23 in paras. 181–192) is adopted, all compensation questions affecting the Industrial Life Offices will be merged in the general problem of the terms on which they shall be replaced by an Industrial Assurance Board. In that case no important problems of compensation for loss of business will arise, except in regard to the proprietary companies now undertaking employers' liability insurance. This problem is limited in scale, since it affects only about 15 per cent. of the total paid as workmen's compensation ; the rest is paid through mutual associations whose supersession may raise questions of compensating for loss of office, but will not raise questions of compensating for loss of business. It would be inappropriate in this Report to make definite proposals as to the treatment of this problem, since it must be considered in relation to the general issue of compensation where action by the State affects private interests. The State cannot undertake to compensate individuals in every case for damage which they may suffer as a result of developments of State policy. To do so would involve compensating all those who were damaged by, say, a change of policy in regard to tariffs or in regard to the use of land for different types of building. All that can be done here is to indicate that there is a problem which will call for consideration, in conjunction with other possible developments of State action, and that in relation to the proposals of this Report this problem can be a comparatively small one.

PROVISIONAL RATES OF BENEFIT AND CONTRIBUTION

401. The provisional post-war rates of benefit, allowance and grant, suggested on tne assumptions as to level of prices stated in para. 231 are as follows :—

Shillings per week.

Unemployment, Disability and Training Benefit.
Man and not gainfully occupied wife (joint benefit) — 40/-
Man with gainfully occupied wife not on benefit ... — 24/-
Single man or woman, aged 21 and upwards ... — 24/-
Single man or woman aged 18—20 ... ... — 20/-
Boys or girls 16—17 ... ... — 15/-
Married woman gainfully occupied when herself on benefit ... ... — 16/-

Retirement Pension (after transition period). *
Man and not gainfully occupied wife (joint pension) — 40/- basic
Single man or woman, man with gainfully occupied wife, woman contributor with husband below pensionable age (single pension) ... ... — 24/- basic
Addition to basic pension for postponement, in respect of each year of postponement—
    On joint pension ... ... — 2/-
    On single pension ... ... — 1/-

Maternity Benefit (13 weeks)
Married woman gainfully occupied whether paying contributions or exempt, in addition to maternity grant ... ... — 36/-

Widow's Benefit (13 weeks) ... ... — 36/-

Guardian Benefit * ... ... — 24/-

Dependant Allowance
Dependant above age for children's allowance of person receiving unemployment, disability or training benefit ... ... — 16/-

Children's Allowance
For each child when responsible parent is in receipt of any benefit or pension, and for each child after the first in other cases, allowances graded by age averaging over all children in addition to existing provision in kind. ... — 8/-

Industrial Pension
For total disability ... ... — Two-thirds of assessed weekly earnings, but not more than £3 a week and not less than would have been paid as disability benefit and dependant allowance if any.

For partial disability ... ... — Pension proportionate to loss of earning power.

Retirement Pension and Guardian Benefit are subject to partial reduction for earnings.

						Grants
Marriage	...	...	...	...	...	Up to £10 according to number of contributions.
Maternity	...	...	...	...	...	£4
Funeral *						
Adults	...	...	...	...	...	£20.
Age 10–20 years	...	...	...	...		£15.
Age 3–9 years	...	...	...	...		£10.
Under 3 years	...	...	...	...		£6.
Industrial	...	...	...	...	...	To be determined in accord with Regulations (para. 334).

402. The rates for particular benefits are based on the following considerations :—

(a) There should be a uniform rate, joint and single respectively, for unemployment, disability and training and the basic rate for retirement pension should be the same as this. The joint rate should apply irrespective of age ; the single rate should be lower for persons below 21 years of age than for adults.

(b) For married women gainfully occupied, maternity benefit should be at a rate materially higher than the single rate for unemployment or disability, while unemployment and disability benefit should be materially below the single rate. These special rates should apply to all married women irrespective of age.

(c) Widows' benefit during the period of re-adjustment should be materially above the single rate for unemployment or disability.

(d) Guardian benefit should be such as to enable the widow, with allowances for every child, to have sufficient for subsistence without earning, and should be subject to reduction of a proportion of any earnings made by her.

(e) The addition to basic pension where retirement is postponed should be less than the full actuarial value of postponement, so that the advantage of postponement is shared between the contributor and the Social Insurance Fund.

(f) The unemployment and disability benefit for boys and girls is put 1/- below the rate of dependant allowance. This will mean that 1/- less is paid when boys and girls are themselves unemployed or sick than if they are dependants and the person upon whom they depend is unemployed or sick. The difference is not a matter of great importance, but is probably right, in view of the fact that boys and girls of this age will be living with older people and while those older people have earnings can be maintained in part from those earnings. When those earnings cease, there must be subsistence both for the dependent boy or girl and for the adult.

---

* Funeral grant is not payable in respect of any person above age of 60 at beginning of scheme.

403. The provisional rates of weekly contribution suggested to secure the provisional scale of benefits are as follows :—

	Male			Female		
	Insured Person	Employers	Joint	Insured Person	Employers	Joint
Class I						
Age 21 and upwards ...	4/3	3/3	7/6	3/6	2/6	6/-
18–20	3/6	2/9	6/3	3/-	2/-	5/-
16–17	2/6	2/6	5/-	2/-	2/-	4/-
Class II						
Age 21 and upwards ...	4/3	—	—	3/9	—	—
18–20	3/6	—	—	3/-	—	—
16–17	2/-	—	—	2/-	—	—
Class IV						
Age 21 and upwards ...	3/9	—	—	3/-	—	—
18–20	3/-	—	—	2/6	—	—
16–17	1/6	—	—	1/6	—	—

NOTE.—If the marriage grant is omitted, the contributions of insured females aged 21 and upwards and 18–20 in Classes I and II can be reduced in each case by 3d.

404. Determination of the relative contributions for men and for women depends on considerations explained by the Government Actuary in regard to the several benefits in paras. 18, 21 and 29 of his Memorandum. In respect of unemployment a change has been made from present practice, by charging the difference between the joint rate for man and wife and the single rate for a man wholly to the man's contribution so as to increase the man's contribution relatively to that of the woman ; this principle has been applied also to disability on the introduction of joint benefit and dependant allowance. The general result is that, in spite of the equalisation of benefit rates for single men and single women, the total contributions proposed for men in the new scheme show a greater increase on present rates than the contributions for women. Thus the joint contribution for an adult man, which is now 44d., is raised to 90d., that is to say to slightly more than double, while the joint contribution for an adult woman, which is now 37d., is raised to 72d., that is to say to rather less than double. The employee's own contribution in the case of a man is raised as from 22d. to 51d. ; in the case of a woman from 19d. to 42d.

405. The contributions shown in para. 403 include contributions assigned for health and rehabilitation services as follows :—

	Male	Female
Age 21 and upwards ...	10d.	8d.
18–21	8d.	6d.
16–18	6d.	6d.

In Class I these contributions are divided approximately as to 1½d. by the employer and the balance of 8½d. or 6½d. by the employee in the case of adults. In Classes II and IV the whole contribution is paid by the insured persons. It is contemplated that in virtue of these contributions insured persons will receive for themselves and their dependants comprehensive medical treatment and post-medical rehabilitation services, including general, specialist, domiciliary and hospital treatment, and nursing and subsidiary services without a charge for treatment. This, as stated, is subject to the further enquiry as to the finance and organisation of the health service suggested in para. 437. If, as a result of that enquiry, it were decided to require some additional payment for hospital treatment, either by way of voluntary contributions or by a charge on treatment, the question would arise of amending the proposed contributions.

406. The rates of contribution suggested for boys and girls, particularly in Classes II and IV, may need further consideration in the light of educational policy. It is desirable that boys and girls should at an early stage be brought

into the Social Security Scheme, and become familiar with it, but exactly how they should be treated depends upon development of educational policy.

407. The benefits and contributions suggested above relate to persons aged 16 and upwards. No specific proposals can be made in regard to boys and girls under 16 until educational policy is decided. The general principle is that up to 16 at least boys and girls should be considered from the educational standpoint. In so far as they work for gain, insurance contributions should be paid by them and their employers. Any payment of cash benefit to them should be combined with continued supervision and education.

408. The general rates of benefit and contribution set out in paras. 401 and 403 should be regarded as subject to investigation of the desirability and practicability of adjustment to special circumstances in the following cases :—

(a) Provision of a lower rate of benefits (other than retirement and industrial pensions) and corresponding lower contribution in particular regions or occupations (paras. 214–215).

(b) Provision of a higher rate of benefits (other than retirement and industrial pension) and corresponding higher contribution in London and in other regions where costs of living are exceptionally high (paras. 214–215).

(c) Different distribution of the joint contribution between employers and insured persons, increasing the employer's share where either (a) a weekly rate of wage is below a certain level, or (b) the sum paid as wages from which deduction of the insured person's contribution has to be made is below a certain point.

(d) Provision of a reduced contribution for a short period of employment e.g. for 2 days or 3 days only.

(e) Provision of reduced contributions for persons working under contracts of apprenticeship.

Practical examination of all these possibilities depends very largely upon the general level of benefit and contribution that may be determined finally. They are appropriate matters for investigation by a Committee analogous to the suggested Social Insurance Statutory Committee.

PART VI

SOCIAL SECURITY AND SOCIAL POLICY

409. Social security as used in this Report means assurance of a certain income. The Plan for Social Security set out in the Report is a plan to win freedom from want by maintaining incomes. But sufficiency of income is not sufficient in itself. Freedom from want is only one of the essential freedoms of mankind. Any Plan for Social Security in the narrow sense assumes a concerted social policy in many fields, most of which it would be inappropriate to discuss in this Report. The plan proposed here involves three particular assumptions so closely related to it that brief discussion is essential for understanding of the plan itself. These are the assumptions of children's allowances, of comprehensive health and rehabilitation services, and of maintenance of employment. After these three assumptions have been examined, general questions are raised as to the practicability of taking freedom from want as an immediate post-war aim and as to the desirability of planning reconstruction of the social services even in war.

Assumption A. Children's Allowances

410. The first of three assumptions underlying the Plan for Social Security is a general scheme of children's allowances. This means that direct provision for the maintenance of dependent children will be made by payment of allowances to those responsible for the care of those children. The assumption rests on two connected arguments.

411. First, it is unreasonable to seek to guarantee an income sufficient for subsistence, while earnings are interrupted by unemployment or disability, without ensuring sufficient income during earning. Social insurance should be part of a policy of a national minimum. But a national minimum for families of every size cannot in practice be secured by a wage system, which must be based on the product of a man's labour and not on the size of his family. The social surveys of Britain between the two wars show that in the first thirty years of this century real wages rose by about one-third without reducing want to insignificance, and that the want which remained was almost wholly due to two causes—interruption or loss of earning power and large families.

412. Second, it is dangerous to allow benefit during unemployment or disability to equal or exceed earnings during work. But, without allowances for children, during earning and not-earning alike, this danger cannot be avoided. It has been experienced in an appreciable number of cases under unemployment benefit and unemployment assistance in the past. The maintenance of employment—last and most important of the three assumptions of social security—will be impossible without greater fluidity of labour and other resources in the aftermath of war than has been achieved in the past. To secure this, the gap between income during earning and during interruption of earning should be as large as possible for every man. It cannot be kept large for men with large families, except either by making their benefit in unemployment and disability inadequate, or by giving allowances for children in time of earning and not-earning alike.

413. In addition to these two arguments, arising directly from considerations of social security, there are arguments arising from consideration of numbers of population and care of children. With its present rate of reproduction, the British race cannot continue ; means of reversing the recent course of the birth rate must be found. It is not likely that allowances for children or any other economic incentives will, by themselves, provide that means and lead parents who do not desire children to rear children for gain. But children's allowances can help to restore the birth rate, both by making it possible for parents who desire more children to bring them into the world without damaging the chances of those already born, and as a signal of the national interest in children, setting the tone of public opinion. As regards care of children, whatever possibilities the future may hold of larger families than now, the small families of to-day make it necessary that every living child should receive the best care that can be given to it. The foundations of a healthy life must be laid in childhood. Children's allowances should be regarded both as a help to parents in meeting their responsibilities, and as an acceptance of new responsibilities by the community.

414. The general principle of children's allowances can by now be taken as accepted. But it is desirable to make suggestions as to the practical form of such allowances from the standpoint of social security. The main points to be settled relate to the source from which allowances should be paid, to the scale of allowances, to the children in respect of whom they should be paid, and to the authority which should administer them.

415. As to the source of children's allowances, the view taken here is that they should be non-contributory, provided wholly out of taxation, and not to any extent out of insurance contributions. The considerations leading to this view are practical. First, the flat rate of contribution required for purposes which should be contributory is about as high as it seems right to propose ; flat insurance contributions are either a poll-tax or a tax on employment, justifiable up to certain limits, but not capable of indefinite expansion. Second, the provision for children should clearly be made to some extent in kind. Though, on the view taken here, children's allowances should be given mainly in cash, the amount of cash at any time must be adjusted to the provision in kind and this adjustment can probably be made more easily, if the cost of allowances is provided from the State than if it forms part of a contributory system. Both these are practical grounds. On principle, it is possible to argue either way. It can be said, on the one hand, that children's allowances should be regarded as an expression of the community's direct interest in children ; it can be argued on the other hand that children are a contingency for which all men should prepare by contributions to an insurance fund. As it is possible to argue on each side in principle, it might be provided in practice that the cost of allowances should be shared. It is in fact proposed below that the first child in each family should be omitted from allowances, while the responsible parent is earning, so that the financial burden of every family is shared between the State and the parents. This involves providing an allowance for the first child whenever the responsible parent is not earning, that is to say providing an allowance for the first child, to be added to unemployment, disability and guardian benefits. Even if the other allowances are provided wholly by the State, the cost of allowances for the first child might well be charged to the Social Insurance Fund, as the cost of the children's allowances now given in unemployment insurance are charged to the Unemployment Fund. On the whole, it appears better to put the whole cost of children's allowances, both when the parent is earning and when he is not earning, upon the National Exchequer, that is to say to make children's allowances non-contributory. The allowances, though non-contributory, may be administered by the Ministry of Social Security. The cost of them should be provided, not from the Social Insurance Fund, but by special Exchequer grant.

416. As to the scale of children's allowances, in paras. 226–228 the allowances required to meet in full the needs of children of various ages for food, clothing, fuel and light are put at figures yielding an average over children of all ages of 7/– a week at 1938 prices. In para. 232, allowing on the one hand for an increase of prices after the war, and, on the other hand, for the provision already being made for children through school meals and supply of free or cheap milk, an average rate of allowance of 8/– per week per child in addition to existing provision is suggested. It does not follow that a cash allowance on this scale should be paid in respect of every child. Two considerations may be urged against such an inference.

417. First, it can be argued that the allowances for children should be regarded only as a help to parents and not as relieving them entirely of financial responsibility. There is substance in this argument. To give full subsistence allowances for all the children of a man or woman at work may be described as wasteful and certainly cannot be described as a measure indispensable for the abolition of poverty ; very few men's wages are insufficient to cover at least two adults and one child. When the responsible parent (that is to say the parent on whom the children depend) is earning, there is no need to aim at allowances relieving the parent of the whole cost of the children. On

the view taken here, it would be wrong to do so—an unnecessary and undesirable inroad on the responsibilities of parents. That is to say, in any system of children's allowances, the cost of maintaining children should be shared between their parents and the community. This can be done in two ways—either by making an allowance for each child which is less than the cost of maintenance, or by making no allowance for one child in each family and a larger or full allowance for each of the other children. The second way is the better and is adopted here, as making a large reduction in the cost of allowances to the community with no hardship to parents, and as increasing the proportion of the total cost borne by the community as the size of the family increases ; this makes the allowances more effective in preventing want and increases whatever influence they may have in encouraging large families.

418. Second, it can be argued that, whatever experts may say, every mother of six knows that six children do not cost six times as much as one child to feed, clothe and warm. Admitting that one child for these purposes will need 7/– at 1938 prices (say 9/– at provisional post-war rates), 42/– for a family of six (54/– at post-war rates) may appear excessive. It is not easy, indeed, to see in the foregoing calculations just where substantial reduction of cost per head for a number of children can be justified. Out of the 7/– pre-war average, 5/11 is for food according to a personal dietary ; there may be less waste in a large family, but the 5/11 includes nothing for waste or inefficiency in buying. The 3d. for fuel has been reached as one-sixth of the recorded difference between two-person and eight-person households. The 10d. for clothing offers a real but small field for economy in large families, by passing clothing from one to another. But against this, the 7/– average takes no account of rent. If having many children makes it possible to reduce slightly the cost of food, clothing and fuel for each child, it can hardly fail to add to the rent. It is probably true that few, if any, parents of large families spend four times as much on essentials for four children as they spend for one, or six times as much on six children as they spend for one. But that may be because very few people are able to afford to do so out of incomes which are in no way related to the number of children.

419. The first of these two arguments, accordingly, is accepted here and the second is rejected. It is proposed, on the one hand, that there should be no allowance for the first child in each family when the responsible parent is earning. It is proposed, on the other hand, that for each of the other children, and for the first child also when the responsible parent is on benefit or pension, there should be an allowance additional to the present provision in kind at the average rate of 8/– a week. The practical effect of this will be that when the parent is earning there will be no allowance in a family with one child only and that, as the size of the family increases, the average allowance for each child will increase in accordance with the following scale :—

No. of children in family	Weekly allowance per family	Average weekly allowance per child
1	Nil	Nil
2	8/–	4/–
3	16/–	5/4
4	24/–	6/–
5	32/–	6/5
6	40/–	6/8

420. Assuming an allowance of 8/– a week per child, omission of one child when the parent is earning reduces the total cost of allowances by nearly £100,000,000 a year, as compared with the cost of including all children at all

times. It would be possible to carry this method of sharing the total cost of the family between the community and the parents a stage further, either by omitting the second child as well as the first, or by giving less than the full allowance for the second child. To give 4/– a week in place of 8/– for the second child when the responsible parent was earning would save a further £23,000,000 a year in the cost of the allowances. But, apart from the undesirability of decreasing the provision for children, this plan is open to the objection that it narrows still further the gap between earnings and income during interruption of earnings. It would mean that a man with two children or more would receive 12/– in respect of those children when on benefit or pension, which he would not be receiving when earning, so that, unless his wages were at least that amount above his benefit or pension, he would not be better off when earning than when unemployed or sick.

421. The allowance proposed for the second and subsequent children when the responsible parent is earning, and for all children when the responsible parent is not earning, has been put at an average of 8/– a week at provisional post-war rates, in addition to existing provision in kind. In practice, the allowances should not be uniform but graded by age, since the needs of children increase rapidly with age. In practice, also, the sum to be given in cash at each age must have regard to the provision in kind at each age. On the view taken here, it would not be desirable to attempt to replace cash allowances for children wholly or even largely by provision in kind. The principle of social policy should not be to remove all responsibilities from parents, but to help them to understand and to meet their responsibilities. But there may prove to be good reasons for a considerable extension of provision in kind, and this may affect differently the cash allowance required at different ages. It is not possible here to do more than indicate at 8/– per week the average additional allowance proposed in cash or in kind.

422. As to the children in respect of whom allowances should be paid, the simplest plan is to make them universal, subject to the omission of the first child when the parent is earning. Little money can be saved by any reasonable income limit. In so far as it appears that children's allowances to all families irrespective of their means would mean giving money to prosperous people without need, this can be corrected by an adjustment of the rebates of income tax now allowed for children. This does not mean that children's allowances should replace tax rebates. The problems of taxation and of allowance are distinct and involve different considerations.

423. The allowances should continue so long as the child is in approved full time education, up to the age of 16. The suggestion sometimes made that allowances should continue during the first six months or year of earning, on the ground that the initial earnings may be insufficient, is open to the objection that it involves a subsidy to juvenile wages and would tend to keep them down. With the growing shortage of juvenile labour in relation to adult labour the wages of the former are likely to rise and should need no subsidy.

424. As to the administration of children's allowances, however the allowances are actually paid—weekly or monthly, by post or in person—there must be some Department with offices in every locality prepared to receive claims and authorise them and to control the payment. The Ministry of Social Security proposed in this Report appears the obvious organ for this purpose, even if the allowances are universal. If they are limited to children after the first, so that allowance for the first child must be added to benefits in unemployment or disability, the case for using the Ministry of Social Security is strengthened. The only alternative appears to be to use the agencies for dealing with childhood—welfare centres for those under five and the schools

for the school-children. Cash allowances for children would thus become part of the system for care of youth. In principle there is something to be said in favour of this. But it is not clear that the administrative machinery for such a plan will be available. The natural plan is to leave the cash payments to the Ministry of Social Security and the care and supervision of children to the authorities concerned with health and education, with arrangements for central and local co-operation between them.

425. The practical conclusions emerging from this discussion are :

(1) Financial provision should be made for children's allowances at the cost of the Exchequer in respect of all children other than the first child when the parent is earning, and of the first child in addition during interruption of earning.

(2) The average amount of such allowances should be 8/- a week in addition to the existing provision in kind. The actual allowance should be graduated according to the age of the child. In so far as provision in kind is extended beyond its present scale, the cash allowances should be reduced.

(3) The cash allowances should be administered by the Ministry of Social Security.

ASSUMPTION B. COMPREHENSIVE HEALTH AND REHABILITATION SERVICES

426. The second of the three assumptions has two sides to it. It covers a national health service for prevention and for cure of disease and disability by medical treatment ; it covers rehabilitation and fitting for employment by treatment which will be both medical and post-medical. Administratively, realisation of Assumption B on its two sides involves action both by the departments concerned with health and by the Ministry of Labour and National Service. Exactly where the line should be drawn between the responsibilities of these Departments cannot, and need not, be settled now. For the purpose of the present Report, the two sides are combined under one head, avoiding the need to distinguish accurately at this stage between medical and post-medical work. The case for regarding Assumption B as necessary for a satisfactory system of social security needs little emphasis. It is a logical corollary to the payment of high benefits in disability that determined efforts should be made by the State to reduce the number of cases for which benefit is needed. It is a logical corollary to the receipt of high benefits in disability that the individual should recognise the duty to be well and to co-operate in all steps which may lead to diagnosis of disease in early stages when it can be prevented. Disease and accidents must be paid for in any case, in lessened power of production and in idleness, if not directly by insurance benefits. One of the reasons why it is preferable to pay for disease and accident openly and directly in the form of insurance benefits, rather than indirectly, is that this emphasises the cost and should give a stimulus to prevention. As to the methods of realising Assumption B, the main problems naturally arise under the first head of medical treatment. Rehabilitation is a new field of remedial activity with great possibilities, but requiring expenditure of a different order of magnitude from that involved in the medical treatment of the nation.

427. The first part of Assumption B is that a comprehensive national health service will ensure that for every citizen there is available whatever medical treatment he requires, in whatever form he requires it, domiciliary or institutional, general, specialist or consultant, and will ensure also the provision of dental, ophthalmic and surgical appliances, nursing and midwifery and rehabilitation after accidents. Whether or not payment towards the cost

of the health service is included in the social insurance contribution, the service itself should

(i) be organised, not by the Ministry concerned with social insurance, but by Departments responsible for the health of the people and for positive and preventive as well as curative measures ;

(ii) be provided where needed without contribution conditions in any individual case.

Restoration of a sick person to health is a duty of the State and the sick person, prior to any other consideration. The assumption made here is in accord with the definition of the objects of medical service as proposed in the Draft Interim Report of the Medical Planning Commission of the British Medical Association :

" (a) to provide a system of medical service directed towards the achievement of positive health, of the prevention of disease, and the relief of sickness ;

(b) to render available to every individual all necessary medical services, both general and specialist, and both domiciliary and institutional."

428. Most of the problems of organisation of such a service fall outside the scope of the Report. It is not necessary to express an opinion on such questions as free choice of doctor, group or individual practice, or the place of voluntary and public hospitals respectively in a national scheme. It is not necessary to express an opinion on the terms of service and remuneration of doctors of various kinds, of dentists and of nurses, except in so far as these terms may affect the possibility of diminishing and controlling sickness and so may affect the finances of the Social Insurance Fund. Once it is accepted that the administration of medical treatment shall be lifted out of social insurance to become part of a comprehensive health service, the questions that remain for answer in this Report are, in the main, financial. Shall any part of the cost of treatment, and if so what part, be included in the compulsory insurance contribution ? But, though that question is in itself financial, the answer to it may affect the organisation of the service and may therefore depend in part upon views as to organisation.

429. In dealing with this financial question, it is desirable to consider separately domiciliary treatment, institutional treatment, special services like dental and ophthalmic treatment, and subsidiary services such as supply of medical or surgical appliances, nursing and convalescent homes.

430. Domiciliary treatment is now paid for by persons subject to health insurance, for themselves by compulsory contributions, for dependants either by a charge for treatment when it is given or more rarely by voluntary contribution through associations for public medical service. There is no obvious reason, apart from a desire to keep the insurance contribution as low as possible, why insured persons should be relieved of this burden wholly, in order that they may bear it as tax-payers. If importance attaches to preserving the contributory principle for cash benefit, it attaches also to contribution for medical treatment. There appears to be a case for including part of the cost of domiciliary treatment in the insurance contribution. This means that a proportion of the receipts of the Social Insurance Fund would be paid by the Fund to the health departments as a grant towards the cost of the medical service. The administration of this money would rest with the health departments.

431. But one consequence of this suggestion has to be noted. The Report proposes a compulsory social insurance scheme without income limits. Its contributing Classes I, II and IV, though they pay different contributions according to the cash benefits for which they insure, are not income classes ;

each contains rich and poor. Any contribution for medical treatment must apply to all these classes, to every one in each of them, and must cover their dependants in Class III (Housewives) and Class V (Children). If a contribution for medical treatment is included in the insurance contribution, contributions will cover not ninety per cent. of the population (the present insured persons and their dependants), as is assumed in the Draft Interim Report issued by the Medical Planning Commission, but one hundred per cent. of the population. This will not, of itself, put an end to private practice. Those who have the desire and the means will be able to pay separately for private treatment, if the medical service is organised to provide that, as they may now pay for private schooling, though the public education system is available for all. But no one will be compelled to pay separately. The possible scope of private general practice will be so restricted that it may not appear worth while to preserve it. If, therefore, it is desired to preserve a substantial scope for private practice and to restrict the right to service without a charge on treatment to persons below a certain income limit, it will not be possible to include a payment for medical service in an insurance contribution which all are required to pay irrespective of income.

432. Institutional treatment is not included in the present health insurance contribution except to a small extent as an additional benefit. It is obtainable by any citizen in a public hospital subject to recovery of the cost, that is to say to payment according to his means, or free if he has no means. It is obtainable in a private hospital, as a rule either in virtue of previous voluntary contribution through a hospital contributory scheme or on payment according to means as agreed with the hospital almoner. The growth of hospital contributory schemes in the years just before this war has been remarkable. They are stated to cover now more than 10,000,000 wage earners and they produce more than £6,500,000 a year for the voluntary hospitals ; the cost of collecting this money is put at about six per cent. ; in London and some other parts of the country contribution to a Hospital Saving Association qualifies the contributor for free treatment either in a voluntary hospital or in a public hospital as may best suit his case. The Ministry of Labour Family Budgets in 1937–38 showed an average payment to hospital saving associations of 3¼d. a week in every industrial household and 3d. a week in every agricultural household. British people are clearly ready and able to pay contributions for institutional treatment. Should a payment for this purpose be included in the compulsory insurance contribution, and be passed on as a grant from the Social Insurance Fund to the health departments towards the maintenance of the institutions ? The answer to this financial question, like the answer to the similar question as to domiciliary treatment, involves problems of organisation as well as finance. If a payment for institutional treatment is included in the compulsory insurance contribution, there will be little or nothing left for which people can be asked to contribute voluntarily, and an important financial resource of the voluntary hospitals will come to an end. It will then be for the health departments to use the grant that they will receive from the Social Insurance Fund in whatever way best fits their hospital policy. If it is not included, people of limited means will have the choice, as at present, of contributing voluntarily beforehand or of paying at the time of treatment, according to means.

433. The main considerations relevant to the choice between these alternatives are :

(i) The importance of securing that suitable hospital treatment is available for every citizen and that recourse to it, at the earliest moment when it becomes desirable, is not delayed by any financial considerations. From this point of view, previous contribution is the ideal, better even than free service supported by the tax-payer. People will take what they have already paid for without delay when they need it, and they pay for it more directly as contributors than as tax-payers. But it can be argued that, under the present system, people do not in practice delay taking hospital treatment when they· need it ; their general practitioner will advise going to hospital, as soon as it becomes necessary, and if they are not voluntary contributors they will be asked to pay only according to their means. It is possible that the main practical reasons which now delay recourse to hospital after it has become desirable are not difficulties about paying for the treatment, but either (a) deficiency of accommodation or (b) unwillingness or inability to give up work or household duties in order to be treated. A suggestion for meeting the last-named difficulty is made in para. 344.

(ii) Hospital policy, particularly in relation to the place of voluntary hospitals, the terms of service and pay of their staffs, and the desirability or the reverse of allowing arrangements whereby individuals, whether through membership of a voluntary association or by special payment, can get choice of specialists or hospitals or special treatment in them.

(iii) Financial policy, and particularly the question of the optimum size of the insurance contribution and of the Security Budget in relation to the ordinary budget.

434. A minor question in the relations of the social insurance scheme and the finance of hospitals is whether persons in receipt of disability benefit, on entering an institution, should be required to make any payment towards the cost of their board as " hotel expenses." With the small benefits provided by national health insurance hitherto, this question could hardly be raised. But, if the social insurance scheme is to provide benefits in future designed to cover the food and fuel requirements of the insured person and his dependants, it may appear reasonable that, while such a person is getting his food and fuel in a hospital and not in his home, the money provided for that purpose should be directed to the hospital. The point is not perhaps of great·import-ance to the finance of institutional treatment ; a sum of (say) 10/- a week is the most that could fairly be regarded as saved in the home by the temporary absence of the insured person in hospital. But if it appears equitable to make such a charge, it may be expedient to make it, if only in order to avoid making it appear profitable to the patient to stay in the hospital when he could go home.

435. Dental and ophthalmic treatment and appliances are now over-whelmingly the most popular of the additional treatment benefits under national health insurance. That is to say,·they are being paid for in part by compulsory contributions and for the rest mainly by a charge when treatment is given. There is a general demand that these services should become statu-tory benefits available to all under health insurance. There appears to be ground for regarding a· development of preservative dental treatment as a measure of major importance for improving the health of the nation. This measure involves, first, a change of popular habit from aversion to visiting the dentist till pain compels into readiness to visit and be inspected periodically ; it involves, simultaneously with creation by these means of a demand for a larger dental service, the taking of steps to organise a larger supply of the service. That the insurance title to free dental service should become as universal as that to free medical service is not open to serious doubt. The only substantial distinction which it seems right to make is in the supply of appliances. To ensure careful use, it is reasonable that part of the cost of renewals of dentures should be borne by the person using them. This might

F

possibly be extended to the original supply. The same holds true of optical appliances.

436. Surgical appliances, convalescent homes and nursing are less widely provided as additional benefits, but are essential to a comprehensive health service. Decision as to making these subsidiary services contributory or non-contributory for the individual depends on the line taken in regard to the major problems of domiciliary and institutional treatment. It is reasonable that insured persons should contribute something for such services, as they have shown themselves able and willing to do in the past ; in regard to appliances of all kinds, the terms of supply and renewal must be such as to give an incentive to careful use. But it would be anomalous to require compulsory contributions for special and subsidiary purposes, if the main services were non-contributory.

437. This review of some of the problems involved in establishing a comprehensive medical service makes clear that no final detailed proposals, even as to the financial basis of this service, can be submitted in this Report. It suggests the need for a further immediate investigation, in which the finance and the organisation of medical services can be considered together, in consultation with the professions concerned and with the public and voluntary organisations which have established hospitals and other institutions. From the standpoint of social security, a health service providing full preventive and curative treatment of every kind to every citizen without exceptions, without remuneration limit and without an economic barrier at any point to delay recourse to it, is the ideal plan. It is proposed accordingly that, in the contributions suggested as part of the Plan for Social Security, there shall be included a payment in virtue of which every citizen will be able to obtain whatever treatment his case requires, at home or in an institution, medical, dental or subsidiary, without a treatment charge. It is proposed that the sums derived from these payments shall be transferred to the Department or Departments concerned with the organisation of the health service to meet part—it can only be part—of the total cost. But these proposals are provisional only, subject to review, in the light of the further enquiry suggested, in which organisation and finance can be dealt with together. The primary interest of the Ministry of Social Security is not in the details of the national health service or in its financial arrangements. It is in finding a health service which will diminish disease by prevention and cure, and will ensure the careful certification needed to control payment of benefit at the rates proposed in this Report.

438. Assumption B covers not only medical treatment in all its forms, but also post-medical rehabilitation. In regard to the latter, as in regard to the former, it would be inappropriate here to discuss details of organisation. During the preparation of this Report, the practical problems of rehabilitation have been under consideration by the Departments concerned and it is hoped that practical measures will follow. Rehabilitation is a continuous process by which disabled persons should be transferred from the state of being incapable under full medical care to the state of being producers and earners. This process requires close co-operation between the health departments and the department concerned with employment, that is to say, the Ministry of Labour and National Service. Whether this co-operation can be secured best by the setting up of an executive organ representative of both sides or by allocation of specific duties to each department, is a problem of departmental organisation on which it would be inappropriate here to express an opinion. It is sufficient to put forward three general propositions :—

 (a) that rehabilitation must be continued from the medical through the
   post-medical stage till the maximum of earning capacity is restored and

that a service for this purpose should be available for all disabled persons who can profit by it irrespective of the cause of their disability.

(b) That cash allowances to persons receiving rehabilitation service should be the same as training benefit, including removal and lodging allowances where required.

(c) That the contributions paid by insured persons should, as in the case of medical treatment, qualify them for rehabilitation service without further payment.

439. It will be consistent with the proposals made here to include part of the cost of post-medical rehabilitation of men injured in scheduled hazardous industries in the industrial levy of these industries, that is to say, to add a contribution towards the cost of this service to the amount of the levy (*see* paras. 279 (iii) and 360).

Assumption C. Maintenance of Employment

440. There are five reasons for saying that a satisfactory scheme of social insurance assumes the maintenance of employment and the prevention of mass unemployment. Three reasons are concerned with the details of social insurance ; the fourth and most important is concerned with its principle ; the fifth is concerned with the possibility of meeting its cost.

First, payment of unconditional cash benefits as of right during unemployment is satisfactory provision only for short periods of unemployment ; after that, complete idleness even on an income demoralises. The proposal of the Report accordingly is to make unemployment benefit after a certain period conditional upon attendance at a work or training centre. But this proposal is impracticable, if it has to be applied to men by the million or the hundred thousand.

Second, the only satisfactory test of unemployment is an offer of work. This test breaks down in mass unemployment and makes necessary recourse to elaborate contribution conditions, and such devices as the Anomalies Regulations, all of which should be avoided in a satisfactory scheme of unemployment insurance.

Third, the state of the labour market has a direct bearing on rehabilitation and recovery of injured and sick persons and upon the possibility of giving to those suffering from partial infirmities, such as deafness, the chance of a happy and useful career. In time of mass unemployment those who are in receipt of compensation feel no urge to get well for idleness. On the other hand, in time of active demand for labour, as in war, the sick and the maimed are encouraged to recover, so that they may be useful.

Fourth, and most important, income security which is all that can be given by social insurance is so inadequate a provision for human happiness that to put it forward by itself as a sole or principal measure of reconstruction hardly seems worth doing. It should be accompanied by an announced determination to use the powers of the State to whatever extent may prove necessary to ensure for all, not indeed absolute continuity of work, but a reasonable chance of productive employment.

Fifth, though it should be within the power of the community to bear the cost of the whole Plan for Social Security, the cost is heavy and, if to the necessary cost waste is added, it may become insupportable. Unemployment, both through increasing expenditure on benefit and through reducing the income to bear those costs, is the worst form of waste.

441. Assumption C does not imply complete abolition of unemployment. In industries subject to seasonal influences, irregularities of work are inevitable ; in an economic system subject to change and progress, fluctuations in the fortunes of individual employers or of particular industries are inevitable ; the possibility of controlling completely the major alternations of good trade and bad trade which are described under the term of the trade cycle has not been established ; a country like Britain, which must have exports to pay for its raw materials, cannot be immune from the results of changes of fortune or of economic policy in other countries. The Plan for Social Security provides benefit for a substantial volume of unemployment. In the industries now subject to unemployment insurance, the finance of the Unemployment Fund has been based by the Unemployment Insurance Statutory Committee on the assumption of an average rate of unemployment through good years and bad of about 15 per cent. In framing the Social Security Budget in Part IV of this Report, it has been assumed that, in the industries now subject to insurance, the average rate of unemployment will in future be about 10 per cent. and that over the whole body of insured employees in Class I unemployment will average about $8\frac{1}{2}$ per cent. It is right to hope that unemployment can be reduced to below that level, in which case more money will be available in the Social Insurance Fund either for better benefits or for reduction of contributions. But it would not be prudent to assume any lower rate of unemployment in preparing the Security Budget. Assumption C requires not the abolition of all unemployment, but the abolition of mass unemployment and of unemployment prolonged year after year for the same individual. In the beginning of compulsory unemployment insurance in 1913 and 1914, it was found that less than 5 per cent. of all the unemployment experienced in the insured industries occurred after men had been unemployed for as long as 15 weeks. Even if it does not prove possible to get back to that level of employment, it should be possible to make unemployment of any individual for more than 26 weeks continuously a rare thing in normal times.

442. Discussion of the methods and conditions of satisfying Assumption C of the Plan for Social Security falls outside the scope of this Report. It may be claimed that the plan will itself have some effect in promoting realisation of this assumption. Payment of unemployment benefit on the most generous scale compatible with preservation of the mobility of labour and of the incentive to seek work and reject idleness will maintain the purchasing power of workpeople, if trade depression begins, and will thus mitigate the severity of the depression. This result is independent of the source from which benefit is paid. If, as is proposed in the plan, benefit is paid not from general taxation, but from a self-contained Social Insurance Fund built up largely by weekly contributions from employers and employees, the effect in stabilising purchasing power and the general demand for labour will be greater. The onset of unemployment will then involve, not only an immediate increase in the expenditure of the Fund, but also an immediate decline in its receipts ; by making surpluses in good times and spending them and even running into debt on its unemployment account in bad times, the Fund may be so operated as to have a further effect in stabilising the general demand for labour. This assumes that no attempt is made by lowering contributions in good times or raising them in bad times to prevent the Fund from alternately accumulating surpluses and incurring debt on its unemployment account. The maximum effect of a social insurance scheme in stabilising employment would be obtained by making contribution rates vary in the opposite way, that is to say, by increasing the contributions in good times and lowering them in bad times. This would increase the rate at which the Fund repaid debt or built up reserves in times of good employment and the rate at which it depleted reserves or borrowed in times of bad employment ; by reducing the contributions of

employers in bad times it would help to restore their demand for labour directly ; by reducing the contributions of employees it would increase their purchasing power over goods and services and thus stimulate the demand for labour indirectly. Whether variation of the insurance contribution in the way suggested is a practical proposition and by what machinery it could be effected are questions falling outside the scope of the Report. They are part of the general problem of financial and budgetary policy after the war, and should be considered in framing that policy.

443. The probable and the possible effects of the Plan for Social Security in stabilising the demand for labour are among its advantages and deserve to be noted. But their importance should not be exaggerated. They are subsidiary measures only ; they do not touch the main problem of maintaining employment. For that other measures are needed. Unless such measures are prepared and can be effective, much that might otherwise be gained through the Plan for Social Security will be wasted.

ABOLITION OF WANT AS A PRACTICABLE POST-WAR AIM

444. The aim of the Plan for Social Security is to abolish want by ensuring that every citizen willing to serve according to his powers has at all times an income sufficient to meet his responsibilities. Is this aim likely to be within our reach immediately after the present war ?

445. The first step in considering the prospective economic resources of the community after the present war is to see what they were just before the war. The social surveys made by impartial investigators of living conditions in some of the main industrial centres of Britain between 1928 and 1937 have been used earlier in this Report to supply a diagnosis of want. They can be used also to show that the total resources of the community were sufficient to make want needless. While, in every town surveyed, substantial percentages of the families examined had less than the bare minimum for subsistence, the great bulk of them had substantially more than the minimum. In East London, in the week chosen for investigation in 1929, while one family in every nine had income below the minimum and was in want, nearly two-thirds of all the families had at least 20/- a week more than the minimum, and nearly a third had 40/- a week more than the minimum ; these were actual incomes after allowing for sickness, unemployment and irregular work.* In Bristol the average working-class family enjoyed a standard of living more than 100 per cent. above its minimum needs ; while one Bristol family in nine in the year 1937 was in sheer physical want, two families out of every five had half as much again as they needed for subsistence.† Similar contrasts were presented in every survey. Another way of putting these contrasts is to compare the surplus of those who had more than the minimum with the deficiency of those who had less. In East London, the total surplus of the working-class families above the minimum was more than thirty times the total deficiency of those below it. In York, where Mr. Rowntree in 1936 used a much higher minimum—the standard of human needs containing more than bare physical necessaries of food, clothing, fuel and housing—the three classes of the working population living above the standard had a total surplus above it at least eight times the total deficiency of the two classes living below the standard. Want could have been abolished before the present war by a redistribution of income within the wage-earning classes, without touching any of the wealthier classes. This is said not to suggest that redistribution of income should be confined to the wage-earning classes ; still less is it said

---

* See *New Survey of London Life and Labour.* Table XVII in Vol. III, p. 91.
† *The Standard of Living in Bristol,* p. 24

to suggest that men should be content with avoidance of want, with subsistence incomes. It is said simply as the most convincing demonstration that abolition of want just before this war was easily within the economic resources of the community ; want was a needless scandal due to not taking the trouble to prevent it.

446. The social surveys showed not only what was the standard of living available to the community just before the war but also that it had risen rapidly in the past thirty or forty years. The recent London and York surveys were designed to provide comparisons with earlier studies. They yielded unquestionable proof of large and general progress. When the New Survey of London Life and Labour was made in 1929, the average workman in London could buy a third more of articles of consumption in return for labour of an hour's less duration per day than he could buy forty years before at the time of Charles Booth's original survey.* The standard of living available to the workpeople of York in 1936 may be put over-all at about 30 per cent, higher than it was in 1899.† This improvement of economic conditions was reflected in improvement of physical conditions. In London, the crude death rate fell from 18·6 per thousand in 1900 to 11·4 in 1935 and the infant mortality rate fell from 159 to 58 per thousand. In York the infant mortality rate fell from 161 per thousand in 1899 to 55 in 1936 ; in the same period nearly 2 inches was added to the height of schoolchildren and nearly 5 lbs. to their weight.‡ Growing prosperity and improving health are facts established for these towns not as general impressions but by scientific impartial investigation. What has been shown for these towns in detail applies to the country generally. The real wages of labour, what the wage-earner could buy with his earnings just before the present war, were in general about one-third higher than in 1900 for an hour less of work each day. What the wage-earner could buy, when earning had been interrupted by sickness, accident or unemployment or had been ended by old age, had increased in even larger proportion, though still inadequately, by development of social insurance and allied services.

447. The rise in the general standard of living in Britain in the thirty or forty years that ended with the present war has two morals. First, growing general prosperity and rising wages diminished want, but did not reduce want to insignificance. The moral is that new measures to spread prosperity are needed. The Plan for Social Security is designed to meet this need ; to establish a national minimum above which prosperity can grow, with want abolished. Second, the period covered by the comparisons between say 1900 and 1936 includes the first world-war. The moral is the encouraging one, that it is wrong to assume that the present war must bring economic progress for Britain, or for the rest of the world, to an end. After four years of open warfare and diversion of effort from useful production to the means of destruction during 1914–18, there followed an aftermath of economic conflict ; international trade was given no chance to recover from the war, and Britain entered into a period of mass unemployment in her staple industries. Yet, across this waste period of destruction and dislocation, the permanent forces making for material progress—technical advance and the capacity of human society to adjust itself to new conditions—continued to operate ; the real wealth per head in a Britain of shrunken oversea investments and lost export markets, counting in all her unemployed, was materially higher in 1938 than

---

* *New Survey of London Life and Labour*, Vol. I, p. 21.
† Rowntree : *Poverty and Progress*, p. 453.
‡ Rowntree, *op. cit.*, pp. 298–302. For Glasgow heights and weights of boys and girls of 5, 9 and 13 years of age from 1910–14 to 1929–33 are given at para. 174 of the Report of the Committee on Scottish Health Services (1936 Cmd. 5204) and show increases in all cases.

in 1913. The present war may be even more destructive. It is likely to complete the work of the first war in exhausting British investments overseas and to deprive Britain largely of another source of earning abroad through shipping services : in these and in other ways it will change the economic environment in which the British people must live and work and may call for radical and in some ways painful readjustments. There are bound to be acute difficulties of transition ; there are no easy care-free times in early prospect. But to suppose that the difficulties cannot be overcome, that power of readjustment has deserted the British people, that technical advance has ended or can end, that the British of the future must be permanently poor because they will have spent their fathers' savings, is defeatism without reason and against reason.

448. The economic argument set out above is in terms not of money, but of standards of living and of real wages. If the argument is sound, it is clear that abolition of want by re-distribution of income is within our means. The problem of how the plan should be financed in terms of money is secondary, though it is a real problem, since the fact that the whole burden, properly distributed, could be borne does not mean that it can be borne unless it is distributed wisely. Wise distribution of the burden is the object of the Social Security Budget as outlined in Part IV. There it is shown that the Plan involves for the National Exchequer an additional charge of at most £86 million in the first year of full operation. It does not seem unreasonable to hope that, even with the other calls upon the Exchequer, an additional expense of this order could be borne when actual fighting ceases. The Budget imposes a much increased burden on the Exchequer in later years to provide retirement pensions ; this is an act of reasonable faith in the future of the British economic system and the proved efficiency of the British people. That, given reasonable time, this burden can be borne is hardly open to question. The exact rate at which the burden will rise is not settled finally in accepting the plan, since the length of the transition period for pensions is capable of adjustment and, if necessary, can be prolonged without serious hardship. As regards the insured person, the Budget requires of him contributions for vital security which together are materially less than he is now paying for compulsory insurance and for voluntary insurance for less important purposes, or on account of medical services for which he pays when he receives them. For the employers, the plan imposes an addition to their costs for labour which should be well repaid by the greater efficiency and content which they secure.

449. The argument of this section can be summed up briefly. Abolition of want cannot be brought about merely by increasing production, without seeing to correct distribution of the product ; but correct distribution does not mean what it has often been taken to mean in the past—distribution between the different agents in production, between land, capital, management and labour. Better distribution of purchasing power is required among wage-earners themselves, as between times of earning and not earning, and between times of heavy family responsibilities and of light or no family responsibilities. Both social insurance and children's allowances are primarily methods of re-distributing wealth. Such better distribution cannot fail to add to welfare and, properly designed, it can increase wealth, by maintaining physical vigour. It does not decrease wealth, unless it involves waste in administration or reduces incentives to production. Unemployment and disability are already being paid for unconsciously ; it is no addition to the burden on the community to provide for them consciously. Unified social insurance will eliminate a good deal of waste inherent in present methods. Properly designed, controlled and financed, it need have no depressing effect on incentive.

450. Want could have been abolished in Britain just before the present war. It can be abolished after the war, unless the British people are and remain very much poorer then than they were before, that is to say unless they remain less productive than they and their fathers were. There is no sense in believing, contrary to experience, that they will and must be less productive. The answer to the question whether freedom from want should be regarded as a post-war aim capable of early attainment is an affirmative—on four conditions. The four conditions are :—

(1) That the world after the war is a world in which the nations set themselves to co-operate for production in peace, rather than to plotting for mutual destruction by war, whether open or concealed ;

(2) That the re-adjustments of British economic policy and structure that will be required by changed conditions after the war should be made, so that productive employment is maintained ;

(3) That a Plan for Social Security, that is to say for income maintenance, should be adopted, free from unnecessary costs of administration and other waste of resources ;

(4) That decisions as to the nature of the plan, that is to say as to the organisation of social insurance and allied services, should be taken during the war.

451. Is there any reason why the fourth condition should not be satisfied here and now ? Re-construction of social insurance and allied services to ensure security of income for all risks is a general aim on which all reasonable men would agree. It involves changes affecting many sectional interests, but it raises no issues of political principle or of party. It involves an immense work of detail in legislation and organisation for which time is essential, for which there may be less time in the uncertain aftermath of war than there is today. If a plan for freedom from want, so far as social security can give it, is to be ready when the war ends, it must be prepared during the war.

452. To give effect to the Plan for Social Security embodied in this Report requires decisions of three kinds : decisions of principle, decisions of execution and detail, and decisions of amount, that is to say of rates of benefit and contribution. Decisions of the third kind, as to rates of benefit and contribution, do not need to be taken now ; they can wait until the probable level of prices after the war is better known. Decisions of the first kind, that is to say decisions of principle, can be taken now and need to be taken, if any Plan for Social Security is to be ready when the war ends. The decisions required are :—

(1) A decision to introduce a unified comprehensive scheme of social insurance embodying the six fundamental principles set out in paras. 303–309 : flat rate of subsistence benefit, flat rate of contribution, unification of administrative responsibility, adequacy of benefit, comprehensiveness and classification ;

(2) A decision to entrust administration of the scheme to a Ministry of Social Security ;

(3) A decision to appoint some person or body to prepare the necessary legislation and bring the scheme into being, so that it is ready when the war ends.

Decisions of this character can be taken by Parliament alone. If His Majesty's Government accept the main recommendations of the Report, it is suggested that the first step would be to submit to Parliament resolutions approving the introduction of a scheme of social insurance and allied services, in accordance with the principles named, and approving the constitution of a Ministry of Social Security. If these resolutions were accepted, there should follow the setting up of some authority—a Minister, a group of Ministers or -a body of Commissioners—to prepare the necessary legislation. The bringing into effect of a scheme on the lines of the Report involves the repeal of many Acts of Parliament and their replacement by one or two Acts of Parliament and a mass of detailed regulations. Consideration of the new legislation proposed would give Parliament a second opportunity of judging the scheme in concrete form. All the detailed Regulations, in accordance with normal practice, would be laid before Parliament before being put into force.

453. Whatever body was charged with the task of preparing the new legislation and Regulations would deal with many questions of detail for which no decisions, or provisional decisions only, are suggested in the Report. There are some matters for which fresh formal investigation might be required. These include :—

(a) The organisation of the national health service forming the first part of Assumption B of the plan. This is a matter for further investigation either by the Departments concerned or by a new independent body, in consultation with the authorities which are concerned outside the Government ;

(b) The organisation of the rehabilitation ·service which forms the second part of Assumption B. This matter is already under examination in the Ministry of Labour and National Service ;

(c) The problem of alternative remedies briefly described in paras. 258–264, and requiring, as is stated there, examination by some body with the requisite technical and practical qualifications and ample time for investigation ;

(d) The fitting of the special provisions for industrial accident and disease into the social insurance scheme ;

(e) The problem of differential rates of benefit and contribution for different parts of the country or different occupations, and the various problems of demarcation between different insurance classes. · These could appropriately be examined by some body which might ultimately become the suggested Social Insurance Statutory Committee.

All these and many other questions require continuous detailed study. That study will come automatically, if once the decision of principle is taken to establish a unified co-ordinated system of social security which shall put an end to physical want.

454. The foregoing outline for procedure does not. mean that the Plan for Social Security is indivisible in time, so that all that is involved ĩn it must be done at one and the same time by one Act of Parliament. There are some parts of the plan which can be dealt with separately and later than the rest, including such matters as transfer of responsibility for public assistance from Local Authorities to a national authority. There are some parts, like children's allowances, which could, if this appeared desirable, be dealt with in advance of the rest. In any case the magnitude of the reconstruction involved makes it inevitable that some of it should be taken by stages. But some parts must be taken together or not at all, and even if reconstruction is by stages it is important that the whole should be dominated by unity of design. To deal piece-meal with particular defects of the present system, and above all to deal piece-meal with deficiencies in the amount of benefit or compensation now provided, in advance of a general decision on the whole plan, involves the risk, almost amounting to certainty, of a continuance of that anomalous and unjust treatment of like cases by different methods which the plan is designed to

remedy. Piece-meal legislation is likely to be less satisfactory and in the end more costly, for less advantage to the community as a whole, than comprehensive unified treatment of the problem of social security.

PLANNING FOR PEACE IN WAR

455. There are some to whom pursuit of security appears to be a wrong aim. They think of security as something inconsistent with initiative, adventure, personal responsibility. That is not a just view of social security as planned in this Report. The plan is not one for giving to everybody something for nothing and without trouble, or something that will free the recipients for ever thereafter from personal responsibilities. The plan is one to secure income for subsistence on condition of service and contribution and in order to make and keep men fit for service. It cannot be got without thought and effort. It can be carried through only by a concentrated determination of the British democracy to free itself once for all of the scandal of physical want for which there is no economic or moral justification. When that effort has been made, the plan leaves room and encouragement to all individuals to win for themselves something above the national minimum, to find and to satisfy and to produce the means of satisfying new and higher needs than bare physical needs.

456. There are some who will say that pursuit of security as defined in this Report, that is to say income security, is a wholly inadequate aim. Their view is not merely admitted but asserted in the Report itself. The Plan for Social Security is put forward as part of a general programme of social policy. It is one part only of an attack upon five giant evils : upon the physical Want with which it is directly concerned, upon Disease which often causes that Want and brings many other troubles in its train, upon Ignorance which no democracy can afford among its citizens, upon the Squalor which arises mainly through haphazard distribution of industry and population, and upon the Idleness which destroys wealth and corrupts men, whether they are well fed or not, when they are idle. In seeking security not merely against physical want, but against all these evils in all their forms, and in showing that security can be combined with freedom and enterprise and responsibility of the individual for his own life, the British community and those who in other lands have inherited the British tradition have a vital service to render to human progress.

457. There are others who, not through lack of faith in Britain's ultimate future, but as a measure of prudence will say that, before committing itself to a scheme as large in total expenditure as that outlined in this Report, the nation should wait to see if in fact its resources grow after the war sufficiently to meet the expenditure. This is natural caution. Those who feel it may, nevertheless, support the plan as a method of organisation, irrespective of the precise rates of benefit and contribution to be written into it or of the number of years chosen for the transition period, during which contributory pensions will rise to adequacy ; that number can be varied and the speed at which expenditure will rise can be increased or decreased. The Plan for Social Security is first and foremost a method of redistributing income, so as to put the first and most urgent needs first, so as to make the best possible use of whatever resources are available. That is worth doing, even if the resources as a whole are insufficient for the standard of life that is desired. But it must be realised that nothing materially below the scales of benefit and pension suggested here can be justified on scientific grounds as adequate for human subsistence. Benefits, allowances or pensions below the proposals of this Report may merely mean that the cost of unemployment or sickness or childhood is being borne not directly in cash, but indirectly in privation and lowered human efficiency.

458. There are yet others who will say that, however desirable it may appear to reconstruct social insurance or to make other plans for a better world of peace, all such concerns must now be put on one side, so that Britain may concentrate upon the urgent tasks of war. There is no need to spend words today in emphasising the urgency or the difficulty of the task that faces the British people and their Allies. Only by surviving victoriously in the present struggle can they enable freedom and happiness and kindliness to survive in the world. Only by obtaining from every individual citizen his maximum of effort, concentrated upon the purposes of war, can they hope for early victory. This does not alter three facts : that the purpose of victory is to live into a better world than the old world ; that each individual citizen is more likely to concentrate upon his war effort if he feels that his Government will be ready in time with plans for that better world ; that, if these plans are to be ready in time, they must be made now.

459. Statement of a reconstruction policy by a nation at war is statement of the uses to which that nation means to put victory, when victory is achieved. In a war which many nations must wage together as whole-hearted allies, if they are to win victory, such a statement of the uses of victory may be vital. This was recognised by the leaders of the democracies east and west of the Atlantic in putting their hands to a charter which, in general terms, set out the nature of the world which they desired to establish after the war. The Atlantic Charter has since then been signed on behalf of all the United Nations. The fifth clause of the charter declares the desire of the American and the British leaders " to bring about the fullest collaboration between all nations in the economic field, with the object of securing for all improved labour standards, economic advancement, and social security." The proposals of this Report are designed as a practical contribution towards the achievement of the social security which is named in the closing words. The proposals cover ground which must be covered, in one way or another, in translating the words of the Atlantic Charter into deeds. They represent, not an attempt by one nation to gain for its citizens advantages at the cost of their fellow fighters in a common cause, but a contribution to that common cause. They are concerned not with increasing the wealth of the British people, but with so distributing whatever wealth is available to them in total, as to deal first with first things, with essential physical needs. They are a sign of the belief that the object of government in peace and in war is not the glory of rulers or of races, but the happiness of the common man. That is a belief which, through all differences in forms of government, unites not only the democracies whose leaders first put their hands to the Atlantic Charter, but those democracies and all their Allies. It unites the United Nations and divides them from their enemies.

460. At the request of His Majesty's Government, the Inter-departmental Committee have pursued the task of surveying the social services of Britain and examining plans for their reconstruction during the most savage, most universal and most critical war in which Britain has ever been engaged. It would be wrong to conclude this Report without expressing gratitude to all those who in such a crisis have, nevertheless, found time and energy to assist the Committee in this task, who, triumphing over difficulties of dispersal, of loss of staff, of absorption in urgent tasks of war, have prepared memoranda, attended to give evidence, and have discussed their problems with so much frankness and public spirit. Naturally the question has arisen at times whether it is possible to give to such problems in war the consideration that they need, whether, both for the sake of concentration on war effort and to make the best in reconstruction, the work of the Committee should not have been postponed to a more leisured season. The question may be asked and can be answered.

The interest that has been shown in the problems of the Committee, by nearly all those who have come before the Committee or have prepared memoranda, is probably a true reflection of the state of public feeling and represents probably a right judgment of the time when reconstruction should be taken in hand. There are difficulties in planning reconstruction of the social services during the height of war, but there are also advantages in doing so. The prevention of want and the diminution and relief of disease—the special aim of the social services—are in fact a common interest of all citizens. It may be possible to secure a keener realisation of that fact in war than it is in peace, because war breeds national unity. It may be possible, through sense of national unity and readiness to sacrifice personal interests to the common cause, to bring about changes which, when they are made, will be accepted on all hands as advances, but which it might be difficult to make at other times. There appears at any rate to be no doubt of the determination of the British people, however hard pressed in war, not to live wholly for war, not to abandon care of what may come after. That, after all, is in accord with the nature of democracies, of the spirit in which they fight and of the purpose for which they fight. They make war, today more consciously than ever, not for the sake of war, not for dominion or revenge, but war for peace. If the united democracies today can show strength and courage and imagination equal to their manifest desire, can plan for a better peace even while waging total war, they will win together two victories which in truth are indivisible.

461. Freedom from want cannot be forced on a democracy or given to a democracy. It must be won by them. Winning it needs courage and faith and a sense of national unity : courage to face facts and difficulties and overcome them ; faith in our future and in the ideals of fair-play and freedom for which century after century our forefathers were prepared to die ; a sense of national unity overriding the interests of any class or section. The Plan for Social Security in this Report is submitted by one who believes that in this supreme crisis the British people will not be found wanting, of courage and faith and national unity, of material and spiritual power to play their part in achieving both social security and the victory of justice among nations upon which security depends.

(Signed) W. H. BEVERIDGE.

20th November, 1942.

APPENDIX A

FINANCE OF THE PROPOSALS OF THE REPORT RELATING TO SOCIAL INSURANCE AND SECURITY BENEFITS

MEMORANDUM BY THE GOVERNMENT ACTUARY

1. I have examined, from the financial aspect, the proposals put forward in Sir William Beveridge's Report in so far as they relate to a scheme of social insurance and security benefits to be financed through a Social Security Budget.

SUMMARY OF PROPOSALS

2. The Social Security Plan considers the needs of the population in six main classes, viz :—

I. Employed persons normally working under contract of service.

II. Other gainfully occupied persons.

III. Housewives (including those who follow a gainful occupation).

IV. Other persons of working age not gainfully occupied.

V. Children below working age.

VI. Persons who have attained pensionable age and have retired from work.

It assumes as necessary prior conditions (A) that an adequate scheme of allowances for children (Class V) will be established, and (B) that the whole population will be covered by a comprehensive scheme of medical treatment and health services.

Under the Social Insurance proposals all persons who have attained the minimum pensionable age, viz. 65 for men and 60 for women, and have retired from work (Class VI) will be entitled to retirement pension if the requisite contributions have been paid by or in respect of them. Those who do not satisfy these conditions will be eligible for an assistance pension dependent on means.

All employed persons (Class I) will be insured for disability benefit, continuing so long as they are unable on account of incapacity to follow a gainful occupation, an industrial pension (of larger amount) being substituted therefor in the case of persons suffering from prolonged disability due to industrial accident or disease. They will be insured also for unemployment benefit, payable so long as they are available for but unable to obtain work.

Other gainfully occupied persons (Class II) will be insured for disability benefit commencing after the first 13 weeks of illness.

The other principal benefits are : a variety of special benefits for married women (Class III) under proposals comprehensively described as a housewife's policy ; pensions of limited character and duration for widows ; and a universal funeral grant.

3. *Rates of Contribution.*—With certain exceptions, all persons in Classes I, II and IV, and gainfully occupied housewives in Class III, must pay contributions related to the benefits for which they are covered ; for this purpose housewives come under Class I or Class II according to the nature of their occupation. The exceptions are :—

(i) A gainfully occupied housewife may elect to be exempt from payment of contributions herself, in which case she is not eligible for unemployment or disability (other than industrial) benefits, but is entitled to (*a*) maternity grant and benefit, and (*b*) other benefits which flow from her husband's insurance ;

(ii) A person in Class II or IV whose total income is less than £75 a year may elect to be exempt from payment of contributions, with loss of the benefit rights resulting from such contributions.

The rates of contribution proposed to be charged for contributors in the various classes are set out below :—

WEEKLY RATES OF CONTRIBUTION

	CLASS I			CLASS II	CLASS IV
	Insured Person	Employer	Joint Contribution		
MEN :—					
Aged 21 and over	4/3	3/3	7/6	4/3	3/9
Between 18 and 21 ...	3/6	2/9	6/3	3/6	3/–
Between 16 and 18 ...	2/6	2/6	5/–	2/–	1/6
WOMEN :—					
Aged 21 and over	3/6	2/6	6/–	3/9	3/–
Between 18 and 21 ...	3/–	2/–	5/–	3/–	2/6
Between 16 and 18 ...	2/–	2/–	4/–	2/–	1/6

4. *Rates and Conditions of Benefit.*—The principal rates of benefit under the insurance proposals are set out below. The rates assumed for this memorandum are those described in the Report as provisional and suggested as appropriate to a post-war position in which the cost of living (including rent) is 25 per cent., or a little more, above the pre-war level. Eligibility for the full rates of benefit is in most cases subject to satisfaction of prescribed conditions as to minimum number of contributions paid under the scheme and annual average of contributions.

Retirement Pensions payable from age 65 (men) or 60 (women) at 24/– a week to a single person and 40/– for a married couple, subject to the following qualifications :—

(i) The married couple's joint pension to be payable irrespective of the age of the wife, but dependent on her not being at work.

(ii) Payment of pension to be dependent on retirement from work.

(iii) Pension to be increased in case of postponement of retirement after 65 or 60 by 1/– a week for a single pensioner or 2/– for a married couple, for each year of such deferment.

(iv) Basic pensions will not be payable at the full rates, i.e. 24/– single and 40/– joint, until the expiry of a transitional period of 20 years from the beginning of the scheme (*see* para. 5*).

Widow's and Guardian Benefits (for widows under age 60) at 36/– a week for the 13 weeks immediately following widowhood ; to be continued as a guardian benefit in the case of widows with dependent children, at the rate of 24/–, subject to reduction for earnings. Apart from these benefits, widows who desire to take up employment are eligible for training benefit (as described under " Unemployment and Disability Benefits ").

Widows who, on the termination of widow's benefit, are unable to take up work on account of permanent disability will be eligible to have their pensions continued at the rate for disability benefit.

Unemployment and Disability Benefits at 24/– a week during unemployment or incapacity for work, without limit as to duration of benefit, subject to the following :—

(i) An allowance at the rate of 16/– a week to be added for a wife (not gainfully occupied) or adult dependant ; the joint benefit for a married couple is thus 40/–.

---

* Throughout this memorandum, references to paragraphs relate to paragraphs of the memorandum and not of the Report.

(ii) Reduced rates of benefit for :

Single men and women aged between 18 and 21 ... ... at 20/–
Boys and girls aged between 16 and 18 ... ... at 15/–
Gainfully occupied married women ... ... at 16/–

(iii) Benefit not to be paid for the first three days of a period of unemployment or incapacity unless it lasts for at least four weeks.

(iv) A training benefit at the same rates, but limited to a maximum of 26 weeks' duration, to be payable in certain circumstances to persons in Classes II, III and IV.

Industrial Pensions.—Where incapacity for work results from an industrial accident or disease, the ordinary rates of disability benefit (including allowance for wife or adult dependant) are to be payable for the first 13 weeks of disability. Thereafter an industrial pension is to be substituted, if more favourable, payable at the rate of two-thirds of estimated full-time earnings in a period preceding incapacitation, subject to a maximum limit of £3 a week, or in cases of partial disability a reduced pension proportionate to the estimated loss of earning power.

Maternity Benefits comprising :—

(i) Maternity grant of £4 available to all married women, and to other women, if insured in Class I or II ; and

(ii) Maternity benefit at 36/– a week for 13 weeks, available to all gainfully occupied women whether paying contributions or exempt:

Marriage Grant, consisting of a payment to a woman, on her marriage, of £1 for each 40 actual contributions paid in Class I or II, subject to a maximum limit of £10.

Funeral Grant, payable to the person responsible for funeral expenses, the amount being £6 on the death of a child under age 3, £10 for a child aged between 3 and 10, £15 for a young person aged between 10 and 21, and £20 for an adult aged 21 or over. At the outset persons then aged 60 or over are to be excluded from this benefit.

5. *Transitional Arrangements for Retirement Pension.*—In the 20-year transitional period, i.e. up to mid-1964 if the Plan is introduced in July, 1944, pensions will be payable at reduced rates, and will be assessed by different methods for those falling into the respective categories :—

(i) Persons paying pensions contributions under the existing system who satisfy the qualifying conditions. This group consists entirely of persons at present insured under the Contributory Pensions Acts, with whom are included persons already in receipt of contributory pensions who have retired ; and

(ii) Persons who will pay contributions for pensions under the Social Security Plan but have not been contributors under the existing system. This group consists of initial entrants in Classes II and IV and employed persons previously excepted from compulsory insurance for contributory pensions and now to be included in Class I.

For the first group, pensions will start in mid-1944 and the proposed rates at the outset are 25/– for a joint pension and 14/– for a single pension. It is further proposed, however, that these rates should be increased by 1/6 and 1/– respectively in mid-1946 and thereafter at two-yearly intervals over a period of 20 years until mid-1964, when the final rates of 40/– joint and 24/– single are reached. The rate of pension payable at any point in this 20-year period will be the same for every pensioner in this group, apart from additions to the basic pension on account of postponement of retirement.

For the second group, pensions will not start until mid-1954, i.e. 10 years after the commencement of the Plan. They will vary according to the year in which retirement takes place but once granted will be fixed and will not increase as do those for group (i) with year of payment. The rates of pension for group (ii) will be 25/- joint and 14/- single in respect of persons retiring in 1954–55, having paid 10 years' contributions under the Plan. The rates for subsequent retirements will be 1/6 or 1/- greater for each year of contribution in excess of 10 years, so that persons retiring with 20 years' contributions in 1964–65 will be granted the final rate of 40/- joint or 24/- single.

The foregoing rates of pension will be subject to addition on account of postponement of retirement, as already stated. In the transitional period this addition will be determined (*a*) for persons in group (i) by the number of years of contribution after age 65 (men) or 60 (women) or after mid-1944 if the pensioner was over age 65 (or 60) at that date ; and (*b*) for persons in group (ii) by the number of years of contribution after age 65 (men) or 60 (women) or after mid-1954 if the pensioner was then over age 65 (or 60). The working of these rules will be clear from the following statement and two examples :—

SPECIMEN WEEKLY RATES OF PENSION PAYABLE, IN THE YEAR SHOWN, TO PERSONS WHO HAVE RETIRED

(i) Persons in existing Contributory Pensions scheme :—

Year of Payment	Basic Pension		Addition for Postponement of Retirement
	Single person	Married couple	
1st (1944–45)	14/-	25/-	Persons who retire after the beginning of the new scheme at an age later than 65 (60 for women) will receive in addition 1/- a week (2/- on joint pension) for each complete year of postponement after 65 (60) for which contributions have been paid under the new scheme, i.e. from July, 1944.
2nd	14/-	25/-	
3rd	15/-	26/6	
4th	15/-	26/6	
5th	16/-	28/-	
11th (1954–55)	19/-	32/6	
16th (1959–60)	21/-	35/6	
21st (1964–65) and thereafter	24/-	40/-	

(ii) Persons not in existing Contributory Pensions scheme :—

Year of Payment	Basic Pension									
	Single person					Married couple				
	Year of retirement					Year of retirement				
	11th	12th	13th	16th	21st	11th	12th	13th	16th	21st
11th (1954–55)	14/-					25/-				
12th	14/-	15/-				25/-	26/6			
13th	14/-	15/-	16/-			25/-	26/6	28/-		
16th (1959–60)	14/-	15/-	16/-	19/-		25/-	26/6	28/-	32/6	
21st (1964–65) and thereafter	14/-	15/-	16/-	19/-	24/-	25/-	26/6	28/-	32/6	40/-

ADDITION FOR POSTPONEMENT OF RETIREMENT :—As for group (i), except that only contributions paid after June, 1954, and subsequent to attainment of age 65 (60), count for this purpose.

Thus, a married man in group (i) who retires at age 65 in 1944-45, will receive, while his spouse survives, 25/- a week during that year and 1945–46, 26/6 a week during 1946–47 and 1947–48, 28/- during 1948–49 and 1949–50, and so on, rising to 40/- a week in 1964–65. If he postpones retirement for two years, until he is aged 67 in 1946–47, he will receive 30/6 (i.e. 26/6 plus 4/- for two years' postponement) a week for that year and 1947–48, 32/- for 1948–49 and 1949–50, rising to 44/- a week in 1964–65.

If the husband dies first and his widow is then aged 60 or more, she will receive the corresponding single pension for life ; if she is then under 60 she is entitled to the normal benefits of a widow. If he is left a widower his pension is then reduced to the single rate.

A married man in group (ii) who retires in 1954–55, being then aged 65 and having paid 10 years' contributions, will receive 25/– a week. If he postpones retirement for two years, continuing meanwhile to pay contributions, and takes his pension at age 67 in 1956–57, he will receive a pension of 32/– a week, made up of 28/– as the basic rate for retirements in that year plus 4/– for two years' postponement. These rates of pension will continue unchanged throughout the lifetime of the pensioner so long as he is married.

6. *Other Security Benefits.*—In addition to the foregoing benefits which are provided on an insurance basis, the Plan includes the following cash benefits :—

(i) *Children's Allowances* for each child under 15 (or 16 if still at school). These are to be paid for all children except the first, at rates averaging 8/– a week, with an additional 8/– for the first child when the parent is in receipt of unemployment or disability benefit, or industrial pension, or is a widow.

(ii) *National Assistance* payments, dependent on the means of the recipient, to meet individual needs where either no insurance benefit is payable or the benefits for which the recipient is qualified require supplementation.

Value of the Benefits Expressed as a Contribution

7. The rates proposed for the joint contribution, payable by the insured person and his employer, in the case of persons falling within Class I are 7/6 a week for men, and 6/– for women, with reduced rates for contributors below age 21. The relationship of these rates to the actuarial value of the benefits is examined in the following paragraphs—and here, perhaps, it is necessary to make a general observation. The reason for considering in detail the relationship of benefits and contributions on the lines adopted in this section, is not the technical interest of an actuarial analysis of the scheme—as if a hypothetical fund were to be built up on the basis of actuarial reserves—but the importance of making abundantly clear (*a*) how and why the proposed rates of contribution for insured persons have been arrived at, and the equity of the proposals as to contributions, and (*b*) the character and extent of the liabilities, not met from these contributions, which the scheme will place upon the State, i.e. liabilities to be met from general taxation.

For the purpose of this analysis the view adopted on similar occasions in the past has been followed, namely, that for assessing the rate of contribution which can equitably be charged in a compulsory scheme of Social Insurance a fair basis is obtained by expressing the value of the future benefits to a new entrant at the minimum age of 16 in terms of the contribution, payable throughout working lifetime, which should be made to insure the benefits on an actuarial basis ; this is commonly termed the actuarial contribution.

The matter may be considered from two points of view : (i) the contribution for 100 per cent. of the cost of benefits, which may be regarded as the maximum contribution which could fairly be charged ; and (ii) the contribution for such a proportion of the benefits under each head as remains after calling upon the State to bear a proportion of the cost for every new entrant to the scheme. If a contribution on the basis in (i) were charged, new entrants at age 16 would be self-supporting in the sense that, if they could be isolated as a class and their contributions accumulated in a separate fund to meet the future cost of their benefits, no State subsidy would be required in respect of them since their pensions, for example, would be met out of the reserves accumulated during the working lifetime of each year's new entrants, which, on the assumptions made, would be exhausted on the death of the last pensioner. If a contribution on basis (ii) is charged, i.e., the contribution which the insured person (jointly with the employer) may reasonably be asked to pay, the extent to which this falls below (i) indicates the liability which is cast upon the Exchequer for every young person who attains the age of 16, now and in the future, apart from the further liability in respect of persons over age 16 when the scheme is introduced—a matter to which reference is made in the next paragraph.

8. The assessment of the contribution, even on the lines of basis (i), i.e. at a rate designed to meet 100 per cent. of the benefit cost to a new entrant, would nevertheless leave a substantial liability to be met from the Exchequer in the case of most of the benefits of the Plan.

The incidence of the risk in respect of retirement pensions, widows' pensions, disability benefits, marriage and maternity benefits and funeral grant, varies substantially and measurably with age ; and a contribution computed as above is sufficient only in the case of those continuously insured from age 16 onwards. For other persons—mainly those brought into the scheme at the outset at an age above the minimum, but at the same rate of contribution—the contribution should be greater. Looking at the matter in another way, there is a deficiency because these persons have not paid the contribution at the new rates continuously in the past from age 16. The resulting excess in the cost of benefits over the income from contributions has to be met from the Exchequer. It has to be remembered always, when reference is made to the full contribution for benefits, that it would be " full " only in the case of entrants at age 16 who are continuously insured ; the population as a whole, taking the joint contributions of employers and insured persons, would not be paying for the full value of their benefits.

The position as regards unemployment benefit is rather different, since the risk cannot satisfactorily be assessed with reference to age but is averaged over the insured population of all ages. There is thus no question of the Exchequer having to meet an extra burden in respect of the extra cost for persons over the age of 16 already in insurance ; the contribution applicable at one age is assumed to be the same as that for another.

9. In the Social Security Plan it is proposed that in addition to the subsidy provided by admitting the bulk of the existing population over age 16 at the flat rate of contribution without reduction of benefits—apart from the effect of the transitional period for pensions in the case of those of fairly advanced ages at the outset—the Exchequer should provide a further subsidy by undertaking the liability for a proportion of the cost for future entrants at the initial age. For the purpose of arriving at suitable rates of contribution the following principles have been adopted, having regard to past practice in regard to Exchequer subsidies under the various schemes of social insurance.

For unemployment benefit there appears to be no reason for departing from the existing arrangement under which the Exchequer bears one-third of the cost of benefits and administration and the employer and insured person share the other two-thirds equally between them.

For most of the other benefits a smaller proportion of the cost of benefits to an entrant at age 16 may fairly be charged to the Exchequer than in the case of unemployment benefit, in view of the heavy liabilities, already referred to, which the scheme imposes upon it. In the case of retirement pensions, widows' benefits and disability benefits*, the contribution has been computed on the basis that the Exchequer meets one-sixth of the liability.

The marriage grant and the funeral grant do not appear to call for a permanent Exchequer subsidy for the new entrant, and accordingly the contribution is framed to meet the full value at 16.

10. The result of my calculations on the foregoing principles is to produce the following weekly rates of contribution for Class I benefits for an entrant

---

*For industrial disability benefits, *see* paras. 36 to 46.

at age 16 ; these are the adult rates payable from age 21 and assume that, as proposed in the Plan, persons between ages 16 and 18 will pay two-thirds of these rates and those between ages 18 and 21 will pay five-sixths of the rates :—

(i) if the contributions pay for 100 per cent. of the insured benefits :
Men, 103·2d. ; Women, 81·6d.

(ii) if the contributions pay for two-thirds of unemployment benefit and five-sixths of all other benefits except marriage grant and funeral grant :
Men, 79·7d. ; Women, 64·1d.
as compared with

(iii) the rates proposed to be charged, viz., 7/6 (men) and 6/– (women) less the contribution towards health services included therein (10d. men, 8d. women—*see* para. 34 below) : Men, 80d. ; Women, 64d.

Thus the contributions proposed are seen—from the relation of (iii) to (ii)—to be approximately adequate in the case of an entrant at age 16 to meet two-thirds of the cost of unemployment benefits and five-sixths of the cost of the other principal benefits. Alternatively—from the ratio of (iii) to (i)—they are equivalent to a little over three-quarters of the over-all value of the Social Insurance benefits.

The position is similar in the case of Classes II and IV, the contributions proposed to be paid from age 21 corresponding as closely as may be to the actuarial contributions appropriate to the benefits for which these classes are insured, having regard to the conditions governing excusal of contributions in certain eventualities and the practical demands of rounding the rates ; Exchequer subsidies similar to those in (ii) above are assumed.

11. On the foregoing basis we have the following comparison for adults in the three contributory classes :—

CONTRIBUTIONS IN PENCE PER WEEK

		Contribution for insurance benefits	Contribution towards health services	Margin (+ or −) to balance	Contribution proposed to be charged
Class I.	Men ...	79·7	10·0	+0·3	90·0
	Women ...	64·1	8·0	−0·1	72·0
Class II.	Men ...	40·5	10·0	+0·5	51·0
	Women ...	37·1	8·0	−0·1	45·0
Class IV.	Men ...	33·7	10·0	+1·3	45·0
	Women ...	26·8	8·0	+1·2	36·0

A more detailed examination of the several actuarial contributions and their relation to the contributions proposed to be charged—including the consideration of the contributions for persons under age 21 and the allocation between employers and insured persons—is set forth in the following paragraphs.

ACTUARIAL BASIS OF THE ESTIMATES

12. The calculations required for this memorandum cover two distinct fields, viz. (i) the composition of the actuarial contribution appropriate to the various benefits, and (ii) the estimation of the expenditure and income expected under the Plan in future years. For both purposes I have made use of the most recent data available for pre-war years in respect of mortality, marriage and other vital statistics. Thus the population figures are based upon the results of the national registration in September, 1939, supplemented by other information. Where, as in the calculation of rates of contribution, the discounting of future liabilities has been necessary, I have assumed compound

interest at the rate of 3 per cent. per annum. I discuss, in the following paragraphs, certain of the more important assumptions made and the considerations on which they are based.

13. In estimating the numbers and age distribution of the population in 1945 (taken as the first complete year of the new Plan), and in 1955 and 1965, I have projected the numbers recorded in the special national registration of 1939, assuming rates of survivorship corresponding to those experienced in Great Britain in the three years 1938-40, the figures for the last of these years being adjusted to exclude war deaths. It is impossible to assess the future casualties in the fighting forces and elsewhere which will be suffered before the close of hostilities ; and I have not attempted to adjust for the effect of the war on the size and constitution of the population surviving at its termination, or, consequentially, on the births and the population in the ensuing period. On the other hand the rates of mortality which I have adopted make no adjustment for the possible improvement in vitality in the future. If the actual rates of mortality experienced in the future are substantially below those on the standard taken, more particularly at the older ages, the population of pensionable age may be materially in excess of my estimates. But the future is obviously very speculative, and after consideration of the statistics of the last thirty years and in view of the uncertainties due to the war I have thought it premature, for the present purpose, to modify the relatively light rates of mortality disclosed in recent years in such a way as to incorporate a loading in the estimates.

In regard to the numbers of births assumed in the future, and the future population of children surviving therefrom, I have based the estimates on the fertility rates for Great Britain in 1938 derived from the more extensive data made available by the Population (Statistics)Act, 1938. The level of the birth rate resulting from these fertility rates corresponds closely to the average of the preceding four years. I have not attempted, in my estimates, to measure the possible effect on the fertility rates in future of changes in economic and social conditions as they may be affected, *inter alia*, by the grant of universal children's allowances.

14. As regards unemployment benefit—the second most important item in the scheme from the point of view of cost—I have assumed, after consultation with Sir William Beveridge, that under normal peace-time conditions the enlarged population insured against unemployment will experience an average rate of 8½ per cent. unemployment and that, as a result of the abolition of a limit on duration of benefit, 95 per cent. of such unemployment will rank for benefit. This matter is discussed further in para. 28 below.

15. As regards disability benefits, I have assumed that an appreciably higher claim rate will be experienced than that now prevailing in the National Health Insurance scheme, *inter alia*, on account of the substantial increases proposed in the rates of benefit. The effect, on the number and duration of claims, of this increase, together with other changes proposed by the scheme, such as the inclusion of " other gainfully occupied persons " for insurance against prolonged disability, is necessarily a matter of speculation, but past experience indicates that the number of weeks of disability benefit will be appreciably higher than would be anticipated on the basis of the experience of sickness and disablement benefit under the existing National Health Insurance system. The point is considered more fully in para. 22 below.

ANALYSIS OF THE ACTUARIAL CONTRIBUTION

16. I propose, in the following paragraphs, to discuss the essential considerations which arise, under the various benefit heads, in arriving at the constituents of the aggregate actuarial contribution. This is, necessarily, a complex matter—especially as regards the principles on which the relative

contributions of men and women should be fixed—the factors involved differing for the several benefits. For convenience, unless otherwise stated, the contributions quoted will be those for adult contributors in Class I.

17. *Pensions.*—The contributions payable up to 1936 under the Contributory Pensions scheme, viz. 9d. for men and 4½d. for women, were originally fixed in relation to the value of widows' and orphans' and age pensions up to age 70, but provision was made for three increases of 2d. for men and 1d. for women, in 1936, 1946 and 1956, with the intention that the entrant in 1956 or later, at the age of 16, should pay approximately for the whole of his or her benefits both before and after age 70. Recently, by the Contributory Pensions Act of 1940, contributions were raised (by 2d. for men and 3d. for women) on account of the reduction to 60 of the pension age for wives and insured women.

The current rates of contribution are thus 1/1 for men and 8½d. for women. If the scheme remained unchanged they would become 1/3 for men and 9½d. for women from 1946, and 1/5 and 10½d. from 1956. It was pointed out, at the time of the 1940 Bill, that these ultimate rates would be equivalent to about 90 per cent. of the full actuarial contribution—rather more in the case of insured men, rather less in the case of insured women—the corresponding proportion on the basis of the 1946 rates of contribution being just over 80 per cent. (*See* Report by the Government Actuary on the Financial Provisions of the Bill, Cmd. 6169.)

18. The fixing of the relative levels of pension contributions for men and women involves the question to what extent the cost of benefits to wives and widows, which arise from their being the dependants of insured men, should be paid for by men. The solution adopted is to assess the contribution for insured women so that, within the limits of practicality, a woman who was insured throughout her working lifetime would pay for her own age pension but would not contribute towards the general cost of wives' and widows' pensions. The contribution for insured men is correspondingly fixed so as to meet the cost of their own pensions, together with so much of the cost of benefits to wives and widows as is not covered by the pre-marriage contributions of insured women who marry and the contributions of employed married women and their employers (or their employers alone if they exercise their option to be exempt persons).

19. The cost of retirement pensions and widow's and guardian benefits* at the rates and under the conditions proposed in the Social Security Plan has been evaluated on the lines indicated in the preceding paragraphs. It is found that the actuarial contribution required to meet the full cost of the benefits, in the case of an entrant to insurance at age 16, would be 39·2d. a week for men (including 4·1d. for widow's and guardian benefits) and 31·8d. for women. These are the contributions for adults, payable from age 21, on the assumption that reduced rates are payable whilst the insured person is under age 21, viz. two-thirds at ages 16–18 and five-sixths at 18–21. Allowing for a State subsidy of one-sixth, the corresponding joint contributions payable by insured persons and their employers to meet five-sixths of the prospective value of these benefits are thus—for adults—32·7d. for men and 26·5d. for women.

These contributions are related to the full rates of pension which will become payable in 1964 when the transitional period has elapsed and not to the reduced rates payable transitionally in the interim. Further, they are on the basis that retirement takes place, and pension is granted, when the minimum pensionable age of 65 (men) or 60 (women) is attained. The financial effect of postponement of retirement and increase of pension in respect of contributions paid after the pensionable age is discussed in the next paragraph.

---

* No allowance has been made in these estimates for the net charge which may arise in respect of the analogous benefits to divorced and separated wives (recoverable, if possible, from their husbands).

It should be noted that the proportion of the liability to be assumed by the Exchequer, viz. one-sixth as proposed, corresponds closely to the position in the existing scheme in 1946 after the second decennial increase of contributions is added, since at that point the contributions charged under the old scheme would represent rather over 80 per cent. of the full actuarial contributions.

20. *Effect of Postponement of Pension.*—The proposals for making the grant of pension dependent on retirement from work and for increasing the rate of pension if retirement is postponed beyond the minimum pensionable age have contrary, but not equal, financial effects. The assumptions which I have made in these respects in my estimates of future expenditure are referred to later, in connection with the examination of the course of pensions expenditure anticipated during the transitional period (para. 54). In calculating the rate of contribution payable for pensions I have made no allowance for the net saving from postponement of pension ; it is worth while considering, however, the relationship of the amount of additional pension proposed for each year of postponement to the amount which could be granted on an actuarial basis.

The Plan gives to a single person 1/- a week extra pension for each year of postponement beyond age 65 (men) or 60 (women). The following statement shows the pension equivalent to (*a*) the final basic rate of 24/-, and (*b*) the initial transitional rate of 14/- payable at 65 (60 for women), which could be paid starting from a later age—and the corresponding addition for each year's deferment—allowing for the actuarial value of deferment of pension and payment of further pension contributions during deferment :—

	24/- Pension		14/- Pension	
Age at retirement	Equivalent rates of pension for age at retirement	Addition for one year's deferment	Equivalent rates of pension for age at retirement	Addition for one year's deferment
Retirement Pension for Man				
65	24/-	—	14/-	—
66	26/11	2/11	15/9	1/9
67	30/5	3/6	17/10	2/1
68	34/6	4/1	20/3	2/5
69	39/4	4/10	23/2	2/11
70	45/2	5/10	26/8	3/6
Retirement Pension for Woman				
60	24/-	—	14/-	—
61	26/2	2/2	15/4	1/4
62	28/8	2/6	16/11	1/7
63	31/6	2/10	18/8	1/9
64	34/8	3/2	20/7	1/11
65	38/3	3/7	22/9	2/2

It will be seen that in the case both of men and of women the grant of an additional 1/- pension for each year of postponement is well below the actuarial equivalent even in the case of a 14/-pension, i.e. the starting transitional rate. The saving due to postponement is thus partly returned to the pensioner in the form of a larger pension and partly a profit to the Social Insurance Fund.

For joint pensions a double addition, viz. 2/- instead of 1/- for each year of postponement, is proposed in the Plan. This can be explained by the fact that though the joint pension is equal to about five-sixths only of two single pensions regard has to be had to the probability of survival of each of the spouses during the period for which the man postpones his retirement.

21. *Disability Benefit.*—The rates of contribution payable under the present Health Insurance scheme have been determined in relation to the full

value of the benefits to an entrant at age 16, the contributions for men and women being separately assessed, having regard to the benefit rates and sickness experience of each sex. The rates were originally designed to represent the full value of the benefits to a new entrant ; a portion of the contributions was, however, earmarked as a sinking fund for the purpose of meeting the deficiency caused by the introduction of initial entrants of all ages at the flat rate of contribution, and though the State grant took the form of a stated proportion of all benefit expenditure (now one-seventh for men and one-fifth for women), this grant in fact enured to the benefit of those who started to contribute when over age 16, new entrants at the minimum age being self-supporting. This principle has been broadly maintained throughout the history of the National Health Insurance scheme as amended from time to time, though some departure from it was found necessary in the case of women, their sickness claims having proved to be substantially greater than had been anticipated. To adjust for this, a special State subsidy was given by raising the proportionate State grant for women.

Under the new Plan it is proposed that the contribution for disability benefit should be equal to only five-sixths of the value of the benefits to an entrant at age 16, the State being responsible for the remaining one-sixth. In addition the State is responsible for (i) any deficiency arising in respect of existing insured persons, owing to the fact that the liabilities as enlarged under the proposals are substantially greater than the reserves accumulated in the past under the existing scheme, and (ii) the new liability in respect of the inclusion of the classes, comprising persons of all ages, brought into insurance at the commencement of the Plan.

22. The main actuarial problem in connection with disability benefits, leaving out of account industrial disability which is dealt with separately in paragraphs 36 to 46, is to decide on appropriate rates of incapacity. The rates of benefit proposed are 24/– a week for a single person (whether adult male or female) and 40/– for a married man—who will receive also an allowance of 8/– for the first child, in addition to the children's allowances payable when he is at work. Moreover, these benefits are payable without reduction in cases of prolonged disability. They are thus much greater than the present Health Insurance rates, viz. 18/– for a man, with no allowances for wife or children (reduced to 10/6 after 26 weeks of incapacity), 15/– for an unmarried and 13/– for a married woman (reduced to 9/– and 8/– respectively after 26 weeks), with small additions if the insured person is a member of an approved society which is able to give additional sickness and disablement benefits. Past experience of sickness insurance—both State and voluntary—leads to the conclusion that, even with the support of a satisfactory system of medical certification and adequate measures of control by sick visiting and by medical referees, these high benefits will result in materially increased claim rates, especially in respect of prolonged incapacity.

While it is true that, as a result of the comprehensive health and rehabilitation service which is to be provided in place of the more limited existing medical benefit, a substantial improvement in the health of the community should be secured in due course, it does not necessarily follow that the cost of benefit will be correspondingly abated. This is due to the fact that under the altered arrangements there may be a tendency on the part of doctors to require longer periods off work in order to secure complete recovery from the effects of an illness, and there will also be less incentive than in the past to return to work owing to loss of income. The combined effect is likely to be an increase in the immediate claim rate, though it is to be hoped that later there will be some reduction in prolonged cases where a permanently incapacitating disease is avoided by more comprehensive and effective treatment at an early stage. It is difficult in framing long-term estimates to strike a balance between these conflicting influences, but in my opinion, however good the administrative arrangements may be, the level of sickness claims deduced from the experience of the past, under materially different conditions, cannot properly be adopted without modification for the new scheme. For the present estimates I have accordingly considered it essential to make a moderate addition to the sickness rates which now form the basis of National Health Insurance finance, increasing them by an average of 12½ per cent., taking a lower figure for the shorter illnesses and a larger for the more prolonged.

The position is definitely speculative, but it is clear to me that the realisation of a level of incapacity as low as that which I have adopted can only be achieved with a full appreciation of their responsibilities on the part of all concerned, that is to say, the active co-operation of the insured persons together with a high standard both of medical certification and of administrative supervision.

23. On this basis the actuarial contribution (for adults) required to meet the cost of the proposed benefits is estimated at 12·9d. a week for men and 10·2d. for women. This does not include the cost of disability due to industrial accident or disease, whether temporary or permanent, which is dealt with later.

These contributions cover five-sixths of the benefit, the balance falling upon the Exchequer. They allow for the special feature of the scheme under which, if a case of disability lasts for at least four weeks, benefit is then payable in respect of the three days' waiting period. They take cognisance also of the reduced rate of benefit payable to married women.

Reference may be made, also, to the fact that, whereas under the existing Health Insurance scheme the rates of benefit do not differentiate between single and married men, under the Plan allowances will be payable for the wives of married men, and adult dependants of other insured persons, who are sick. In the computation of the rates of contribution the cost of these allowances has been treated as an addition to the disability benefit of the insured person concerned, the result being a substantial addition to the man's contribution and only a small addition to that of women.

24. *Maternity Grant and Benefit.*—The lump sum grant on a married woman's confinement is met from the man's contributions. The weekly benefits before and after confinement to gainfully occupied women, whether married or single, and the cost of maternity grant to single women, are met from the woman's contributions. The actuarial contributions equivalent to these liabilities are 1·1d. a week on the man's contribution and 1·7d. on the woman's ; these relate to five-sixths of the cost.

25. *Marriage Grant.*—This has been treated as a separate benefit payable on marriage to women who have paid contributions whilst in Class I or II and the contribution has been assessed as the sum which, if paid from age 16 by all women contributors in these classes, would be equivalent to the cost of the benefit. The requisite contribution, payable under Class I conditions, to meet the full cost is estimated to be 2·8d. a week, there being no Exchequer subsidy towards this benefit. This assumes that the contribution forms part of the Social Security contribution throughout and, as such, is payable by women in Classes I and II of all ages and whether single or married unless exempt from payment of contributions. It would seem that this is a necessary assumption, since it would be impracticable to reduce the aggregate contribution payable to take account of a woman's individual position in regard to this particular benefit.

It will be seen that while the grant payable on marriage is equal to 6d. for each contribution paid, with a maximum of £10 (i.e. for 400 contributions), the actuarial contribution is about one-half of this figure for adults, with proportionately lower amounts for girls and young women. The reason for this is first, that the contributions as paid are assumed to be accumulated at interest ; secondly, that where marriage is deferred beyond about age 25, the maximum having been reached, no further accretions occur ; and thirdly, that if a woman never marries her contributions enure to those who do.

26. *Funeral Grant.*—This is a universal benefit. The finance of the scheme provides that a contribution towards its cost shall be part of the Social Security contribution wherever payable. For the full benefit of £20 in respect of the death of an adult at any age over 21 (£15 in case of death between 16 and 21) the equivalent contributions payable from age 16 to 65 (60 for a woman) under the conditions appropriate to Class I would be 1·1d. a week both for a man and for a woman, assuming that the two-thirds rate was payable to age 18 and five-sixths rate to 21. The premiums for men and women are about equal because the effect of their cessation five years earlier in the case of women is, roughly, offset by the lighter mortality of the sex.

The figure of 1·1d. has been taken as the appropriate contribution for women, but for men an addition is necessary (i) to make good the deficiency due to non-payment of contributions by housewives who are not gainfully occupied, or otherwise claim exemption, and (ii) to meet the liability in respect of the grants payable at reduced rates on the deaths of dependent children. Allowance for these liabilities raises the actuarial contribution for men to 1·8d. a week.

These, it may be noted, are net rates of contribution, which—like all the actuarial contributions quoted in this memorandum—do not include any provision for expenses. Further they are related to the full cost, there being no Exchequer subsidy towards this benefit in the case of new entrants. This does not mean that the Exchequer is free of any charge for the funeral grant ; on the contrary, a deficiency of substantial amount will fall upon the Exchequer since the present value of funeral grants for persons of all ages between 16 and 60 (and for their dependent children) brought in at the outset is substantially larger than the present value of the contributions they will pay. It is estimated that the amount of this initial deficiency, expressed as a capital sum, is about £150 millions ; it will, however, emerge gradually over a long period.

27. *Unemployment Benefit.*—The principle of an actuarial contribution at age 16 related to the prospective future liability is not appropriate to this benefit. As a corollary, it cannot be said that an Exchequer liability arises on account of new classes of persons brought into unemployment insurance because of an absence of reserves which should have been accumulated from contributions in the past. The contribution is in fact obtained by averaging the estimated annual cost of the benefit over all contributors insured for it, i.e., all persons in Class I, without regard to the effect of any tendency of the risk to increase with age or to the relative amounts of unemployment for which benefit is drawn by the two sexes. In this process allowance is made for the following considerations, viz. (i) that, as in the existing system, the Exchequer is assumed to bear one-third of the cost, (ii) that an appropriate relationship is fixed between the rates to be charged to men and women, and (iii) that reduced contributions are payable under age 21.

28. The estimate of the cost of unemployment benefit depends upon two factors, namely the average proportion of the insured population who are out of work and the proportion of these who qualify for benefit. As regards the first, which is highly speculative, assumption (C) of the three basic assumptions underlying the Social Security Plan, i.e. the exercise of the full powers of the State to maintain employment, implies that long-term unemployment would be reduced to a negligible amount. I have consulted Sir William Beveridge on this, and he is of opinion that it would be reasonable, in the circumstances which he envisages in the Report, to contemplate an average rate of unemployment of the order of 10 per cent. among the industries at present covered by the General Scheme of Unemployment Insurance. Merging with these rates the lighter risks of persons now insured under the Agricultural Scheme, and

including also private domestic servants and the other classes coming within Class I who are at present excepted from insurance against unemployment (railwaymen, central and local government officials, etc.), the average rate for the whole population paying contributions under Class I has been taken at 8½ per cent.

The proportion of the unemployed who would qualify for benefit under the new conditions cannot be estimated from past experience, for the new benefit is to continue without limit during unemployment (subject to the fulfilment of appropriate conditions) whereas at present insurance benefit is normally terminated after about 26 weeks and thereafter recourse has to be had to Unemployment Assistance. Broadly speaking, under the new Plan all unemployed persons will be able to obtain insurance benefit except for a very small group, mainly composed of persons incurring odd days of unemployment (not linked up) or otherwise serving waiting days, and persons in course of transfer away from employee occupations. I have accordingly assumed that 95 per cent. of unemployment will rank for benefit, making due allowance for the changed arrangements relating to waiting time.

29. The fixing of the relative contributions of men and of women is a matter of some difficulty. The woman's contribution has, in the past, been only a few pence below the man's rate, reflecting perhaps the difference between their nominal benefit levels but not the difference between the effective levels if benefits for dependants are averaged over the class of insured persons—men or women—in respect of which they arise. The difference in contribution rates according to the basis adopted is of course considerable; moreover, it is widened if account is taken of the rate of benefit for married women, which is to be appreciably lower than that for single women, thus depressing the women's average. Taking into account allowances for wives and adult dependants, the average rate of benefit payable under the Plan to an adult man is estimated at 32/10 a week. For adult women the average rate is estimated at 21/8, taking due proportions of single women and married women claimants at their respective benefit rates and giving effect to the assumption that one-half of gainfully employed housewives will secure exemption from contributions under Class I and thus from insurance against unemployment.

I think a fair allocation of the cost as between men and women is to be obtained by fixing their respective contribution rates in proportion to these average benefit rates. On this basis the appropriate contributions for unemployment benefit are estimated at 24·8d. a week for men and 16·4d. for women, reducible below age 21 as proposed. These rates leave one-third of the cost of the benefit to be met from the Exchequer.

30. *Industrial Disability Benefit (and Pension)*.—The cost of these benefits and the proposed methods of financing them are discussed in a separate section of this memorandum (paras. 36 to 46). It will be seen that, apart from the portion of the total cost to be defrayed by a special levy on the hazardous industries, the full cost is represented by weekly contributions of 3·3d. for an adult man and 2·2d. for an adult woman (with proportionately lower sums for persons under age 21). These sums are estimated to cover the liability for non-hazardous industries together with a share (one-third) of the excess cost in hazardous industries, the balance thereof being met by a special levy on the employers in those industries. Deducting the proposed Exchequer grant of one-sixth of the above contributions, the net sums to be included in the Social Insurance contributions for Class I are thus 2·8d. and 1·8d. respectively for adult men and women, divisible between the workers and their employers.

31. *Expenses of Administration*.—All the contributions given in the preceding paragraphs are net, that is to say, they have not been loaded to

include an allowance for the related expenses of administration. This subject is discussed later, in para. 70, where it is estimated that an aggregate sum of £18 millions a year would be required for the administration of Social Insurance benefits and grants. It has been assumed that the Exchequer would discharge one-third of these expenses in so far as they relate to unemployment benefit and one-sixth in so far as they relate to other benefits. The balance of the cost, if spread evenly over the contributions of men and women, is equivalent to a contribution of 3·6d. a week (reducible under age 21).

32. *Division of the Contribution between Insured Persons and Employers.*— Before summarising the foregoing results it is necessary to discuss the principle on which the contribution for persons in Class I is to be allocated between the insured person and the employer. In the existing schemes of Contributory Pensions, Health Insurance and Unemployment Insurance the joint contribution is shared equally between the two except where, for convenience in the division of a penny, the contribution of one party has been made ½d. or 1d. greater than that of the other. Following this precedent the contributions under the Social Security Plan, so far as they relate to retirement pensions, widows' benefits, unemployment benefit and disability benefit, are assumed to be shared equally between the insured person and the employer, and the same division has been made in the case of the contribution for the industrial disability benefit—in so far as this is met by contributions and not by levy— and for the weekly maternity benefit. The lump sum maternity grant is in a somewhat different category and the small contribution in respect of this benefit has been placed upon the insured person. The marriage grant, again, and the funeral grant are thought to be benefits for which the employer should not be asked to take any financial responsibility and the contributions for these have been placed upon the insured person. Finally, the contribution to cover cost of administration is divided equally between the two parties.

SUMMARY OF CONTRIBUTION RATES

33. The constitution of the actuarial contribution appropriate to Class I for the Social Insurance benefits, and its division between the three parties concerned, the insured person, the employer and the State, may now be set out (*see* table on page 188). The contributions shown are those payable from age 21 on the assumption that from age 16 to 18 two-thirds of these rates are paid and from age 18 to 21 five-sixths of the rates. Allowance is made for the conditions for payment of contribution in Class I in regard to excusal of contributions in periods of disability and unemployment.

It is important to note that, although the Exchequer's share of the actuarial contribution is shown in the table as an addition to the contributions, this is probably not the procedure which would be adopted in practice. The Exchequer subsidy would presumably be an annual payment—probably fixed, periodically, for a span of years—related to the emerging expenditure and would comprise in principle (i) the equivalent of the various proportions (one-sixth, etc.) of the cost in respect of all insured persons plus (ii) the further sum required in respect of the additional liability, already mentioned in para. 8, in respect of those coming into the new scheme at ages above the minimum entry age.

34. The rates of contribution proposed to be paid for all classes include a contribution towards the cost of health services, viz., 10d. for an adult man and 8d. for an adult woman, with reduced sums of 8d. for a young man aged between 18 and 21 and 6d. for young persons aged between 16 and 18 and young women aged between 18 and 21. In all these contributions the employer's share has been taken as 1½d., this being approximately the contribution which employers now pay towards the medical benefit of their employees

RATES OF CONTRIBUTION IN PENCE PER WEEK FOR AN ADULT IN CLASS 1 (*see* para. 33)

	Full Actuarial Contribution	Share of		
		Insured Person	Employer	Exchequer
MEN				
Retirement Pensions	35·1	14·7	14·6	5·8 (1/6th)
Widow's and Guardian Benefits...	4·1	1·7	1·7	·7 (1/6th)
Unemployment Benefit	37·2	12.4	12·4	12·4 (1/3rd)
Disability Benefit	15·5	6·4	6·5	2·6 (1/6th)
Industrial Disability Benefits ...	3·3	1·4	1·4	·5 (1/6th)
Maternity Grant and Benefit ...	1·3	1·1	—	·2 (1/6th)
Marriage Grant	—	—	—	—
Funeral Grant	1·8	1·8	—	—
Cost of Administration	4·9	1·8	1·8	1·3*
Total for Social Insurance Benefits ...	103·2	41·3	38·4	23·5
WOMEN				
Retirement Pensions	31·8	13·3	13·2	5·3 (1/6th)
Widow's and Guardian Benefits...	—	—	—	—
Unemployment Benefit	24·6	8·2	8·2	8·2 (1/3rd)
Disability Benefit	12·2	5·1	5·1	2·0 (1/6th)
Industrial Disability Benefits ...	2·2	·9	·9	·4 (1/6th)
Maternity Grant and Benefit ...	2·0	·9	·8	·3 (1/6th)
Marriage Grant	2·8	2·8	—	—
Funeral Grant	1·1	1·1	—	—
Cost of Administration	4·9	1·8	1·8°	1·3*
Total for Social Insurance Benefits ...	81·6	34·1	30·0	17·5

* The Exchequer share of cost of administration is taken at one-third for unemployment benefit and one-sixth for other benefits.

under the present National Health Insurance scheme. For Class I, therefore, the make-up of the contributions (for adults) of 7/6 (men) and 6/– (women) is as follows :—

ALLOCATION OF CLASS I RATES OF CONTRIBUTION (ADULTS), IN PENCE PER WEEK, BETWEEN INSURED PERSON AND EMPLOYER

	MEN			WOMEN		
	Insured Person	Employer	Total	Insured Person	Employer	Total
Contribution :						
(1) for Social Insurance Benefits... ...	41·3	38·4	79·7	34·1	30·0	64·1
(2) towards Health Services ...	8·5	1·5	10·0	6·5	1·5	8·0
Margin	+1·2	−0·9	+0·3	+1·4	− 1·5	−0·1
Contribution proposed to be charged ...	51·0	39·0	90·0	42·0	30·0	72·0

It will be seen from the above that the actuarial contributions for the benefits, together with the sums proposed to be taken for health services, absorb, with little or no margin, the proposed contributions of 7/6 and 6/– and that the allocation between insured person and employer does not diverge materially from the results obtained on the principles envisaged in the Report.

35. *Contributions for Classes II and IV.*—Rates of contribution for Classes II. and IV have been computed on similar principles, allowing for the more limited benefits for which these classes are to be insured, and assuming that they receive the same Exchequer subsidy as Class I for each benefit. A small sum has been included in the contributions for these classes in respect of the training benefit available to them in lieu of unemployment benefit. It should be borne in mind that the disability benefit for Class II, unlike that for Class I, is payable only after disability has lasted for 13 weeks. These contributions take account of the slightly different conditions for payment of contributions, as set out below :—

Class I.—Contributions are excused during unemployment or disability (including industrial disability) and, in the case of a woman, during payment of the weekly maternity benefit.

Class II.—Contributions are excused during disability after the first 13 weeks of an attack and, in the case of a woman, during payment of the weekly maternity benefit.

Class IV.—Contributions are payable without any excusal, except, in the case of a woman, during receipt of widow's or guardian benefit.

The actuarial contributions for the three classes, payable under these conditions, are given in the statement below, which also shows the amounts of the reduced contributions for persons under 21 and the margins in the contribution proposed to be charged in each case.

RATES OF CONTRIBUTION, IN PENCE PER WEEK, FOR JUVENILES, YOUNG PERSONS AND ADULTS, IN CLASSES I, II AND IV

	MEN			WOMEN		
	Under 18	Between 18 & 21	21 and over	Under 18	Between 18 & 21	21 and over
Class I :						
For Benefits and administration ...	53·1	66·4	79·7	42·7	53·4	64·1
Towards Health Services	6·0	8·0	10·0	6·0	6·0	8·0
Margin	+0·9	+0·6	+0·3	—0·7	+0·6	—0·1
Contribution to be charged	60·0 (5/–)	75·0 (6/3)	90·0 (7/6)	48·0 (4/–)	60·0 (5/–)	72·0 (6/–)
Class II :						
For Benefits and administration ...	27·0	33·7	40·5	24·7	30·9	37·1
Towards Health Services	6·0	8·0	10·0	6·0	6·0	8·0
Margin	—9·0	+0·3	+0·5	—6·7	—0·9	—0·1
Contribution to be charged	24·0 (2/–)	42·0 (3/6)	51·0 (4/3)	24·0 (2/–)	36·0 (3/–)	45·0 (3/9)
Class IV :						
For Benefits and administration ...	22·5	28·1	33·7	17·9	22·3	26·8
Towards Health Services	6·0	8·0	10·0	6·0	6·0	8·0
Margin	—10·5	—0·1	+1·3	—5·9	+1·7	+1·2
Contribution to be charged	18·0 (1/6)	36·0 (3/–)	45·0 (3/9)	18·0 (1/6)	30·0 (2/6)	36·0 (3/–)

This statement shows that for Classes II and IV, as for Class I, the contributions proposed to be charged correspond closely to the appropriate actuarial contributions, together with the suggested contributions towards health services, except in the case of persons under age 18. For the latter, substantial deficiencies are shown, but the special circumstances of juveniles in Classes II and IV appear to call for nominal rates of contribution, viz. 2/– in Class II and 1/6 in Class IV.

INDUSTRIAL DISABILITY

36. The principal proposals in regard to industrial compensation are as follows :—

(i) During the first 13 weeks of disability due to industrial accident or disease payments to be made at the ordinary rates of disability benefit (single or joint according to the injured person's status).

(ii) If incapacity continues beyond this period disability benefit to be replaced by an industrial pension payable so long as disability continues. The amount of this pension to be two-thirds of the earnings of the workman when in full employment, subject to a maximum of £3 and to a minimum of the ordinary rate of disability benefit, or, in cases of partial disability, a reduced pension proportionate to the estimated loss of earning power.

(iii) In the case of fatal injuries :—

(a) the ordinary funeral grant and widow's or guardian benefit to be payable, and in addition,

(b) a lump sum grant in respect of a widow or other person wholly or mainly dependent on the deceased workman.

(iv) Certain industries to be scheduled as hazardous, and two-thirds of the excess cost of compensation in each such industry over the level of the other (non-hazardous) industries to be met by the employers concerned, the remaining third being shared by employees, all employers and the State. The three parties will thus pay for compensation at the non-hazardous level and also for a share of the excess cost in hazardous industries, while the employers in each such industry will be liable also for the balance of the cost of compensation for their own industry.

In the following paragraphs I examine the financial implications of these proposals in the following order :—

(a) the estimated gross cost arising under (i), (ii), (iii) (b), for all industries together—the funeral grant and widows' and guardian benefits under (iii) (a) are assumed to be covered by the ordinary contributions for these services ;

(b) the division of industries between hazardous and non-hazardous ;

(c) the cost of compensation, at the non-hazardous level, in all industries taken together ;

(d) the excess cost in hazardous industries ;

(e) the ordinary contribution required to defray (c) and one-third of (d) and the additional contributions required from the employers in the hazardous industries.

In the first instance, the position is examined for a normal year, and the cost of the proposals is compared with that of the existing scheme. Finally, special problems arising in the transition from the old to the new Plan are considered.

37. The estimates which follow are based on the annual statistical reports of the Home Office, being built up on the average for the three years 1936-38, modified to give effect to the substitution of disability benefit at the rates proposed and industrial pensions (assuming rates of wages at about 25 per

cent. in excess of their level in 1938) in place of the rates of compensation payable in the three years 1936–38. Further, it is assumed that before the new scheme is introduced peace-time conditions will have been restored.

The detailed statistics contained in the Home Office reports relate to seven large groups of important industries, viz. mines, quarries, railways, factories, docks, constructional work and shipping. In the three years 1936–38 the average numbers employed in these industries were about 8,000,000 and the total compensation paid was about £6 millions in cases of disablement and about £700,000 in fatal cases. There were 400,000 new cases of disablement (resulting from accidents or disease) each year, representing an annual rate of 5 per cent. of the number of employees. This rate varied considerably in the different industries and ranged from 3½ per cent. in the factories group to over 18 per cent. among miners.

It was estimated that allowing for all other industries and employments not included in these seven large groups but of which no details were available, the total amount spent on compensation (excluding administrative expenses and the profits of insurance companies) was in the region of £10 millions. On this basis, and assuming that 10 per cent. related to fatal cases, the total cost of disablement compensation before the war may be taken as £9 millions, of which the seven large industries accounted for £6 millions and all other industries and employments accounted for the balance of £3 millions.

38. The first important change made by the new scheme is the payment of disability benefit at the ordinary rates for industrial disability of less than 13 weeks' duration in place of compensation based on a proportion of earnings. From the Home Office figures it would appear that of men who are disabled by industrial accident (or disease) about 90 per cent. recover within 13 weeks and that in about 10 per cent. only of the cases will industrial pensions become payable. While the rate of accident varies considerably between one industry and another, the proportion of cases where incapacity continues beyond 13 weeks does not show such wide variations. For example, in the case of the mining industry, the proportion of claims lasting over 13 weeks is about 12 per cent., or 2 per cent. more than the average for all industries for which statistics are available.

The effect of a change in a rate of benefit based on wages depends upon the distribution of the persons affected according to rates of wage. While it is recognised that this distribution may be different in the various industries, it has not been found practicable to give effect to this point, and the estimates of cost have been arrived at on the basis of an estimated distribution of the wage-earning population as a whole.

39. On the foregoing basis I estimate the annual expenditure on weekly allowances to employees incapacitated by industrial accident or disease for all industries together at about £14·2 millions, nearly three-quarters of which is represented by the cost of industrial pensions. The remaining quarter is the cost of disability benefit to persons who draw the full 13 weeks and then qualify for industrial pensions, and to others for shorter periods. Adding £800,000 for lump sum grants in fatal cases, taken at an average of £300 for each fatal accident where a total dependant is left, with proportionately reduced amounts in cases of partial dependency, a total annual expenditure of approximately £15 millions is reached, exclusive of cost of administration and with no allowance for any additional cost due to claims at Common Law.

40. The seven industries covered in the Home Office returns include the majority, but not all, of the notably hazardous industries ; but some of the ten subsidiary groups into which the main factories group is sub-divided show a comparatively light rate of disablement. Among the notably hazardous

industries not included may be mentioned the building industry (some sections of which are understood to be particularly hazardous), agriculture and cartage contracting. For the purpose of the present estimates, in which differentiation between non-hazardous and hazardous industries is required, it has been assumed that all the subsidiaries in the factories group where the claim rate was under $3\frac{1}{2}$ per cent. (and averaged $2\frac{1}{2}$ per cent.), accounting for nearly two-thirds of the total number of employees in that group, may be classed as non-hazardous. On the other hand, it has been assumed that industries which should be classed as hazardous but are not included in the seven groups may comprise some $1\frac{1}{2}$ million employees. The net result is that in the present estimates rather less than one-third of the total number of employees has been assumed to be employed in these industries, with a predominating proportion of men.

41. Apportioning the total cost of £15 millions between the two groups it is estimated that the cost of compensation will be about £5 millions for all the non-hazardous industries taken together and about £10 millions for the hazardous group. It will be observed that although the former industries are taken to cover over two-thirds of the total numbers employed, they account for only one-third of the total cost. In this connection it is to be noted that although the Home Office statistics relating to the seven industries are fairly extensive, no similar details are available regarding the other industries. At the outset the scheduling of industries to be classed as hazardous will present some difficulties and must necessarily be tentative. Moreover, as experience accumulates the constitution of the two groups will no doubt vary, as the relative cost in particular industries improves or deteriorates and, as the case may be, warrants their removal from or their inclusion in the hazardous list.

42. If all employees were in non-hazardous industries I estimate that a total contribution of about $2\frac{1}{2}$d. a week would be required in respect of an adult man and two-thirds of this sum for an adult woman, with proportionately lower contributions in respect of boys and girls under 18 and young persons of 18 but under 21. The produce of these contributions is estimated at about £7·4 millions. The excess cost in respect of the hazardous industries is thus about £7·6 millions. On the assumption that one-third of this excess is pooled among all workers and employers and the State, the ordinary contribution required is accordingly raised to 3·3d. for an adult man and 2·2d. for an adult woman, and the aggregate amount of the additional contributions to be levied on the employers in the hazardous industries is approximately £5 millions. Assuming a State grant of one-sixth, the sum to be included in the Social Insurance contribution for Class I is 2·8d. a week for an adult man, divisible equally between the worker and his employer, with proportionately lower amounts for adult women and for persons under age 21.

43. On this basis the apportionment between the several parties of the total cost of compensation payable throughout industry is as follows :—

Non-hazardous Industries :

	£ millions
Workers' contributions	2·7
Employers' contributions	2·7
Proportionate State grant	1·1
	6·5
Cost of Compensation	4·9
Surplus, i.e. subsidy to hazardous industries	1·6

Hazardous Industries :					£ millions
Workers' contributions					1·4
Employers' contributions (ordinary)				1·4	
(additional)				5·1	
					6·5
Proportionate State grant (ordinary contributions) ...					·6
Surplus from other industries					1·6
Cost of Compensation					10·1

44. The raising of the basic weekly contribution required to provide the benefits in the non-hazardous industries from 2·5d. to 3·3d., in order to subsidise the cost in the hazardous industries to the extent of one-third of the extra charge which otherwise would fall on these industries will have differing effects in the various industries.

The position may be illustrated by the following figures showing the approximate results in the mining industry, which gives rise to relatively the heaviest charge.

					£ millions
Workers' contributions					·2
Employers' contributions (ordinary)				·2	
(additional)				2·7	
					2·9
Subsidy from other industries and the State					1·3
Cost of Compensation					4·4

45. As indicated above, of the total annual compensation under the proposals, viz., £15 millions, as estimated, the workers will pay £4·1 millions, employers £9·2 millions and the State £1·7 millions. In comparing this with the present scheme I have brought into account the expected expenditure under the Workmen's Compensation Acts in force before the war as extended by the Act passed in 1940. Under that Act, in general, the compensation to a totally disabled workman was increased by 5/- a week, and weekly allowances were provided in respect of the workman's children while under age 15. Further, by the Act of 1941, the scope of liability was extended to include non-manual workers up to a remuneration limit of £420, instead of £350.

For a normal year the expenditure of the pre-war scheme as enlarged by these amending Acts may be put at about £12½ millions, of which probably over half a million pounds is in respect of the children of disabled workers and the orphan children left after fatal accidents. The cost, on the present scales, exclusive of provision in respect of children, who will in future be provided for under the proposed national scheme of allowances for children, is thus about £12 millions for compensation. The average annual cost of compensation in 1936–38 was about £10 millions. The enlargement under the present proposals is thus about £5 millions above the pre-war level, of which about two-fifths has already been granted by virtue of war-time legislation.

46. At the commencement of the new scheme the employers will have incurred liabilities in respect of accidents which had occurred previously and they (or their insurers) will have set aside reserves to meet outstanding claims to the injured men. These, however, will be on the basis of the existing law and if the compensation rates for current claims are increased to the new scales of industrial pension (after 13 weeks of disability), the cost of this concession has to be provided for. The additional sum required may be computed very roughly at about £2 millions in 1945, diminishing gradually thereafter as these claims terminate, and when the scheme is worked out in

detail it will be necessary to decide what part of these transitional liabilities should be borne by the Social Insurance Fund and what part by way of additional charge on employers. Hitherto industry has normally made provision in each year for the capital cost of the accidents arising in that year, but in future it will probably be thought appropriate for the Social Insurance Fund to collect sufficient income for the actual expenditure of the year. It would seem likely, therefore, that the strain due to the concessions given to existing cases can be met without material adjustment of the balance of charge as it will ultimately be when the new scheme has reached maturity.

Classification of the Population under the Plan

47. In the middle of the year 1944 (taken as the date of commencement of the Plan) the population of Great Britain, making no allowance for future war deaths—a factor which cannot be assessed—is estimated at about 47 millions. Making the necessary assumption that, when the scheme starts, peace-time conditions will have been restored to the extent of a more or less normal division of the population by occupational status, the estimated population may be allocated as follows to the six " security classes " of the Plan :—

Class	Numbers in thou ands		
	Men	Women	Total
I. Employed persons...	13,350	4,750	18,100
II. Others gainfully occupied ...	2,150	450	2,600
III. Housewives, including those gain- fully occupied	—	9,450	9,450
IV. Other persons of working age ...	1,000	1,300	2,300
V. Children under 15, or 15–16 at school	5,000	4,800	9,800
VI. Persons above working age who have retired	1,200	3,550	4,750
	22,700	24,300	47,000

48. This division is based upon the application of 1931 Census occupational data to the estimated population in age groups at mid-1944, with an adjustment for assumed changes since 1931 in the proportions of the population who follow a gainful occupation and in the relative proportions of employers, employees and persons working on their own account. The adjustment can only be made on very broad lines, since the Census information is more than ten years old, but regard has been had to the indications afforded by National Health and Unemployment Insurance data.

No attempt has been made to allow for changes during the war such as the increase in the size of the Armed Forces, the increase in the proportion of the population of working age who are following a gainful occupation and the change to paid employment from other gainful occupations—in particular, the marked increase in the employment of women (especially married women). These changes, it may be expected, will be in a large measure temporary ; in any event it would seem inappropriate for the present purpose to attempt to measure what changes in the peace-time occupational constitution of the population, as compared with the pre-war position, will result from the war. It is to be noted, further, that :—

(i) the numbers employed or otherwise gainfully occupied are prior to adjustment for the estimated effect of the grant of pensions conditional on retirement ;

(ii) the numbers shown in Class I include those pensioners under the existing scheme who are at work ;

(iii) all gainfully occupied housewives, of whatever age, are included under Class III ;

(iv) Class V includes all under age 15, on the assumption that the minimum school-leaving age will have been raised to 15. Children aged between 15 and 16 who have left school are included, not in Class V, but in the appropriate one of Class I, II or IV—those over 16 in full-time education being included in Class IV ;

(v) blind and crippled persons and invalids, if under pension age, are included in Class IV ;

(vi) the numbers in Class I include, in respect of the Armed Forces, an assumed peace-time strength of 500,000 men ; as indicated in the Report, special arrangements will be made for these, and suitable allowance is made in the estimates for the fact that, while serving, their contributions will presumably be fixed in relation to their pro-spective benefits after discharge only.

49. It is of interest to make a rough comparison of the above estimates of the numbers of contributors to be insured for pensions (Classes I, II, III and IV), disability (Classes I, II and III) and unemployment (Classes I and III) with the corresponding numbers under the existing system. For this purpose it is necessary to make various adjustments to the existing data of insured persons.

Under current conditions as to insurability, and with the present school-leaving age of 14, out of 47 millions population of Great Britain, as estimated at mid-1944, about 19·9 millions would, on a peace-time basis, be insured between the ages of 16 and 65 (60 for women) under the existing Health and Pensions schemes and ·9 millions aged between 14 and 16 would be insured for medical benefit only. Of the numbers counted as insured, however, about ·9 millions normally consist of persons who, having ceased to be insurably employed, would be in process of passing out of insurance ; further, probably about ·3 millions would have become permanently incapable of work on account of accident or disease. Thus, the net number of contributors for pensions, subject to temporary abstention due to sickness or unemployment, may be put at 18·7 millions above age 16.

Not all of these persons will come within the new Class I. The numbers include about ·8 millions of voluntary contributors, who, though they were at one time employed persons, may now belong to any one of the three Classes I, II or IV. On the other hand, they do not include some ·3 millions of persons, coming within Class I, II or IV, who are insured for pensions only under the Special Voluntary Contributors scheme established in 1938 for the purpose of making pension provision for persons of small income not eligible for insur-ance as employed or voluntary contributors under the main Contributory Pensions scheme.

50. It will be evident that the differences in categorisation between the existing and the proposed schemes are such as to make a precise analysis of the position for each class impossible. Broadly, however, it may be said that the effect of the proposals, as estimated, will be to increase the numbers of potential contributors under one head or another between the ages of 16 and 65 (60 for women) as follows :—

For pensions :   from 19 millions to 22½ millions.
For disability benefits :   „   18¼ „   „ 20¾   „
For unemployment benefits :   „   15½ „   „ 18¼   „

In this statement, in order to obtain the maximum degree of comparability, juvenile contributors aged 14–16 under the existing scheme are excluded ; persons in the Armed Forces are included in both series of numbers ; and persons at work over age 65 (60 for women) are excluded in both series. Also, persons in Classes II and IV who are over 55 (50 for women) at the beginning of the new scheme, persons in Classes II and IV with incomes under £75 a year, and gainfully occupied married women—all of whom have certain options to be exempt from contributions under the new scheme—are included in the numbers, although in considering the probable number of actual contributors a reduction should be made for these classes.

ESTIMATED EXPENDITURE UNDER THE PLAN

51.   The annual expenditure under the Plan has been estimated for three individual calendar years, viz., 1945, 1955 and 1965.   An assumption has to be made regarding the actual date of commencement of the Plan since this affects not only the date when the necessary qualifying contributions' for disability, unemployment and other benefits will have been paid by persons newly brought into insurance for these benefits but also the number of contributions paid, and hence the rate of pension granted, in the case of persons in the new classes retiring and claiming pension during the transitional period. For this purpose July, 1944, has been taken as the commencing date.

Even by 1965 the expenditure in respect of retirement pensions will not have reached its full magnitude owing to the operation of the transitional arrangements (*see* para. 5)—quite apart from the effect of increasing numbers of the aged population.   In other respects, however, 1955 and 1965 will include a full year's expenditure, and 1945 will be deficient only to the extent that persons not previously insured will not have qualified for benefit in respect of prolonged disability, because they will not have been able to pay three years' contributions as required by the Plan.

52.   The expenditure on benefits under each head, in respect of the estimated population covered for the particular benefit, has been computed on the same actuarial basis as that adopted in calculating the contributions and described in the relevant sections of this memorandum.   The only matters which require special comment here are the probable effects on the cost of retirement pensions of (i) the operation of the transitional arrangements and (ii) the provision for increasing the rate of pension by postponement of retirement.

53.   *Retirement Pensions : Transitional Arrangements.*—As will be evident from the description of the transitional arrangements and the addition to pension on account of postponement given in para. 5, it is necessary, in obtaining the cost of pensions in the first 20 years of the Plan, to divide the pensionable population (making appropriate deduction for those persons of pension age who have not yet retired and claimed pension) according as they would or would not be qualified for pension under the present Contributory Pensions scheme.   For those who are so qualified the pensions cost is estimated by applying to the numbers surviving in each of the three years of estimate the basic rate of pension appropriate to that year plus an addition for the effect of postponement on the pension rate.   For those who have not qualified for contributory pension, the population of pensionable age in the year of estimate has to be considered separately according to year of retirement and appropriate pension rates applicable to that year, together with an allowance for the effect of postponement, since a pension once granted is not subsequently increased.

Although by 1964–65 the rate of pension granted to new pensioners will have reached the final rate, the average pension for all pensioners then existing will not have reached this level, since those persons among the pensioner population who were not previously insured for contributory pensions will not have had their pensions increased year by year but will retain the fixed reduced rate awarded at the time of their retirement.   The saving in pensions on this account in 1965 is not substantial in relation to the total charge, amounting to about £15 millions on a total pensions charge of £300 millions (*see* table on page 199).

The Report makes an alternative suggestion regarding the grant of pension to persons in the existing Contributory Pensions scheme who retire before the end of the transition period.   Under this proposal such persons would retain the reduced rate awarded at the time of retirement without the subsequent biennial increases provided for under the Plan (*see* first part of the table in para. 5 above). Thus, a pensioner who retired in the first year of the Plan, or had retired previously, would receive a joint pension of 25/- or a single pension of 14/-, which would remain unaltered. Under this arrangement there would be no saving at the outset, but by 1965 there would be a net saving of £30 millions, allowing for the cost of additional assistance, on the total pensions charge of £300 millions.

54. *Retirement Condition.*—The effect of postponement of pension on account of a retirement condition is to reduce the number of incumbent pensioners, but to increase the average rate of pension for the reduced numbers. Its effect on the number of pensioners has been assessed as follows on the basis of the somewhat inconclusive statistics which are available. On the one hand, the Census figures are over ten years old and, moreover, in these the number of aged persons described as still gainfully occupied is probably overstated owing to misdescription. On the other hand, the statistics relating to the number of persons at work deduced from the surrender of stamped insurance cards may be expected to understate the position, owing to the possible failure, in some cases, of the employer to affix stamps on the special card for this class, or of the employee to surrender his card. It would appear, however, that prior to the war about 55 per cent. of men in receipt of contributory pensions remained at work on reaching age 65, and the percentage declined gradually with advancing age until by age 75 there were only about 12½ per cent. still at work. Under the conditions proposed in the Report, a man will be able to retire more readily, since his pension will be much more substantial than at present, especially in the case of the man aged 65 with a wife aged under 60—and he cannot obtain his pension without retiring. But there is the inducement to continue at work provided by the bonus for postponement of retirement. On balance it appears to me likely that in the case of employed persons the tendency to retire will be somewhat stronger than under the present scheme. Accordingly I have assumed for the purpose of the estimates that in the case of Class I, 50 per cent. of both men and women will give up work immediately after reaching pensionable age (65 for men and 60 for women), that a further 25 per cent. will retire during the ensuing five years, and that the balance of 25 per cent. will have ceased work by age 75 (men) or 70 (women). For gainfully occupied persons who do not work for an employer the position is rather different, and it has been thought not unreasonable to assume that, apart from breakdown in health, both men and women will continue in their occupation for five years after reaching the minimum pensionable age.

The net effect on current expenditure, setting off the saving due to withholding the pension until retirement against the additions granted on account of postponement, is a saving in the pensions charge of the order of £5 millions at the outset, increasing gradually as the scheme becomes more mature. By 1965 it is estimated that the net saving on this account will amount to about £30 millions a year.

55. *Treatment of Existing Beneficiaries.*—There will at the outset of the scheme be a substantial number of beneficiaries of a more or less permanent status under the existing schemes of Health and Pensions Insurance for whom definite benefit conditions under the new scheme must be laid down. Similar cases arise in respect of unemployment and short-term sickness, but these do not present the same problems. The general assumptions made for the purpose of estimating cost are as follows :—

Contributory age pensioners : Their pensions will be continued at the present rates if they are at work. If they have retired, or retire in future, they will receive the appropriate rate of retirement pension. Contributory widow pensioners over age 60 come into this category.

Means pensioners : Their pensions will be continued as such or as assistance pensions, and in either case will be accounted for under national assistance.

Widow pensioners (under age 60) : Their pensions will be continued at the present rate to age 60 unless they are qualified for the higher rates of benefit under the new proposals for widow's and guardian benefits. It is assumed that after age 60 they will come within the scope and the conditions of retirement pensions.

Disability benefits : Existing beneficiaries will have their present benefits raised to the higher levels proposed in the Plan ; for an alternative method of treatment see next paragraph.

56. *Alternative Transitional Plan for Disability Benefit.*—The estimates of cost of disability benefit given in this memorandum are based on the assumption that persons who were in receipt of sickness or disablement benefit at the beginning of the new scheme will, like those who claim these benefits later, be granted the new disability benefit at the full basic rate (40/- for a married man, 24/- for a single man or woman). Under an alternative plan, referred to in the Report, transitional arrangements similar to those suggested for retirement pensions might be made under which, in cases of prolonged or permanent disability, the full rate would not be granted unless the person had fulfilled new qualifying conditions by payment of contributions under the scheme. Disabled persons who did not satisfy the prescribed conditions would receive benefit at a rate equal to the current pension rate, i.e. starting at 25/- for a married man in 1944 and rising biennially as is proposed for pensions.

The saving in the first year due to this limitation, on the assumption that it starts six months after the beginning of illness, may be put at about £10 millions on the total cost of £57 millions for disability benefit (*see* table on page 199). In subsequent years the savings would gradually drop from the initial figure, the further savings due to new cases where the qualifying conditions had not been fulfilled being less than the gradual diminution of the saving on initial cases as a result of deaths and recoveries among them. There would, however, be some set-off to these savings in respect of national assistance for those who needed supplementation.

SUMMARY OF EXPENDITURE

57. In the following statement (*see* page 199) I have brought together the estimated annual expenditure on the various Social Insurance benefits, and in order to show the total expenditure in the proposed Social Security Budget I have added the sums payable in respect of national assistance, children's allowances and health services. For a description of these three items, and comment on the trend of their cost, see paras. 59 to 68 below.

58. It will be seen that the total expenditure starts at £697 millions in 1945 and rises to £764 millions in 1955 and £858 millions in 1965, i.e. an increase of £67 millions (or 10 per cent.) in the first ten years and £94 millions (or 12 per cent.) in the next ten years. These increases are more than accounted for by the expansion of Social Insurance benefits, the cost of which, starting at £367 millions, rises by £75 millions (or 20 per cent.) in the first ten years and £111 millions (or 25 per cent.) in the next ten years. The increase in the first ten years is due in part to the fact that the full cost of disability benefit will not be experienced in 1945 (*see* para. 51). The main cause of increase, however, is the rising cost of retirement pensions, due partly to the natural increase in the number of pensioners, partly to the inclusion of persons in Classes II and IV from mid-1954 and partly to the rise in the rate of transitional pensions —the transitional arrangements having by that time run through half their period. In the ten years from 1955 to 1965 the increase in cost is almost

SOCIAL SECURITY BUDGET : ESTIMATED EXPENDITURE (*see* para. 57)

	1945 £millions	1955 £millions	1965 £millions
SOCIAL INSURANCE BENEFITS.			
Retirement Pensions	126	190	300
Widow's and Guardian Benefits	29	26	21
Unemployment Benefit	110	109	107
Disability Benefit	57	68	71
Industrial Disability Benefits	15	15	15
Maternity Grant and Benefit	7	6	6
Marriage Grant	1	3	3
Funeral Grant	4	7	12
Cost of Administration	18	18	18
Total for Social Insurance Benefits	367	442	553
NATIONAL ASSISTANCE.			
Assistance Pensions	39	33	25
Other Assistance	5	5	5
Cost of Administration	3	3	2
Total for National Assistance	47	41	32
CHILDREN'S ALLOWANCES.			
Allowances	110	108	100
Cost of Administration	3	3	3
Total for Children's Allowances	113	111	103
HEALTH SERVICES.	170	170	170
Total Expenditure	697	764	858

entirely due to retirement pensions, the main reasons being the same as those which operate in the first ten years of the scheme.

The variations in the cost of the other Social Insurance benefits are not important. They reflect, for the most part, changes in the size of the population eligible for the particular benefit. There is, however, a rise, throughout the period, in the cost of the funeral grant which deserves comment ; this is due to the fact that persons aged over 60 at the beginning of the scheme are to be excluded from this benefit, thus involving a gradually increasing expenditure on funeral grant.

NATIONAL ASSISTANCE

59. As indicated in para. 6, the Report envisages that the Social Insurance provisions of the Plan will, even when fully mature, require to be supplemented by assistance, since (i) even in respect of pensions, for which the widest coverage is provided, the Plan does not provide a universal benefit, but contemplates that certain individuals and classes of persons will not have paid the necessary insurance contributions, and (ii) the subsistence benefits provided will not cover entirely a marginal group of persons with abnormal needs. The sums required for this purpose will be provided entirely from the Exchequer. It is assumed that the scales of supplementary pensions and assistance now (November, 1942) in operation will continue in force.

The cost of assistance pensions has been estimated to fall from £39 millions in the first year to a figure of £25 millions, necessarily very speculative, in 1965, and it may be expected to show a further substantial decline in the following ten years. Nevertheless there will probably always be a not insignificant charge under this head, as is indicated by the following analysis of the position.

At the outset expenditure for assistance arises from two main classes of approximately equal size, viz. :—

(i) Pensions (at 10/–) of existing means pensioners, plus cost of supplementation in a little over one-half of the cases.

(ii) Cost of supplementation of the retirement pensions (at new rates) of those existing and new contributory pensioners who require supplementation of the reduced transitional pensions up to the level on which, at present, the grant of supplementary pensions is based.

These classes will have fallen to very small proportions by 1965, the first by death of the pensioners, the second by increase of their pensions to the full basic scales. But there are two other classes of importance, viz. :—

(iii) Cost of assistance pensions to persons in Class II or IV who, being aged between 55 (50 for women) and 70 at the outset, elect not to pay contributions, but require assistance at the beginning of the scheme or, later, on attaining age 65 (60 for women).

This class are, in type, successors of the existing means pensioners and include some who have recourse to public assistance pending attainment of age 70. Their cost is not inappreciable in 1945, owing to the substitution of national assistance for public assistance ; it rises considerably to 1955 when it accounts for about one-half of the total for assistance pensions, the persons concerned being then mostly aged over 70 (65) and having left work ; and it then declines, as the group is reduced by death, until in 1965 it accounts for about one-fourth of the total.

(iv) Cost of assistance pensions to other persons who, whilst in Class II or IV, elect not to contribute on grounds of insufficiency of income and on attaining age 65 (60) require full or partial assistance pensions.

This is a permanent class, resulting from the option given to persons of limited income in Classes II and IV to obtain exemption from payment of insurance contributions. It will probably be made up to a large extent of women (a) who never take up a paid employment but live, usually, with relatives and may thus never pay any insurance contributions, or (b) who return home, or to a relative, after one or more spells of employment not sufficient to build up a substantial insurance qualification. In addition there are among those who follow a gainful occupation and are included in Class II, many, both men and women, whose incomes will be such as to enable them to obtain exemption, either occasionally or regularly, if they so desire, e.g. small-holders, crofters, hawkers, seamstresses, outworkers and other casual workers. The financial effect of these mixed categories can only be conjectured on broad lines, but it is thought that it might account, financially, for the equivalent of some 15,000 new cases of full assistance pensions each year. On this basis the cost of the group rises gradually to a round £15 millions in 1965.

The balance of the cost of assistance pensions after allowing for these four classes is due to minor items, such as the cost of supplementing the pensions of persons with abnormal needs.

The figure of £5 millions for " Other Assistance " is a token figure covering a number of categories of persons under pensionable age requiring assistance. There are no means of assessing the probable cost with any precision.

60. As already indicated, the estimate of the cost of national assistance when the scheme has become mature must necessarily be speculative, depending as it does not only on the income distribution of substantial classes of the population but also on the attractiveness, to those with limited incomes who do not work for an employer, of the option not to contribute under the Plan, at the price of forgoing pension as of right (and, for Class II, disability benefits) but not the health services or assistance benefits. If the numbers claiming exemption were substantially smaller than I have assumed there would be a transfer of cost from national assistance to Social Insurance benefits, bearing in mind that the persons covered belong to the poorer classes and will, largely, qualify for full assistance. On the other hand there would be an addition, of much smaller amount, to the contribution income of the scheme : the aggregate Exchequer liability would not, therefore, be very materially diminished as a result of the smaller numbers obtaining exemption.

HEALTH AND REHABILITATION SERVICES

61. The second of the three assumptions stated in the Report to be essential to the institution of the Plan of Social Security is :—

(B) Comprehensive health and rehabilitation services for prevention and cure of disease and restoration of capacity for work, available to all members of the community.

The general principles underlying this assumption are given in Part VI of the Report, but it is there indicated that most of the problems of organisation in such a service fall outside the scope of the Report. The cost of such a comprehensive scheme clearly cannot be estimated with precision until the proposals have taken more definite shape. It is proposed that the cost should be defrayed out of public funds, subject to a substantial grant-in-aid from the Social Insurance Fund.

62. As indicated in para. 34, the sum available for allocation out of the contributions at the rates proposed is 10d. a week for each adult male contributor in Class I, II or IV, and 8d. for each adult woman in these classes, the corresponding rates for contributors under age 21 being 6d. for a boy under age 18, 8d. for a young man of 18 and under 21, and 6d. for a girl or young woman under age 21.

I estimate that the annual income from contributions at the rates stated will amount to about £40 millions in 1945.

On the basis described in para. 34 above relating to the division of the total contributions in Class I between employers and workers, it is estimated that about £6 millions will be paid by employers, about £26 millions by employees in Class I, and the remainder, about £8 millions, by contributors in Classes II and IV.

63. While, as indicated above, a precise estimate cannot be framed of the gross cost of a comprehensive scheme of the services in question, it is essential at the present stage, in order to measure broadly the liabilities of the Exchequer and other parties arising under the Social Security Plan as a whole, to include an estimate in the Social Security Budget, where the expenditure arising among the various heads is brought together. After consultation with the Ministry of Health and the Department of Health for Scotland, a round figure of £170 millions a year has been taken as a suitable measure for this purpose.

Assuming a grant-in-aid from insurance contributions of £40 millions, the net annual cost to public funds would thus be in the neighbourhood of £130 millions, or rather over three-quarters of the total expenditure.

64. In view of the fundamental changes involved in the substitution of a comprehensive health service, covering the whole population of all ages, for the present arrangements under which, apart from the medical benefit provided for the insured persons themselves, but not their dependants, under the National Health Insurance scheme on the one hand and the various public health services on the other, medical treatment is secured under private arrangements, it is not thought appropriate in the present memorandum to attempt a financial comparison of the two systems. In considering, however, the proposed charge on public funds it is necessary to have regard to the existing charges on the national and local exchequers in regard to analogous services. Before the war the charges on public funds for the services in question may be put at about £45 to £50 millions. Making some allowance for development and for increased prices, it is thought appropriate for comparative purposes to put the cost of the existing services at about £60 millions in a post-war year. The net increase in the cost to public funds is thus of the order of £70 millions.

CHILDREN'S ALLOWANCES

65. The Report postulates the establishment of a system of children's allowances, not as insurance benefits financed in whole or part by contributions, but as security benefits financed entirely from the Exchequer but

coming within the Social Security Budget. The proposal is that cash payments should be made in respect of all children under the age of 15 (or 16 if in full-time education) other than the first child in the family when the parent is not in receipt of a Social Insurance benefit, but including the first child when the parent is in receipt of disability or unemployment benefit or, in the case of a widow, widow's or guardian benefit.

The allowances are to be on a scale varying with the age of child but taken for convenience in these estimates as a flat 8/– per child. The precise scale would affect the cost, and the effect would not be quite proportionate for alternative schemes (a) excluding one child in family, and (b) including all children, since the average rate of allowance per child on the two bases would be appreciably different.

66. I estimate the cost of these allowances, apart from administration, to be £110 millions in 1945. Their cost in later years will depend increasingly upon the future trend of the fertility rate, i.e. upon the number of births per married woman at each age. How far this trend would be affected by the introduction of children's allowances and other proposed changes can only be a matter for conjecture. If the fertility rate after the war were stabilised at about the pre-war level, the cost of these allowances would fall gradually to £108 millions in 1955 and to £100 millions in 1965. To these figures must be added the cost of administration of the benefit, which I have taken at £3 millions a year for the purpose of the Social Security Budget.

The corresponding figure for 1945 if the allowances were payable for all children would be about £208 millions as compared with £110 millions above, i.e. a difference of £98 millions. This is the net effect of (i) the exclusion of the first child in all circumstances, accounting for £116 millions, less (ii) the cost of providing the allowances in such cases where the parent is in receipt of Social Insurance benefit, estimated at £18 millions.

If it were decided, as an alternative plan, in addition to excluding the first child while the parent is earning, to reduce the grant to 4/– a week for the second child whilst retaining 8/– for the third and subsequent children, the cost would be reduced at the outset by about £23 millions. Under this alternative it is assumed that the supplementary payment to the parent who was in receipt of unemployment or other benefit would be 8/– for the first child and 4/– for the second.

67. It has been suggested in some quarters that the payment of universal family allowances should not be additional to the income tax relief given in respect of children, and the question of linking family allowances with income tax relief was discussed in paras. 13, 32 and 33 and the Annex to the recent White Paper on Family Allowances (Cmd. 6354). The Report does not consider this question and the estimates given above assume the continuance unchanged of the income tax arrangements. It is evident that if, in consideration of the grant of children's allowances, the system of income tax rebates were modified there might be a substantial saving to the Exchequer to set against the cost of the new allowances.

68. The cost is not entirely a new charge. Under the present system juvenile dependants' allowances in Unemployment Insurance and Assistance, children's allowances and orphans' benefits in Contributory Pensions, and children's allowances under Workmen's Compensation, would cost about £11 millions a year in 1945, met partly from the contributions of insured persons. These would no longer be required under the new conditions.

EXPENSES OF ADMINISTRATION

69. Until the details of the scheme and its administration have been worked out, the amounts which will be required for the expenses of administration under the various heads must be largely speculative. Not only are some of the benefits new and complex in character, calling for the development of new methods of administration, but also it is proposed to reorganise the

whole machinery of administration of the Pensions and Health Insurance schemes, if not of the Unemployment scheme. On balance is appears unlikely that there will be a saving, at any rate for a considerable time to come.

70. For the existing schemes of Health, Pensions and Unemployment Insurance the aggregate cost of administration for the latest pre-war year (1938) appears to have been about £13 millions apart from the cost of administering medical benefit, at present included therein. To this has to be added the cost of operating the present Workmen's Compensation scheme by employers (or insurers on their behalf). Full information as to this is not available, but it appears to have been rather less than £3 millions a year. The aggregate expenses under all these schemes taken together may thus be put at about £16 millions a year (pre-war).

Taking into consideration the increased numbers insured under the Plan, the greater complexity of administration involved in some of the benefits (e.g. the retirement condition), and the inclusion of benefits not previously covered, as well as the change in costs, wages, etc., since the war, and setting off against these the economies resulting from unifying the collection of contributions and the administration of the scheme generally (where there is now overlapping or duplication), I do not think it would be wise to put the probable expenditure on administration at less than a round figure of £18 millions a year for the insurance benefits. It will be appreciated that an increase in the weekly rate of benefit does not of itself involve any increase in administrative cost.

71. The figure of £3 millions for administration of national assistance is based on the experience of the Assistance Board and should be reasonably accurate.

72. The administration of children's allowances is likely to be more expensive than might, *prima facie*, be expected. The changes in the size of the family, variations in the rate of allowance with age of child, and the intermittent payment of allowances for the first child where the parent is unemployed, disabled, etc., will necessitate very frequent administrative action. In these circumstances I think a figure of £3 millions, representing under 3 per cent. on the cost of allowances, is reasonable. Much will depend, however, on the extent to which this work can be dovetailed in with other parts of the administration.

73. The amounts suggested above do not include any sums in respect of capital liabilities which might arise at the outset of the scheme, whether in respect of the acquisition or construction of buildings, the payment of compensation or other similar items.

COMPARISON OF EXPENDITURE UNDER PROPOSED PLAN AND EXISTING SYSTEM

74. I now proceed to compare the estimated expenditure which will be incurred in the first full year (1945) under the Social Security Plan with the corresponding expenditure under the various Social Insurance schemes, and on other services so far as met from central and local public funds, which would arise in the same year if the existing system remained in force. With these is included Workmen's Compensation which, though not provided for under a Social Insurance scheme, is a legal liability analogous to that covered by National Health Insurance in the case of non-industrial accident and disease.

The comparison cannot be made in great detail, for a number of reasons. The nature and grouping of the benefits has changed in various respects; the populations covered for insurance are different; the method of meeting certain needs has changed, and, in some cases, the extent to which they are met respectively from State insurance, private insurance, national and local assistance, etc. Nevertheless, the following statement, in which the costs in main groups of services under the existing and new arrangements are given, is thought to provide a fair picture of the effect of the Plan.

COMPARATIVE STATEMENT OF ESTIMATED EXPENDITURE IN 1945

Under Present Social Insurance Schemes and Allied Services		Under Social Security Plan	
	£ millions		£ millions
PENSION BENEFITS		Retirement pensions... ... 126 ⎱	
Contributory pensions :		Widows' and Guardian	
Age and widows', over 60 94 ⎫		benefits ... ... 29 ⎰ 194	
Widows', under 60 ... 12 ⎬ 163			
Non-contributory pensions 10		Assistance pensions ... ... 39 ⎰	
Supplementary pensions ... 47 ⎭			
UNEMPLOYMENT		Unemployment and training	
Insurance and assistance		benefit	110
benefits	84		
SICKNESS (including Industrial and Maternity)			
National Health Insurance :		Disability benefit ... ... 57 ⎱	
Sickness and disablement		Industrial disability benefit	
benefits ... ... 27 ⎫		(including pensions) ... 15 ⎬ 79	
Maternity benefit ... 3 ⎬ 43			
Workmen's compensation 13 ⎭		Maternity grant and benefit 7 ⎰	
CHILDREN'S BENEFITS		Universal children's	
Children's allowances		allowances	110
payable under above schemes	11		
OTHER ASSISTANCE		National assistance	5
Public assistance	15	(apart from assistance pensions)	
OTHER CASH BENEFITS			
		Marriage grant	1
		Funeral grant...	4
ADMINISTRATION			
Cost for above services ...	20	Cost for above services ...	24
HEALTH SERVICES			
Included in National Health 19 ⎫		Comprehensive national scheme	170
Insurance ... ... ⎬ 79			
Others, met from public funds 60 ⎭			
Total ...	415	Total ...	697

75. It will be seen that the aggregate expenditure is estimated to be increased from £415 millions under existing arrangements to £697 millions under the Social Security Plan, i.e. an increase of about 70 per cent. Of the increase of £282 millions, two-thirds is due in almost equal proportions to (i) the introduction of a scheme of universal children's allowances in place of the small allowances now payable where the parent is in receipt of workmen's compensation, unemployment benefit or a widow's pension, and (ii) the enlargement of the general practitioner service included in National Health Insurance, and the health services provided by local authorities, etc., into a comprehensive national scheme of health and rehabilitation services.

The balance of about £90 millions increase in expenditure is distributed over the various services. Expenditure on pensions is increased by about 20 per cent., due mainly to the raising of rates of pension from the present 10/- a week (20/- for a married couple), supplemented in case of need, to the starting transitional pension rate of 14/- (25/- for a married couple) also supplemented in case of need. In this, the first, year of the scheme the additional expenditure due to bringing new classes within the scope of insurance will be negligible.

The increase in expenditure on unemployment by about 30 per cent. is due in the main to raising the rates of benefit, but in part also to bringing into insurance certain classes of employed persons not at present insured for unemployment.

The increase in expenditure on disability benefits by over 80 per cent. is due mainly to the raising of the rates of benefit and the inclusion of an allowance for wives and adult dependants not given under the present National Health

Insurance system, and, to a less extent, to the inclusion in insurance of new classes and the substantial expansion of maternity benefits.

The sum now payable for public assistance is not properly comparable with that estimated to become payable in respect of national assistance, but the decline in this expenditure reflects the extent to which the abnormal needs not met by insurance will be diminished by the provisions of the new scheme, including the transfer of certain classes from public assistance to national assistance.

Estimated Income Under the Plan

76. *Income from Contributions.*—The income from the contributions of insured persons and employers for the three years 1945, 1955 and 1965, has been estimated by applying to the numbers of the contributing population in each class the rates of contribution proposed to be charged, assuming non-payment of contributions during sickness, unemployment, etc., as permitted in the conditions for excusal of contribution appropriate to the respective classes. Allowance has been made for the loss of income due to (i) married women who choose to be exempt from contributing although gainfully occupied, (ii) persons over age 55 (men) and 50 (women) at the outset and not within the present scheme, who take advantage of the initial option given to them, and (iii) other persons, in Classes II and IV, who exercise their option not to contribute on the ground of insufficiency of income.

The amount of the resulting annual income over the 20-year period shows little variation, being £325 millions in 1945, £326 millions in 1955 and £319 millions in 1965, of which approximately 60 per cent. is paid by insured persons and 40 per cent. by employers.

In addition, employers pay about £5 millions a year in respect of the levy for excess cost of industrial disability benefits in hazardous industries (*see* para. 42).

Treatment of Existing Assets

77. Additional income to the Social Security scheme will be derived from the assets of the existing Social Insurance schemes. The three existing systems—Health, Pensions and Unemployment Insurance—have each accumulated in the course of their operations, in diverse ways, funds of substantial amount.

78. In the case of Health Insurance the aggregate of these invested assets amounted at the end of 1941 to about £225 millions at present market prices, yielding an average interest income of about 3¼ per cent. on this valuation. These funds are held partly by the Approved Societies themselves and partly by the Central Departments (or the National Debt Commissioners) on their behalf and on account of certain central funds. They have arisen mainly from the contributions allocated for the building up of reserves to meet the needs of later life for all insured persons due to the excess cost of benefits over the then current contribution income, and from marginal contributions earmarked for contingencies. Further, the accumulated reserves have been augmented by profits due to favourable experience as compared with the financial basis. These surpluses accrued to a large extent many years ago and have been only partly absorbed by the grant of additional benefits, the remainder carried forward. By mid-1944 the aggregate assets of the National Health Insurance scheme may be expected to amount to about £240 millions, invested to produce an annual income of rather more than £7½ millions.

79. In the case of the Contributory Pensions scheme—except for the Special Voluntary Contributors scheme—the financial arrangements are not run as an accumulative fund, and the Exchequer subsidy takes the form broadly of defraying year by year the deficiency of each year's contribution income as compared with expenditure on pensions. Up to March, 1946, however, the State grants to the Treasury Pensions Account have been prescribed in the

Statute on a fixed scale ; thereafter the amount of the Exchequer grant is to be redetermined by Parliament. Balances in the Pensions Accounts amounting to about £50 millions had accrued at 31st March, 1942, the prescribed scale of grants having proved to be somewhat in excess of the difference between current income and current expenditure to date, mainly owing to adventitious causes such as light unemployment during the war. By mid-1944 these invested balances will probably have increased to about £70 millions, and if the present scheme continued they would be used in abatement of the Exchequer charge in future years.

80. The Unemployment Fund held balances at October, 1942, amounting to about £145 millions, which are invested in short-term securities yielding an average rate of interest of nearly 2½ per cent. These are primarily due to the maintenance of the rates of contribution on the basis of the hypothetical cycle of unemployment, averaging 15 per cent., adopted before the war, although unemployment during the war and for some time before the war has been at a much lower level. Moreover, the rates of contribution were fixed when the Fund was in debt and include a provision for the extinction thereof : the debt has been paid off and replaced by invested reserves. These balances will continue to grow at the rate of about £6 millions a month so long as the present abnormal conditions continue, but its subsequent course depends largely on the measures taken to deal with post-war demobilisation and unemployment. The probable amount of the balances at mid-1944 is thus uncertain, but for the present estimates it seems not unreasonable to assume that they will be not far short of £250 millions.

81. In total, therefore, the invested assets set free by the supersession of the existing systems may be of the order of £550 millions, earning interest amounting to about £15 millions a year. The precise method of utilisation of the accumulated resources of the old schemes, when absorbed in the Social Insurance Fund to be set up under the enlarged and reconstructed Social Security Plan, would no doubt have to be determined later. In view of the greatly increased liabilities of the Exchequer resulting from the enlargement of benefits for existing insured persons it would seem equitable that the Exchequer should have the advantage of the existing reserves. In the statements of income for the years stated, credit has been taken only for the interest yielded by these funds on the basis that they are maintained as reserves.

SUMMARY OF INCOME

82. Bringing together the various sources of income, it is estimated that the expenditure under the scheme, including not only the insurance benefits but also health services, national assistance and children's allowances, would be met in the following way :—

SOCIAL SECURITY BUDGET : ESTIMATED INCOME

	1945		1955		1965	
	£ mills	Percent-age of total	£ mills	Percent-age of total	£ mills	Percent-age of total
Contributions from :—						
Insured Persons	194	28	196	25	192	22
Employers	131 ⎫		130 ⎫		127 ⎫	
Industrial disability levy on employers*	6 ⎬	20	5 ⎬	18	5 ⎬	15
	⎭		⎭		⎭	
Interest on existing funds ...	15	2	15	2	15	2
Balance of expenditure, to be met from Exchequer (or local rates)	351	50	418	55	519	61
Total	697	100	764	100	858	100

*Including, in 1945, payments from reserves held by employers (or their insurers) for compensation on the old scales to persons injured before July, 1944.

In this statement the employers' share of contributions is less than the insured persons', partly because the Class I contribution is shared between insured person and employer in the ratio 51d. : 39d. (for men), but also because contributors in Classes II and IV have no employer and pay the whole contribution themselves.

COMPARISON WITH EXISTING POSITION

83. An exact comparison of the income under the Plan with the income, from each source, to meet corresponding charges under the present Social Insurance schemes—so far as they exist—though not entirely valid owing to the great change in the character of the services and the extent to which they are met from contributions for State insurance and by charges on public funds (either central or local) gives material for broad generalisations. The following statement has been prepared, therefore, contrasting the figures given in the preceding paragraph for the year 1945 with the aggregate sums estimated to be payable in that year in contributions for Health, Pensions and Unemployment Insurance under the existing schemes, the interest yielded on the funds of these schemes, and the estimated aggregate charge on the Exchequer and other public funds.

In order to make the basis of comparison as satisfactory as possible, this last item comprises not only the sum of Exchequer payments to the three Insurance schemes but also expenditure from central and local funds on unemployment assistance, supplementary pensions, hospital services, public assistance, etc. Further, the cost of workmen's compensation has been added to and included with the contributions of employers for social insurance ; this is the main reason why the employers' share of contributions is shown to be appreciably greater than insured persons', although the normal division of the present social insurance contributions is equally between the two.

COMPARATIVE STATEMENT OF ESTIMATED INCOME IN 1945

	Under Present Social Insurance Schemes and Allied Services		Under Social Security Plan	
	£ millions	Percentage of total	£ millions	Percentage of total
Contributions from :—				
Insured Persons	69	16	194	28
Employers (including payments for industrial disability)	83	19	137	20
Interest on existing funds	15	4	15	2
Expenditure to be met from Exchequer (or local rates)	265	61	351	50
	432	100	697	100

In considering the figures of expenditure and income for 1945 under the existing schemes, given in the comparative statements here and in para. 74, it will be observed that the estimated income, viz., £432 millions, exceeds the expenditure, viz. £415 millions, by £17 millions. This is partly accounted for by the fact that the present National Health Insurance scheme is framed on an accumulative plan and the reserves are still increasing, but is mainly due to the material changes which have occurred in the financial position of the Unemployment Insurance scheme as the result of the war.

84. It is to be noted that the aggregate expenditure in 1945 would be much greater than that in the immediate pre-war years even if no further changes were made in the system. Since 1939, the rates of benefit in Health and Unemployment Insurance have been raised, the pension age for women has been reduced from 65 to 60, and the system of Supplementary Pensions has

been inaugurated. For these and other reasons, the expenditure under all heads is estimated at nearly £90 millions more in 1945 than in 1938–39.

Provision for the additional income necessary to meet this increase in expenditure has been made to the extent of about 40 per cent. by raising the rates of Health, Unemployment and Pensions contributions on account of the increase in benefits, taken in conjunction with the inclusion in those schemes of employed persons whose remuneration is between £250 and £420 a year. The remaining 60 per cent. is met by increased Exchequer grants to the various schemes.

85. The statement in para. 83 shows that the introduction of the Social Security Plan would increase the income applied to Social Insurance, etc., purposes in 1945 by £265 millions, of which £179 millions would be obtained from contributions of insured persons and their employers and £86 millions from the Exchequer. Thereby the proportion of total expenditure met from the Exchequer would fall temporarily from 61 to 50 per cent.

Looking to the future, however, it will be seen from the statement in para. 82 that whereas the contribution income received each year from insured persons and their employers remains more or less stationary, the balance of expenditure to be provided from the Exchequer rises steadily. In 1965 the Exchequer will be paying £168 millions more than in 1945 under the new Plan, an increase of 48 per cent., and will be providing 61 per cent. of the total income under the Plan.

The Social Security Budget

86. In Part IV of the Report the finance of the Plan is considered from the point of view of framing a Social Security Budget, bringing together for individual years, on the one hand, the expenditure under all heads, whether for insurance or for other Security benefits, and on the other the income from contributions and interest and the balance of expenditure falling upon the Exchequer (or local rates).

This is not to be taken as indicating the form in which the financial arrangements of the scheme would necessarily be carried through. Numerous considerations, which need not be elaborated at this stage, will arise in determining the most satisfactory form in which to cast the financial provisions of a Plan covering so many benefits, and of so diverse a character ; in particular, the consideration of appropriate arrangements for meeting the Exchequer liabilities under the various heads will be a matter of the first importance.

It is useful, however, to bring together the estimates for the various sections of the Plan, and this has been done separately for expenditure and income in paras. 57 and 82 above. I now give a summary (*see* page 209) in the form of a Budget showing expenditure and income side by side for the first calendar year (1945) and the twenty-first year (1965) of the scheme. In this statement, in order to simplify the presentation, I have grouped together the minor insurance benefits under one head, viz., " Other insurance benefits " ; the group comprises widow's and guardian benefits, maternity grant and benefit, marriage grant and funeral grant.

87. The salient features of these estimated figures as regards expenditure have already been pointed out in para. 58. It is sufficient here to refer to certain outstanding points which emerge clearly from this further statement.

Over the twenty years from 1945 to 1965 the various heads of expenditure, other than retirement pensions, show relatively small increases and decreases. Pensions, however, much more than double their cost—increasing from £126 millions (or 18 per cent. of the total budget) in 1945 to £300 millions (or 35 per cent. of the total budget) in 1965. This is partly due, as already stated, to the saving—very considerable at the outset and gradually declining—under the provisions for reduced pensions in a transition period of 20 years.

The increase from 1945 to 1965 of £161 millions in the total budgeted

SOCIAL SECURITY BUDGET: ESTIMATED EXPENDITURE AND INCOME IN 1945 AND 1965

EXPENDITURE	1945	1965	INCOME	1945	1965
	£ millions			£ millions	
Retirement Pensions ...	126	300	Contributions of Insured Persons	194	192
Unemployment Benefit ...	110	107			
Disability Benefit (including Industrial Disability)	72	86	Employers' Contributions (including Industrial Disability Levy) ...	137	132
Other Social Insurance Benefits	41	42	Interest on Funds ...	15	15
National Assistance ...	44	30	Charges upon Exchequer	351	519
Children's Allowances ...	110	100			
Cost of Administration of above	24	23			
Health Services	170	170			
Total ...	697	858	Total ...	697	858

expenditure is, in fact, due entirely to the increase in pensions expenditure, viz., £174 millions.

On the other side, as the Plan is framed, the increase in expenditure will fall to be met entirely from the Exchequer—the charge on which increases by £168 millions during the period—whereas the income from contributions declines very slightly.

88. In connection with the foregoing examination of the Exchequer liability under the Social Security Budget as a whole, it is of interest to examine separately the position in regard to insurance benefits and other benefits and services.

In 1965 the expenditure on social insurance benefits (and their administration) will amount to £553 millions. In that year the insured persons and their employers will be paying £324 millions of which £39 millions will be allocated to the health services, i.e. £285 millions net for insurance benefits. Allowing for £15 millions interest on the reserves held, the balance of expenditure falling on the Exchequer will thus be £253 millions, or 46 per cent. of the total charges on the Social Insurance Fund.

At the same time the Exchequer will be meeting the whole of the cost of children's allowances and national assistance, £135 millions, and the balance of the cost of health services, viz., £131 millions, not met by the £39 millions contributions mentioned above.

In the whole Social Security Budget the Exchequer will thus be paying 46 per cent. of insurance benefits, 100 per cent. of children's allowances and national assistance, and 77 per cent. of health services, or 61 per cent. over all, as shown in the table in para. 82.

89. The proportion met by the Exchequer in the case of Social Insurance benefits, viz., 46 per cent., is of course very much greater than the part of the actuarial contribution allocated to the Exchequer, viz., about one-quarter of the aggregate contribution (see para. 10). The reason for this is that in addition to this one-fourth subsidy the Exchequer takes the strain of admitting the existing population of all ages for the ordinary benefits of the Plan at the same rate of contribution as is charged to new entrants at age 16. Further, owing to the fact that it does not extinguish its liability by a series of deficiency payments to an accumulative fund, but makes good the annually emerging

excess of current expenditure over current income, there is a deficit in perpetuity, the charge on the Exchequer not being reduced when, in due course, the present insured population has passed away.

90. *Position after* 1965.—I have not carried my estimates beyond the year 1965. There is no doubt, however, that estimates of the position after that year would show a further growth in the proportion of Social Security expenditure to be provided from the Exchequer as compared with the proportions met from the contributions of insured persons and their employers, for the following reasons. First, the cost of the scheme will still be increasing substantially, mainly on account of pensions, because (i) the aged population will be increasing and (ii) the average rate of pension will be rising, as pensioners then existing and receiving a reduced transitional rate are replaced by others receiving the full rate. Second, the contributing population will probably be stationary or declining. Thus, for many years at least, the whole of the additional expenditure, i.e. a growing proportion of the total expenditure, will fall to be met from the Exchequer under the method of finance envisaged in the Plan.

PERIODICAL ACTUARIAL REVIEW

91. In calculating the contributions appropriate to the varied types of benefits provided in the Plan, and in estimating the charges likely to arise under the scheme during the first twenty years, account has had to be taken of many factors and attempts have been made to forecast the effect of changes which are constantly taking place in conditions affecting the social and economic state of the people. Moreover, the estimates have had to envisage a peacetime basis which was perforce related to that obtaining before the beginning of the war.

Clearly it is impracticable at the present time to attempt to measure with any precision the changes which may occur between the social constitution of the population as it is now (or immediately before the war) and as it will be found after the immediate disturbances due to the war have passed away. Many of these conditions will no doubt have indirect consequences which may materially affect the realisation of the estimates. As instances, reference may be made to (i) the future level of disability benefit, in respect of which, as explained in para. 22 above, conditions will differ radically from those under which the available sickness tables have been compiled, and (ii) the effect on the cost of pensions of making pension dependent on retirement from work, as to which no past experience under comparable conditions is available.

In the circumstances, having regard to the fundamental nature of the changes from the various schemes of Social Insurance now existing for Contributory Pensions, National Health Insurance and Unemployment Insurance— the past experience of which has had to be used, with modifications, as the basis of the new estimates—it will be appreciated that the actual experience when the scheme is in operation may prove to differ materially from the assumptions made. There is, therefore, more than the usual need for an actuarial review to be made, at regular intervals, of the working of the Plan. This review should be directed not only towards reporting on the adequacy or otherwise of the rates of contribution in relation to the benefits provided— in order that any necessary changes to restore equilibrium in this respect may be made—but also on the future cost to the Exchequer and the most suitable rates of subsidy in order to meet its growing liabilities under the Plan.

G. S. W. EPPS.

Government Actuary's Department,
London, S.W.1.
November, 1942.

APPENDIX B

THE PRESENT SCHEMES OF
SOCIAL INSURANCE AND ASSISTANCE

SECTION I.—DEVELOPMENT OF THE SOCIAL INSURANCE AND ASSISTANCE
SCHEMES

1. To give a full and balanced account of the development of the existing national schemes of social insurance and assistance and their varied aspects is, for the purpose of this Report, an unnecessary undertaking. This note, therefore, picks out the significant dates and illustrates the development of the schemes by reference to the main statistics.

2. The Poor Relief Act, 1601, though not the first statute to deal with the relief of destitution can be regarded as the starting point of State provision for social security. For over 300 years the poor law authorities have had the responsibility for the relief of destitution. Since 1601 there have been several changes in the type of authority given this responsibility. There have also been great developments in the social services concerned with Public Health and Education. The poor law authorities played a part in the inception of these new services which have now become separate and important functions of local government.. Since the beginning of the present century and particularly since the Report of the Royal Commission on the Poor Laws and Relief of Distress (1909) there has been a strong movement against the form and spirit of the old poor law. There has been a development of compulsory insurance and of assistance administered on a national basis.

3. In 1897 the Workmen's (Compensation for Accidents) Act made provision for compensation to be paid for death or incapacity suffered as a result of an accident in certain specially dangerous industries (roughly—employment on, in or about railways, factories, mines, quarries, building operations and structural engineering). Agriculture was added in 1900, and an Act of 1906 extended the scheme to cover practically every case in which two people stand to each other in the relation of master and servant ; non-manual workers whose remuneration exceeded £250 a year (raised to £350 in 1923 and £420 as from January, 1942), outworkers and certain employments were excluded. Further the Act of 1906 provided an extension of the compensation to cases of scheduled industrial diseases and made provision for the inclusion of further industrial diseases in the schedule by administrative order. The 1897 Act did not provide a State-administered scheme nor did the State or the workmen contribute towards the cost of compensation as in the case of Unemployment Insurance. The significance of the Act was that from that time onwards people who became partially or totally incapacitated as a result of an industrial accident were entitled to receive a weekly payment or a lump sum. The widows and dependants of workmen killed as a result of an industrial accident also became eligible for compensation.

4. The first real departure from the Poor Law occurred with the passing of the Old Age Pensions Act, 1908. There had been considerable agitation in favour of old age pensions since the latter part of the 19th Century. A Royal Commission on the Aged Poor had reported on the question in 1895 but had concluded that no fundamental change was needed in the existing system of Poor Relief. In 1896 the Treasury appointed a Committee on Old Age Pensions whose report was followed by a Select Committee in 1899 and a Departmental Committee in 1900. Finally, in 1908, an Act to provide for Old Age Pensions was passed. It is noticeable that the scheme was not financed by compulsory contributions and the main effect was to enable people to receive a pension of 1/- to 5/- a week on reaching the age of 70 subject to a means test, but not subject to the stigma of poor relief, nor was destitution made a condition. By the end of March, 1909, some 500,000 old persons were receiving these new pensions.

5. In 1911 the two important contributory schemes of insurance against ill health and unemployment were enacted. The National Insurance Act, 1911, was described in its preamble as " an Act to provide for insurance against loss of health and for the prevention and cure of sickness and for insurance against unemployment and for purposes incidental thereto." The scheme, which came into operation on the 15th July, 1912, provided for the payment of sickness, disablement and maternity cash benefits and for a general practitioner and certain medical benefit for the insured person. The scheme was compulsory and contributory, and, with certain exceptions, covered all those between the ages of 16 and 70 who were employed under a contract of service in manual labour or in non-manual employment if receiving a rate of remuneration not exceeding £160 a year. The National Health Insurance Act, 1919, raised the remuneration limit to £250 a year, and the limit became £420 a year as from January, 1942.

6. Part II of the 1911 Act introduced a limited scheme of Unemployment Insurance. Provision was made for a compulsory and contributory scheme of insurance against unemployment in certain skilled industries in which marked fluctuations in employment were known to occur, viz. building, construction of works, shipbuilding, mechanical engineering, iron founding, construction of vehicles and certain classes of saw-milling ; in all about 2¼ million workers. The scheme came into operation in July, 1912. The scheme was extended in 1916, to cover some 1½ million further workpeople. The Unemployment Insurance Act, 1920, superseded the original scheme and extended unemployment insurance to cover over 11 million workers. The 1911 Act did not apply unemployment insurance to non-manual workers, but these were brought in by the 1920 Act, where their rate of remuneration was not more than £250 a year. This limit was raised to £420 a year as from September, 1940. The scope of the scheme has been extended from time to time, and in 1936 a special scheme was started for agricultural workers.

7. The main changes since 1920 have, however, turned on the treatment of long-term unemployment. It is unnecessary here to refer to the many changes which have occurred in benefit conditions, and in particular in the relation between contribution record and the length of benefit for which the unemployed person was eligible. The most significant events were the introduction of Transitional Payments in 1931, a scheme under which the responsibility for the needs of the long-term unemployed was placed directly on the Exchequer subject to a means test, and the taking over of this class by the Unemployment Assistance Board on 7th January, 1935. On 1st April, 1937, a further 100,000 cases of persons who were within the scope of unemployment assistance were taken over by the Board directly from the Public Assistance Authorities. Up to 1941 assistance to this class which comprised, broadly, all able-bodied people who were accustomed to earn their living by working for wages was administered on the basis of a household means test under which part of the resources of the household in which an unemployed man was living were regarded as available to meet his needs. By the Determination of Needs Act, 1941, a personal means test based on the circumstances in which the applicant was living but taking no account otherwise of the resources of his household was substituted for the household means test.

8. In 1925 the Widows', Orphans', and Old Age Contributory Pensions Act provided the first national scheme of contributory pensions. The benefit provisions of the Act came into force in three stages, viz.:—

(i) As from 4th January, 1926, pensions at the rate of 10/- a week (with allowances for young children) became payable to the widows of insured men dying on or after that date, while in the case of motherless children orphans' pensions at the rate of 7/6 a week became payable to their guardians.

(ii) As from 2nd July, 1926, old age pensions at 10/- a week were granted, without any question of means, to persons then over the age of 70, or who attained that age between such date and 2nd January, 1928—if they had been insured under the Health Insurance scheme prior to attaining 70.

(iii) As from 2nd January, 1928, pensions to insured persons then of ages 65–70 began to be paid ; and from that date each insured person reaching the age of 65 received a pension of 10/- a week. The wife of an insured man received a pension as a concomitant of her husband's insurance, when she attained age 65 or as soon thereafter as her husband reached that age.

9. Provision was also made by the 1925 Act for the payment of pensions to certain persons who would have been entitled to a contributory pension if the scheme had been in force before 1926. Under this provision, widows with children of or under school age were, from 4th January, 1926, granted pensions and allowances at the ordinary rates if it could be shown, broadly, that the husband had followed an occupation which would have been insurable under the scheme. These non-contributory widows' pensions were of strictly limited duration, being terminated six months after the youngest child reached the age of 14.

10. The Pensions Act of 1929 extended very considerably the scope of pensions to widows. It granted pensions, payable from the attainment of age 55, to the widows of men of the insurable class who died before 4th January, 1926, and these pensions began to be paid generally from 1st January, 1931, but widows who were already over age 60 at 1st July, 1930, or who reached that age between these two dates, were given their pensions on the earlier date, or the 60th birthday (if later).

11. In 1937 the benefits of voluntary insurance for widows', orphans' and old age pensions were extended to persons with small incomes, whether working on their own account or not, who had not the qualifications of insurable employment essential to insurance under the main scheme. Previously the opportunity to become a voluntary contributor was, in general, confined to persons who had been insured under the compulsory scheme. The 1937 Act also broke the interlocking of Health and Pensions

insurance, so far as voluntary contributors were concerned, allowing such persons to select the insurance most suited to their needs. In so doing, the Act for the first time enabled married women to become voluntary contributors for pensions.

12.   The Old Age and Widows' Pensions Act, 1940, provided that, as from 1st July, 1940, the old age pension of 10/– a week should be payable as from the age of 60, instead of 65, to an insured woman and to the wife of an insured man who has himself attained the age of 65.

13.   The Act also introduced the system of supplementary pensions. It provided for supplementation in case of need of the pensions of old age pensioners and to widow pensioners over the age of 60. The significance of the Act was that it placed on the Assistance Board (until that time called the Unemployment Assistance Board) the responsibility of dealing with old age and widow pensioners who were in need. The Act came into operation in August, 1940, so far as supplementary pensions were concerned. It removed about 250,000 cases from Public Assistance though the number of pensioners who applied for and obtained a supplementary pension was considerably greater.

14.   In 1920 as a result of the Blind Persons Act the non-contributory old age pension became payable to blind persons at the age of 50 ; it was reduced to 40 in 1938. In addition, the 1920 Act imposed a duty on the Council of each County and County Borough to make arrangements to the satisfaction of the Ministry of Health and Department of Health for Scotland for promoting the welfare of blind persons in their areas. The Blind Persons Act, 1938, among other things provided that all assistance by Local Authorities to blind persons, other than assistance in an institution or medical assistance, should be provided exclusively by virtue of the Blind Persons Acts and not by way of poor relief. Thus, since 1938, blind persons and their dependants, apart from certain exceptional needs, have been removed entirely from the ordinary public assistance provisions.

15.   Though they do not fall directly under the heading of social insurance and assistance, it is necessary to mention the great expansion of the Health, Education, Housing and other social services. Most of these provide treatment or a service which does not place any cash in the citizen's pocket in the same sense as, say, does unemployment benefit. But their significance for the purpose of this brief history is that they represent another method of meeting need outside the Poor Law—rent rebates, provision of school meals, free or cheap milk, hospital and medical services have been provided as part of a health or education service and not as part of the Poor Law.

Increase in Number Insured and Cash Benefits

16.   Table XVII shows the growth in the numbers covered by the three national contributory schemes. The steady increase in the number of contributors is partly due to an increase in number of workers, but in the main is due to extensions of scope. The numbers covered at the present time are, of course, much higher, due to the large recruitment of women for war factories, etc.

Table XVII—Social Insurance Schemes
Numbers Insured in Great Britain, 1914–1938 (figures in 000's)

At 31st December (a)	Unemployment	Health (b)	Widows, Orphans and Old Age
1914	2,500	13,689	—
1921	11,081	15,165	—
1926	11,774	16,375	17,089
1931	12,500	17,353	18,513
1936	14,580	18,081	19,651
1938	15,395	19,706	20,678

(a) In July of each year for Unemployment.
(b) Excluding persons over 65 years of age.

The main groups which are covered for widows, orphans and old age pensions, but not for unemployment are : private domestic servants, nurses, sharefishermen, outworkers, civil servants, railwaymen, etc., about 2¾ million ; voluntary and special voluntary contributors, nearly 1 million ; and persons retained (permanently or temporarily) in contributory pensions (e.g., women recently married) about 1¼ million.

17.   The great increase in the amount of cash benefit and assistance paid out under the different schemes is shown in Table XVIII below.

Table XVIII

Cash Benefit(a) Paid under Social Insurance and Assistance Schemes, in Great Britain, 1900–1939 £000's.

Financial Year (b)	Unemployment	Health	Widows, Orphans and Old Age Pensions		Public Assistance (Out-relief)	Unemployment Assistance	Blind Persons Assistance	Workmen's Compensation(d)	Total
			Contributory	Non-Contributory					
1900–1901	—	—	—	—	3,281	—	—	(e)	3,281
1910–1911	—	—	—	7,300	3,743	—	—	2,700	13,743
1914–1915	419(c)	8,010	—	10,021	3,246	—	—	3,465	25,161
1921–1922	52,848(c)	13,153	—	21,940	17,691	—	—	5,509	111,141
1926–1927	49,549	20,482	10,814	27,390	27,862	—	—	6,056	142,153
1931–1932	80,169	18,907	54,066	22,197	15,790	30,742(f)	—	6,114	227,985
1936–1937	35,332	18,896	71,568	16,561	25,801	37,428	—	6,448	212,034
1938–1939	55,081	18,600	78,772	15,302	24,189	35,331	2,077	6,765	236,117

Note.—(a) Excluding cost of treatment under Health Insurance and cost of administration in all cases, (except Public Assistance).

(b) The figures for Health Insurance benefits and Workmen's Compensation relate to Calendar years.

(c) Insurance years ending in July.

(d) Compensation paid in seven groups of industries (mines, quarries, docks, railways, shipping, factories and constructional work) for which returns were collected. The total amount of workmen's compensation paid in 1938–39 was about £10 million.

(e) Not available.

(f) Transitional payments.

In 1900–01 only poor relief and workmen's compensation were available and some £4 million was paid for these items. By 1914–15 non-contributory pensions, and unemployment and health insurance had been added; the total cash benefits had increased to £25 million. By 1921–22 the schemes had been extended in scope and the rates of benefit increased so that the money paid out had now risen to £111 million. Contributory pensions started to be paid in 1926 and increased rapidly. Cash benefits and assistance in 1938–39 were thus about nine times the 1914–15 figure and about 70 times the 1900–01 figure.

Changes in Rates of Benefit

18. The increase in the amount of cash benefits paid under the various schemes is due partly to the increased number of persons eligible for benefit and partly to the increased rates of benefit. Without enumerating all the minor changes the following are the main developments in rates of benefit :—

(i) *National Health*

(a) *Ordinary Rate* (payable after 104 weeks' insurance and 104 contributions).

	1911 Act (July, 1912)		As from July, 1920		As from Jan., 1933			As from Jan., 1942		
						Woman			Woman	
	Man	Woman	Man	Woman	Man	Married	Other	Man	Married	Other
Sickness ...	10/–	7/6	15/–	12/–	15/–	10/–	12/–	18/–	13/–	15/–
Disablement	5/–		7/6		7/6	5/–	6/–	10/6	8/–	9/–

(b) *Reduced Benefit* (payable after only 26 weeks' insurance and 26 contributions).*

	As from July 1918		As from July 1920		As from Jan. 1942	
	Man	Woman	Man	Woman	Man	Woman
Sickness	6/–	5/–	9/–	7/6	12/–	10/6

* The National Health Insurance Act, 1918, raised the qualifying period to 104 weeks' insurance and 104 contributions for ordinary benefit and provided for a reduced sickness benefit where only 26 weeks' insurance and 26 contributions had been paid. Previously the scheme provided for reduced benefits temporarily for unmarried miners and permanently for late entrants.

(c) *Maternity Benefit*

The 1911 Act provided 30/– maternity benefit after 26 weeks' insurance. The qualifying period was raised to the present 42 weeks in 1918. The benefit became 40/– in 1920.

(ii) *Old Age, Widows and Orphans Pensions*

(a) *Non-contributory Pensions* (1908 *Act*)

The 1908 Act fixed the full rate pension as 5/– and provided for a pension at reduced rates of 4/– to 1/– according to a scale of means. From the 2nd January, 1920, the full rate was increased to 10/– and the reduced rates became 8/– to 1/–. The means test has also been modified and is now more generous than under the original Act.

(b) *Widows and Orphans*

The 1925 Act provided for 10/– a week for the widow and 5/– per week for the eldest child plus 3/– per week per child for each other child. In the case of motherless children orphan's pensions at 7/6 per week per orphan were payable.

(c) Contributory Old Age Pensions

The 1925 Act provided for 10/– per week.

(d) Supplementary Pensions

These are based on need. For a person without other resources, the normal weekly rates, inclusive of the contributory or non-contributory pension, when the scheme was introduced in August, 1940, were 19/6 for the single applicant living alone, and 32/– for man and wife where both were pensioners. There were other rates for applicants who were members of households and additional sums might be paid to meet high rent and special circumstances.

The basic normal rates were in 1942 increased by 2/6 per week for the single applicant and by 5/– for a man and wife.

(iii) Unemployment Insurance

In the original scheme of unemployment insurance the rate of benefit was 7/– for man or woman. This was raised to 11/– in December, 1919. In November, 1920, a differentiation was made between men and women, and the rate for the former was increased to 15/– and for the latter to 12/–. In November, 1921, dependant's allowances were introduced at the rate of 5/– for the wife or adult dependant and 1/– a week for each dependent child. In August, 1924, there was a general increase in rates to 18/– for a man, 15/– for a woman, and 2/– for each child. The 18/– was reduced to 17/– in 1928. The adult dependant's allowance was raised to 7/– in 1928 and to 9/– in 1930. These rates then remained in force, except for a cut between 1931–1934 of roughly 10 per cent. under the National Economy Order, until the children's allowance was raised to 3/– per week in 1935 and the adult dependant's allowance to 10/– in 1939. There was a general increase in rates in August, 1940, when, under the general scheme, 20/– became the rate for a man, 18/– for a woman, and 4/– for each of first two children.

There have also been changes and increases of benefit for boys and girls and for agricultural workers. The original scheme provided for 3/6 a week benefit for boys and girls, but this was increased in 1919 and 1920. In 1928 benefit rates for non adults were made to vary according to age, and in 1930 the present classification was adopted. The adult rates under the Agriculture scheme as introduced in 1936 were 14/– for men and 12/6 for women as against the present figures of 18/– for men and 15/– for women.

(iv) Unemployment Assistance

When the unemployment assistance scheme came into force in 1934, the rates of allowances, subject to a test of means, were 24/– for a man and wife, 15/– for a man living alone, and 14/– for a woman living alone (increased to 15/– in 1936). There were other rates for persons living as members of households and for dependants of applicants, the allowances for dependent children ranging from 3/– for children under five years of age to 6/– for children aged 14 to 16. Provision was also made in the scheme for adjustment of the basic allowances to meet high rent or other special circumstances.

The basic rates were increased in 1939, and again in 1940, when the allowance for man and wife was raised to 28/– and for a man or woman living alone to 17/6, with proportionate increases in other rates. In 1941, the rate for man and wife was increased to 30/–. In 1942 there have been further general increases, the present rate for a man and wife being 35/– and for a man or woman living alone 20/–. The present rates for children range from 4/9 for children under 5 to 7/9 for children aged 14 to 16.

(v) Workmen's Compensation

The 1897 Act provided, for total incapacity, a weekly payment subject to a maximum of £1 and not exceeding 50 per cent. of the workmen's average weekly earnings during the previous twelve months or shorter period under the same employer. For partial incapacity a weekly payment was provided, taking account of the difference between the pre-accident earnings and amount which the workman was earning or able to earn after the accident. The Workmen's Compensation (War Addition) Act, 1917, provided for an addition of 25 per cent. to the amount of the weekly payment during total incapacity; this was raised to 75 per cent. in 1919. These Acts, which were temporary, were repealed in 1923, but the maximum weekly payment was then raised to 30/– per week and provision was made, in the case of workmen earning less than 50/– a week, for the payment of a higher percentage of his earnings fixed with a sliding scale ranging from 50 per cent.

to 75 per cent. From the 19th August, 1940, the weekly compensation for total incapacity for cases occurring on or after 1st January, 1924, was increased by a supplementary allowance of 5/– a week plus, in the cases of male workmen, a children's allowance of 4/– for each of the first two children, and 3/– a week for each additional child. Cases of partial incapacity received proportionate additional allowances. In cases of death the 1897 Act provided, where total dependants were left, for three years' earnings of the workman under the employer (maximum £300, minimum £150), but subject to deductions for weekly payments of compensation made during the workman's lifetime ; where only partial dependants were left, a reasonable and proportionate sum ; where no dependants, medical and burial expenses up to £10. The Act of 1923, while retaining the maximum of £300, raised the minimum to £200 and provided that weekly payments made during the workman's lifetime could be deducted but not so as to reduce the amount below £200. The 1923 Act also provided, where the dependants included a child or children under the age of 15 as well as a totally or partially dependant widow or some other member of the family over the age of 15, for an additional allowance in respect of each child, varying according to the child's age so, however, that the total compensation payable to the dependants, including the children's allowance, should not exceed £600.

CHANGES IN RATES OF CONTRIBUTIONS

19. Along with these increased rates of benefit have gone increased contributions for Health and Unemployment.

The original and present rates of contributions for adults are as follows :—

		Contributions fixed by 1911 Act		Present rate of Contributions	
		Man	Woman	Man	Woman
Health : Employer	... ...	3d.	3d.	5½d.	5½d.
Employee	... ...	4d.	3d.	5½d.	5d.
Total	...	7d.	6d.	11d.	10½d.
Unemployment : Employer	... ...	2½d.	2½d.	10d.	9d.
Employee	... ...	2½d.	2½d.	10d.	9d.
Total	...	5d.	5d.	1/8	1/6

The joint contribution from employer and employee for widows, orphans and old age pensions has risen from 9d. for men and 4½d. for women under the original (1925) Act to 1/1 for men and 8½d. for women at the present time ; the employee's share being now 6½d. in the case of men and 5d. in the case of women.

In total, therefore, taking a person, e.g. an engineer, who came under both the Health and Unemployment sections of the National Insurance Act, 1911, his total weekly contributions for all schemes has risen from 6½d. in 1912 to 1/10 at the present time. The corresponding figures for a woman are from 5½d. to 1/7 a week.

Put another way, employees and employers together contributed £18½ million in 1914, £56½ million in 1921, £79¾ million in 1928, and nearly £108 million in 1938.

POOR RELIEF

20. Notwithstanding the big increase in State insurances, the numbers in receipt of poor relief are not materially different from what they were before these important new schemes of insurance and assistance were put into operation. The numbers on domiciliary

and institutional relief in Great Britain in various years are given in the following table :—

TABLE XIX.—NUMBER OF PERSONS (INCLUDING DEPENDANTS) RELIEVED IN GREAT BRITAIN

	Domiciliary 000's	Per 10,000 Population	Institutional 000's	Per 10,000 Population
1900	584	158	227	61
1910	628	155	304	75
1920	369	88	195	46
1925	1,064	243	229	52
1930	1,018	228	233	52
1939	1,156	249	169	36
1942	462	98	143	30

21. The number on domiciliary relief in 1942, was abnormally low owing to the war having caused a greatly increased demand for labour of all kinds. If allowance is made for this factor, it is probable that the number in 1942 would be higher than the number relieved in 1900. The institutional figure for 1942 is also affected by the war, but since the Local Government Act, 1929, under which many poor law hospitals and their inmates were transferred to the Public Health service, the number on institutional relief has been falling. The number of cases of institutional relief is thus substantially lower than at the beginning of this century.

22. It is interesting to ask why, notwithstanding the great increase in insurance and other forms of cash assistance, outdoor relief continues at such a comparatively high level. At the beginning of 1942 there were the following numbers receiving other forms of State benefit or assistance :—

	Approximate numbers
Unemployment Benefit and Assistance	140,000
National Health : Sickness and Disablement Benefit ...	800,000
Pensions : Old Age	3,620,000
Widows' (under 60)	440,000
Workmen's Compensation	100,000
	5,100,000

The number in receipt of unemployment benefit or assistance at the beginning of 1942 was exceptionally low owing to the war.

23. To a small extent the classes overlap, for it is possible, for example, to receive both unemployment benefit and workmen's compensation. The number of supplementary pensioners has been excluded because the recipients must already be included in the number of contributory or non-contributory pensioners.

24. Again, it is estimated that some 90,000 or about 40 per cent. of the cases in receipt of outdoor relief were receiving it in supplementation of some form of State benefit or workmen's compensation. It is probable, therefore, that, if double counting were excluded, the number of recipients of all forms of benefit and assistance would be around 5 million.

25. It must be pointed out that the receipt of benefit or pension does not mean that these people would otherwise be destitute as is the case of the recipient of outdoor relief. About ¾ million contributory old age pensioners are also employed, and the number of workmen's compensation cases includes workmen who are only partially incapacitated and are at work.

26. An analysis of Public Assistance cases for March, 1942, is given in the last section of this Appendix, and it is interesting to attempt a contrast with a year in the early part of the century. The Royal Commission on the Poor Laws obtained for England and Wales a detailed census of outdoor relief at 31st March, 1906.* Unfortunately, the classification was not on the same basis as the analysis made for the Inter-departmental Committee, but by a broad grouping it is possible to attempt some comparison. Table XX shows an analysis for 1906 and 1942.

---

* Appendix, Volume XXV, Cd. 5077.

TABLE XX.—ANALYSIS OF OUT-RELIEF IN ENGLAND AND WALES—1906 AND 1942

Type of Case	1906		1942		Change since 1906
	Number of Cases	Percentage of Total	Number of Cases	Percentage of Total	
Able-bodied unemployed :—					
Men	3,200	1·0	1,000	0·6	— 2,200
Women	2,700	0·8	600	0·3	— 2,100
Temporary, permanent, or chronic sickness or disablement, or mentally handicapped	51,400	15·5	107,600	59·9	+ 56,200
Widows, separated and deserted wives	40,200	12·1	36,500	20·3	— 3,700
Old persons (men 65 and over, women 60 and over)	219,800	66·2	26,000	14·5	— 193,800
Others	14,800	4·4	7,800	4·4	— 7,000
Total out-relief cases	332,100	100·0	179,500	100·0	— 152,600

27.   The comparison must be treated with some caution because of possible differences between the two years in the compilation of the statistics.   Furthermore because of the war 1942 was a time of very low unemployment, a fact which considerably reduces the number of all types of poor relief cases.   But, broadly speaking, the comparison shows the following results :—

(i) The various Old Age Pensions Acts, including supplementary pensions, have removed the main cause of outdoor relief.   The number of old persons remaining on outdoor relief is accounted for by the gap between 65 (60 for women) and the qualifying age of 70 for the non-contributory pension.   This gap accounted for 12 per cent. of all cases of outdoor relief in 1942.

(ii) The number of widows on outdoor relief has been decreased by the provision of widows' pensions, but there are still 18,000 widow pensioners under 60 who also receive out-relief.   In addition, there are now a large number of deserted wives in receipt of out-relief.

(iii) As a result of the war few, if any, able-bodied men are unemployed, and those who are now receive either unemployment insurance or assistance.   The few still remaining on outdoor relief are those out of scope of the insurance Acts, e.g. persons formerly working on own account.

(iv) There has been an increase in the number of cases of temporary and chronic sickness in receipt of out-relief notwithstanding the introduction of health insurance.   The majority of these 1942 cases was also receiving sickness or disablement benefit.

28.   One important general factor which affects the contrast is the increase in number of old persons.   In 1901 there were in England and Wales about 2 million men aged over 65 and women aged over 60, or about 1 in 16 of the total population.   In 1941 the number was nearly 5 million or nearly 1 in 8 of the total population.   When it is remembered that in 1906 half the pauperism was due to old age and that nearly 1 in 3 of the people aged over 70 were in receipt of poor relief, it can be seen that had it not been for the introduction of pension schemes there would have been a very big increase in the number of paupers.

29.   But probably the most important general factor has been the more generous and sympathetic administration of poor relief.   In 1906, according to evidence available to the Royal Commission, few Boards of Guardians had defined scales of relief.   In some Unions only completely destitute people were eligible for assistance, in others out-relief was only given if the applicant was already receiving sick pay from a Friendly Society, or had " shown signs of thrift," or was earning some minimum amount.   In some Unions relief was not paid to persons living " in cottages rented above the average rent of the neighbourhood," or paying rent above a certain amount, while in other districts out-relief was not given unless there was already sufficient income to pay rent.   These were no doubt extreme cases, but in most Unions nothing at all was allowed to an able-bodied widow in respect of herself and her first child, relief being paid only for children after the first.   Where there were defined scales of benefit the Royal Commission found that one Union

granted an adult only 1/– a week and 5 lb. of flour or its equivalent in bread. The more usual scale was 2/6 a week for an adult though in a few Unions it might be as high as 4/– or 5/– a week. The usual rate for a child was 1/– a week and one or two loaves. In most Unions nothing was allowed for a widow in respect of herself and her first child, relief being paid only in respect of the second child. To quote two cases from one Union, in 1906 a woman aged 73 earning 2/6 a week received 1/6 in relief ; and a widow—blind, with no income, living with a daughter who was a charwoman—received 2/6 a week relief.

30. Since 1906 and particularly in recent years Public Assistance scales have been made increasingly generous, and, though they vary from area to area, in general they tend to be fixed around subsistence level. As a result they are generally much higher than sickness and disablement benefit and the widow's pension. Furthermore, a large number of people with small earnings, who at the beginning of the century would have been refused poor relief, now have their income supplemented from this source. In general the poor law is no longer administered in the same deterrent manner as it was in the earlier part of the century.

31. Finally, it must be borne in mind that though there have been big extensions of State insurance the schemes do not cover either all the gainfully occupied or all classes of risk. Small shopkeepers, hawkers, middle-aged spinsters, and separated or deserted wives generally must have recourse to the Poor Law if they lose their source of income. Public Assistance Authorities are still responsible on the one hand for giving relief in cases of sudden and urgent necessity and on the other for meeting the needs of everybody who does not qualify for benefit under any other scheme.

SECTION 2. SUMMARY AND ANALYSIS OF EXISTING SCHEMES OF SOCIAL INSURANCE AND ASSISTANCE ADMINISTRATION

	Unemployment Insurance	Health Insurance	Contributory Pensions (Old Age and Widows and Orphans)	Non-Contributory Pensions (Old Age and Blind Pensions)	Supplementary Pensions
Central Department	Ministry of Labour and National Service	The Ministry of Health; Department of Health for Scotland; and Welsh Board of Health, are responsible for their particular countries. But for the purpose of securing co-ordination the responsible Ministers act together as a Joint Committee	Same as for Health Insurance	Commissioners of Customs and Excise	Assistance Board
Assessment Agency	Local Insurance Officers of the Ministry of Labour and National Service	Approved Society* of which the Insured person is a member	Appropriate Central Department	Investigation by local Pension Officer (of Customs and Excise) Assessment by Local Pension Committee (appointed by County Councils and by Boroughs and Urban Districts with population over 20,000—in Scotland by all Burghs)	Assistance Board Area Officers
Payment Agency	Local Offices of Ministry of Labour and National Service		Post Office	Post Office	Post Office
Other Administrative Bodies		Insurance Committee (for Medical Benefit) for the County or County Borough in which the insured person is resident			
Appeal Tribunal	Appeals against an Insurance Officer to a Court of Referees. Appeal against Court of Referees to the Umpire	If dispute between insured person and Approved Society is not settled by arbitration under the Society's rules Department may appoint a referee	Panel of Referees	By claimant or Pensions Officer to Ministry of Health, or Department of Health for Scotland	Local Appeal Tribunal
Statutory Consultative or Advisory Bodies	Unemployment Insurance Statutory Committee	Consultative Councils for National Health Insurance (Approved Societies' Work). One for England and Wales and another, for Scotland			Local Advisory Committees

Dental Benefit Council and the Ophthalmic Benefit Approved Committee

* The benefits of Deposit Contributors (persons who are not members of Approved Societies) are administered by Insurance Committees and the Central Departments.

ADMINISTRATION—*Continued*

	Blind Persons Assistance	Unemployment Assistance	Public Assistance	War Pensions			Workmen's Compensation
				Services	Mercantile Marine	Civilians	
Central Department	Ministry of Health, Department of Health for Scotland and Welsh Board of Health (Board of Education for Education and Training)	Assistance Board	Ministry of Health, Department of Health for Scotland and Welsh Board of Health	Ministry of Pensions	Ministry of Pensions	Ministry of Pensions	Home Office.
Assessment Agency	County Council, County Borough Council and the City of London; or, in Scotland, County Councils and large Burghs	Assistance Board Area Officers	Public Assistance Committee of County or County Borough Council	Ministry of Pensions	Ministry of Pensions	Ministry of Pensions	Settled by agreement between employer and workman, or, in default of agreement, by arbitration, generally, in the County Court, (in Scotland the Sheriff Court). Disputes on medical issues may be referred through the County (or Sheriff Court) to a medical Referee, whose certificate is conclusive.
Payment Agency		Ministry of Labour Local Offices; Assistance Board Area Offices		Post Office (Paymaster General for Officers' War Pensions)	Post Office	Post Office	—
Other Local Agencies	Powers delegated to Voluntary Associations in many cases	—	—	—	—	—	—
Appeal Tribunal	—	Local Appeal Tribunals	Ministry of Health, Department of Health for Scotland and Welsh Board of Health	Pensions Appeals Tribunal (still available for the few Great War widows' cases) Central Advisory Committee Special Grants Committee (for Great War cases)	—	—	Appeals on points of law to Court of Appeal (in Scotland, Court of Session) with further appeal to House of Lords.
Statutory Consultative or Advisory Bodies	Advisory Committee on the Welfare of the Blind	Local Advisory Committees	—	War Pensions Committees (local) for applications arising out of Great War. (Non-statutory: At request of Minister these Committees afford same facilities to present war applicants). (Non-statutory: Panel of independent Medical Experts).	(Non-statutory: Civil Injuries Advisory Committees)	(Non-statutory: Civil Injuries Advisory Committees)	

Scope of Unemployment, Health and Contributory Pensions Schemes.

Compulsory Contributors

A.   All persons engaged under a contract of service or as apprentices receiving a money payment are compulsorily insurable under the Unemployment, Health and Contributory Pensions Insurance Schemes.

The general exceptions to this rule are :—

(1) Men aged 65 or over and women aged 60 or over.(a)

(2) Non-manual workers whose rate of remuneration exceeds £420 a year.

(3) Husbands employed by their wives and wives employed by their husbands.

(4) Persons who receive no money payment and are the children of or maintained by their employers.

(5) Agents paid by commission, fees or share in profits, or partly one or the other who are :—

    (a) Mainly dependent upon earnings from some other occupation, or
    (b) employed as an agent by more than one employer and are not mainly dependent on the earnings from any one agency.

(6) Persons casually employed (otherwise than for the purpose of the employer's trade or business, or for the purposes of any game or recreation where the employees are engaged or paid through a club).

(7) Teachers who are in contributory service within the meaning of the Teachers (Superannuation) Act, 1925 (or Education (Scotland) (Superannuation) Acts, 1919–25).

(8) Pupil and student teachers in a public elementary school (or a State aided school in Scotland).

(9) Persons engaged in occupations specified by Special Order as being of a subsidiary character and not as the principal means of livelihood.

(10) Masters and seamen who are neither domiciled nor have a place of residence in the United Kingdom. (b)

(11) Persons engaged in certain employments under local authorities specified in a Special Order.

B.   The following classes of employment are *within* the scope of *Compulsory Health and Pensions Insurance*, but *not* of *Unemployment Insurance* :—

(1) Certain classes of employment which, although not under contract of service, is akin to employment under such a contract and is performed for a recognisable employer.

These classes of employment are :—

    (i) Outworkers (i.e., persons who take out work to be done in their own homes and not under the control or supervision of the employer) (but in the rare case where the outworker can be shown to be under contract of service with the employer who gives out the work he is insurable under Unemployment Insurance).
    (ii) Cab drivers and others plying for hire with a vehicle or vessel obtained under a contract of bailment.
    (iii) Employment by way of manual labour under a contract for the performance of such labour for the purposes of any trade or business but which is not employment under a contract of Service.
    (iv) Crews of fishing vessels wholly remunerated by shares of profits or gross earnings.

(2) Employment in private indoor domestic service.

(3) Certain part-time cleaners who are employed wholly outside the business hours of their employer or for a comparatively short time inside those hours.

(4) Certain domestic servants in universities, schools, colleges and certain other residential educational establishments.

(5) Employment as a female professional nurse for the sick and female probationers undergoing training.

(6) Certain kinds of employment by Government Departments, local authorities, railway companies, etc., which are excluded from unemployment insurance either specifically or by certificates of exception from such insurance, but are not excluded by corresponding certificates for health insurance.(c)

(7) Employment in work provided by a Local Authority in consequence of an arrangement made between that Authority and a Poor Law Authority, if the latter makes a contribution towards remuneration, except where the person employed has previously been in receipt of unemployment benefit and is employed in full time work provided by the Local Authority.

(8) Employed persons in receipt of a Blind Person's pension.

(9) Persons employed in agriculture who are not domiciled in, and ordinarily resident outside, the United Kingdom (but may be excluded from health insurance by the operation of the Subsidiary Employments Order (d)).

(10) Employment in agriculture, horticulture or forestry where the persons employed bear certain relationships to the employer, e.g., son, parent, grandparent.

(11) Persons employed in inconsiderable employment, i.e., persons not under the age of 16, employed (except as dockers), less than 4 hours in any week by any individual employer ; or employed only on a Sunday or Monday in certain circumstances ; or employed as a snow clearer on not more than 4 days in the week.

(12) Persons serving in the Naval, Military or Air services of the Crown. On discharge, however, a credit of Unemployment contributions is given subject to certain conditions to all such persons.

(13) Persons employed ordinarily for not more than 30 hours a week whose employment began since 3rd September, 1939, and whose services are not ordinarily performed by persons rendering not more than 30 hours a week or would not be so performed but for circumstances arising out of the war.

C. The following classes of employment are *within* the scope of *Compulsory Employment Insurance*, but *not* of *Health and Pensions Insurances* :—

(1) Certain employment excluded from health insurance by certificates of exception, but not from unemployment insurance either by certificates of exception, or specifically.

(2) Persons engaged under certain conditions for employment outside the United Kingdom by persons resident in or having their principal place of business in Great Britain.

(3) Employment on an agricultural holding, where there is no money payments and the employer is the occupier of the holding.

(4) Employment in the United Kingdom as a master or a member of the crew of a British ship registered outside Great Britain, not being a ship engaged in regular trade with ports outside the British Isles.

(5) Employment for the purpose of any business of which, within a period of two years immediately preceding the date on which the employment began, the employed person was the owner or part owner, being employment of that person either by a relative or by a company in the case of which the majority of the voting power or shares is in the hands of the employed person or his relatives or of nominees of the employed person or his relatives.

D. The following classes are *within* the scope of Pensions Insurance, but not of *Unemployment Insurance* or *Health Insurance* :—

(1) Certain kinds of employment, in general, pensionable by Government Departments, local authorities, railway companies, etc., which are excluded from unemployment insurance either specifically or by certificates of exception, and are also excluded from Health Insurance by a certificate of exception.

(2) Certain persons though engaged in insurable employment are entitled, if they so desire, to claim exemption from the payment of the employee's share of the contributions payable in respect of unemployment, health(e) and old age pensions, but men who obtain exemption in this way are compulsorily insurable for widows' and orphans' pensions.

The condition subject to which such exemption may be granted is that the person must be

(a) in receipt of a pension or independent income of not less than £26 a year, or
(b) dependent, ordinarily and mainly, upon some other person for his livelihood, or
(c) in insurable(f) employment for less than 18 weeks in a contribution year, or
(d) ordinarily and mainly dependent upon some non-insurable employment for his livelihood.

NOTE.—During the war no exemption can be granted otherwise than by way of renewal of a certificate of exemption issued before 3rd September, 1939.

PERSONS ENTITLED TO BE VOLUNTARY CONTRIBUTORS

There is no provision for the voluntary payment of Unemployment Insurance Contributions.

For persons becoming voluntary contributors after 2nd January, 1938, health insurance and pensions insurance are distinct from and independent of each other, and contributions under one scheme are payable separately from contributions under the other.

Persons who have been compulsorily insured for health insurance and pensions or for pensions alone and have ceased to be so insured by reason of having ceased to be employed, or having become subject to a change in the conditions of their employment (e.g., by having their rate of remuneration for non-manual employment increased above the rate of £420 a year), or having entered excepted employment, which may or may not be insurable for pensions, or having become exempt persons, may become voluntary contributors for the benefits for which they were compulsorily insured and have ceased to be so insured, if they were employed in the employment in respect of which they were insured for those benefits for at least 104 weeks since last entry into insurance. The only exception to this rule is that a married woman cannot become a voluntary contributor for health insurance.

Thus :—

(1) Employed contributors compulsorily insured for health insurance and pensions on ceasing to be so insured may, if they satisfy the employment condition, become voluntary contributors for health insurance and/or pensions insurance.

A person who becomes a voluntary contributor for health insurance remains a member of the Approved Society (if any) to which he belonged as an employed contributor, but voluntary insurance for pensions is administered by the Central Departments.

(2) Persons excepted from health insurance but compulsorily insurable for all pensions may in the circumstances stated above become voluntary contributors for all pensions.

(3) Married women previously compulsorily insurable for health insurance and pension may become voluntary contributors for pensions.

(4) Men excepted from compulsory health and old age pensions insurance and men holding exemption certificates, all of whom are compulsorily insurable for widows' and orphans' pensions, may, on ceasing to be compulsorily insurable, become voluntary contributors only for widows' and orphans' pensions.

SPECIAL VOLUNTARY CONTRIBUTORS FOR PENSIONS

These are persons, not entitled to become voluntary contributors by virtue of the qualification of previous compulsory insurance, who at date of application

(i) are under age 40.

(ii) have been resident in Great Britain for the last 10 years,

(iii) are, in the case of men, in receipt of total incomes not exceeding £400 a year of which not more than £200 a year is unearned and in the case of women in receipt of total incomes of not more than £250 a year of which not more than £125 a year is unearned.

Men.—May insure either for Widows, Orphans and Old Age Pensions or Widows and Orphans pensions only.

Women.—May insure for Orphans and Old Age Pensions only.

Certain classes of men, e.g., teachers in recognised or contributory service, are entitled to become special voluntary contributors but only for widows and orphans pensions.

SCOPE OF EMPLOYMENT COVERED BY WORKMEN'S COMPENSATION

In general any person who has entered into or works under a contract of service or apprenticeship with an employer is within the scope of Workmen's Compensation. The specific exceptions to this general rule are :—

(1) Non-manual workers whose remuneration exceeds £420 a year. (Also excluded from Unemployment, Health and Pensions Insurance.)

(2) Person whose employment is of a casual nature and who is employed otherwise than for the purposes of the employer's trade or business, not being a person engaged for the purposes of any game or recreation or paid through a club. (Also excluded from Unemployment, Health and Pensions Insurance.)

(3) Outworkers. (Also excluded from Unemployment Insurance except where under contract of service with employer who gives out the work, but not from Health and Pensions Insurance.)

H

(4) Member of employer's family dwelling in his house. (Compare items A (3) and (4) and item B (10).

(5) Member of a Police Force. (Normally excepted from insurance for Unemployment, Health and Pensions.)

(6) Persons in the Naval, Military or Air Service of the Crown. (See item B (12).

(7) Fishermen who are remunerated wholly or mainly by shares in the profits or gross earnings of the vessel except so far as provided by Order. No such Order has been made. (Fishermen remunerated by shares in the profits or gross earnings of the vessel are not excepted from Health and Pensions Insurance.)

SCOPE OF EMPLOYMENT COVERED BY UNEMPLOYMENT ASSISTANCE

Normal occupation of applicant for Unemployment Assistance must be employment in respect of which contributions are payable under the Widows, Orphans and Old Age Contributory Pensions Acts. A person who has not normally been engaged in remunerative employment since the age of 16 may be admitted if he might reasonably have expected that he would have qualified as above but for the industrial circumstances of the district in which he resides.

SCOPE OF ALL OTHER SCHEMES

Not confined to particular types of employment but available to all who satisfy the general conditions, e.g., blindness in the case of Blind Persons Pensions.

(a) The employer's share of the contributions is payable by the employer in respect of these persons.

(b) Contributions are payable at the employer's rate for the purposes of Health and Unemployment Insurance but not for purposes of Pensions Insurance.

(c) The criterion for exception from Health Insurance is that the terms of service must be such as to secure provision in respect of sickness and disablement on the whole not less favourable than that made in the Health Insurance Act. For exclusion from Unemployment Insurance the employment must be permanent in character; the employed person must have completed 3 years service in the employment; and the other circumstances of the employment must make it unnecessary for it to be insured for unemployment purposes.

(d) Employer's contribution is payable for Unemployment Insurance.

(e) Such persons are entitled to medical benefit subject to certain conditions.

(f) The employment must be seasonal in the case of Unemployment Insurance.

TABLE XXI.—PRESENT SCHEMES OF SOCIAL INSURANCE

WEEKLY RATES OF CONTRIBUTIONS, 1942

Type of Contributor	Unemployment			Health			Pensions			Total		
	Employer	Employee	Total	Employer	Employee	Total	Employer	Employee	Total	Employer	Employee	Total
	d.	d.	s. d.	d.	d.	d.	s. d.	d.	s. d.	s. d.	s. d.	s. d.
GENERAL WORKERS (a)												
Men Aged 21–65	10	10	1 8							1 10	1 10	3 8
Women Aged 21–60	9	9	1 6							1 6	1 7	3 1
Young Men and Women between the ages of 18 and 21 :												
Men	9	9	1 6	(b) Men 5½	5½	11	Men 6½	6½	1 1	1 9	1 9	3 6
Women	8	8	1 4	Women 5½	5	10½	Women 3½	5	8½	1 5	1 6	2 11
Young People between the ages of 16 and 18 :												
Boys	5	5	10							1 5	1 5	2 10
Girls	4½	4½	9							1 1½	1 2½	2 4
Boys and Girls under the age of 16	2	2	4	2	2	4	—	—	—	4	4	8
Persons over age 65 (men) or 60 (women) in employment :												
Men	10	—	10	—	—	—	1 0	—	1 0(c)	1 10	—	1 10
Women	9	—	9	—	—	—	9	—	9(c)	1 6	—	1 6

(a) In the case of workers over the age of 18 who are remunerated at more than 3/– and not more than 4/– a day, and whose remuneration does not include the provision of board and lodging by the employer, the employer's contribution for Health Insurance is increased by 1d. a week and the worker's contribution is reduced by the same amount, while in the case of such workers who are remunerated at not more than 3/– a day, the employer is required to pay the whole of the worker's Health contribution in addition to his own.

(b) For masters and seamen serving on foreign going ships, the employer's Health contribution is 3d. less.

(c) These contributions are the sum of the rates payable by the employer in respect of employed persons for Health and Pensions. The Health portion of the contribution is transferred from the Pensions Account to the Health Insurance Funds.

WEEKLY RATES OF CONTRIBUTIONS—(*continued*)

Type of contributor	Unemployment			Health			Pensions			Total		
	Employer	Employee	Total	Employer	Employee	Total	Employer	Employee	Total	Employer	Employee	Total
EXEMPT PERSONS	*d.*	*d.*	*d.*	*d.*	*d.*	*d.*	*d.*	*d.*	*d.*	*s. d.*	*d.*	*s. d.*
Men aged 21 to 65	10	—	10		—		4½	2½	7	1 8	2½	1 10½
Women aged 21 to 60	9	—	9		—		2½	—	2½	1 5	—	1 5
Young men aged 18–21 ...	9	—	9	5½	—	5½	4½	2½	7	1 7	2½	1 9½
Young women aged 18–21 ...	8	—	8		—		2½	—	2½	1 4	—	1 4
Boys aged 16–18	5	—	5		—		4½	2½	7	1 3	2½	1 5½
Girls aged 16–18	4½	—	4½		—		2½	—	2½	1 0½	—	1 0½
AGRICULTURAL WORKERS (*d*)												
Men aged 21–65	3½	3½	7							1 3½	1 3½	2 7
Women aged 21–60	3	3	6							1 0	1 1	2 1
Young men aged 18–21 ...	3	3	6	M. 5½	5½	11	6½	6½	1 1	1 3	1 3	2 6
Young women aged 18–21 ...	2½	2½	5	W. 5½	5	10½	3½	5	8½	11½	1 0½	2 0
Boys aged 16–18	2	2	4							1 2	1 2	2 4
Girls aged 16–18	1½	1½	3							10½	11½	1 10
Boys under 16	1½	1½	3	2	2	4	—	—	—	3½	3½	7
Girls under 16	1	1	2	2	2	4	—	—	—	3	3	6
Men aged 65 or over ... ... (in employment)	3½	—	3½	—	—	—	1 0	—	1 0 (*e*)	1 3½	—	1 3½
Women aged 60 or over ... (in employment)	3	—	3	—	—	—	9	—	9	1 0	—	1 0
Members of the Forces of the Crown — Men ...	—	—	—	4	—	4	6½	6½	1 1	10½	6½	1 5
Members of the Forces of the Crown — Women	—	—	—	3½	—	3½	3½	5	8½	7	5	1 0

	s. d.	s. d.	s. d.	s. d.	s. d.	d.	d.
Persons excepted from Health and Unemployment Insurance :							
Men excepted from old age pensions contributions ...	7	3½	3½	7	3½	—	—
Not excepted from old age pensions contributions } Men ...	1 1	6½	6½	1 1	6½	—	—
} Women	8½	5	3½	8½	5	—	—
(f) VOLUNTARY CONTRIBUTORS:							
Insured for health purposes only, total income not over £420 a year } Men ...	—	—	—	—	—	11	11
} Women	—	—	—	—	—	10½	10½
Insured for health purposes only, total income over £420 a year } Men ...	—	—	—	—	—	8	8
} Women	—	—	—	—	—	7½	7½
Insured for widows orphans and old age pensions only } Men ...	1 1	—	—	1 1	—	—	—
} Women g	1 1	—	—	1 1	—	—	—
Men insured for widows and orphans pensions only ...	7	—	—	7	—	—	—
Insured for health and pensions purposes under combined Scheme, total income not over £420 a year } Men ...	2 0	8½	—	2 0	8½	—	—
} Women g	1 7	8½	—	1 7	8½	—	—
Insured for health and pensions purposes under combined scheme, total income over £420 a year } Men ...	1 9	8½	—	1 9	8½	—	—
} Women g	1 4	8½	—	1 4	8½	—	—

(d) For Unemployment Insurance the contributions in respect of exempt persons are those payable by the employer. For Health and Pensions Insurance they are the rates already listed.

(e) These contributions are the sum of the rates payable by the employer in respect of employed persons for Health and Pensions. The Health portion of the contribution is transferred from the Pensions Account to the Health Insurance Funds.

(f) Special Voluntary Contributors are insured only for Pensions and pay varying rates of contribution. For men they vary from 10d. to 2/11, according to class of insurance and age at entry (for women rates vary from 6d. to 11d.), and are payable up to 65 years of age.

(g) Women are not insured for the purposes of widows' pensions.

TABLE XXII.—PRESENT SCHEMES OF SOCIAL INSURANCE AND ASSISTANCE
WEEKLY RATES OF BENEFIT

	Unemployment Insurance		Health Insurance (a)		Contributory Pensions (d)			Non-Contributory Pensions and Blind Persons' Pensions
	General	Agricultural	Sickness	Disablement	Old Age	Widows	Orphans	
Men 65 and over	—	—	—	—	10/-	—	—	10/- (e) (Non-contributor at 70, Blind at 40)
Men 21–65	20/-	18/-	18/- (c)	10/6	—	—	—	
Men 18–21	16/- (g)	15/- (g)			—	—	—	
Boys 17–18	9/-	7/6			—	—	—	
Boys 16–17	6/-	5/-			—	—	—	
Women 60 and over	— (f)	— (f)	—	—	10/-	—	—	10/- (e) (Non-contributor at 70, Blind at 40)
Women 21–60	18/-	15/-	single 15/- (c)	single 9/-	—	10/-	—	
Women 18–21	14/- (g)	12/- (g)	married 13/-	married 8/-	—	—	—	
Girls 17–18	7/6	6/-			—	—	—	
Girls 16–17	5/-	4/-			—	—	—	
Allowances for Dependants:— Wife or other adult dependant	10/-	9/-	—	—	—	—	—	
Children's Allowances (b):—								
First ...	4/-	4/-				5/-	7/6	
Second ...	4/-	4/-				3/-	7/6	
Third, etc. ...	3/-	3/-				3/-	7/6	
Maximum benefit ...	—	41/- or 6/10 a day						

(a) These rates may be increased by additional cash benefits or reduced on account of unpaid arrears.
In addition to sickness and disablement benefit the scheme provides for the payment of a maternity benefit of £2 which may be increased by additional benefit.
(b) Age limit unless otherwise stated is 14 (or 16 in case of children receiving whole time education).
(c) Until 104 contributions have been paid and 104 weeks of insurance have been completed the rate of sickness benefit is reduced to 12/- for men and 10/6 for women.
(d) The rates of pension shown in these columns may be reduced where the title for pension is based on the insurance of voluntary contributors for pensions who have not maintained an average of at least 50 contributions a year over the whole period of insurance.
(e) This is the maximum rate and lower scales apply where means are higher. The lowest rate is 1/-.
(f) The appropriate unemployment benefit rate for women 21–60 is applicable to women between 60 and 65 who qualify under the special transitional provision ending on June 30th, 1945.
(g) These rates are increased to the full adult rates if dependants' benefit is also allowed.

	Supplementary Pensions — Present Normal Weekly Rates (h)			Unemployment Assistance — Present Normal Weekly Rates (j)			Public Assistance and Blind Persons Assistance
	Householder in household	In household but not householder	Not member of a household	Householder in household	In household but not householder	Not member of a household	
	To arrive at the amount of Supplementary Pension, the basic Old Age or Widow's Pension must be deducted.						The scale (if any) for any particular area is determined by the Public Assistance Authority (or the Blind Persons Acts Authority) for that area, and the application of the scale in any particular case depends upon the needs of the applicant.
Married couple	If both are pensioners 37/- If only one is a pensioner 36/-	31/- plus rent allowance (maximum 7/-)	—	35/-	28/- plus rent allowance (maximum 7/-)	—	
Single applicant: Male ...	22/-	16/- plus rent allowance (maximum 5/-)	22/-	20/6	21 or over:— 14/6 plus rent allowance (maximum 5/-) 18–21:— 12/6 plus rent allowance (maximum 5/-) 16–18:— 12/6	20/-	
Female ...	21/-	15/- plus rent allowance (maximum 5/-)	22/-	19/6	21 and over:— 13/6 plus rent allowance (maximum 5/-) 18–21:— 12/6 plus rent allowance (maximum 5/-) 16–18:— 12/6	20/-	
Allowances for dependants: Adult	If not already included above and 21 or over:— Man 14/- Woman 13/-			If not already included above and 21 or over Man 14/6 Woman 13/6			
Children's allowances: 16–21...	12/-			12/6			
14–16...	7/9			7/9			
11–14...	6/3			6/3			
8–11...	5/9			5/9			
5–8...	5/3 (i)			5/3 (i)			
Under 5	4/9 (i)			4/9 (i)			
Maximum benefit	—			In the absence of special circumstances an allowance must not exceed the amount which the applicant might reasonably expect to earn if in employment in his normal occupation.			

(h) These normal rates comprise the basic Scale Rates plus additions to Scale Rates at present prescribed by Regulation and which may be varied from time to time. They may be adjusted on account of (i) rent, (ii) resources available to applicant in addition to Old Age or Widow's Pension, (iii) special circumstances.

(i) 5/9 if only one child and not more than two adults in household.

(j) These normal rates comprise the basic Scale Rates plus additions to Scale Rates prescribed at present by Regulation and which may be varied from time to time. They may be adjusted on account of (i) rent, (ii) resources available to applicant, (iii) special circumstances.

WEEKLY RATES OF BENEFIT (*continued.*)

	War Pensions (Services, Mercantile Marine and Civilians)			
	Services		Mercantile Marine	Civil Defence Personnel and gainfully occupied civilians
	Great War	Present War	Present War	Present War
DISABLEMENT (100% rates)(a)				
Man	40/- (b)	37/6 (b)	37/6 (b)	{ 18 and over 37/6 / Under 18 18/9
Woman	—	27/6 (b)	27/6 (b)	{ 18 and over 27/6 / Under 18 15/-
Additional allowances (a)				
Wife	10/-	9/2	9/2	9/2
1st child	7/6 (c)	7/1 (c)	7/1 (c)	7/1 (c)
2nd child	6/- (c)	5/5 (c)	5/5 (c)	5/5 (c)
3rd child and others (each)	6/- (c)	5/5 (c)	5/5 (c)	5/5 (c)
WIDOWS' PENSIONS AND ALLOWANCES				
Over 40 years of age / All ages with children eligible for allowances	26/8 (b)	25/- (b)	25/- (b)	25/-
Under 40 without eligible children	20/- (b)	17/6 (b) (d)	17/6 (b) (d)	17/6 (d)
Separated wives	3/6–13/9	up to 17/6	up to 17/6	up to 17/6
UNMARRIED DEPENDANTS LIVING AS WIVES	12/-	11/-	11/-	
CHILDREN'S ALLOWANCES				
1st Child	10/-	9/6	9/6	9/6
2nd Child	7/6	7/-	7/-	7/-
3rd Child	6/-	5/6	5/6	5/6
TOTAL ORPHANS				
1st Child	12/-	11/-	11/-	11/-
2nd Child and others each	11/- (e)	11/-	11/-	11/- (b)
DEPENDANTS				
Parents	5/- to 20/-	5/- to 10/- for 1 / 5/- to 12/6 for 2 (Plus an addition not exceeding 6/6 in special circumstances)		
Other Dependants	Up to 20/-	Up to 5/- for 1 / Up to 10/- for more than one		

(a) For lower percentages of disablement, rates are correspondingly less.

(b) Rates applicable to the private soldier, etc., subject to increases in the form of allowances for higher ranks.

(c) If no wife's allowance, the rate for the first child is that of the wife, for the second child that applicable to the first, and so on.

(d) If physically or mentally incapable of self-support, widow is eligible for " over 40 " rate.

(e) If each orphan is in a different household, each is granted the rate applicable to the first child.

WORKMEN'S COMPENSATION (f)

	During Total Disablement	During Partial Disablement
MAN OR WOMAN	(i) Average weekly earnings from 50/– upwards—a weekly payment not exceeding 50% of earnings with maximum of 30/– (ii) Average weekly earnings below 50/– proportion varies from 50% to 75%.	One half (or such other proportion as under (ii) opposite) of the difference between the pre-accident earnings and what the workman is earning or is able to earn in some suitable trade or business after the accident, subject to the maximum of 30/–
ADDITIONAL ALLOWANCES	In addition to the weekly payments as above, a supplementary allowance of 5/– a week is payable making the maximum 35/–. Male workmen with children under 15 years of age are also entitled to allowances for such children as follows :— First and second child, 4/– a week each. Third child and others, 3/– a week each.	In addition, the same proportion of the supplementary allowances as his weekly payment bears to the weekly payment payable in case of total incapacity.
MAXIMUM BENEFIT	The weekly payment and supplementary allowances together not to exceed seven-eighths of average weekly earnings.	The weekly payment and allowances together not to exceed seven-eighths of the difference between pre-accident and post-accident earnings.
WIDOWS OR OTHER TOTALLY DEPENDENT PERSONS	Where injury results in death and the workman leaves dependants wholly dependent on his earnings, the compensation is £200 or three years' earnings, whichever is the larger, up to a maximum of £300 (g) Where a workman leaves a child or children under the age of 15, as well as a widow or other members of his family over the age of 15, wholly or partially dependent on his earnings, there is payable in addition an allowance in respect of each child varying according to the child's age and the workman's earnings. The total compensation not to exceed £600 (h).	
PARTIAL DEPENDANTS	Where the workman leaves persons partially dependent on him for the ordinary necessaries of life, suitable for persons in his class or position, the compensation is such sum not exceeding £300 as is reasonable and proportionate to the loss sustained by such dependants.	
NO DEPENDANTS	Reasonable expenses of medical attendance and burial, up to a maximum of £15.	

(f) The rates apply in every case, irrespective of age, but where the workman was, at the date of the accident, under 21 years of age he can, after six months, have the compensation reviewed on the basis of what he would probably have been earning at the date of review if he had remained uninjured ; but application must be made before or within six months after the workman attains the age of 21.

(g) Any weekly payments (excluding supplementary allowances) paid to the workman in the interval between the accident and death have to be deducted, but not so as to reduce the amount below £200. If the workman has been paid a lump sum in redemption of the weekly payments, the whole amount so paid is deducted.

(h) Deductions cannot be made from the children's allowances except where a lump sum has been paid in redemption of the weekly payments.

CONDITIONS OF BENEFIT

	UNEMPLOYMENT INSURANCE. GENERAL AND AGRICULTURAL SCHEMES.	HEALTH INSURANCE				
		Sickness Benefit (a)	Disablement Benefit (a)	Maternity Benefit (b)	Medical Benefit (c)	Additional Benefit (d)
General qualifications to be satisfied before drawing benefit.	*First Statutory Condition.* 30 contributions (20 in case of the Agricultural scheme) to be paid for two years before the claim. A claimant who has been at any time during the two years in receipt of a disability pension for a disability contracted during the late War (1914–18) and whose failure to satisfy this condition is due to his disability, need only prove the payment of 10 contributions instead of 30 or 20 as the case may be. If during any period within the two years a person has been unfit for work by reason of sickness or has been in employment which is excepted from the unemployment insurance scheme, the period of two years may be extended by the period of sickness or of employment in excepted work, up to a maximum of four years. When once the First Statutory Condition has been satisfied it is held to remain satisfied until the end of the benefit year. In the case of a woman between the ages of 60 and 65, only contributions paid in respect of the period prior to her 60th birthday, or 1st July, 1940, whichever is later, count towards the satisfaction of this condition. *Second Statutory Condition.* That he has made application for benefit in the prescribed manner and proves that since the date of the application he has been continuously unemployed. (A period of unemployment is not deemed to commence until the insured contributor makes application for benefit in the prescribed manner. *Third Statutory Condition.* That he is capable of and available for work. *Fourth Statutory Condition.* That if required to attend an authorised course of training he proves that he duly attended or had good cause for not attending. *Freedom from Disqualification.* In general, persons are disqualified for benefit for varying periods:— (i) during a stoppage of work due to a trade dispute; (ii) if discharged for misconduct; (iii) after leaving voluntarily without just cause; (iv) for refusing suitable employment; (v) while receiving sickness or disability benefit under the National Health Insurance Acts; (vi) while in a public institution or residing outside Great Britain.	26 weeks' insurance and 26 contributions qualify for reduced rates of benefit. The normal rates become payable only after the insured person has been insured for 104 weeks and has paid 104 contributions.	104 weeks' insurance and 104 contributions.	42 weeks' insurance and 42 contributions.	Available immediately on becoming insured. But not available to voluntary contributors whose total income from all sources exceeds £420 per annum.	Treatment: January of the 3rd year after that in which person concerned becomes a member of the Approved Society. For additional cash benefits the qualifying time is the January of the 5th year after that in which person concerned becomes a member of the Approved Society, but for the purposes of cash additional benefits membership before the age of 16 is disregarded.

These benefits are available only to insured persons. A person who ceases to be insurably employed normally remains in insurance for a period of between 18 and 24 months, during which he continues to be entitled to all benefits subject to the conditions set out below. At the end of that period his insurance ceases unless he has resumed insurable employment, or has become a voluntary contributor or, having been insured for at least ten years when he ceased employment, he shows that since ceasing employment he has been available for but unable to obtain employment. In the last-mentioned event, subject to proof of genuine unemployment, his insurance can be extended year by year indefinitely; but, while so insured, he is not entitled to sickness and disablement benefits.

Voluntary contributors for Health Insurance who do not pay at least 45 contributions in any year (26 in the case of men over age 60, or women over age 55, who have been insured for 10 years) are not allowed to continue to be voluntary contributors and their insurance ceases after 18 to 24 months from the date of the last contribution paid.

Juvenile Contributors (i.e. employed persons under the age of 16) are entitled only to medical benefit.

A Deposit Contributor (i.e. an insured person who has not joined an Approved Society) is entitled to receive cash benefits to the extent to which the value of his contributions (plus State grant) will allow, the first charge on his account being for medical benefit and administration expenses.

Sickness Benefit (a)	Maternity Benefit (b)	Medical Benefit (c)	Additional Benefit (d)
(a) Sickness and disablement benefits are payable in respect of periods of incapacity for work caused by some specific disease or by bodily or mental disablement. These benefits are not payable or may be payable at a reduced rate (i) if there is title to compensation or damages under the Workmen's Compensation Acts or otherwise, or (ii) in respect of incapacity caused by injury or disease due to the war for which injury Allowance or War Pension may be granted.	(b) Maternity benefit is payable in respect of the confinement of the wife or widow of an insured man, or of any woman who is herself an insured person.	(c) Medical benefit consists of the provision of free medical treatment (including medicines) and attendance such as is normally provided by a general medical practitioner.	(d) These benefits are provided by approved Societies out of disposable surplus, if any, which is revealed in quinquennial valuation. Treatment additional benefits consist of payments towards the cost of forms of treatment, e.g. dental ophthalmic, hospital, or convalescent home treatment or of medical or surgical appliances. Cash additional benefit consists of additions to the normal statutory cash benefits. The choice of additional benefits is left to the individual Approved Society and the extent to which they can be provided depends on the amount of the disposable surplus.

CONDITIONS OF BENEFIT—(continued)

Payment of benefit commences.	The first three days of a continuous period of unemployment are a waiting period for which no benefit is payable. The rule regarding continuity of unemployment is as follows:— (1) Any two or more days of unemployment, whether consecutive or not, within a period of six consecutive days is treated as a continuous period of unemployment, and (2) Any two such continuous periods of two or more days are treated as continuous with one another if they are separated by not more than ten weeks.	4th day of incapacity.	After payment of 26 weeks of sickness benefit. (e)	—	—	—
Payment of benefit ceases.	(1) After a certain number of days have been drawn:— (i) Normally, the maximum number of days receivable in a Benefit year under the General Scheme is 156 with additional days varying according to the employment record; under the Agricultural Scheme the whole number of days receivable depends upon the employment record, subject to a maximum of 300 days in any benefit year. (ii) During the war the number of days receivable under the General Scheme is 180 and that under the Agricultural Scheme 90. (2) After attaining a certain age, namely, 65 in the case of men and 60 in the case of women (up to 30th June, 1945, there is a special transitional provision relating to women aged 60 to 65).	(1) After payment for 26 weeks. (e) (2) After attaining age of 65 (60 in case of women, up to 30th June, 1945, there is a special transitional provision for certain women aged 60 to 65).	After attaining age of 65 (60 in case of women, although up to 30th June, 1945, there is a special transitional provision for certain women aged 60 to 65).	—	—	—

(e) In calculating the 26 weeks, periods of incapacity separated by intervals of less than 12 months are linked together and treated as though they formed a single illness.

CONDITIONS OF BENEFIT—(continued)

	CONTRIBUTORY PENSIONS		NON-CONTRIBUTORY PENSIONS	SUPPLEMENTARY PENSIONS
	Old Age	Widows and Orphans (incl. children's allowances)	Old Age	(Old Age and Widows)
General qualifications to be satisfied before drawing benefit.	The *qualifying conditions* for the 65 (or 60 for women) to 70 pensions are that :— (i) that claimant must be an insured(a) person on reaching pensionable age and have been insured for at least five years up to that date ; (ii) at least 104 contributions must have been paid ; and (iii) the number of contributions, weeks of incapacity and weeks of genuine unemployment for the three contribution years immediately before reaching pensionable age must represent a yearly average of at least 39. If condition (i) is not satisfied at the date of attaining pensionable age the applicant may become eligible for a pension provided he subsequently completes five years of insurance before age 70; the other conditions then apply as at the date of completion of five years' insurance. Condition (iii) does not apply to a person who on reaching age 60 had been continuously insured for 10 years. If the man was 62 years of age or over when he married, his wife will not be entitled to an old age pension in right of his insurance before the expiration of three years from the marriage unless immediately before the marriage she was (or but for any disqualification would have been) in receipt of a widow's pension. A married woman is entitled to an old age pension at age 60 in right of her husband's insurance if when she reaches that age he is alive and is himself entitled to an old age pension. If her husband is under age 65 when she attains age 60 she does not become entitled to an old age pension in right of his insurance until he reaches age 65, but she can become entitled at age 60 in right of her own insurance if she is an insured person and satisfies the conditions. For special Voluntary Contributors the Pension age for both men and women is 65 and the qualifying period is 10 years' insurance immediately before age 65 and payment of 260 contributions. A person is disqualified for receiving, or continuing to receive a pension while— (i) an inmate of a workhouse or other Poor Law institution unless he has become an inmate for the purpose of obtaining medical or surgical treatment in which case he is not disqualified so long as he continues to require such treatment ; (ii) detained in a mental hospital or maintained in any place as a rate-aided person of unsound mind. (This disqualification applies only to the very limited class of pensioners whose title to pension is not derived from payment of pensions contribu-	Title to a widow's pension *always depends on the insurance of her deceased husband. The qualifying conditions are* that the husband must be insured(a) at the date of death, and that 104 weeks must have elapsed and 104 contributions have been paid since his last entry into insurance. There is a further condition that if the husband dies before or after attaining age 65, whichever happens first, the number of contributions, weeks of incapacity and weeks of genuine unemployment for the three contribution years preceding his death, or his 65th birthday, as the case may require, must represent a yearly average of at least 26. (This condition does not apply, however, if the husband was over age 60 at death, and was continuously insured for a period of ten years up to reaching that age ; or if at the time of death he was entitled to a contributory old age pension under the scheme). A widow whose deceased husband was aged 60 or more at the date of marriage cannot become entitled to a widow's pension in respect of his insurance unless one of certain additional conditions is satisfied. For special Voluntary Contributors the qualifying period of 104 weeks of insurance and payment of 104 contributions. A *widow is disqualified* from receiving, or continuing to receive, a pension while she—(i) is cohabiting with a man as his wife ; (ii) is an inmate of a workhouse or other Poor Law Institution unless she has become an inmate for the purpose of obtaining medical or surgical treatment, in which case she is not disqualified so long as she continues to require such treatment ; (iii) detained in a mental hospital or maintained in any place as a rate-aided person of unsound mind ; (iv) is being maintained in any place as a criminal lunatic, or (v) is undergoing a term of imprisonment without the option of a fine. Disqualifications (ii) and (iii) apply also to orphans' pensions and children's allowances. Disqualification (iii) applies only to the very limited class of pensioners whose title to pension is not derived from payment of pensions contributions.	1. Must have attained age 70. 2. Must have been a British Subject for at least 10 years up to date of receipt of pension. 3. Must have resided in U.K. for 12 years after 50, and, if not a natural born British Subject, for 20 years in all. 4. Income calculated in the prescribed manner, must not exceed £49 17s. 6d. a year, after deducting such part, if any, not exceeding £39 as is derived from any source other than earnings. A person is disqualified by law for receiving or continuing to receive, a pension while— (i) an inmate of a workhouse or other Poor Law Institution, unless he has become an inmate for the purpose of obtaining medical or surgical treatment, in which case he is not disqualified so long as he continues to require such treatment ; (iii) detained in a mental hospital or maintained in any place as a rate-aided person of unsound mind ; (iii) being maintained in any place as a criminal lunatic ; (iv) undergoing a term of imprisonment without option of a fine ; (v) having been convicted at the age of 60 or over he is liable to have a detention order made against him under the Inebriates Act, 1898, and the Court has ordered³ that he is to be disqualified.	Any person (other than a blind person) who is entitled to weekly payments on account of an old age pension or (in the case of a widow of 60 years of age or more) who is entitled to weekly payments on account of a widow's pension under the Contributory Pensions Act, and is *in need.*

CONDITIONS OF BENEFIT—(continued)

Benefit commences.	(iii) being maintained in any place as a criminal lunatic; or (iv) undergoing a term of imprisonment without the option of a fine. On attaining age 65 (or 60 in case of women insured otherwise than as special voluntary contributors). In case of a woman claiming by virtue of her husband's insurance, when he attains 65 or when she attains 60, whichever is the later. If, however, the husband is insured as a special voluntary contributor the woman must wait until she also attains the age of 65.	On widowhood. Orphans' pensions become payable at death of widow or widower.	On attaining age of 70.	On satisfying general conditions.
Benefit ceases.	(1) On attaining age of 70 when the pension is automatically replaced by a non-contributory old age pension without means, residence or nationality tests. (2) If disqualified as mentioned above.	Widow's pension ceases :— (1) On re-marriage. (2) On attaining age of 70 when the pension is automatically replaced by a non-contributory old age pension without means, residence or nationality tests. (3) If disqualified as mentioned above. Orphans and other children : payment continues until the child attains age of 14, or for so long as he remains under full-time instruction in a day school, but not beyond the end of July next following the date on which he attains the age of 16.	(1) If income, calculated in the prescribed manner, rises to over £49 17s. 6d. a year, after making deduction referred to at 4 above. (2) If disqualified as mentioned above.	On ceasing to satisfy general conditions.

(a) "Insured" in this connection normally means "insured under the Health Insurance Scheme other than as a voluntary contributor." Special provisions are made for the continuance of Pensions Insurance in the case of exempt and excepted persons and of voluntary contributors for pensions. In general, such persons are entitled to a free period of insurance, after ceasing to pay contributions, of 18 to 24 months.

CONDITIONS OF BENEFIT—(continued)

	Blind Persons Pensions	Blind Persons Assistance	Unemployment Assistance	Public Assistance (Non-Institutional)
General qualifications to be satisfied before drawing benefit.	The general conditions for the grant of pensions to persons who are "so blind as to be unable to perform any work for which eyesight is essential," are the same as for non-contributory old age pensions with two exceptions :— (a) A blind person must have reached the age of 40 instead of 70. (b) A blind person, if a natural-born British subject, must have resided in the United Kingdom for at least 12 years in all since the age of 20. The disqualifications are the same as for non-contributory old age pensions.	Domiciliary financial assistance is available to blind persons based on the needs of the blind persons and members of his household who are dependent on him.	(i) Aged 16 or over but not yet 65 years of age. (ii) His normal occupation is (a) employment in respect of which contributions are payable under the Contributory Pensions Acts; or (b) employment in respect of which by virtue of Section 4 of the Unemployment Insurance Act, 1940, contributions are payable under the Unemployment Insurance Acts, 1935–1940; (if person has not normally been engaged in any remunerative occupation since reaching the age of 16 years he may be admitted if he might reasonably have expected to qualify under (a) but for the industrial circumstances of the district in which he resides). (iii) Is capable of and available for work; and (iv) Is not affected by certain provisions relating to stoppages of work due to trade disputes. (v) In need, and has no work, or only such part-time or intermittent work as not to enable him to earn enough for his needs, and is registered for employment.	Outdoor relief (other than medical relief or relief in cases of sudden and urgent necessity) may not be granted (i) to persons receiving (a) unemployment benefit; (b) unemployment assistance ; or (c) Supplementary pensions. (ii) to blind persons (this must be provided under the Blind Persons Act). (iii) o an able-bodied man in receipt of wages.
Benefit commences.	(1) On becoming blind, if at a later age than 40. (2) On attaining age of 40.	On satisfying general conditions.	On satisfying the above conditions.	On satisfying general conditions.
Benefit ceases.	Same as for non-contributory old-age pensions.	On ceasing to satisfy general conditions.	On attaining age of 65 ; or on ceasing to satisfy the above conditions.	On ceasing to satisfy general conditions.

	Members of the Naval, Military and Air Forces	Mercantile Marine	Civil Defence Personnel and Civilians	Workmen's Compensation
General qualifications to be satisfied before drawing benefit.	Disablement must be attributable to war service or must have been aggravated thereby : to a material extent and death must be attributable to war service or materially hastened thereby. Additional requirements as regards wives and dependants. (1) Wives and Children.—Broadly marriage must have taken place before the disability was incurred and children must have been born within nine months of the termination of service. (2) Separated wives.—Support by the husband or entitlement to support under a Separation Maintenance Order. (3) Unmarried dependants living as wives.—Maintenance on a *bona fide* domestic basis for six months prior to the member's death and dependence on the member at that date. (4) Parents of deceased members.—Pecuniary need arising from old age, infirmity or other adverse condition, not of a temporary nature. (5) Other dependants.—Dependence for six months prior to the member's death, pecuniary need and incapacity for self-support. No award can be made if pension granted under (1), (2), (3) or (4).	Disablement or death must be attributable to "war injury" or war risk injury (physical injury due to a specific war-like act by the enemy or to substantially increased risks from war conditions) or detention by the enemy. (1) The service rules apply, but the determining date is that of the injury or commencement of detention. (2) As for service cases. (3) do. 4) do. (5) do.	Disablement or death must be attributable to a "war injury" (a physical injury due to war-like "operations" (i.e. in the case of a civil defence volunteer a "war service injury," (a physical injury arising out of and in the course of the performance of duties as a member of a civil defence organisation): (1) Civil Defence personnel and gainfully occupied persons. As in Service cases but the determining date is the date of injury. (2) do. do. (3) Ineligible. (4) Civil Defence personnel and gainfully occupied persons as in service cases, but there must be dependence for one year before death. (5) Do. do. Juvenile orphan brothers and sisters. NOTE.—The widows and children of non-gainfully occupied persons must be in need owing to the cessation of a pension or other income on death.	*Death or Disablement :—* (1) *Due to accident :—* (i) the accident must arise out of and in the course of the employment. (ii) If the injury is due to serious and wilful misconduct on the part of the injured workman, compensation is not payable unless the injury results in death or serious and permanent disablement. (2) *Caused by certain specified industrial disease.* The disease must :— (i) have been scheduled under the Act ; (ii) be due to the nature of some employment in which the workman has been employed during the previous 12 months.
Benefit commences.	Disablement.—From the date of the member's discharge from the service or where the claim is made considerably later, from the date of application. Death.—From the termination of the 13 weeks during which family or dependants' allowances continue to be paid.	Disablement.—From the date fo the injury or the cessation of one month's "extra pay" which is continued in certain circumstances. Death.—From the day following death.	Disablement.—Injury allowances from date of incapacity for work if incapacity lasts for a week. Disablement pension from the date of cessation of injury allowance. Death.—From the day following death.	(1) The injury or disease must disable the workman for at least 3 days from earning full wages at the work at which he was employed. (2) If the disablement lasts less than 4 weeks, no compensation is payable in respect of the first 3 days. (3) When the injury or disease results in death and dependants are left, the compensation is not paid to the dependants direct, but must be paid into the County Court (in Scotland the Sheriff Court) to be invested, applied or otherwise dealt with in such manner as the Court thinks best for the benefit of the dependants.

CONDITIONS OF BENEFIT—(continued)

	War Pensions			Workmen's Compensation
	Members of the Naval, Military and Air Forces	Mercantile Marine	Civil Defence Personnel and Civilians	
Benefit ceases.	(1) Disablement pensions or allowances.—When no appreciable disablement remains from the effects of war service.	Same rules apply.	Same rules apply, but compensation ceases when disablement is assessed at less than 20 per cent.	On recovery by the workman of his pre-accident wage-earning capacity, or on redemption or commutation of the liability to make weekly payments in accordance with prescribed procedure.
	(2) Widow's pension.—On re-marriage when a widow (or separated wife) receives a gratuity of one year's pension. This gratuity is not payable to a widow of an officer, but in the event of her becoming a widow again, the question of restoration in whole or in part can be considered in the light of her pecuniary circumstances.	Same rules apply.	Pension ceases on re-marriage. No re-marriage gratuity.	
	(3) Allowances for children normally cease at the age of 16 (18 in the case of officers' children) and are not affected by re-marriage.	Same rules apply.	Allowances terminate at the age of 15 or 16 if still at school.	
	(4) Unmarried dependants.—12 months after the date of the member's death unless there are children in her charge or she is incapable of self-support or on marriage.	Same rules apply.	Ineligible.	
	(5) Parents.—When need no longer exists. Pension to a widowed mother ceases on re-marriage.	Same rules apply.	Same rules broadly apply.	
	(6) Other dependants.—When no longer in need or incapable of self-support and in the case of a female dependant on marriage. In the case of juvenile dependants, pension normally ceases at 16 (18 in the case of officers).	Same rules apply.	Pensions of juvenile dependants cease at the age of 15 or 16 if still at school.	
	(7) Payment is also terminated if a widow or female dependant is held to be unworthy to receive a pension from public funds.	Same rules apply.	Same rules apply.	

TABLE XXIII.—SOCIAL INSURANCE AND ASSISTANCE (EXCLUDING WORKMEN'S COMPENSATION) GREAT BRITAIN.

RECEIPTS AND PAYMENTS IN THE YEAR ENDING 31ST MARCH, 1939

| | RECEIPTS £000 | | | | | | | | PAYMENTS £000 | | | | | |
| | Contributions | | Ex-chequer contri-bution | Local Rates | Income from Invest-ments | Other Receipts | Balance on Year | Total | Benefit or Assistance | | Admin-istration | Other Pay-ments | Balance on Year | Total |
	Employ-ers	Employ-ees							Cash	Treat-ment				
Unemployment Insurance:—														
General	21,902	21,601	21,902	—	1,359	1	1,056	67,821	54,209	—	6,186	7,426 (a)	—	67,821
Agricultural	617	617	617	—	62	—	—	1,913	872	—	231	2	808	1,913
Health Insurance	14,575	15,284	7,696	—	6,379	413	—	44,347	18,600	15,361	5,976	442	3,968	44,347
Contributory Pensions:—														
Widows	15,852	16,649	17,000	—	791	—	—	50,292	24,226	—	1,468	294	2,291	50,292
Orphans									320	—				
Old Age									21,693	—				
Special Voluntary Contributors (b) ...	—	682	(b)	—	—	—	—	682	—	—	158	—	524	682
Old Age Pensions (paid by virtue of Contributory Pensions Acts)	—	—	32,533	—	—	—	—	32,533	32,533	—	(c)	—	—	32,533
Non Contributory (Old Age) Pensions ...	—	—	15,871	—	—	—	—	15,871	14,517	—	569	—	—	15,871
Blind Persons Pensions	—	—		—	—	—	—		785	—		—	—	
Blind Persons Assistance	—	—	—	2,077	—	—	—	2,077	2,077	—	(d)	—	—	2,077
Unemployment Assistance	—	—	39,635	—	—	—	—	39,635	35,331	—	4,304	—	—	39,635
Public Assistance (Outdoor Relief) ...	—	—	—	24,189	—	—	—	24,189	24,189 (c)	—	(e)	—	—	24,189
	52,946	54,833	135,254	26,266	8,591	414	1,056	279,360	229,352	15,361	18,892	8,164	7,591	279,360

(a) Including £3 million applied towards reduction of debt.
(b) The scheme for Special Voluntary Contributors commenced on 1st January, 1938, and the figures of receipts and payments, therefore, cover the first 15 months.
(c) The Exchequer Contribution started to be paid in 1939–40.
(d) The administrative cost of these pensions is included in the cost of administration shown for contributory and non-contributory pensions.
(e) Included in the general administrative costs of Local Authorities.
(e) Includes about £2 million of administrative costs.

SECTION 3. ANALYSIS OF PUBLIC ASSISTANCE CASES. MARCH, 1942

BASIS OF THE STATISTICS

1. A detailed return of the number of persons in receipt of Public Assistance in their area during the first week of March has been obtained from 20 Local Authorities. The 15 Local Authorities in England and Wales were the County Councils of Breconshire, Derbyshire, Glamorgan, Kent, Lancashire, London, Middlesex, Somerset and the West Riding of Yorkshire, and the County Borough Councils of Bristol, Leicester, Manchester, Rotherham and Sheffield.

In Scotland the Local Authorities were the Burghs of Aberdeen, Dundee, Glasgow and Edinburgh, and the County Council of Lanark.

2. The proportion of the total* number of persons in receipt of out relief, covered by these 20 returns, was about 38 per cent. in the case of England and Wales, and 59 per cent. for Scotland. The corresponding figures for institutional relief were 33 and 37 per cent.

3. The selected areas in England and Wales may be regarded as a fair sample of the whole country, and the percentages used may be taken as affording a reasonably accurate indication of the total numbers in each category. The selected areas in Scotland include Glasgow, which is a preponderating influence not only in relation to these areas but also to the country as a whole, but any distortion of the total figures due to the inclusion of Glasgow in the sample is unlikely to be of material importance.

4. These percentages have, therefore, been used to rate up the numbers shown under the various headings included in the questionnaire for the selected areas in order to obtain estimated numbers under the corresponding heads for the whole of Great Britain. The results are given in Table·XXIV ; they are, of course, approximations subject to a margin of error.

ANALYSIS OF DOMICILIARY RELIEF

5. The distribution of persons in the main categories of outdoor relief in March, 1942, was as follows :—

Category	Percentage of cases relieved (excluding dependants)			Percentage of persons relieved (including dependants)		
	England & Wales	Scotland	Great Britain	England & Wales	Scotland	Great Britain
1. Receiving relief in supplementation of benefit or pension (including workmen's compensation) ...	42·3	31·8	40·0	51·6	40·6	49·2
2. Chronic sickness, cripples, physically and mentally handicapped (excluding cases in receipt of disablement benefit	21·3	21·0	21·3	15·2	17·7	15·8
3. Widows (not in receipt of pension) ; separated and deserted wives ...	9·7	11·8	10·1	10·0	12·4	10·5
4. Old Persons (men 65–70, women 60–70) ...	13·4	7·6	12·1	7·8	4·4	7·1
5. Cases relieved pending settlement of claims for other forms of benefit	2·2	2·7	2·3	2·7	4·1	3·0
6. All other cases (including able-bodied unemployed, old persons over 70, etc.) ...	11·1	25·1	14·2	12·7	20·8	14·4
	100·0	100·0	100·0	100·0	100·0	100·0

(*) The total figures for England and Wales are for the 28th February, 1942, and for Scotland are for the 15th January, 1942.

6. There are differences in the law of Public Assistance between England and Wales and Scotland and this may account for some of the differences revealed by the analysis of the two areas. The Scottish relief system has always been predominantly an outdoor relief system and has not depended to nearly the same extent as in England on the use of institutions such as workhouses. The ratio of out-relief cases to institutional cases in Scotland was about 5½ to 1, whereas it was less than 1½ to 1 in England and Wales. This, no doubt, goes some way to explain the higher percentage of cases in category 6 in Scotland.

SUPPLEMENTATION OF INSURANCE BENEFIT

7. The analysis of persons who, though in receipt of one or other insurance benefits, had to have recourse to the Poor Law can be examined from two viewpoints :—
   (i) By how much was their insurance benefit supplemented ?
   (ii) What proportion of insured persons in receipt of benefit had to have their incomes supplemented by Public Assistance ?

(i) *Degree of Supplementation*

8. The average amount of supplementation per case (to the nearest 6d.) during the week in question and the average number of dependants covered were as follows :—

	Average amount of relief granted per case	Average number of dependants per case	
		Adults	Children
Sickness benefit—Men	28/–	0·90	1·63
Women	18/6	0·03	0·22
Disablement benefit—Men	28/6	0·73	0·70
Women ...	18/–	0·04	0·05
Widows' pension	14/–	0·04	1·03
Workmen's compensation	15/6	1·00	1·77

9. It is not possible without a great deal of further investigation to make a reliable estimate of the total income received by an average family relieved under one of the above headings. Public Assistance scales and the assessment of any resources the applicant may possess vary from area to area. The following points can, however, be made :—

   (a) The amount of supplementation for disablement benefit cases is practically the same as that for sickness benefit cases though the insurance benefit is 7/6 per week lower for a man and 6/– per week lower for a single woman. The explanation lies in the greater number of dependants possessed by the sickness benefit cases. Assuming (i) the adult dependant in the case of a man to be his wife ; (ii) the difference between the number of cases and the number of adult dependants to be the number of single men ; and (iii) a wife and a child respectively to receive one-half and one-quarter of the man's share, the following estimates can be made :—

	Sickness			Disablement		
	Public Assistance	Insurance benefit	Total benefit and Assistance	Public Assistance	Insurance benefit	Total benefit and Assistance
Single men ...	15/–	18/–	33/–	18/6	10/6	29/–
Married man with one child ...	26/6	18/–	44/6	32/6	10/6	43/–

   (b) The average family receiving both a widow's pension and outdoor relief is composed of a widow and one dependent child receiving 14/– a week in relief. This with a pension of 10/– and a child's allowance of 5/– would give 29/– per week as the total income received from these two sources.

   (c) It is impossible to estimate the average income of persons in receipt of workmen's compensation and Public Assistance, as there is no fixed weekly amount of compensation. The average family receiving compensation and public assistance consists of a man, wife and 1·77 dependent children receiving in assistance an average of 15/6 a week.

(*d*) The cost to Local Authorities of supplementing benefit (including workmen's compensation) was about £109,000 per week or, if the first week in March was an average week, about £5½ millions per annum.

(ii) *Numbers receiving benefit and assistance*

10. The following table shows the proportion of benefit cases receiving Public Assistance :—

Benefit	Estimated number in receipt of benefit	Estimated number in receipt of Public Assistance	Percentage of cases of benefit in receipt of Assistance
Sickness—Men	250,000	24,000	9·6
Women	175,000	2,500	1·4
Disablement—Men	225,000	31,000	13·8
Women	150,000	9,700	6·5
Widow pensioners (under 60) ...	440,000	23,300	5·3
Workmen's compensation	100,000	1,500	1·5

In addition there were :—

(*a*) About 370,000 widows under 60 not in receipt of a widow's pension of whom 9,500 or 2½ per cent. were on Public Assistance (out relief) ;

(*b*) About 650,000 persons in receipt of Great War wounds or disability pensions, including widows and dependants of men who have died, of whom 5,000 or about ¾ per cent. were on Public Assistance (out relief) ;

(*c*) About 240,000 men aged 65–70 not in receipt of an old age pension of whom 9,800 or 4 per cent. were on Public Assistance (out relief) ;

(*d*) About 1,100,000 women aged 60–70 not in receipt of an old age pension of whom 18,000 or about 1½ per cent. were on Public Assistance (out relief).

It must be remembered that persons eligible for or in receipt of unemployment assistance or supplementary pension cannot receive outdoor relief except in cases of sudden and urgent necessity and for medical needs.

INSTITUTIONAL RELIEF

11. Altogether about 70,000 old persons (men 65 and over, women 60 and over) were receiving institutional relief.

The number of old persons receiving institutional relief in relation to the total number of old persons was as follows :—

Category	Estimated number in category	Estimated number receiving institutional relief*	Percentage of category in institutions
(a) *Receiving Old Age Pension*			
Men 65–70	580,000	2,600	0·5
Men 70 and over	800,000	11,000	1·4
Women 60–70 (including widows) ...	1,100,000	2,700	0·2
Women 70 and over	1,140,000	13,500	1·2
Total ...	3,620,000	29,800	0·8
(b) *Not receiving Old Age Pension*			
Men 65–70	240,000	7,700	3·2
Men 70 and over	220,000	12,700	5·8
Women 60–70 (including widows) ...	1,100,000	7,800	0·7
Women 70 and over	330,000	11,400	3·5
Total ...	1,890,000	39,600	2·1

*These figures do not include old persons in mental asylums.

TABLE XXIV—ANALYSIS OF PERSONS IN RECEIPT OF PUBLIC ASSISTANCE DURING THE FIRST WEEK OF MARCH, 1942, IN GREAT BRITAIN

(Estimate Based on Returns from 15 Public Assistance Authorities in England and Wales and 5 in Scotland)

TYPE OF CASE	ENGLAND AND WALES				SCOTLAND				GREAT BRITAIN				
	No. of Cases	Dependants Adults	Children	Total Relief Paid (b) £	No. of Cases	Dependants Adults	Children	Total Relief Paid (b) £	No. of Cases	% of Total	Dependants Adults	Children	Total Relief Paid (b) £
OUT RELIEF (a)													
1. *Able-bodied Unemployed*—out of scope of U.A. Acts — Men	987	528	849		620	138	308		1,607	.7	666	1,157	
Women	593	8	160		313	—	7		906	.4	8	167	
2. *Temporary Sickness*:—													
(a) Not in receipt of N.H.I. Sickness Benefit — Men	5,421	3,582	6,210		1,670	846	2,123		7,091	3.1	4,428	8,333	
Women	2,675	89	836		893		197		3,568	1.6	89	1,033	
(b) Receiving Relief in supplementation of N.H.I. Sickness Benefit — Men	20,087	18,352	32,478	27,767	3,703	3,074	6,322	5,752	23,790	10.3	21,426	38,800	33,519
Women	2,136	81	513	2,002	434	—	44	359	2,570	1.1	81	557	2,361
3. *Permanent or Chronic Sickness* (including cripples and physically and mentally handicapped):—													
(a) Not in receipt of N.H.I. Disablement Benefit — Men	18,579	8,554	7,232		5,609	2,275	4,063		24,188	10.5	10,829	11,295	
Women	19,727	691	762		4,964	7	372		24,691	10.7	698	1,134	
(b) Receiving Relief in supplementation of Disablement Benefit — Men	26,118	19,180	16,946	36,949	5,034	3,559	4,883	7,341	31,152	13.5	22,739	21,829	44,290
Women	8,131	355	389	7,426	1,609	2	94	1,377	9,740	4.2	357	483	8,803
4. *Industrial Accident and Disease*:— Persons receiving relief in supplementation of Workmen's Compensation	1,472	1,482	2,570	1,149	55	50	129	33	1,527	.7	1,532	2,699	1,182
5. *Widows*:—													
(a) Not in receipt of Widows' Pension	7,144	478	5,133		2,406	3	2,255		9,550	4.1	481	7,388	
(b) Receiving Relief in supplementation of Widows' Pension	18,058	962	18,591	13,268	5,221	27	5,373	3,050	23,279	10.1	989	23,964	16,318
6. *Separated or Deserted Wives*:—	10,196	512	13,025		3,521	7	3,953		13,717	6.0	519	16,978	
7. *Others*: (a) Dependants of persons in hospital	3,482	704	5,348		726	399	1,114		4,208	1.8	1,103	6,462	
(b) Receiving relief in supplementation of Wounds or Disability Pensions	1,328	836	1,122		686	451	720		2,014	.9	1,287	1,842	
(c) All others	4,290	922	4,791	1,662	7,345	17	1,302	929	11,635	5.1	939	6,093	2,591

TABLE XXIV   ANALYSIS OF PERSONS IN RECEIPT OF PUBLIC ASSISTANCE DURING THE FIRST WEEK OF MARCH, 1942, IN GREAT BRITAIN
—(continued)

(Estimate Based on Returns from 15 Public Assistance Authorities in England and Wales and 5 in Scotland)

TYPE OF CASE	ENGLAND AND WALES				SCOTLAND				GREAT BRITAIN				
	No. of Cases	Dependants Adults	Dependants Children	Total Relief Paid (b) £	No. of Cases	Dependants Adults	Dependants Children	Total Relief Paid (b) £	No. of Cases	% of Total	Dependants Adults	Dependants Children	Total Relief Paid (b) £
8. *Cases Relieved pending Settlement of Claims for other forms of Benefit :—*													
(a) Pending settlement of Old Age Pension	969	300	39		192	39	2		1,161	·5	339	41	
(b) Pending settlement of N.H.I. Sickness Benefit	1,149	760	1,527		641	437	1,011		1,790	·8	1,197	2,538	
(c) Pending settlement of Widows' Pension	1,077	71	1,340		313	3	488		1,390	·6	74	1,828	
(d) Pending settlement of Workmen's Compensation	808	639	1,159		242	172	421		1,050	·5	811	1,580	
9. *Old Age* Men 65—70	8,275	3,293	213		1,538	374	49		9,813	4·3	3,667	262	
Women 60—70	15,724	936	47		2,300	3	2		18,024	7·8	939	49	
Men 70 and over	610	226	5		187	84	—		797	·4	310	5	
Women 70 and over	467	16	—		222	—	—		689	·3	16	—	
TOTAL OUT-RELIEF … … …	179,503	63,557	121,285	90,223(b)	50,444	11,967	35,232	18,841(b)	229,947	100·0	75,524	156,517	109,064(b)
INSTITUTIONAL RELIEF(c)													
10. *Old Persons :—*													
(a) Receiving Old Age Pension Men 65—70	2,186				393	21	—		2,579	1·8	21	—	
Women 60—70	2,619				106	—	—		2,725	1·9	—	—	
Men 70 and over	9,609				1,338	13	—		10,947	7·8	13	—	
Women 70 and over	12,686				854	—	—		13,540	9·7	—	—	
(b) Not receiving Old Age Pension Men 65—70	7,148				506	19	—		7,654	5·5	19	—	
Women 60—70	7,200				607	—	—		7,807	5·6	—	—	
Men 70 and over	12,031				680	13	—		12,711	9·1	13	—	
Women 70 and over	10,761				626	—	—		11,387	8·1	—	—	
11. *Others* … … …	66,675	30	2,566		4,002	38	241		70,677	50·5	68	2,807	
TOTAL INSTITUTIONAL RELIEF(c) … …	130,915	30	2,566		9,112	104	241		140,027	100·0	134	2,807	

(a) Out-Relief cases are included under the heading which denotes the primary cause of chargeability, and no cases are included under more than one heading. All *old persons* except those falling in class 8 (a) are included under heading 9. Persons receiving domiciliary medical relief only are excluded.

(b) Estimated relief paid in respect of items 2 (b), 3 (b), 4, 5 (b), 7 (b) only.

(c) Rate-aided patients in mental hospitals are excluded.

APPENDIX C

LIST OF ORGANISATIONS AND INDIVIDUALS (OTHER THAN GOVERNMENT DEPARTMENTS) SUBMITTING WRITTEN OR ORAL EVIDENCE.

*Accident Offices Association.
Assistance Board Departmental Whitley Council (Staff Side).
*Association of Approved Societies.
*Association of Counties of Cities in Scotland (Aberdeen, Dundee, Edinburgh and Glasgow).
*Association of County Councils in Scotland.
Association of Deposit Societies.
*Association of Municipal Corporations.
Association of Superannuation and Pension Funds.
*Association of Trade Mutual Insurance Societies.
Banking Unemployment Insurance Board.
Bolton and District Old Age Pensioners Association.
Bristol Council of Social Service.
British Dental Association.
*British Employers' Confederation.
British Federation of Social Workers.
*British Iron and Steel Federation.
Central Council for the Care of Cripples.
Charity Organisation Society (in conjunction with the Institute of Sociology).
College of Teachers of the Blind (Scottish Branch).
*Convention of Royal Burghs in Scotland.
*Cotton Spinners and Manufacturers Association.
*County Councils Association.
Cowdenbeath Town Council.
Dagenham Borough Council (and certain other Local Authorities in the London area).
Dame Georgiana Buller.
Diabetic Association.
Dr. Frank Ellis (Sheffield Radium Centre).
East Ham Insurance Committee.
Educational Institute of Scotland.
Electrical Industries Benevolent Association.
*Engineering and Allied Employers' National Federation.
Edinburgh Women Citizens' Association.
*Fabian Society.
Family Endowment Society.
Federation Committee of English, Scottish and Welsh Associations of Insurance Committees.
*Federation of Master Cotton Spinners' Associations, Ltd.
Friendly Societies Medical Alliance.
Sir Ian Fraser, M.P.
Gardner's Trust for the Blind.
Guild of British Dispensing Opticians.
Guild of Public Pharmacists.
Incorporated Dental Society.
*Industrial Life Offices Association.
Insurance Unemployment Board.
Insurance Unions Congress.
Insurance Unions Joint Consultative Committee.
*International Group of Non-Surplus Approved Societies.
International Labour Office.
Joint University Council for Social Studies and Public Administration.
*Joint Committee of Approved Societies and National Union of Holloway Friendly Societies (Mr. Percy Rockliff).
Leicestershire Insurance Committee.
Lever Brothers and Unilever, Ltd.
*Liberal Parliamentary Party.
Life Offices Association and Associated Scottish Life Offices.
*Lloyd's.
Local Government Clerks' Association.
*London County Council.
London Old Age Pensions Committee.
Married Women's Association.
Middlesex Insurance Committee.
Midland Employers' Mutual Assurance, Ltd.
*Mining Association of Great Britain.
*Mutual Insurance Companies Association.
National Association of Administrators of Local Government Establishments.
National Association of Local Government Officers.

National Association of Maternity and Child Welfare Centres and for the Prevention of
Infant Mortality.
National Association of Relieving Officers.
National Association of Workshops for the Blind Incorporated.
*National Conference of Friendly Societies.
*National Conference of Industrial Assurance Approved Societies.
National Council of Social Service.
*National Council of Women of Great Britain.
National Cripples Reform League.
National Federation of Business and Professional Women's Clubs of Great Britain and
Ireland.
*National Federation of Employees' Approved Societies.
*National Federation of Old Age Pensions Associations.
National Federation of Professional Workers.
National Federation of Provident Associations of Clerks and Warehousemen.
*National Federation of Rural Approved Societies.
National Federation of Women's Institutes.
National Institute for the Blind (Mr. W. McG. Eagar).
National Institute for the Deaf.
*National Labour Organisation.
National League of the Blind.
National Spinsters' Pension Association.
National Special Schools Union (Incorporated).
National Union of Railwaymen.
National Union of Seamen.
National Union of Teachers.
National Union of Women Teachers.
National Welfare Association.
Northern Counties, Southern Regional and Western Counties Associations for the Blind.
Nuffield College Social Reconstruction Survey.
Ophthalmic Benefit Approved Committee.
*Parliamentary Committee of the Co-operative Congress.
Pedestrians' Association.
*P.E.P. (Political and Economic Planning).
Pharmaceutical Society of Great Britain and the National Pharmaceutical Union.
*Prudential Assurance Company, Ltd.
Prudential Staff Union.
Public Dental Service Association of Great Britain, Ltd.
Queen's Institute of District Nursing.
Railway Clerks' Association.
Railway Companies Association.
Royal College of Nursing.
Royal Seamen's Pensions Fund.
*Scottish Association of Friendly and Approved Societies.
Scottish Association of Home Teachers of the Blind.
Scottish Federation for the Welfare of the Blind.
Scottish Midwives' Association.
*Scottish Miners' Federation Approved Society.
Scottish Rural Workers' Approved Society.
*Shipbuilding Employers' Federation.
*Shipping Federation, Ltd., and the Liverpool Steam Ship Owners' Association (and
National Council of Port Labour Employers).
Sight-Testing Opticians—Organisations on List of Ophthalmic Benefit Approved Com-
mittee, viz. :—
The Spectacle Makers Company, The British Optical Association, The National
Association of Opticians, The Scottish Association of Opticians, The Joint
Council of Qualified Opticians, and The Society of Opticians. The Institute of
Chemist Opticians. The Institute of Ophthalmic Opticians.
Six Point Group.
Society of Public Assistance Officials of Scotland.
South Metropolitan Gas Co.
South Wales and Monmouthshire Clerks' Association.
Surrey Insurance Committee.
*Trades Union Congress, Scottish Trade Union Congress, and National Association of
Trade Union Approved Societies.
*United Women's Insurance Society.
Wales and Monmouthshire Regional Council for the Blind.
Women's Co-operative Guild.
Women's Freedom League.
Women's Pension League (Scotland).

---

*Memoranda submitted by these organisations have been printed as Appendix G to
Sir William Beveridge's Report and are published in a separate volume (Cmd. 6405,
price 2s. 0d.).

APPENDIX D

THE PROBLEM OF INDUSTRIAL ASSURANCE

1. General Features

1. Life assurance means paying agreed premiums at regular intervals to an insurance office in order to obtain, when the person whose life is insured dies or attains an agreed age, payment by the office of an agreed sum. The person whose life is insured is described as the " life assured " ; the person who undertakes to pay the premiums is described below as the " proposer." Industrial assurance is that class of life assurance in which the premiums are payable at intervals of less than two months and are received by means of collectors who make house to house visits for that purpose. This class of life assurance can be carried on either by an assurance company within the meaning of the Assurance Companies Act, 1909, or by a Friendly Society registered under the Friendly Societies Act of 1896. A company which carries on this business is termed " an industrial assurance company " ; it must be registered under the Companies Acts or the Industrial and Provident Societies Acts or be incorporated by special Act. A Friendly Society which carries on this business is termed a " collecting society." There are at the present time 14 companies and 146 societies conducting industrial assurance.

2. The primary distinction between industrial assurance and other classes of life assurance is in the method by which the premiums are paid. There is also a distinction in the purposes for which insurance may legally be undertaken. In all forms of life assurance, every person may legally insure his or her own life or that of a wife or husband without restriction on the sum insured. Beyond that, in ordinary life assurance, direct pecuniary interest must exist in each case at the time when the insurance is effected, and the sum insured may not be greater than the pecuniary interest. In industrial assurance, by Section 3 of the Industrial Assurance Act, 1923, among the purposes for which societies and companies entitled to conduct that business may issue policies there is included " insuring money to be paid for the funeral expenses of a parent, child, grandparent, grandchild, brother or sister." This Section reproduces in substance Section 36 (1) of the Assurance Companies Act, 1909. Before 1909, in the absence of direct pecuniary interest to be proved in each case, the only permitted insurance on the life of another was that of a child by its parents under the Friendly Societies Act of 1896 for funeral expenses, restricted in amount so long as the child was under ten. Industrial assurance began as insurance for funeral expenses by persons whose means were so limited that they could not feel sure of meeting them out of current resources when need arose. As it was put by the Royal Commission on Friendly Societies which reported in 1874, " the great bulk of collecting societies are burial societies, the great bulk of burial societies are collecting societies." The function of industrial assurance, in meeting this need among persons of limited means to provide in advance for funeral expenses, has been recognised, by legalising for insurance effected through collectors, policies which would not be legal under ordinary insurance, that is to say, without collectors. The circumstances under which the powers of industrial assurance offices were extended in 1909 and the nature of that extension are discussed in paras. 54–57 below in dealing with insurance of life-of-another. Under the Industrial Assurance and Friendly Societies Act of 1929 the powers of industrial life offices were extended further by permitting the same range of relations as those authorised to insure for funeral expenses under the Act of 1923 to take out endowment policies for their own benefit on each other's lives.

3. In addition to the legal distinctions between ordinary and industrial life assurance, in respect of methods of collecting premiums and permitted purpose of insurance, there are important practical differences in the treatment of proposals for insurance :

(a) There is in general no medical examination of the person whose life is to be assured under an industrial policy. The proposer is required by all offices to give an absolute warranty of good health in a policy on his own life ; by most offices, with a few exceptions of which the Prudential Company is the most important (accepting a warranty of knowledge and belief), he is required to give an absolute warranty of good health in assurance on the life of another. By section 20 (4) of the Industrial Assurance Act, 1923, where, as is commonly the case, the proposal form is wholly or partly filled in by the agent of the assurance office, in the absence of fraud on the part of the proposer, the validity of the policy cannot be questioned on the ground of any mis-statement in the proposal relating to the state of health of the life assured, unless the question is raised within two years from the date of the issue of the policy, and during these two years the policy can only be questioned on the ground of a mis-statement in the proposal, relating to the state of health at the date of the proposal.

(b) The consent of the person whose life is to be assured in an industrial policy is not required. In ordinary life assurance this consent is normally involved in the holding of a medical examination or in the measures necessary to establish insurable interest.

(c) Industrial policies carry no right to a share of profits disclosed on a valuation, that is to say the with-profit policies which form so large a part of ordinary life assurance do not exist in industrial assurance. But in the case of collecting societies surpluses belong to the members, and it is the practice to distribute some portion as bonus to the members. The largest of the companies moreover—the Prudential —since 1907 has, by an arrangement now embodied in its articles of association, assigned a share of the profits—now 75 per cent. of what remains after providing a specified sum free of tax for dividends—to the policy-holders. The other companies also as a rule allocate part of their profits to the policy-holders, though in most cases a smaller proportion than with the Prudential.

4. The practice of collecting premiums for burial insurance is more than 100 years old, the oldest of the surviving societies, the Preston Shelley, having been founded in 1831 and the largest of the companies—the Prudential—having been established in 1854. The business has attained its present stature only in recent times; in 1910 the total premium income of all industrial assurance offices was barely a quarter of what it was in 1939. Today the business is immense. In 1939 there were 103,000,000 policies of industrial assurance in force, more than two-and-a-quarter policies for every man, woman and child in Britain. The sums assured amounted to £1,668,000,000, and the Assurance funds to £455,000,000. The amount paid in claims on death was £24,000,000 and the amount paid in claims on maturity was nearly £11,500,000. The premiums received were over £74,000,000 and the expenses of management were nearly £24,000,000, exclusive of dividends to shareholders amounting to over £1,750,000 after payment of £1,600,000 as income tax. In addition to premiums, the companies and societies received in 1939 nearly £20,000,000 as interest on investment.

5. The premium income £74,000,000 in 1939 is built up of pennies, sixpences and shillings, collected for the most part week by week from a large proportion of all the households of Britain. The tables issued by the offices show the sums that can be assured for so many pence a week at each age : 1d. a week for £15 in the case of children under 10 ; 4d. a week for entry at age 30 for £31 8s. 0d. ; 9d. a week at 50 for £31 1s. 0d. ; 1/2 a week at 60 for £30 2s. 0d., and so on. Such rates relate to whole-life policies, about 85 per cent. of the whole number of paying policies ; the average premium on such policies in 1940 in 19 of the largest offices was about 3d. a week and the average sum assured, including bonus, was just under £15. Most of the remaining policies are endowment assurances, with an average premium in 1940 of about 8d. a week and an average sum assured, including bonus, of just under £23. The large total number of policies in relation to the population is accounted for partly by the fact that many people take out successive policies on their own or their spouse's life, as their resources increase, partly by the fact that under the powers for insurance on life of another it is common for more than one relative to insure for the funeral expenses of the same person.

Companies and Societies

6. Of the total business, about four-fifths is done by the 14 companies, and one-fifth by the 146 collecting societies. This proportion applies almost exactly to the premiums, to the sums assured and to the claims on death. The companies pay a larger proportion— seven-eighths—of the claims on maturity, indicating their greater development of endowment insurance ; they have a smaller proportion—about three-quarters—of the number of policies, indicating that on the average their policies are for slightly larger amounts. The collecting societies are subject to restrictions not applying to companies ; they cannot issue any policy, even an own life policy, for more than £300, or allow a person to insure even a spouse for more than reasonable funeral expenses. Each collecting society is subject to its rules, pays no shareholders' profits and is exempt from income-tax. These societies are registered under the Friendly Societies Acts and most of them use the term " friendly " in their title, as well as the term " collecting " which is required by statute. To avoid confusion, they are described here simply as collecting societies and the term Friendly Society is reserved for societies which do not collect and in the main are concerned with provision for sickness as well as for funerals.

7. One of the companies, the Prudential Assurance Co., Ltd., is much larger than any of the others, having a third of the total premiums paid for industrial assurance. The business of this company differs in important respects from that of the others. Of the remaining two-thirds of industrial assurance business, the great bulk is conducted by 25 companies and societies associated in the Industrial Life Offices Association. These offices and the Prudential between them employed in September, 1939, a field staff of nearly 60,000 full-time agents (16,249 in the Prudential and 43,300 in the Industrial Life Offices Association) ; the Prudential had in addition about 120 part-time staff and the Industrial Life Offices Association had 5,949 spare-time and part-time staff. The remaining offices between them had about 5,000 full-time agents, of whom about 3,500 were employed by the company described as the Co-operative Insurance Society, Ltd., The total number of full-time agents at the outbreak of war may be put at 65,000.

8. Most of the companies and larger collecting societies, in addition to industrial assurance, do ordinary life assurance, which to a large extent is business with persons who already hold industrial policies, is for relatively small amounts and is undertaken through the collectors. It ranks as ordinary business because the premiums are payable at quarterly or longer intervals ; it differs from the business of companies not doing industrial assurance because the sums assured are normally much less and because the premiums are often collected in place of being sent through the post. In the Prudential more than three-quarters of the ordinary branch policies are for sums of less than £300 ; the ordinary branch premiums have grown from £4,812,268 in 1911 to £14,598,391 in 1941, and are thus nearly 60 per cent. of the industrial assurance premiums. In the Industrial Life Offices Association a very large proportion of the ordinary business is on policies for £200 or less ; the ordinary branch premiums have grown in the past 30 years at twice the rate of the industrial branch premiums, and at the figure of £18,167,112 reached in 1941 are about 40 per cent. of the latter. The Prudential and the Industrial Life Offices Association between them do about one-third of the ordinary life assurance in the country. Some of the companies undertake other classes of insurance business on a large scale, at home and abroad.

9. Most of the principal companies and societies, during the last thirty years of their most rapid growth, have been associated closely with the administration of National Health Insurance under the Act of 1911. That is to say, they have formed Approved Societies which are administered in connection with their main business and through the same staff of collectors. Approved Societies of this type now include nearly half the whole number of persons covered by health insurance.

10. In addition to earlier investigations by commissions such as that which examined Friendly and Benefit Building Societies in 1872-74, and by a Select Committee of the House of Commons in 1889, the business of industrial assurance has been the subject of two official enquiries specially devoted to it within the past quarter of a century. One enquiry was made by a Departmental Committee on Industrial Assurance Companies and Collecting Societies, under the chairmanship of Lord Parmoor, which reported in 1920 [Cmd. 614]. The second enquiry was made by a Departmental Committee on Industrial Assurance and Assurance on the Lives of Children under ten years of age, under the chairmanship of Sir Benjamin Cohen, which reported in 1933 [Cmd. 4376].

2. The Collectors and their Terms of Service

11. The distinguishing mark of industrial assurance is the use of collectors to receive premiums by house to house visits. These collectors are also the principal, though not the sole, agents for extending the business. Their remuneration is a large part of the total administrative cost and the terms of their remuneration affect materially the conduct of the business.

12. In considering the agents and their terms of service, a distinction may be made between the Prudential, other companies and collecting societies

13. The Prudential operates on a block system, that is to say for each block of streets it has only one agent. These agents are remunerated in every case by a fixed salary, by a payment for work done in connection with the Approved Societies under national health insurance, by commission on ordinary branch and general branch business and by a share of profits. The make up of the average weekly remuneration of all agents in the income-tax year 1938/39 is shown in the following table :—

Fixed salary ...	...	...	...	...	...	£3 15 3
Approved Society ...	...	...	...	...	11 11
Ordinary branch commission		...	...	...	4 8
General branch commission ...		...	...	...	5 4
						£4 17 2
Share of profits (1938)	...	...	...	...	16 2
						£5 13 4

The share of profits allotted to each agent is related to the amount of business done by him, and to this extent, as well as in his hopes of promotion, his financial position depends on his results in respect of industrial assurance, as well as in respect of other work. But in the main his work for industrial assurance is done for a fixed salary in a defined area. This statement describes the position just before the war ; recently, as a war measure, the terms of remuneration have been modified in some respects.

14. In the other companies methods of remuneration vary. A common arrangement in the larger offices is for the agent to receive both a salary, rising and falling with the amount of his " debit," that is to say with the amount of premiums which he is due to collect, and a payment of 18 to 24 times the premium on new business sustained, that is to say on new policies written in excess of lapses. One at least of the other companies— the Refuge—operates a block system.

15. In the collecting societies, a special form of remuneration exists. The general practice of the five largest collecting societies as described by the Cohen Committee " is to pay the agents 25 per cent. of the premiums on whole-life policies carrying weekly premiums which have passed through the ' new business ' stage. On new business the agents take as fees the whole of the first 13 to 16 weeks' premiums and in certain cases bonuses are also paid periodically on the ' increase ' of premiums collected. Further the agents are paid for re-writing their collecting books half-yearly (a custom which also obtains in the case of some of the companies)." The present Committee were informed by the Industrial Life Offices Association that this description by the Cohen Committee holds true today. To complete it, however, reference is required to a distinction between payment for new business by " times down " and payment for new business by " times as collected." The former means that as soon as a policy has been taken up a payment of so many times (perhaps twelve times) the agreed weekly premium is made to the agent, even if no further premiums are paid. The latter means that the agent takes the whole of so many weeks of premiums, but takes them only if and as they are paid. The former is a simple procuration fee. The latter is a procuration fee which is not paid unless the premiums at least equal to the fee are paid. There are differences of practice between the societies in the choice of these two methods, and differences of view as regards them between the management and the staff.

Book Interest

16. Another vital element in the finance and management of collecting societies is " book interest." This means the right conferred by the rules of the society on the agent, or in the event of his death on his legal personal representative, to nominate his successor. The society may reject any particular nominee as unsuitable, but the right of nomination in effect puts the agent in a position to sell his book, and books are advertised for sale in trade journals at prices commonly of about thirty times the weekly premiums represented by it. That is to say a book representing premiums of £15 a week, and worth to the agent holding it a remuneration of all kinds of something under £5 a week, would be saleable for £450 ; exceptionally a book may sell for as much as £1,000. Book interest exists not only in all the large societies but in companies like the Royal London Mutual and the Blackburn Philanthropic, which were formerly societies, and in the Co-operative Insurance Society Limited. It was estimated by the representatives of the Industrial Life Offices Association that book interest applies now to slightly more than one-third of the total premium income of industrial assurance and represents a capital value of upwards of £12,000,000 in the hands of the agents. In connection with each of the three largest mutual offices—Liverpool Victoria, Royal London Mutual and Royal Liver—there are associations, now registered as companies, for the purpose of financing the purchase of books. These associations, confined to past or present members of the staff of each Office, lend money for the purchase of books, usually at 7 or 8 per cent., and obtain this money, either as share capital on which usually something in the neightbourhood of 8 per cent. is paid, or by borrowing.

17. Book interest is a matter on which strongly differing views have been expressed by reasonable men, both outside the business of industrial assurance and within it. In the view of the Cohen Committee, book interest represents " the capitalized value of the excess of the agents' commission over the market value of the services he renders " (Cohen Committee, para. 38). The Parmoor Committee said practically the same thing in a few more words. On the other hand, book interest can with equal plausibility be compared to the power of a doctor to sell his practice, whether he has built it up himself or has bought it from a predecessor, or it can be compared to the goodwill of an insurance broker's business. From within the business Sir Joseph Burn, as general manager of the Prudential, giving evidence to the Cohen Committee, described the system as " bad " on the ground that with it " there is considerably less opportunity of improving the conditions of industrial assurance " (Cohen Committee Evidence, Qu. 2971–72). The same point had been made to the Parmoor Committee by the representative of the Refuge in saying that book interest " rather eliminates the power of the company to control the staff " ; the Refuge at that time had just initiated a block system and, as is shown below, has been able to reduce its expense ratio almost as much as the Prudential. On the other hand, the Co-operative Insurance Society, in entering the industrial assurance field seriously about 25 years ago, adopted book interest as a means of securing good responsible agents.

18. The various organisations of agents generally favour the system of book interest ; apart from giving them greater independence in relation to their employers, they claim for it that it gives the agent an interest in building up business that is sound and likely to last ; the agent has his own motive for increasing his business and is at the same time in a better position to resist pressure from his employers to get business at all costs. The issue in some ways is like that between the multiple shop and the small shopkeeper ; each form of organisation has its advantages and its disadvantages. From the point of view of the policy-holder, the significance of book interest lies in its making practically unchangeable the terms of service of the agent and by consequence the administrative cost of

insurance. Many of the present agents have invested their savings in buying books; all of them look forward to selling or bequeathing their books when they retire. Recognition of book interest turns the right to collect into a property with a market value, which depends on the conditions of service of the agent. These conditions cannot in practice be changed without his consent except on payment of compensation, and the societies have no funds from which compensation could be paid.

19. The methods of remuneration now in force show a considerable though unequal move from former methods. At the time of the Parmoor Report, agents in nearly all cases were paid partly by a percentage on the amount collected each week, varying from 25 per cent. in the societies to 15 or 20 per cent. in the companies, and partly by payments for " new business." Sometimes the agent took the whole of the premiums during an agreed period following the issue of new policies, say the first 13 weeks ; sometimes lapses were set off against fresh policies so that " new business " pay depended on net increase. Thus the Prudential at that time paid ten times the weekly premium on each new policy, provided it were kept in force for 13 weeks, and 18 times the net increase in the weekly debit ; this payment for new business represented more than a quarter of the total remuneration of the Prudential agents. The whole system, while varying in detail, gave the strongest possible incentive to agents to push their business at all costs ; in many cases they could not live without doing so. The Parmoor Committee found that for collecting a £10 book a Prudential agent would be paid 32/6 a week. " If a man with such a book is to obtain a wage on which he can maintain himself and his family it is clear that he must secure and keep securing a large number of new customers." The Committee flatly recommended " the prohibition of the payment to agents of procuration fees for new business, and the substitution of a minimum weekly wage, based on a fixed collection per week, with a commission on all sums collected above that amount." (Parmoor Committee, paras, 14 and 42.)

20. This recommendation found no place in the Industrial Assurance Act of 1923 which followed the Parmoor Report, so that it is surprising that Lord Parmoor in speaking in the House of Lords of that measure should have declared himself unable " to find a single instance in which a reform we suggested has not found its place in the present Bill."* But, as appears above, the recommendation has been adopted very fully by the Prudential Company. It has been adopted in part by other companies, in so far as new business payment has come to mean payment for increase after deduction of lapses. In the principal societies, which still allow the agent to retain the premiums of the first weeks, irrespective of lapses, it has not been adopted at all. The history of these societies, with their barely changed systems of remuneration, confirms the view expressed successively by the Parmoor Committee (para. 21) and the Cohen Committee (para. 37) that the control of the organisation in all the large societies has been secured by the agents.

21. The collecting societies are, in theory, mutual associations controlled by those who insure through them as members. Collectors, both in societies and in companies, are debarred by Section 33 of the Industrial Assurance Act from membership of the Committee of Management or Board of Directors ; they may hold no other office in the society or company except that of superintending collector within a specified area ; they may not be present at any meeting of the society or company. The methods by which, nevertheless, control of societies by their staff has been achieved, through the influence exercised on their clientele by the collectors, were described frankly to the Cohen Committee by a representative of the National Amalgamated Union of Life Assurance Workers, when under examination by Sir Alfred Watson (Cohen Committee Evidence, Qu. 5555–5566). If the matter is looked at realistically, there is nothing surprising in this. Both the Parmoor Committee and the Cohen Committee admitted that there was no evidence of any desire on the part of the members to govern themselves or take an interest in the affairs of their society ; ordinary citizens have not the time to be positively democratic about their burial insurance. It was inevitable that the democracy of the collecting societies should become a syndicalist organisation of agents, an association of the sellers of insurance rather than of its buyers. This was bound to happen irrespective of book interest and to make difficult any large changes in the organisation of those societies. In practice, in all the larger societies, book interest enters as a further obstacle to change, and these societies, in spite of the recommendations of the Parmoor Committee, have maintained their methods of remuneration with little change. The agent still keeps in whole or in part the first premiums on new policies, even though the new policies lapse almost as soon as they have been effected.

Pressure for Increase

22. In the Prudential and to a less extent in the other companies, the methods of remuneration have been changed, so as to have less direct relation to the amount of new business procured. This has not meant that the procuring of new business has ceased

---

* Cited in *Industrial Assurance* by Sir Arnold Wilson and Professor H. Levy, p. 92.

in any of the offices to be an important—indeed an essential—part of the agent's duties. The National Amalgamated Union of Life Assurance Workers, whose evidence has been mentioned above, emphasised " pressure for increase " of business as the predominant feature of the agent's life, pressure coming upon him from his office and transmitted to the public. They gave instances of what they regarded as undue pressure as much in companies like the Prudential and the Pearl, which had rationalised their business and altered their terms of remuneration, as in other offices. The greater part of the staff of the Industrial Life Offices are organised not in this union, but in staff unions confined to particular offices which are associated in the Insurance Unions Congress. The representatives of this Congress, when before the Cohen Committee, were not so outspoken as the representatives of the National Amalgamated Union, but did not deny that there was " severe pressure by the offices upon agents to obtain new business " (Cohen Committee, Qu. 5897). . " While the general administration of the Insurance Industry will compare favourably with that of other industries touching the industrial population, there are certain defects inherent in the intensive competitive methods prevalent, which we know from practical experience are operating to the prejudice of the public and collecting staffs." (Memorandum of Insurance Unions Congress to Cohen Committee, p. 3.) Industrial assurance has always been and remains a highly competitive industry primarily dependent on salesmanship. Even if the agent gains nothing by writing new business which does not stick, he loses, if he does not get new business in one way or another, for that is what he is appointed to do. As it was put to the Cohen Committee by the representative of the Industrial Life Offices Association, " I consider what is alleged to be ' undue pressure ' is nothing more than ordinary business methods of conducting a business successfully." (Cohen Committee Evidence, Qu. 8572.)

23. The collectors are not the sole agents for extending the business. At the time of the Cohen report, the industrial offices engaged 2,675 persons other than agents, district managers or superintendents in canvassing. The activity of these special canvassers was emphasised by the representatives of the National Amalgamated Union as a main factor in what they regarded as over-selling of insurance.

3. ADMINISTRATIVE COSTS

24. During the four years 1937-40, the industrial assurance companies and collecting societies paid on an average £23,809,000 each year as commission and management expenses. The proprietary companies paid £1,805,000 a year under a heading described in the reports of the Industrial Assurance Commissioner as " Shareholders' dividends, etc." They paid also £1,535,000 a year as income-tax. This tax in the case of life assurance companies is based on their investment interest less their expenses of management, with the proviso that the income-tax paid must not be less than the tax on their trading profits. In the case of industrial assurance, the management expenses are so high that the proviso nearly always comes into operation, that is to say the income-tax paid is in effect a tax on trading profits.. In one company only, the Prudential, in the last few years before the war was interest so high in relation to management expenses and trading profits that tax was charged upon the interest less expenses and not under the proviso.

Cost Ratio and Expense Ratio

25. From the point of view of the companies neither dividends nor income tax are an expense of management ; profits to be distributed as dividends are one of the objects for which expense is incurred and income tax is an unavoidable incident in making profits. From the point of view of the industrial policy-holder, both dividends and income tax are part of the administrative cost of securing the protection of insurance ; if there were no profits or tax, he could get the same protection for lower premiums. Both dividends and income tax, accordingly, must be brought into account in comparing industrial assurance with other forms of insurance, or in comparing the costs of collecting societies which do not pay dividends or tax with companies which do pay them. The heading used by the Industrial Assurance Commissioner of " shareholders' dividends, etc.," is not, of course, identical with " dividends." It is described as including " all appropriations from the Industrial Assurance Fund to shareholders' dividends and any amounts transferred from that Fund to the Profit and Loss Account which are not earmarked for other purposes, e.g., for investment reserves. All transfers which are so earmarked are included under ' miscellaneous expenditure.' " This heading therefore does not necessarily include all dividends paid to shareholders in proprietary companies undertaking industrial assurance, because they may receive dividends from business other than industrial assurance. It may, on the other hand, occasionally include sums which, though not earmarked for investment reserves when made, are used later either for that purpose or in some other way which directly or indirectly benefits the policy-holders. In the main, however, this heading represents sums which go elsewhere than to the advantage of the policy-holders, and sums entered under it, together with income tax, must be added.to the management expenses, in order to obtain the total administrative cost of industrial assurance from the point of view of the policy-holder. This total

TABLE XXV.—INDUSTRIAL ASSURANCE IN 1912-17 AND 1937-40.

Office	Type	Premiums £000		Expenses of Management, £000		Dividends to shareholders, etc., £000		Income Tax, £000	Administrative Cost, excl. Tax £000		% of Premiums		Total Cost Ratio incl. Tax
		Mean of 1912-17	Mean of 1937-40	Mean of 1912-17	Mean of 1937-40	Mean of 1912-17	Mean of 1937-40	Mean of 1937-40	Mean of 1912-17	Mean of 1937-40	Mean of 1912-17	Mean of 1937-40	Mean of 1937-40
(1)	(2)	(3)	(4)	(5)	(6)	(7)	(8)	(9)	(10)	(11)	(12)	(13)	(14)
Prudential	P.C.	8,437·3	23,600·1	3,302·8	6,049·5	448·0	813·1	908·0	3,750·8	6,862·6	44·4	29·1	32·9
Co-operative... ...	—	14·3	5,339·9	7·1	1,768·3				7·1	1,768·3	49·7	33·1	33·1
Refuge	P.C.	2,258·2	6,016·1	1,017·1	2,006·1	34·0	64·5	79·7	1,051·1	2,070·6	46·5	34·4	35·7
Pearl	P.C.	2,631·2	9,189·7	1,094·7	2,762·3	55·6	532·5	296·3	1,150·3	3,294·8	43·7	35·9	39·1
Royal Liver	C.S.	1,147·1	4,220·0	453·1	1,658·9				453·1	1,658·9	39·5	39·3	39·3
Liverpool Victoria ...	C.S.	1,633·8	6,888·6	718·7	2,766·8				718·7	2,766·8	44·0	40·2	40·2
Royal London Mutual	M.C.	1,405·5	5,221·5	601·2	2,105·6				601·2	2,105·6	42·8	40·3	40·3
Scottish Legal ...	C.S.	429·3	1,485·3	176·6	599·8				176·6	599·8	41·1	40·4	40·4
Wesleyan & General ...		779·9	1,442·9	355·8	584·3				355·8	584·3	45·6	40·5	40·5
Britannic	P.C.	1,082·4	4,031·1	437·7	1,319·0	20·8	222·5	135·4	458·5	1,541·5	42·4	38·2	41·6
Royal Co-operative ...	C.S.	88·8	404·6	46·4	171·3				46·4	171·3	52·2	42·3	42·3
Salvation Army ...	P.C.	312·7	981·2	141·0	337·1	0·1	50·0	29·6	141·1	387·1	45·1	39·5	42·5
Blackburn Philanthropic	P.C.	101·5	615·7	43·5	231·3		25·3	17·0	43·5	256·6	42·9	41·7	44·5
Pioneer Life... ...	P.C.	78·5	128·0	42·0	49·0	1·2	4·5	3·8	43·2	53·5	55·0	41·8	44·8
London & Manchester ...	P.C.	696·6	1,912·8	295·1	760·7	3·7	91·9	64·7	298·8	852·6	42·9	44·6	48·0
15 Offices		21,097·1	71,477·5	8,733·0	23,170·0	563·3	1,804·3	1,534·5	9,296·3	24,974·3	44·1	34·9	37·1
Other Companies		567·1	474·5	268·7	254·6	0·6	0·3	1·0	269·3	254·9	47·5	53·7	53·9
Other Societies		298·9	1,043·0	115·2	384·8				115·2	384·8	38·5	36·9	36·9
All Offices		21,963·1	72,995·0	9,116·9	23,809·4	563·9	1,804·6	1,535·5	9,680·8	25,614·0	44·1	35·1	37·2

For notes to this Table see next page.

Notes to Table XXV:

The offices are of three main types : Proprietary Companies (P.C.), Mutual Companies (M.C.) and Collecting Societies (C.S.). Neither the Co-operative nor the Wesleyan and General falls exactly into any of these classes. The former is a company registered, not under the Companies Acts, but under the Industrial and Provident Societies Acts, and has a small paid-up capital on which is based a limited dividend, but this dividend does not come from the Industrial Branch. In the Wesleyan and General, valuation surpluses of the industrial branch are distributed, not only among industrial policy holders, but in part among the holders of ordinary branch policies participating in profits. The amount so transferred from the industrial to the ordinary branch in 1937–40 averaged £21,000 a year. This should be added to the administrative cost of the Wesleyan and General in 1937–40, which would make it 42·0 instead of 40·5 per cent. But this correction is not made in the table above, since it is uncertain how transfers to the ordinary branch were treated in the table of the Parmoor Committee for 1912–17.

The total Cost Ratio including Tax is the sum of cols. 9 and 11 expressed as a percentage of col. 4.

The figures now included in the Reports of the Industrial Assurance Commissioner as " Shareholders' Dividends, etc." include all appropriations from the industrial assurance fund to shareholders' dividends and any amounts transferred from that fund to the profit and loss account which are not earmarked for other purposes, e.g., for investment reserves. These are the figures used above for 1937–40. The figures used for 1912–17 are taken from the column in the Parmoor Report headed " Dividends to Shareholders." It is possible, though there is no positive reason for believing it, that these dividends were provided in part either from other classes of business than industrial assurance or from interest earned on reserve funds. In so far as the figures in these columns at the two periods are not exactly comparable, it is likely that they are unduly large in the earlier period, i.e., that the table overstates the administrative cost of companies in the earlier period and by consequence overstates the reduction of the cost ratio between the two periods. But any error is likely to be small.

The four companies doing business in 1937–40 which were not in business in 1912–17 are the Cremation, Nation Life, Shield and United Friendly with the annual premium income and administrative cost shown at the foot of the table against the heading " other companies."

Eight companies appearing in Appendix B of the Parmoor Report are no longer in separate existence. Their annual premium income and administrative cost and those of the four " other companies " of 1937–38 are shown at the foot of the table in separate lines, as they are not comparable with one another. The figures for " other societies " in 1912–17 and 1937–40 are shown in the same way for the same reason.

Appendix B of the Parmoor Report contains an arithmetical error giving the total premiums of the Co-operative in 1912–17 at ten times the correct figure and using this wrong figure in reaching the totals for all companies and societies. The administrative costs are stated correctly. Correction of this mistake by reducing the total of premiums increases the expense percentage for all companies in 1912–17 from 44·2, as printed in the Parmoor Report, to 44·5 and for all companies and the four societies from 43·9 as printed to 44·1.

in 1937-40 was accordingly £27,149,000 a year, that is to say 37·2 per cent. of the premium income of £72,995,000. The "expense ratio" in the Industrial Life Offices, as it is estimated by them omitting dividends and income tax is materially less. The "cost ratio" for the policy-holder as estimated above is 37·2 per cent., or nearly 7/6 in the or 4½d. in the shilling of the premiums received.

26. This is an average figure for all the offices taken together in 1937-40. It is important to consider the principal offices and types of offices separately and also to compare the present costs with those of earlier periods. Material for both these comparisons is given in Table XXV, showing for each of the eleven companies in existence both in 1912-17 and in 1937-40 and for the four chief collecting societies, the average annual premiums, management expenses, dividends to shareholders, sum of these last two as administrative costs, and the proportion borne by administrative costs to premiums. The few companies excluded as not in existence at both epochs and the numerous smaller collecting societies are statistically unimportant. The offices directly compared in Table XXV have 98 per cent. of the total premium income in 1937-40, and had 95 per cent. of the total number of full-time agents in 1937. The figures for the earlier period—derived from a table printed in the Report of the Parmoor Committee—do not include income tax; complete cost-ratios including tax where it is paid are given, for the later period only, in a final column and the offices are arranged in the order of these ratios, beginning with the Prudential as the lowest. For comparing 1912-17 with 1937-40 the costs without tax must be used.

27. This comparison shows that in about twenty-four years the administrative cost (exclusive of tax) of industrial assurance has fallen from 44 per cent. of the premiums to 35 per cent., from 8/10 in every £ paid by the insured persons to 7/– in the £. The reduction of the total cost ratio, including tax, would be somewhat less than this, since the rate of tax was higher in the later period. The most interesting feature, however, of the comparison between 1912-17 and the years just before this war, lies not in the totals, but in the contrasted histories of different types of office. This feature is brought out by Table XXVI summarising the results for the Prudential, the Co-operative, the Refuge, the six other large proprietary companies, and five large mutual offices of which four are collecting societies. Leaving the Co-operative for consideration later as an interesting special case, it will be seen that the Prudential in 1912-17 had administrative costs (excluding tax) just above the average at 44·4 per cent. of the premiums ; it has now reduced this percentage by a third to 29·1, well below that of any other office. The Refuge in 1912-17 had administrative costs (excluding tax) well above the average at 46·5 per cent. of the premiums ; it has now reduced this percentage by a quarter to 34·4 per cent. The six other proprietary companies had an administrative cost, excluding tax, of 43·6 per cent., this has fallen by about an eighth to 37·9 per cent. The five mutual offices in 1912-17 had a cost ratio below that of the offices at 42·4 per cent. ; in twenty-four years this has hardly fallen at all and remains at 40·1 per cent. These mutual offices used to take 8/6 in the £ of their members' contributions to pay their staff ; they now take 8/– out of each of nearly four times as many £'s as before.

Growth of Different Types of Office

28. This last fact calls attention to one of the most striking features in Table XXVI. The Prudential has for long given better terms than almost any other office in respect of forfeiture ; it does not demand an absolute warranty of health in proposals for life of another policies, as most of the other offices do ; it can work at about three-quarters of the administrative expense of the societies and more cheaply than any other company ; it alone of all the large companies guarantees to its policy-holders, by its articles of association, a share of profits. It might have been expected that the Prudential would tend to drive its rivals from the field, and would certainly grow more rapidly than they. Column 3 of the table shows the opposite tendency. Between the two epochs compared the office which can do best for its policy-holders has increased its premium income less than three times ; that of the six other proprietary companies which are combined in the table has increased nearly three and a half times ; the business of the collecting societies, who have failed to any great extent either to change their method of remuneration with its direct incentive to get new business or to reduce their ratio of expenses, has grown nearly four times. The experience of the Refuge gives a second illustration of the same paradox— of a large reduction of administrative costs and a specially favourable treatment of policy-holders in sharing profits, combined with a slower expansion of business. Rapid expansion and high cost of administration in the collecting societies have a mutual relation of cause and effect. The terms of remuneration giving procuration fees for new business stimulate expansion ; if expansion follows, new business forms a larger proportion of the whole business and, being more expensive, raises the expense ratio of the society.

29. In addition to the Prudential and the Refuge, the Co-operative Insurance Society, Ltd., is shown separately in Table XXVI. This company is unusual in several ways : as the only industrial assurance company registered under the Industrial and Provident Societies Acts, as having next to the Prudential the lowest expense ratio of any industrial office, and as showing spectacular growth. Yet another exceptional feature

I

TABLE XXVI.—SUMMARY OF INDUSTRIAL ASSURANCE, 1912-17 AND 1937-40

Office	Annual Premium Income			Annual Administrative Cost					
	£000		Rate of increase (2)÷(1)	(excluding tax)				(including tax) 1937-40	
				Actual (£000)		Per cent. of premiums			
	1912-17	1937-40		1912-17	1937-40	1912-17	1937-40	Actual (£000)	Per cent. of premiums
	(1)	(2)	(3)	(4)	(5)	(6)	(7)	(8)	(9)
Prudential	8437·3	23600·1	2·8	3750·8	6862·6	44·4	29·1	7770·6	32·9
Co-operative	14·3	5339·9	373·4	7·1	1768·3	49·8	33·1	1768·3	33·1
Refuge	2258·2	6016·1	2·7	1051·1	2070·6	46·5	34·4	2150·3	35·7
Six other proprietary companies	4902·9	16858·5	3·4	2135·5	6386·1	43·6	37·9	6932·9	41·1
Five mutual offices	4704·5	18220·0	3·9	1996·0	7302·4	42·4	40·1	7302·4	40·1
Other offices	1645·9	2960·4	1·8	740·3	1224·0	45·0	41·3	1225·0	41·4
All offices	21963·1	72995·0	3·3	9680·8	25614·0	44·1	35·1	27149·5	37·2

about this company is that in England it is no longer associated with the administration of health insurance, that is to say its agents in England do not combine industrial assurance with work for an Approved Society. The company was registered so long ago as 1867 but so late as 1918 its premium income was about £20,000. The Co-operative Movement with which it is connected decided then to develop industrial assurance, and co-operative societies throughout the country have given to it special facilities for approaching their members. The company has a nominal capital of £105,000 held by the two Co-operative Wholesale Societies as shareholders. Of this nominal capital one-quarter or about £26,000 has been called up, but the dividend of 5 per cent. on this capital is paid, not from the industrial assurance branch, but from other branches of the company's business. The surpluses of the industrial assurance branch are divided among the policy-holders after certain superannuation provision for the staff. The company employs now about 3,600 agents, remunerated on specially favourable terms including 50 per cent. of the premiums for the first 40 weeks, and entitled to book interest. The low expense ratio achieved is presumably due, among other things, to its having a selected clientele and exceptionally easy means of canvassing. Its progress may fairly be attributed to combination of three factors : appeal to co-operative sentiment, favourable terms to the policy-holders, and the strong incentive given to the agents by their terms of remuneration and by book interest to develop their business.

30. Correct comparison of different types of offices, from the point of view of the policy-holder, requires that account should be taken of the trading profits of companies which make profits, and the sums which have to be paid away as income-tax. This comparison is presented in the final columns of Tables XXV and XXVI. Inclusion of income tax brings the total cost ratio of the Prudential practically to the same level as that of the Co-operative which makes no profit for shareholders from its industrial branch and pays no tax ; the total cost in each is nearly one-third of the premiums ; what the Prudential saves on expenses as compared with the Co-operative goes in dividends and tax. The Refuge, with a relatively small allocation to dividends comes next, with a ratio of 35·7—materially below any other office. Except for three relatively small companies with higher costs, the ratios for all the other large offices range only from 39·1 to 42·5, with no important difference between the six proprietary companies, the mutual companies and the societies. Taken together the six proprietary companies grouped together in Table XXVI have substantially lower expense ratios than the five mutual offices, but they make up for this and a little more by what they spend on dividends and tax.

Comparison with 1887

31. It is possible and interesting to carry the history of the cost ratio back to an even earlier period than 1912–17. This is done in Table XXVII below, giving figures for 1887 from information obtained by the Select Committee of the House of Commons which in 1889 examined the working of industrial assurance. Table XXVII shows the cost ratio of the principal mutual offices falling in fifty years from 44·2 to 40·0 while the premium income rises from less than £1,000,000 to nearly £18,000,000 ; this can hardly represent more than the spreading of central office expenses over a business expanded eighteen times. It shows the cost ratio of the proprietary companies at first stationary and higher than that of the mutual offices, then falling rapidly, with the dividend ratio rising throughout ; in the fifty years premium income has multiplied between eleven and twelve times (i.e., less than with the mutual offices), management expenses have multiplied between seven and eight times, and shareholders' profits have multiplied nearly thirty times.

TABLE XXVII.—INDUSTRIAL ASSURANCE : PROPRIETARY COMPANIES AND MUTUAL OFFICES IN 1887, 1912–17 AND 1937–40 (ANNUAL MEANS)

Type of Office	Pre-miums £000	Expenses incl. commission		Dividends to shareholders, etc.		Expenses and Dividends	
		£000	% of Pre-miums	£000	% of Pre-miums	£000	% of Pre-miums
Proprietary Cos.—							
1887	4032·1	1773·4	44·0	60·9	1·5	1834·3	45·5
1912–17	15905·8	6524·6	41·0	563·4	3·5	7088·0	44·6
1937–40	45859·0	13283·7	29·0	1779·0	3·9	15062·7	32·9
Mutual Offices—							
1887	984·4	435·0	44·2	—	—	435·0	44·2
1912–17	4615·8	1949·6	42·2	—	—	1949·6	42·2
1937–40	17815·4	7131·1	40·0	—	—	7131·1	40·0

NOTE.—The Proprietary Companies in 1937–40 are the Britannic, London and Manchester, Pearl, Pioneer, Prudential, Refuge and Salvation Army. In 1912–17 they are the same with the addition of the British Legal (absorbed later in the Britannic) and the British Widows and London General (whose business was transferred later to the Prudential). The seven companies named first are the only companies undertaking industrial assurance in both periods which paid a dividend in either period, except the Blackburn Philanthropic which had been a collecting society and became a company in 1913. The Proprietary Companies in 1887 are British Workman's and British Legal (both subsequently merged in Britannic) ; London and Manchester ; London, Edinburgh and Glasgow (subsequently absorbed by Pearl) ; Pearl, Prudential, Refuge and United Kingdom (which was absorbed by the London, Edinburgh and Glasgow in 1889 so that later it became part of the Pearl). These are the only companies other than the Wesleyan with premiums above £10,000. Most of the remaining companies were moribund in 1887.

The Mutual Offices are three large societies—Liverpool Victoria, Royal Liver and Scottish Legal—and the Royal London Mutual which was a society till 1908 when it became a company paying no dividend. The four offices including the Royal London Mutual had 86·6 per cent. of the premium income of all societies in 1887, and 92·5 per cent. of the premium income of all societies plus the Royal London Mutual in 1937–40. They are thus fully representative of mutual business. The year 1887 happened to be the year in which the Prudential declared the results of its quinquennial valuation and allocated to shareholders £249,600 and to the ordinary branch £35,400 ; one-fifth of the sum of these two amounts (£57,000) is reckoned as the dividends of the Prudential in 1887. For the other companies the actual dividends of 1887 are taken.

Dividends in Proprietary Companies

32. Table XXVII shows the persistence of methods and costs in the collecting societies. It shows also the rising tide of dividends to shareholders in the proprietary companies as their success became established, from being about £61,000 a year or 1·5 per cent. of the premiums in 1887, to being £1,779,000 a year or 3·9 per cent. of the premiums in 1937–40. In making any comparison between 1912–17 and 1937–40 regard must be had to the fact that the earlier period includes 2½ years before war and 3½ years of war with reduced dividends, while the later period includes 2⅜ years before war and 1¼ years of war. If comparison is limited to the pre-war years, say 1912–13 and 1937–38, it is found that the amount devoted to dividends rose about as much as the premiums and kept the same proportion to the premiums.

33. The Parmoor Committee gave special attention to the question of dividends in industrial assurance. They stated it as " evident that the share capital of industrial assurance companies exercises much less important functions than that of commercial or manufacturing undertakings " and declared that " in these circumstances the case for high dividends appears . . . to rest upon somewhat slender foundations." Their examination of witnesses, following up an earlier investigation by the Select Committee of 1889, established the fact that the hard cash subscribed as share capital to the Prudential had been £5,839* ; all the rest of its paid-up capital, then put at £1,000,000, represented bonuses distributed to shareholders out of the profits of the business ; many of the existing shareholders might have paid high prices for their shares in the market, but their money went to those from whom they bought, not to strengthen the capital resources of the company. At the time of the Parmoor Committee the Prudential had a premium income of over £8,000,000 a year and was distributing £400,000 a year to shareholders after paying income tax. Obviously no additional capital has been needed since then. An issue of capital was made in 1929 under circumstances described and criticised by the Cohen Committee (Report, para. 43), while the premium income has grown to £23,000,000, with over £800,000 a year going as dividends after more than £900,000 a year has been paid as tax. The view of the Parmoor Committee as to the small function of capital in industrial assurance cannot well be disputed ; the view of the Parmoor Committee has been confirmed amply since their Report by the spectacular growth of the Co-operative from an annual premium income of less than £20,000 to one of over £5,000,000 in twenty years, without need to pay any dividends at all on this business.

34. In judging the cost of industrial assurance to the policy-holder it is necessary to adopt the procedure of the preceding paragraphs and look at the total cost ratio including dividends and income-tax. To the Industrial Life Offices themselves their costs are something different ; their interest is in their expenses of management and their aim is to reduce these expenses. Led by the Prudential, most of the larger companies in the last twenty-five years have made vigorous efforts to rationalise their work and to bring

---

* Evidence of Mr. T. C. Dewey (General Manager of the Prudential) to Select Committee of 1889 (particularly Qu. 4769–70, 4942–45, 4960–75) and of Sir George May (Secretary of the Prudential) to the Parmoor Committee (particularly Qu. 3512–14, 3522–24).

about economies of staff. The results are shown in Table XXVIII, which gives for each of the fifteen offices the expenses of management shown in Table XXV as percentages of the premium income; the offices are arranged in the order of success in reducing their expense ratios. The figures for the Co-operative have no great significance, since the high figure for 1912–17 relates to a very small premium income, and the Pioneer Life is a small office with extremely high expenses in 1912–17. Among the other offices, the expense ratio of the Prudential has fallen by about one-third; that of the Refuge, Pearl and Salvation Army by about one-quarter; that of the Royal Co-operative and Britannic by about a fifth. In the mutual offices at the foot of the table, from Liverpool Victoria to Royal Liver, the expense ratio is the same as the cost ratio; the reduction between 1912–17 and 1937–40 is markedly less than with the principal proprietary companies. This is true also of the London and Manchester, which is a proprietary company.

TABLE XXVIII.—INDUSTRIAL ASSURANCE—EXPENSES OF MANAGEMENT AS PERCENTAGE OF PREMIUMS, 1912–17 AND 1937–40

	1912–17	1937–40
Co-operative	49·7	33·1
Pioneer Life	53·5	38·3
Prudential	39·1	25·6
Refuge	45·0	33·3
Pearl	41·6	30·1
Salvation Army	45·1	34·4
Royal Co-operative	52·2	42·3
Britannic	40·4	32·7
Blackburn Philanthropic	42·9	37·6
Wesleyan & General	45·6	40·5
Liverpool Victoria	44·0	40·2
London & Manchester	42·4	39·8
Royal London Mutual	42·8	40·3
Scottish Legal	41·1	40·4
Royal Liver	39·5	39·3
15 Offices	41·4	32·4
All Offices	41·5	32·6
Premium Income (£000)	21,963	72,995
Expenses of Management (£000)	9,117	23,809

35. The high proportion of the premiums paid by the poorest classes that became absorbed in the expenses and profits of industrial assurance has been the subject of adverse comment by every independent body that has investigated the subject, from the Royal Commission on Friendly Societies which reported in 1874 to the Cohen Committee which reported in 1933. As is shown in paragraph 34, since the date of the Parmoor Report a vigorous and successful attempt has been made by most of the proprietary companies to reduce their expenses, but from the point of view of the policy-holder this has been offset to some extent by increases in the amounts paid as dividend and tax. It has left the total cost ratio of all the proprietary companies taken together at 36·3 per cent. of a premium income three times as large as at the beginning of this attempt. The mutual companies and the chief collecting societies have made no similar attempt and no significant change of methods; on a premium income expanded more than three and a-half times, they have reduced their cost ratio only from 42·4 in 1912–17 to 40·1 in 1937–40; fifty years ago, at the time of the Select Committee of 1889, these offices had practically the same ratio.

Comparison with Other Forms of Insurance

36. It is urged sometimes in defence of the cost ratio of industrial assurance that it is not higher than is found in many other classes of insurance. As appears from the comparison of administrative costs of various forms of insurance made in Appendix E, this is true of insurance against fire, accidents, motor risks and employers' liability; the cost ratio for such classes of insurance, calculated so far as possible in the same way, is actually higher than in industrial assurance. But these classes of business are not in any way comparable; they involve administrative work in adjusting premiums, determining liability and assessing damage more complicated than arises in any form of life assurance; some of this work, such as the imposition of safety precautions against fire, though it swells the administrative cost, is a direct benefit to the policy-holder. Industrial assurance is the life assurance of the man of limited means; ordinary life assurance, in spite of growing charges for commission, costs the policy-holder not 7/6 in the £ of premiums but about 3/2 in the £.

TABLE XXIX.—INDUSTRIAL AND ORDINARY LIFE ASSURANCE IN CERTAIN OFFICES, 1937

| | Industrial Branch | | | | | Ordinary Branch | | | | | Sum of expenses and dividends % of Premiums | |
| | Premiums | Expenses of management | | Dividends to shareholders, etc. | | Premiums | Expenses and commission | | Dividends to shareholders | | Indus-trial | Ordi-nary |
	£000	£000	% of Premiums	£000	% of Premiums	£000	£000	% of Premiums	£000	% of Premiums		
Blackburn Philanthropic	588·6	226·1	38·4	26·0	4·4	123·4	16·0	13·0	6·6	5·3	42·8	18·3
Britannic	3908·4	1321·6	33·8	240·0	6·1	1387·5	186·4	13·4	39·2	2·8	39·9	16·2
London & Manchester	1850·3	773·0	41·8	98·5	5·3	1402·3	204·5	14·6	35·0	2·5	47·1	17·1
Pearl	8778·5	2689·7	30·6	480·0	5·5	5301·0	629·0	11·9	209·0	3·9	36·1	15·8
Pioneer	126·6	49·2	38·9	10·0	7·9	44·5	5·7	12·8	7·0	15·7	46·8	28·5
Prudential	22296·7	5768·0	25·9	894·1	4·0	13726·2	1851·1	13·5	288·2	2·1	29·9	15·6
Refuge	5853·7	1966·5	33·6	48·6	0·8	4627·8	669·2	14·5	101·4	2·2	34·4	16·7
Salvation Army	935·0	313·7	33·6	64·5	6·9	366·3	48·5	13·2	8·4	2·3	40·5	15·5
Eight companies	44337·8	13107·8	29·5	1861·7	4·2	26979·0	3610·4	13·4	694·8	2·6	33·7	16·0
Royal London Mutual	4992·4	2039·9	40·9	—	—	1746·5	299·1	17·1	—	—	40·9	17·1
Wesleyan	1405·5	582·4	41·5	—	—	760·6	129·9	17·1	13·1	1·7	41·5	18·8
All collecting societies	13440·6	5334·2	39·7	—	—	1526·8	281·6	18·4	—	—	39·7	18·4
Two companies and all societies	19838·5	7956·5	40·1	—	—	4033·9	710·6	17·6	13·1	0·3	40·1	17·9
Ten companies and all societies	64176·3	21064·3	32·8	1861·7	2·9	31012·9	4321·0	13·9	707·9	2·3	35·7	16·2

37. The industrial offices themselves do a large and growing volume of ordinary life assurance. Just before the present war, they had a premium income in their ordinary branches of over £30,000,000 a year—more than a third of all the premiums paid for ordinary life assurance in Britain. To a large extent this business is done with the same persons as hold industrial policies, a large proportion of the ordinary policies being for sums of £200 or less. It is undertaken also in the main by the same staff of agents, and the premiums are often collected by the agents, though at intervals of more than two months. Table XXIX compares for the year 1937 the industrial and ordinary branches of each of the companies which have any substantial volume of ordinary business, and of the collecting societies as a whole. Ordinary life assurance is in the main a function of the companies rather than of the societies. The principal features of the comparison are as follows :—

(a) The cost ratio (exclusive of tax) for the ordinary business of industrial life offices (16·2 per cent. in 1937) is less than half the corresponding ratio for their industrial business (35·7 per cent.) and is comparable to that of ordinary life assurance as a whole (see Appendix E, para. 10).

(b) The dividends to shareholders in the proprietary companies are a materially larger proportion of the premiums in the industrial branch—4·2 per cent.—than they are in the ordinary branch—2·6 per cent. This arises presumably from the fact that in ordinary life assurance holders of with-profit policies are normally entitled to 90 per cent. of the valuation surplus, while industrial policies carry no such rights.

(c) On the ordinary, as on the industrial side, the mutual companies and collecting societies have expenses of management exceeding the expenses plus dividends of the companies. What is saved by them in dividends goes not to policy-holders but to staff, in ordinary life assurance as it does in industrial assurance.

4. THE PROBLEM OF LAPSES

38. One of the features of industrial assurance is the large number of policies which fail to reach maturity. The Parmoor Committee reported in 1920 that " Under the system of industrial assurance as it is practised, the great majority of the policies effected lapse within a short time," and gave as typical the experience of one office—the Refuge—which in the ten years 1909–18 had issued 9,322,336 policies and had 6,426,313 lapses. They made two distinct proposals for dealing with this evil. The first and fundamental remedy was to abolish procuration fees for new business. " . . . the Committee are satisfied that so long as procuration fees are paid for new business, it will be to the interest of agents to attach undue importance to this side of their activities, looking only to the amount of the new business they can get instead of to its value to the assured and the likelihood of its permanence, and the present waste and loss will continue." This remedy, as stated above, has been tried fully by the Prudential, partly by most of the other proprietary companies, and not at all by the large collecting societies. The second proposal was to provide for the compulsory grant of free policies of reduced amount or of surrender values, after premiums had been paid for a certain number of years. This measure was embodied in the Industrial Assurance Act of 1923, and most of the larger offices have gone beyond their statutory obligations, granting free policies or surrender values after much shorter periods than those required by the Act. The Prudential and the Liverpool Victoria now grant free paid-up policies of reduced amount after premiums have been paid for one year ; a like concession is made by most of the other large offices after premiums have been paid for two years. As a consequence of these concessions a large number of policies which would have appeared among the lapses before 1920 appear now among those surrendered or replaced by free policies for reduced sums.

39. Nevertheless, the number of lapses, that is to say outright forfeitures, remains formidable. The Cohen Committee obtained a special return from all companies and societies as to the numerical movement of assurances in the year 1929 and tabulated the results in their Appendix A. They summarised the table in the following terms : " The figures indicate that as against nearly 10 million policies issued in that year (excluding ' not taken up ' cases) the number discontinued was somewhat over 6 million in the case of 1¼ millions of which, however, free policies or surrender values were granted, leaving the number of ' lapsed ' policies as 4¾ millions."

40. The present Committee obtained information as to the numerical movement of assurances in a number of years subsequent to 1929, from six of the largest offices—the Prudential, Britannic, Liverpool Victoria, Pearl, Refuge, and Royal London. This information is summarised below in Table XXX with corresponding information for 1929 from the Cohen Report, and so far as possible for 1909–18 from the Parmoor Report. The practice of different offices in regard to the issue of policies differs ; some do not regard policies as issued till a premium has been paid upon them ; some regard policies as issued as soon as the proposal has been accepted and record those on which no premium

is paid as " not taken up." The Cohen Committee in the passage quoted above disregarded policies " not taken up," and this appears to be the best procedure ; it confines examination of lapses to policies on which a premium has been paid. But the Parmoor Committee included policies issued but not taken up as having lapsed ; there is some justification for this procedure, in so far as administrative expenditure will have been incurred on these policies. With a view to getting figures so far as possible comparable with those of the Parmoor Committee, their method has been adopted in Table XXX, though the numbers of policies not taken up are also given separately. The broad results would not be very different whatever the method adopted.

Lapse Proportions at Various Dates

41. Table XXX shows a fall in the proportion of lapses to policies issued from 1909–18 to 1929 and again to 1937–39, combined with a rise in the proportion of policies ended prematurely in other ways—by being made free for a reduced sum or being surrendered for cash. This reflects the operation of the concessions progressively made by the offices since the Parmoor Report. Taking all causes of premature ending together the proportion so ended is a little higher in each of the years 1937 to 1939 than in 1929—68 per cent. as compared with 64 per cent. Complete comparison cannot be made with 1909–18 as information as to the number of surrenders is lacking, but from information as to the amounts paid out on surrenders it is possible to estimate the numbers and reach an approximate figure for the total of premature endings from all causes. This estimate suggests that for 1909–18 the policies issued and ended otherwise than by claim on maturity were about 72 per cent. of the total numbers issued as compared with the 68 per cent. twenty or more years later.

42. The figures for 1941 show a marked decline in the proportion of lapses and of surrenders on a smaller total of policies issued. This reflects both the diminution of unemployment and the arrangements made to help members of the Forces to meet their commitments for rent and insurance by war grants administered through the Ministry of Pensions. These arrangements are very extensive and cover a substantial proportion of the whole of the armed forces. Under these arrangements all premiums in respect of life, endowment or educational insurance policies taken out not less than six months before call-up or enlistment are normally accepted as commitments, provided that they are not considered unreasonable in relation to his pre-service earnings, and grants are made to meet these premiums, so far as this is necessary to maintain a net weekly income of not less than 16/- a week for each adult and 8/- a week for each child under 14 years of age. This is the minimum standard to which the net income of the serving man's household must be brought, even in cases where the standard of living prior to his service was lower. Where, however, the pre-service standard represented more than 16/- for each adult the grant is related to a proportionately higher standard. These arrangements must clearly have a very considerable effect in preventing lapses during the present war. The corresponding arrangements for dealing with the liabilities of servicemen during the war of 1914–18 were not nearly so extensive. The commitments for rent and rates were dealt with as from the beginning of the war by the National Relief Fund and later by a War Pensions Statutory Committee and a Special Grants Committee, but till March 1918 these bodies took no account of insurance premiums. From May 1916 onwards the Civil Liabilities Committee was prepared to deal with liabilities of all kinds, but sitting centrally confined its activities in the main to liabilities larger than those involved in industrial assurance. Extensive maintenance of industrial assurance policies in the last war does not appear to have begun till March 1918. It is probable, nevertheless, that for other causes lapsing tended to diminish during the last war, though not so much as in the present war and that, therefore, the fall from 72 per cent. as the average rate of abortive insurance in 1909–18 to 68 per cent. in 1937–39 understates slightly the extent of improvement.

43. Industrial assurance, however, must be judged, not by its working in the abnormal conditions of the war, but by its working in peace. The significant comparison is between the figures obtained by the Cohen Committee for 1929 and those obtained by the present Committee for 1937–39. The last line of the table giving comprehensive figures for 1929 shows that the proportion of premature endings was much the same in all the offices taken together as in the six large offices and that these had nearly three-quarters of the whole business. It may be estimated accordingly that in the last years before the present war, about 10 million policies on an average were issued each year, and about 6¾ million policies were ended prematurely each year. Of these ¾ of a million were policies not taken up ; about 3¼ million represented outright forfeitures after the policy had been taken up, and premiums paid upon it ; and about 2¾ million were converted into free policies for reduced sums or surrendered for cash. These are the figures for 1937–39, for comparison with those for 1929 given by the Cohen Committee and cited in para. 39 above.

TABLE XXX.—POLICIES ISSUED AND ENDED OTHERWISE THAN BY CLAIM ON MATURITY IN 1909-18, 1929, 1937 AND LATER

Period	Numbers of Policies (thousands)						Per Cent. of Numbers Issued			
	Issued incl. not taken up	Lapsed incl. not taken up	Made Free Reduced Sum	Surrendered for Cash	Total ended not by Claim (Sum of 3,4,5)	Not taken up	Lapsed incl. not taken up	Made Free Reduced Sum	Surrendered for Cash	Total ended not by Claim
(1)	(2)	(3)	(4)	(5)	(6)	(7)	(8)	(9)	(10)	(11)
Six Large Offices Mean of 1909-18	5793·1	3688·7	111·7	?	?	?	63·7	1·9	?	?
1929	7522·1	3808·2	325·4	702·0	4835·6	652·7	50·7	4·3	9·3	64·3
1937	7026·6	2777·7	969·1	1034·3	4781·1	547·9	39·5	13·8	14·7	68·0
1938	7791·9	3174·7	1082·6	1083·2	5340·5	564·0	40·7	13·9	13·9	68·5
1939	6954·7	2752·6	1063·9	899·0	4715·5	502·8	39·6	15·3	12·9	67·8
1941	5094·5	1418·5	668·8	297·3	2384·6	304·6	27·9	13·1	5·8	46·8
All offices 1929	10708·9	5602·2	404·2	889·1	6895·5	756·7	52·3	3·8	8·3	64·4

Note.—The six offices are the Prudential, Britannic, Liverpool Victoria, Pearl, Refuge, and Royal London. Information for Liverpool Victoria is not available in 1909-18 and the figures relate to five offices only. Policies made free for reduced sum and full sum respectively are not distinguished in the Prudential after 1929 ; the numbers made free for full sum have been estimated at 140,000 in 1938 on information supplied by the company, at 130,000 in each of 1937 and 1939 and 100,000 in 1941 and deducted from the total of free policies.

K

44. The Parmoor Committee showed that the bulk of lapses occurred within the first few months ; about 80 per cent. occurred within two years of the issue of the policy. This also holds true to-day. An analysis of lapses in one of the important offices in 1941 showed that 44·9 per cent. of the forfeited policies had been issued in 1941 and 39·5 per cent. in 1940, that is to say at least 84·4 per cent. were less than two years old.

45. Both the Parmoor Committee and the Cohen Committee discussed at some length whether lapsing of policies was profitable or the reverse to the industrial offices, and were sceptical of the claim that the offices made no gain by lapses. It is unnecessary to renew that discussion to-day. It can be accepted that the offices, as they stated in evidence to the present Committee, dislike lapses and would gladly see them diminished. It remains true, as the Parmoor Committee put it in para. 41 of their Report that " whoever gets the benefit of the premiums paid, whether the companies or their agents, it is certain that the public loses heavily by lapses."

46. The general result of the comparison is that up to the outbreak of the present war the proportion of policies issued which failed before maturity showed no substantial change. The palliative proposed by the Parmoor Committee, of grant of free policies or surrender values, had been applied. The fundamental improvement of restricting the issue of policies to those with a good chance of survival has not been achieved. As the Cohen Committee pointed out, the practical value of a free policy perhaps for a few shillings or a pound or two, payable thirty years hence, is not very great. All such policies and all surrendered policies have borne their share of the heavy costs of issue and of collection of premiums.

Over-selling as Cause of Lapsing

47. It is argued on behalf of the industrial offices that life assurance is a form of instalment buying and that some failures to maintain instalments are inevitable incidents of such a business, particularly in a society subject to unemployment. This is true. The question remains whether it is socially desirable that instalment business in the form of life assurance should be pushed to an extent producing failure to complete the purchase in two-thirds of the cases and outright forfeiture after some payments have been made in half of this two-thirds. The Parmoor Committee had no doubt that the business was being pushed too far and would continue to be pushed while procuration fees remained, as they remain in all the large collecting societies today. In giving evidence to the Cohen Committee a dozen years later the National Amalgamated Union of Life Assurance Workers declared that " much lapsing is due to over-selling." Some years later still, at the outbreak of the present war, the scale of abortive insurance was as large as ever, though its form had altered.

48. In some offices there seems to have been not even a change of form. Nearly eighty years ago in 1864, Mr. Gladstone, in urging the Bill for Post Office Insurance, tried to shock the House of Commons by giving to them what he regarded as almost incredible figures. " The Royal Liver Society," he said, " issued 135,000 policies last year and had in the same time 70,000 lapsed policies." That is a lapse proportion of 52 per cent. in 1863. In 1929, the Royal Liver Society—one of the large collecting societies which have preserved their methods of remuneration and payment for procuring new business in spite of the Parmoor Report—issued 811,545 policies and had 444,829 lapses, excluding in each case policies not taken up ; another 46,080 policies were made free for reduced sums or surrendered for cash. That is a lapse proportion of 55 per cent. in 1929 with another 6 per cent. of insurance abortive in other ways. What Mr. Gladstone regarded as an incredible scandal in 1864 was reproduced in 1929 six times greater in scale and slightly worse in degree.

5. Insurance on Life-of-Another

49. Industrial assurance began as burial insurance, as the method by which men of scanty means might provide for the inevitable expense of burial and avoid for themselves and their dependants the indignity of a " pauper grave." It has developed into the general life assurance of men of limited incomes, giving the opportunity of saving for all purposes in a great variety of forms. It is sufficient here to distinguish three main classes—endowment assurance, whole life assurance on the proposer's own life or that of a spouse, and insurance on the life-of-another. Endowment assurance as the way of combining provision for the proposer s later years with provision for earlier death is now the most rapidly growing class of business. In the 19 offices of the Industrial Life Offices Association, the premiums for endowment assurance and endowments were over a quarter of the total premiums in 1940, and had increased about 124 per cent in ten years while whole life premiums had increased only 21 per cent. In the Prudential in 1941 62 per cent. of the premiums for new business were for endowment assurances, effected either by adults on their own lives or on behalf of children on their own lives. Whole life insurance on own life or that of a spouse, may provide both funeral expenses—the original object of industrial assurance—and something for the needs of dependants ; this

class of insurance accounted for a little more than 22 per cent. of the new industrial premiums of the Prudential in 1941. Insurance on life-of-another, i.e. of a person other than the proposer or a spouse, is, in industrial assurance, insurance for funeral expenses ; including infantile assurance, it accounted for less than 16 per cent. of the new premiums of the Prudential in 1941.

Relative Importance of Funeral Expense Insurance

50. It might be thought that insurance for funeral expenses was by now a relatively unimportant part of industrial assurance. But this view would be wrong for several reasons. First, the Prudential for which these percentages have been given, is not typical ; it has a larger proportion both of endowment and of own life policies than the other offices. Second, the percentages relate to new business only ; in the whole body of assurances effected over many years in the past the proportion of endowment assurance, in the Prudential, as elsewhere, is much less. Third, the importance to the offices of insurance for funeral expenses is not measured by the statistical relation between the premiums paid specifically for that purpose and the premiums paid for other purposes. Provision for funeral expenses as a requirement whose need is recognised by all is the natural starting point from which the agent can lead his clients to saving and insurance for other less urgent purposes. In this respect insurance for funeral expenses still forms the foundation of industrial assurance. A policy intended to cover such expenses may be taken out by the proposer to provide for his own funeral or that of a spouse under the common law covering insurance in all forms. A policy to provide the funeral expenses of any other person is a policy on the life-of-another, valid only by statute and only for the special form of insurance described as industrial assurance, with premiums collected at the door.

51. Issue of policies on life-of-another, that is to say, of some person other than the proposer or spouse, to specified relatives for funeral expenses, is a feature peculiar to industrial assurance, in derogation of the law governing insurance generally. The extent to which industrial assurance depends on the power given by Section 36 (1) of the Assurance Companies Act, 1909, now Section 3 of the Act of 1923, for insurance on life-of-another, is shown by the following table. This gives the distribution of premium income on policies of whole life assurance effected on lives over ten years of age by groups of important companies in two weeks of August, 1931, and two weeks of March, 1942, respectively, with corresponding figures for the Co-operative Insurance Society, Ltd., in February, 1932 and August, 1942.

TABLE XXXI.—DISTRIBUTION OF NEW INDUSTRIAL ASSURANCE
BUSINESS BY RELATIONSHIP OF PROPOSER

Relationship of Proposer to Life Assured (1)	Premiums in two or three weeks' new Whole-Life Assurance on lives over 10 expressed as percentages of premiums on all such policies				Average sum assured
	27 offices Aug., 1931 (2)	19 offices Mar., 1942 (3)	Co-operative Feb., 1932 (4)	Co-operative Aug., 1942 (5)	Co-operative Aug., 1942 (6)
					£
Self, husband or wife ...	45·3	42·8	48·5	54·9	21·36
Son or daughter ...	41·8	44·3	25·3	35·8	10·50
Parent	5·8	5·2	23·4	5·6	17·87
Brother or sister ...	4·5	5·4	1·9	2·7	12·83
Grandchild	2·5	2·2	0·9	1·0	8·16
Grandparent	0·1	0·1	0·0	—	14·26
	100·0	100·0	100·0	100·0	

52. The offices are not precisely the same in August 1931 and March 1942 (numbering twenty-seven including the Prudential and Co-operative at the earlier date, and nineteen excluding the Prudential and Co-operative at the later date) ; the distribution of the Co-operative's business in 1932 is materially different from the general average. For this and for other reasons, such as the growth of endowment insurance on own life, differences between the two sets of percentages in cols. 2 and 3 are of no great significance. The main result is to show that at each date about half the new premiums were in respect of life-of-another policies, that is to say were valid only under the special powers given by Section 3 of the Act of 1923 for policies to provide funeral expenses.

53. These expenses are of two kinds. There is the direct cost of the funeral, which must be borne by someone and which need not vary greatly from one death to another. There are the personal expenditures which relatives and friends of the dead person may wish to incur in showing their respect, by mourning garments, by attendance at the funeral involving perhaps travelling costs and loss of wages, by sending of flowers, and in other ways. These expenditures depend both on the numbers and on the feelings of those who feel bound to incur them. The first kind may, for convenience, be described as direct funeral expenses ; the second kind as indirect expenses on death.

Illegal Policies and the Act of 1909

54. Industrial assurance began as a means of meeting direct funeral expenses ; in the words already quoted from the Royal Commission of 1874 the bulk of the collecting societies were burial societies. Much of this insurance took the form of own life policies needing no special legal authority ; beyond this, friendly societies, whether using collectors or not, were authorised by statute to provide money for the funeral expenses of the husband, wife or child of a member and companies could issue policies for the same purpose to the parents of children under ten years of age. These powers, the only ones existing before 1909, did not cover direct funeral expenses in all cases, and they made no provision at all for the indirect expenses on death which might be incurred by relatives other than a parent or spouse. But both companies and societies before 1909 had become accustomed to issue policies, some of which, while on the face of them they might appear to be own-life policies, were, in fact, taken out by persons who had no insurable interest, with a view to receiving a payment on the death of the life assured. Such policies were illegal under the Act of 1774. In introducing in 1909 the Bill which became the Assurance Companies Act, the President of the Board of Trade (Mr. Winston Churchill) estimated that of 35,000,000 industrial assurance policies then in existence, about 10,000,000 were illegal.

55. A situation had been created by the Industrial Life Offices with which Parliament was forced to deal. Parliament dealt with it in two stages under sub-sections (1) and (2) of Section 36 of the Assurance Companies Act of 1909 as set out below :—

(1) Amongst the purposes for which collecting societies and industrial assurance companies may issue policies of assurance there shall be included insuring money to be paid for the funeral expenses of a parent, grandparent, grandchild, brother or sister.

(2) No policy effected before the passing of this Act with a collecting society or industrial assurance company shall be deemed to be void by reason only that the person effecting the policy had not, at the time the policy was effected, an insurable interest in the life of the person insured, or that the name of the person interested, or for whose benefit or on whose account the policy was effected, was not inserted in the policy, or that the insurance was not one authorised by the Acts relating to friendly societies, if the policy was effected by or on account of a person who had at the time a *bona fide* expectation that he would incur expenses in connection with the death or funeral of the assured, and if the sum assured is not unreasonable for the purpose of covering those expenses, and any such policy shall enure for the benefit of the person for whose benefit it was effected or his assigns.

(3) Any collecting society or industrial assurance company which, after the passing of this Act, issues policies of assurance which are not within the legal powers of such society or company shall be held to have made default in complying with the requiements of this Act ; and the provisions of this Act with respect to such default shall apply to collecting societies, industrial assurance companies and their officers, in like manner as they apply to assurance companies and their officers.

The first of these sub-sections dealt with the future ; it recognised the need for extended powers of insurance by named relatives for funeral expenses ; this sub-section was reproduced in substance by Section 3 of the Act of 1923, which by adding " child " to the list of permitted relationships consolidated therewith powers of insurance on children given under earlier Acts of 1896. The second sub-section dealt with the past ; it validated insurances made with a *bona fide* expectation of incurring expenses in connection with the death or funeral of the assured, but only if such insurances had been made before 3rd December, 1909 ; this whitewashing sub-section was reproduced in substance by Section 31 of the Act of 1923. What was the intention and what has been the effect of this legislation ? There has been much legal argument as to the precise meaning and effect of sub-section (1), but three propositions may be laid down as beyond dispute by reasonable men.

56. First, " the funeral expenses " for which continuing insurance is permitted under sub-section (1) are something different from and narrower than the *bona fide* expectation of incurring expenses in connection with a death or funeral, insurance which in the past is validated by sub-section (2). Parliament does not use entirely different words in the same Act to mean the same thing. A supporting argument for strict interpretation of sub-section (1) is that no condition is imposed there as to the amount assured being " not

unreasonable " as it is imposed in sub-section (2). One way of making the necessary distinction between the two sub-sections is to interpret " the funeral expenses " of a deceased person as meaning the direct cost of the funeral, exclusive of personal expenditures occasioned by a death, on mourning or attendance at the funeral. This is the most natural sense of the term " funeral expenses," and the sense in which the term is used for purposes of estate duty excluding such expenditures as the provision of a tombstone or mourning. That for the purpose of industrial assurance funeral expenses do not include mourning expenses was made clear by the Court of Appeal in 1915 ; they held that it was a fraud for an agent to describe a policy for funeral expenses as covering mourning expenses (*Tofts* v. *Pearl Assurance Co.* [1915] 1 K.B. 189). Another way of distinction is to treat policies for funeral expenses as policies of indemnity, that is as policies in which the insured person may recover only the amount actually spent by him, with the sum assured as maximum. This is the view favoured by some of the judges in two cases decided soon after the Act of 1909 (*Wolenberg* v. *Royal Co-operative Collecting Society* [1916] W.C. and Ins. R. 346, and *Goldstein* v. *Salvation Army Assurance Society* [1917] 2 K.B. 291). The view that policies under Section 36 (1) of the Act of 1909 were contracts of indemnity was not necessary to the decision in either case and is therefore still open to argument ; an elaborate legal argument against regarding such policies as contracts of indemnity was submitted by the Prudential to the Cohen Committee. What is not open to argument is that, either in this way or another way, Parliament intended in 1909 to distinguish sharply between the business that it authorised for the future under sub-section (1) and that which it whitewashed in the past under sub-section (2).

57. Second, the industrial assurance companies and collecting societies have conducted their business since 1909 in such a way as to ignore the distinction drawn by Parliament. They have treated Section 36 (1) as authorising the issue of a life-of-another policy to any of the named relatives up to a limit fixed by themselves, in most cases now about £30, without taking any steps to discover at the time that the proposer has any liability for the funeral expenses for which he is insuring, or to ensure later that he devotes money paid on the policy to that purpose. They now in all cases require a proposer to declare whether he has any policies on the same life in another office, but they take no responsibility for checking the correctness of this declaration when death occurs. They resist the interpretation of funeral expense policies under Section 36 (1) either as policies of indemnity or as policies for direct funeral expenses. In other words they interpret " funeral expenses " in sub-section (1) as meaning any " expenses in connection with the death or funeral of the assured " which the relative insuring may expect or desire to incur up to an amount of £30. More accurately they treat it as meaning any money up to that limit which the proposer may wish to get when his relative dies. In giving evidence to the Cohen Committee the representatives of the Co-operative Insurance Society Ltd. agreed frankly that they ignored any distinction between the wording of the two sub-sections ; they stated also that this was common throughout the business and that in practice the Act has not been obeyed (Cohen Committee, Qu. 3667–72). The evidence of the other offices—including the Prudential and the Industrial Life Offices Association—as well as of the Insurance Unions Congress, if less frank, was just as revealing. It took the form of suggesting an amendment of the law by substituting " expenses in connection with the death or funeral " for " the funeral expenses " ; no doubt was left that this would merely give legal cover to the established practice of all the offices and their agents.

Direct and Indirect Expenses on Death

58. Third, provision for direct funeral expenses and provision for personal expenditure in connection with a death or funeral are in fact distinct purposes and need different kinds of insurance. No person can have more than one funeral. On every death, therefore, a sum of money sufficient for the funeral expenses of that person should be available for the person who pays the funeral expenses, but only one sum of money should be available for this purpose. Money for direct funeral expenses should not on any death be paid to more than one person. On the other hand, the number of persons who on the occasion of a death may desire to incur personal expenditure in buying mourning, in sending flowers or other tokens of respect, in travelling to the funeral and perhaps losing earnings for that purpose, is uncertain and variable. But such expenditure can only be incurred by those particular persons ; since it depends on their personal relation to the deceased, policies intended to cover it should not be transferable to others.

59. Insurance for " the funeral expenses " of a dead person and insurance for personal expenses which a living person may expect or desire to incur " in connection with the death or funeral " are distinct purposes. They are combined in practice, only because the companies and collecting societies in issuing and dealing with funeral expense policies issue those policies and pay on them without making any attempt to ensure that the person receiving the money will have any funeral expenses to meet. The companies and societies limit the amount of any insurance that A can put upon the life of B both by declining themselves to issue policies for more than a certain amount and by requiring

disclosure of similar policies with other companies. But this does not, and cannot, prevent many persons from taking out policies with the same company or with different companies on the same life, nor does it prevent many policies on the same life accumulating ultimately in the hands of one person, since such policies are treated as transferable and not terminating in any case on the death of the person who took out the policy.

60. The result is that on the occurrence of a death money may be paid, and undoubtedly is in a large number of cases paid, for which there is no obvious need either in meeting direct funeral expenses (since these may be covered several times over by different policies taken out by different persons), or in meeting personal expenditure of relatives (since one surviving relative may have accumulated policies which would have covered the personal expenditure of many relatives). Insurance money for funeral expenses may fall due at a death in such amounts that there is no choice between extravagant spending and making a profit out of insurance on the life-of-another, that is to say turning insurance into gambling. Insurance money may be paid to one relative but the actual cost of the funeral may fall on another who is not insured at all. Money for funeral expenses may be spent in other ways, leaving the funeral unpaid for.

61. It is clear that to make the distinction intended by Parliament in 1909 between " the funeral expenses " and personal expenditure " in connection with the death or funeral " of the life assured would have been troublesome to the Industrial Life Offices. They would either have had to make enquiries at the time of a proposal as to other funeral expense policies held by any person on the life assured, or to have treated such policies at the time of claim as policies of indemnity ; they would have had to apply to policies on the life-of-another something of the care that is applied to such policies in ordinary insurance. It can be argued, and is argued by the offices, that this would have prevented them from meeting a real demand for the means of defraying personal expenditure in mourning or attending funerals. It can be claimed finally that if the offices were doing wrong it was for the public authorities charged with their supervision to bring them to book. The Act of 1909, in Section 36 (3) quoted above, had penal provisions expressly directed against the issue of illegal policies ; the Board of Trade with whom the enforcement of those provisions rested never questioned the proceedings of the industrial offices. The Act of 1923, repeating in substance the whole of Section 36 from the Act of 1909, set up an Industrial Assurance Commissioner with new powers of inspection for discovering just what the offices were doing and ample means for challenging any doubtful procedure ; the Industrial Assurance Commissioner took no action, though when the Cohen Committee came he stated expressly that in his view many of the industrial policies being issued were illegal. The Cohen Committee agreed with this view ; they agreed also with the Industrial Assurance Commissioner of that time that some modification of the law was desirable. They made recommendations described in the following paragraphs, which would have legalised some but not all things which the Industrial Life Offices were doing but would have legalised them on conditions which the offices rejected. The Government took no action on the Report of the Cohen Committee and the offices went on just as before ; they have now been left unchallenged for more than thirty years. All this can be claimed by them with force and justice ; it is an illustration of the fact that in face of a powerful economic motive incomplete remedies are dangerous. There should be no lack of completeness in what is proposed for the future. This calls for further consideration of the recommendations of the Cohen Committee.

Recommendations of Cohen Committee

62. That Committee, while emphasising the disregard of law involved in the practice of the Industrial Life Offices since 1909 and before that date, accepted the argument of the offices that there was a genuine demand by the public for policies to cover not direct funeral expenses merely but personal expenditure on mourning, attendance at the funeral and the like. They proposed that any person should be allowed to insure the life of any of his relatives named in Section 3 of the Act of 1923 up to a maximum of £20, without specifying the purpose of the policy ; that is to say, within a certain range of relationship there should be a statutory insurable interest. They made this suggestion subject to two conditions :—

(1) That insurance should require the consent of the person whose life was being insured ;

(2) That if the proposer died before the life assured, the policy should become the property of any permitted relation provided the transferred policy would not bring his total assurances on the life over the permitted limit of £20. If it did or there was no permitted relation who desired to take over the policy, a surrender value would be paid.

63. The industrial offices and their agents objected to the suggested limit of £20 and proposed £50 instead. As regards the first of the two conditions proposed by the Cohen Committee, the offices argued that to require the consent of the life assured would prevent many assurances from being effected, since consent would be refused and that this

would lead to deaths without provision for the cost of the funeral. It is not easy to believe that any appreciable proportion of people would object to co-operate in steps to ensure them a decent funeral ; it may well be that those who already had this ensured would object to assisting relatives to secure the chance of a new outfit of clothes or a jaunt on the occasion of their deaths. The objection of the offices has some validity in respect of personal expenditure insurance ; it has little or none in respect of provision for direct funeral costs, a serious purpose for which people starve and stint themselves. Undoubtedly to require the consent of the life assured would diminish the amount of industrial assurance, by checking multiple and therefore excessive insurance on the same life by several different relatives. From the point of view of public policy it would probably be worth while to secure that check, even at the risk of some genuine funeral expense going unprovided. But as is suggested in para. 65 below there is no need to take this risk.

64. As regards the second condition the offices appear not to have expressed a definite view but they objected to restricting the transferability of policies, on the ground that the proposer might die when the person assured was so old that no fresh insurance could be taken out on him by another proposer ; there might thus be no provision at all for his funeral. This argument has validity in respect of insurance for direct funeral expenses ; it has none in respect of personal expenditure insurance.

65. Examination of the proposals made by the Cohen Committee and of the objections raised to these proposals by the industrial offices illustrates from another angle the undesirability of combining, as the Industrial Life Offices, in defiance of the clear intention of Parliament have combined, the necessary and important business of providing for decent burial with the secondary business of providing for personal expenditure occasioned by a death. The first is a fit subject for compulsory social insurance and can be done through that agency for a tenth or a twentieth of the administrative cost involved in doing it through industrial assurance. The second is a fit subject for voluntary insurance conducted with a rigid adherence to the rules which separate insurance from gambling.

66. The Chairman of the Departmental Committee, Sir Benjamin Cohen, described the right of insuring for funeral expenses conferred by Section 3 of the Industrial Assurance Act of 1923 as " a right given to the poor man and not to the rich. The rich man cannot assure for the funeral expenses of his relatives, the working class can assure lives in which they have no insurable interest." (Cohen Committee, Qu. 3361.) It is true that insurances may be effected through industrial assurance which are not permissible in any other way, but this is hardly a right given to poor men and denied to rich men. There is nothing to prevent a rich man from taking out a policy for funeral expenses with an Industrial Life Office, that is to say he can assure provided he pays for collection. The true state of affairs is that liberty to insure for funeral expenses—something needed by the poor man though not by the rich man—is now given to rich and poor alike only on condition of insuring through collectors, that is to say of insuring in a way which absorbs in administration 7/6 out of every £ paid as premiums.

6. Results of Earlier Enquiries

67. All the three independent committees which in the course of about forty years investigated the business of industrial assurance, while recognising the need for the service rendered by it in providing for burial expenses, made strong criticisms both on the conduct of the business and as to the cost of the service.

68. The House of Commons Select Committee of 1889 were concerned largely with cases of what at this interval of time may without impropriety be described as sharp practice or even fraud. On industrial assurance in general they expressed a carefully balanced judgment in the following terms : " It must be regarded as a means, for which at present there is no effective substitute, of inducing very large numbers of the working classes to make some provision for burial or for benefit to survivors at death, who would otherwise make none ; and so far these societies and companies may be regarded, when well managed, as commendable institutions, always subject to the consideration that, owing to the commission charged by collectors (from 20 to 25 per cent.), added to the ordinary cost of management, it often happens that nearly half the premium income never goes to the benefit fund." They expressed also the opinion that the method of collecting societies was " of no value whatever towards education in thrift," and called attention to the " very acute " competition between these societies as a source of danger.

69. The Departmental Committee of 1919–20 under the chairmanship of Lord Parmoor described the industrial assurance system as one which " lends itself to abuse in many directions." In using these words they had in mind gross abuses of adventure and extravagance and harsh contracts, and they made recommendations for dealing with these abuses, most of which were embodied in the Industrial Assurance Act of 1923. The more general subjects of their criticism were the high administrative cost, the high rates of dividend or remuneration of directors in the proprietary companies and the excessive proportion of lapses ; among these three they laid special emphasis on the last, attributing it in the main to the pressure to increase business involved in the terms of remuneration to agents.

70. The Departmental Committee of 1931–33 under the chairmanship of Sir Benjamin Cohen, among many criticisms of detail, repeated much of what had been said by the Parmoor Committee as to the high cost of administration and lapses. They were severe—perhaps unduly severe—in what they said of the institution of book interest. But in the main, they attributed what they regarded as the principal defects of the business, not as the Parmoor Committee had done to the precise methods of remuneration, but to excessive competition among the offices. " Our survey of the business of industrial assurance has led us to the conclusion that excessive competition with its almost feverish pressure for ' increase,' firstly by the offices upon their staffs, and secondly by the latter upon the working class population, is responsible for the principal defects of the business. To this competition and pressure must be ascribed the masses of uneconomical contracts (many of them of doubtful legality) into which people are induced to enter and the inordinate number of lapses which ensue, with the heavy losses resulting from them."

71. Criticisms of this character repeated by one independent body of investigators after another are weighty.* Naturally they have had their weight and have led to changes. Many of these changes have been embodied in legislation. At least as important are the steps which have been taken by the Industrial Life Offices themselves to deal with matters not touched by legislation.

First, during the past twenty-five or thirty years there has been a determined and successful attempt by the principal companies, through re-organisation of their staffs and otherwise, to reduce their expenses of management. The leader in this has been the Prudential, but other companies, like the Refuge and the Pearl, have not been far behind.

Second, practically all the important companies and societies have gone far beyond their statutory obligations for the issue of free paid-up policies or grant of surrender values as an alternative to lapsing completely where the premium ceased to be paid.

Third, all or nearly all the companies have followed the lead of the Prudential in distributing part of the profits, to which legally only the shareholders were entitled, to policy-holders, or have in other ways given to the policy-holders more than they were entitled to by their contracts.

72. These changes to meet criticisms are important and must be put on record. There must be added to the record recognition of the positive achievements of industrial assurance. It has met an essential need of the British people of provision for direct funeral expenses and needs less essential, but real, for personal expenditure in connection with death and for insurance and saving for a great variety of purposes. It has developed the desirable habit of putting money away for a rainy day, that is to say, in spite of the contrary judgment of the Select Committee of 1889, it has encouraged thrift. Finally, the agents as knowledgeable, hard working citizens have become in many cases the friends of the families with which they deal and have rendered them many informal services.

73. To deny the good that there is in the development of life assurance by persons of limited means would be absurd. The question remains whether the defects of the business, as they have been pointed out by one independent enquiry after another, have now been remedied as completely as is possible or are likely to be remedied in time if the business continues on its present lines. The answer to that question, in view of the facts submitted above, must be negative, in relation both to cost of administration and to the extent of abortive insurance.

Need for Further Reforms

74. The cost ratio of industrial assurance from the point of view of the policy-holder, that is to say the proportion of the premiums diverted to purposes other than his benefit, at the time of the Select Committee of 1889 was just over 45 per cent. In 1931 it was nearly 40 per cent. In 1937–40 it was over 37 per cent. This is a fall in 50 years from a

---

* The Select Committee of 1889 consisted of twenty-one members of the House of Commons under the Chairmanship of Sir Herbert Maxwell. The Parmoor Committee consisted of Lord Parmoor, K.C.V.O. (Chairman), Mr. W. T. Carr, M.P., Mr. H. S. Cautley, K.C., M.P. (now Lord Cautley), Major Evan Hayward, M.P., The Rt. Hon. John Hodge, M.P., Mr. H. A. Payne, C.B., Mr. G. Stuart Robertson (now Sir George Robertson), Sir Alfred W. Watson.

The Cohen Committee consisted of Sir Benjamin Cohen, K.C. (Chairman), Mr. John G. Archibald, Miss Dorothy Evans, M.A., Mr. Fred Kershaw, O.B.E., J.P., Mr. Stewart Macnaghten, Sir Alfred Watson, K.C.B., Mr. J. J. Wills, Sir John Fischer Williams, C.B.E., K.C.

The Reports both of the Parmoor Committee and of the Cohen Committee were unanimous, signed by all the members.

charge of about 9/- in the £ of premium to nearly 7/6 in the £, while the number of £s on which the charge falls has multiplied more than twelve times. Such reduction of costs, moreover, as has been achieved is largely the work of a few companies ; in the mutual offices there has been little change and there is little prospect of change in the future. Even at its present level life assurance through collectors still costs more than twice as much in administration as ordinary life assurance. It is not sufficient, however, to dwell on the high administrative cost of industrial assurance. It is necessary to show if possible that the cost could be less. The cost comes in the main through the use of collectors. Could the same needs be met more cheaply ? The answer to that question can be given in stages.

75. First, the essential universal need for direct funeral expenses, which is the starting-point of industrial assurance, can be met at a very small fraction of the cost of industrial assurance by compulsory social insurance. This is the ground for the proposal made as Change **18** in Part II, to include a universal funeral grant in the social insurance scheme. It is hard to see how the administrative cost of this could amount to more than about 6d. in the £, 2½ per cent. as compared with more than 37 per cent.

76. Second, the other needs—for personal expenditure in connection with death, for life assurance and for saving generally, being less uniform and less universal, are subjects for voluntary action rather than for compulsion. Voluntary insurance is necessarily and reasonably more costly in administration than compulsory insurance. But at least three great voluntary organisations now at work in Britain show the possibility of encouraging voluntary insurance or saving on a large scale among persons of limited means at a cost ratio far below that of industrial assurance. As is shown in Appendix E, the centralised Friendly Societies, with a membership of nearly 4,000,000, obtain contributions and administer a far more complicated system of benefits than that of industrial assurance at not much more than a quarter of the administrative cost of industrial assurance, 10 per cent., or 2/- in the £ of contributions. The Hospital Contributory Schemes, covering before the present war about 10,000,000 wage-earners, were obtaining about £6,500,000 a year from them mainly in weekly subscriptions at an administrative cost of about 6 per cent. The War Savings Committee, in peace as in war, has proved its ability to collect small savings from all classes at an insignificant cost. Neither of the two organisations last named performs the same function as industrial assurance, with contracts for whole life or many years. And none of the three covers so large a proportion of the whole population. But, as is suggested below, there is little doubt that some of the existing industrial assurance is socially undesirable, because made at the cost of more essential needs. And the success of all three of these organisations makes it hard to accept an argument that the naturally thrifty British people cannot be persuaded to save except at the present administrative cost of industrial assurance.

77. Third, even assuming the need for weekly collection of premiums, the contrast between the Prudential and the other Industrial Life Offices shows that the work could be done more cheaply than at present. No one can suggest that the Prudential renders less efficient service to its policy-holders than do its rivals. But for its actual expenses of management the Prudential needs little more than a quarter of its premiums ; only the profit which it distributes to shareholders and the income-tax which it pays brings its total cost ratio up to nearly one-third of the premiums. Even assuming weekly collection just as at present, the cost of industrial assurance could be materially less if it were conducted on the lines of the Prudential by a monopoly corporation.

78. In the light of these considerations it is not possible either to accept what has been accomplished in reducing the cost of administration as adequate or to look forward to any substantial change in the future.

79. In regard to abortive assurance, the position is much the same as in regard to cost of administration. There has been an improvement, but the improvement still leaves serious evils without remedy. There has been an improvement, in so far as outright lapses have been replaced to a substantial extent by grant of free policies for reduced sums or of surrender values when premiums cease to be paid, but that is nearly the whole of the improvement. In relation to the number of policies issued each year the number failing before maturity right up to the beginning of the present war was nearly as high as in the days of the Parmoor Committee and higher than in 1929. During the war the proportion of failures has fallen markedly but this is the result of special circumstances. Judgment must rest on what was accomplished up to the war. It is doubtful if in this respect there has been any large improvement since long before that time. A form of insurance in which the number of policies failing before maturity each year is two-thirds of the policies issued each year, while more than half of that two-thirds lapsed completely, cannot be regarded as satisfactory. It is clear evidence of over-selling, of a business so organised that more policies are taken out than is desirable in the public interest or in the interests of those who take them.

Drain on Limited Incomes

80. The same thing is shown in another way by the evidence as to the large proportion of the incomes of the poorest classes that is devoted to industrial assurance. Some of the money which goes to build the immense funds and premium income of industrial life offices has come and still continues to come from people with less than the means of bare subsistence. Mr. Rowntree in 1936, in a special study of 267 poor families in York, found that out of an average weekly income of 34/9—far below the poverty line—they were contributing on an average 2/1 a week per family for death insurance ; 30 of these families were devoting up to one-fifth or more of their whole income to this purpose.* The Unemployment Assistance Board in 1938 found that premiums for life, burial and endowment insurance were being paid by more than three-quarters of all their applicants ; more than three-quarters of this three-quarters were paying 1/- or more each week. Their total payments for this purpose amounted to about £1,750,000 a year. The smaller the income, the larger in general is the proportion of the whole that is spent on burial insurance ; in the language of economists, burial insurance behaves like a necessity— bread or rent—not a luxury. Table VI in para. 209 shows voluntary insurance payments, which are practically all industrial assurance premiums, of 2/3 a week or 7½ per cent. of the total income paid from incomes of less than 40/- a week, while those with £4 to £5 of income pay 2/10 a week or only 3 per cent. of their income. A table given by Drs. McGonigle and Kirby, for Stockton-on-Tees,† shows families with an income of 25/- to 35/- a week paying on an average 1/6½ or 4·9 per cent. of their net income for such insurance, while families with 70/- or 80/- a week pay on an average 2/9¼ a week or 3·6 per cent. ; contributions on this scale are, of course, far more than could be needed to cover reasonable funeral expenses. Hundreds of thousands of families with less than enough to live on contribute substantial proportions of their incomes to industrial insurance. From 30 per cent. to 40 per cent. or more of what they contribute goes in administrative expenses and profits.

81. Both the extent of abortive assurance and the evidence of the social surveys show the amount of industrial assurance today as excessive. That excess follows from the fact that it is a business with a strong internal pressure to develop in the interests of the staff or the interests of shareholders. Some amount of abortive insurance is inevitable in the life assurance of persons of limited means exposed to economic insecurity. That fact is a reason for keeping the amount of life assurance within the capacity of the buyers of insurance and removing the pressure to over-insurance which comes from the natural desire of the sellers of insurance for business gain.

82. The criticisms made upon industrial assurance in the past have not been met, and cannot be met while the system remains, as at present, a competitive business. The best hope of meeting them lies in following out some of the ideas which were present to the minds of the Cohen Committee. That Committee, while ruling out nationalisation of industrial assurance " as it now exists " as not a practical proposition, added " Some of us, however, consider that the possibility of widening the scope of the present State Insurance Schemes so as to cover the contingencies now met by industrial assurance should be fully explored." The Committee added as a final sentence to the main body of their Report, " we are convinced that if the changes which the due protection of the assuring public demands cannot be effected by less drastic measures the difficulties in the transference of the business to a single organization to which we have referred at length will ultimately have to be faced."

7. Proposal for an Industrial Assurance Board

83. The exploration suggested by " some " of the Cohen Committee has been carried out in the course of the present enquiry ; that exploration leads to the proposal as Change 18 in Part II, that the main purpose for which industrial assurance came into being, of providing for direct burial expenses, should be included in the unified scheme of compulsory insurance. This is the " effective substitute " which the Select Committee of 1889 could not find, but clearly desired to find, for burial insurance through collectors, as they saw it in action. In the course of the exploration leading to this proposal, the general problem of industrial assurance has been reviewed, in the light of the earlier enquiries and of events since the date of the Cohen Committee. This review leads to the suggestion that the only satisfactory solution of the problem of industrial assurance, retaining the good while curing the defects of the present system, will lie in following out the final hint of the Cohen Committee and converting industrial assurance from being a competitive sellers' business to being a monopoly consumers' service.

84. This suggestion involves no general conviction in favour of public monopolies or against private competition. Today it is recognised among reasonable men that there is a place for each of these methods in its appropriate sphere, and the choice between

---

* *Poverty and Progress* (1941), p. 213.
† *Poverty and Public Health* (1936), pp. 222-4.

the two methods should depend upon the character of the work to be done. The proposal that life assurance among persons of limited means should be a public service rather than a competitive private business is based upon the special character of industrial assurance, as a business in which competition leads to over-selling and as a business in which the seller's interest presents special danger to the consumer. Life insurance is not like other commodities, because those who insure make their choice once for all when they take out a policy. They cannot buy less insurance or another form of insurance next day or change their assurance company without loss, as next day they can substitute bacon for beef or change their grocer without loss. Industrial assurance, that is to say life assurance among people of limited means, is so different from most other commodities that it cannot safely be treated as an article of commerce. Industrial assurance is different from ordinary life assurance, because those who undertake the latter have both, as a rule, less limited means and the possibility of recourse to independent advice. The consumers of industrial assurance have not this recourse ; they should be guided in their choice of insurance by advice that is wholly disinterested.

85. From these general arguments, the case for following to its logical conclusion of public monopoly the tendency of thought apparent in the Report of the Cohen Committee is strong in itself. The case is reinforced on practical grounds by consideration of two proposals made on other grounds, for changing the present system of Approved Societies (Report, paras. 48–76) and for providing a funeral grant for every death as part of compulsory insurance (Report, paras. 157–160). Both these proposals are an essential part of the Plan for Social Security. In theory, on the introduction of these measures, the Industrial Life Offices might be left in their present form to cover the large and growing field that remains for voluntary insurance by persons of limited means. This includes insurance on own life or that of a spouse under whole life or endowment policies, insurance for meeting reasonable personal expenditure involved in the death or funeral of another, and insurance against general risks, such as fire or theft, or for education of children. For the second of those purposes—insurance against indirect personal expenses on a death—the Industrial Life Offices, in substitution for Section 3 of the Act of 1923, might be authorised to issue policies on life-of-another within the prescribed relationship, up to a maximum of say £10 or £15, terminating on the previous death of the proposer or transferable subject to the conditions suggested by the Cohen Committee (see para 62 above).

86. Such a solution of the problem of industrial assurance is possible. It would, it is suggested, be unsatisfactory for several reasons. First, it breaks the connection between industrial assurance and health insurance. There is no escape from breaking this connection, if industrial assurance remains a competitive business for gain, but if it becomes a public service it can be kept as part of the general organisation of social security. All that there is of permanent value in the " home service " rendered by the collectors on the side of health insurance can be continued. Second, it would not be fair to the life offices and their staffs without compensation for the interference with their business. But, owing to the partial nature of the interference, assessment would present extremely difficult problems. Third, it would leave the present defects of industrial assurance—of over-selling and excessive cost—in a narrower sphere, indeed, but unremedied. The way to economy in the use of collectors lies in rationalisation and monopoly, not in competition. But a monopoly cannot be allowed to work for profits without control. The way to replacing the costly system of collectors gradually by more economical forms of insurance and saving is blocked so long as so many livelihoods depend on collection. Fourth, voluntary insurance enabling the individual to make provision above the minimum for his special needs is an integral part of social security. The work of the Industrial Life Offices, though marred by serious defects, though representing today an excessive drain on the limited resources of wage-earners, has made a contribution of great value in using and stimulating the spirit of thrift throughout the people. It has brought into being an army of collectors who in thousands of cases have become the friends of their clients. They can be used and should be used to better purpose than is the case today, to encourage fruitful saving, to play their part in bringing security to all.

87. In the field of sickness insurance the Friendly Societies should be used to administer the subsistence benefits of compulsory insurance to their members, because in doing so they will have the occasion to develop voluntary insurance beyond that minimum. The Friendly Societies can be used as they stand, because and in so far as they are mutual associations serving only their members. In the field covered by industrial assurance, particularly though not exclusively in its later developments of endowment assurance, there is ample room and need for continuing voluntary insurance ; there are other problems of supplementary insurance against unemployment and against economic insecurity of independent workers. The Industrial Life Offices cannot be used just as they stand for dealing with such problems ; they cannot be used while they are businesses working for shareholders, or are associations of agents investing capital in books. But the men in these offices, their energies, abilities and experience should be used, for what they can do is needed.

88.   These considerations lead to the proposal for setting up an Industrial Assurance Board with a statutory monopoly of the use of collectors.   The Board would take over all the existing policies of industrial assurance and honour them.   It would employ or compensate the staff.   It would compensate the shareholders.   It would take over all or part of the ordinary life assurance business of the Industrial Life Offices, as might be found most convenient in each case.   It would be authorised for the future to undertake new life assurance, whether with or without collection of premiums, subject to a limit of the amount assured, designed to restrict its clientele to persons of limited means ; something like the present limit of £300 imposed on collecting societies would probably fit the case.   The Board would work steadily to substitute direct payment of premiums for collection, to encourage socially desirable forms of insurance and thrift, to provide ways of insurance free from serious risk of lapsing.   It would work under the general supervision of the Minister of Social Security but with a large measure of practical independence.   It would use to the utmost the skill and energy which have gone to build up the Industrial Life Offices.   It would be not a Government department but a public service run on business lines.

89.   This proposal is put forward, not as an essential part of the Plan for Social Security, but as one of the bracketed proposals.   It is not the only possible solution of the problem of industrial assurance and it is not free from difficulties.   But it is put forward as the best solution in the interests alike of the public and of the staff—as the solution which, while giving better results than any other, will probably in the end present fewer and less intractable difficulties.   That is to say it will probably be found easier to take over industrial assurance, and such part of the other work of the offices undertaking it as goes conveniently with it, than to divorce these offices themselves from health and burial insurance.

90.   The working out of this proposal would be an immense practical task to be confined to a special body with adequate powers and experience.   It will be necessary and relatively easy—to settle terms of compensation to shareholders.   It will be necessary to settle terms for the staff, including fair compensation for book interest, and the steps to be taken gradually to reduce the number of collectors without hardship.   It will be necessary to settle terms for the policy-holders, including such matters as claims to bonus.   It will be necessary to frame measures not only for the taking over of the large offices of national scope, but for dealing with the numerous local societies.   The practical problems are numerous and intricate.   But it cannot seriously be suggested that they are insoluble.   Companies have been taken over by other companies in the past.   Today 88 per cent. of industrial assurance is concentrated in 8 out of the 160 Industrial Life Offices ; 98 per cent. is concentrated in 15 of them.   This is the time for solution of problems, for turning the business of industrial assurance, with its chequered history of good and bad, into one of the great social services of the future.

APPENDIX E

ADMINISTRATIVE COSTS OF VARIOUS FORMS OF INSURANCE

1. In this Appendix the information available as to the administrative cost of five different types of insurance, in relation to the premiums or contributions paid by or on behalf of the insured persons, is summarised. The five types of insurance compared are :—

(a) *Ordinary commercial insurance*, that is to say voluntary insurance through business undertakings of various kinds outside the direct scope of the Inter-departmental Committee, including fire, accident and general (excluding employers' liability insurance business within the United Kingdom), motor and ordinary life assurance.

(b) *Industrial assurance*.

(c) *Employers' liability insurance*, that is to say insurance against liabilities for industrial accident and disease within the United Kingdom, both under the Workmen's Compensation Acts and apart from these Acts.

(d) *Voluntary insurance through Friendly Societies*.

(e) *Compulsory State insurance* against unemployment, sickness and old age and widowhood.

2. The question of what should be included in administrative costs must be answered differently according to the point of view from which it is regarded. From the point of view of an office conducting insurance the costs are the expense of getting business (usually entered under the head of commission) and the expense of management ; income tax and other taxes are elements of which account must be taken to the extent that they are not recovered out of dividends to shareholders. Profits distributed to shareholders are not part of the cost, but one of the objects for which expenses are incurred. From the point of view of the insured person profits are not an object of insurance, but part of its cost, and in making comparisons for him between insurance conducted for profit and insurance on a mutual basis whether voluntary or compulsory, what goes to the shareholders should be included as part of the costs. But the practice of different forms of insurance and of different companies in reckoning profits and in the source from which they take profits differs, so that an attempt to bring into account shareholders' profits on a uniform basis for all forms of insurance presents difficulties. The comparisons made below must be read subject to this caution.

3. The treatment of legal and medical expenses incurred by companies or mutual associations which insure employers against liability for accidents or disease among their employees raises a similar question. The insurance companies and associations normally and naturally treat medical and legal expenses in handling claims to compensation as part of the service rendered by them to their clients, that is to say the employers, and not as expenses of management. From the point of view of the person claiming compensation, however, they are, in the case of legal expenses wholly, and in the case of medical expenses mainly, costs of administration and not money expended for that person's benefit. They have been treated as costs accordingly in this comparison. The extent of possible error in respect of medical expenses which are of direct benefit to the injured employee is discussed in the paragraphs dealing with this subject. The employer's liability costs shown are exclusive of those borne by the claimant or his trade union or other society in enforcing a claim. Strictly these should be included, but no estimate of them can be made.

4. In calculating the cost of State insurance against unemployment, sickness and old age and widowhood, an estimate of the costs incurred by employers in dealing with insurance documents, affixing insurance stamps, and making deductions from wages, has been added to the costs incurred by the Government Departments in administering these schemes. Costs are incurred by employers also in relation to workmen's compensation, but no estimate of these is possible.

5. In all cases the administrative costs have been shown as proportions of the sums paid by or on behalf of insured persons as premiums or contributions. In some forms of insurance there are substantial receipts also as interests on investments. These receipts are shown in relation to premiums or contributions in para. 31.

6. Most of the figures relate to a year or years just preceding the war or to 1939. In one case, for special reasons, 1940 has been included. In nearly all cases, both of voluntary and of State insurance, administrative costs in relation to contributions or premiums have fallen during the war, partly through increase of contribution rates, and partly through other causes. Thus in unemployment insurance the administrative cost in 1941 was about 4·8 per cent. of the contributions in place of 10 per cent. in 1938 ; this reflects both the raising of rates of contribution and benefit and the decline of unemployment. Changes in respect of some of the other types of insurance are noted in the appropriate places. For all types of insurance war conditions are abnormal, though to differing degrees, and make fair comparisons impossible.

7. A difference between two types of insurance in the administrative cost per cent? of premiums does not mean that the one with higher percentage cost is less efficiently managed. The work involved in different forms of insurance differs, both on the side of obtaining the premiums and on the side of paying claims. In the obtaining of premiums, compulsory insurance by the State has an outstanding advantage over any form of voluntary insurance. It can dispense with commission and collectors. On the side of meeting claims, compulsory insurance for most of the purposes for which it has been introduced up to the present has a more complicated task to perform than that of most, though not all, forms of voluntary insurance. Life insurance, for instance, whether in its ordinary form or in the form of industrial assurance, involves in general one claim only on each policy to be paid on an event which can be established without difficulty. In other forms of commercial insurance such as those dealing with fire, accidents or motor risks, not only is the settlement of claims more difficult, but in some at least of these, notably fire insurance, some of the expenses are of a character beneficial to the policy-holder, being designed for the prevention of fires. In the different forms of compulsory insurance there are equally marked differences in the complexity of the work involved. Administration of unemployment insurance, for instance, involves a large number of claims in relation to the number of policies—in normal times before the war something like thirty claims each year for every hundred insured persons. On each of these numerous claims the facts as to unemployment, as to fitness and availability for work, and as to cause of leaving employment have to be established, possibly with considerable dispute. When they have been established payments on the claim have to be made week by week in small sums. Sickness insurance has comparable, though different, complexities of adminis-tration. Pensions insurance is relatively simple.

8. Comparison of unemployment and of health insurance illustrates another point which must be borne in mind in comparing administrative costs, namely, the scale of benefits. It costs as much to pay out 15/– a week as to pay out 30/– or 40/–. It costs as much to collect a contribution of 3d. as to collect a contribution two or three times as great. This point is relevant to comparisons between ordinary and industrial life assurance and also to comparisons between the administrative costs of workmen's com-pensation in different industries. Apart from all other factors, a high risk of accident as in mining, and a consequent large expenditure on compensation, tends to make the cost of administration a smaller part of the whole cost of insurance.

A. Ordinary Commercial Insurance

9. The following table shows the main classes of commercial insurance, other than industrial assurance, employers' liability insurance (dealt with below) ordinary life assurance and marine insurance (where premiums are commonly stated after deducting commission). The figures are taken from *Policy Holder Journal Tables* published by the Policy Holder Journal Company, Ltd. They relate to 1937 and represent £'000.

Table XXXII.—Fire, Accident and Motor Insurance, 1937

Class of Business and No. of Companies	Prem-iums.	Inter-est (net)	Com-mission	Manage-ment	Under-writing Profit	% of Premiums	
						Com-mission and Manage-ment	Under-writing Profit
Fire—71 tariff	48,749	1,771	9,954	13,336	4,957	47·8	10·2
Fire—32 non-tariff ...	2,769	13	553	710	462	45·6	16·7
Accident and General—							
66 tariff	56,150	1,549	9,620	12,436	3,060	39·3	5·4
35 non-tariff	19,275	407	3,363	3,756	136	36·9	0·7
Motor—							
54 tariff	24,420	410	4,432	5,405	280	40·3	1·1
25 non-tariff	12,429	157	2,417	2,478	—68	39·4	—0·5
Total	163,792	4,307	30,339	38,121	8,827	41·8	5·4

The underwriting profit in most cases of commercial insurance other than ordinary life assurance is not in general distributed to the proprietors, but is put into the business and so adds to the security of the policy-holders. Moreover, estimates of the amount of underwriting profit depend on the assumptions made as to the provision required in respect of unexpired risks and unsettled claims. It does not seem right accordingly to add it to the commission and management as part of the administrative cost and it is shown separately. As is seen from the foot of the table, if the figures for fire, accident and motor business are added together they yield a percentage of commissions and management in relation to premiums of 41·8 per cent. The interest described as " net " is interest after deduction of income tax.

10.   For ordinary life assurance the following figures are taken from page 664 of the Assurance Companies Return for 1938 published by the Board of Trade.   The figures relate to 1937 and represent £'000 :—

Premiums and Payments for Annuities	Interest	Commission	Management	Shareholders' surplus and Transfers to Profit and Loss Account	% of Premiums	
					Commission and Management	Commission, Management and Profit
99,739	38,903	4,680	8,295	1,574	13·0	14·6

The total in the first column, covering business both within and without the United Kingdom, includes about £87·9 million of premiums and about £11·8 million as payments for annuities which, coming in large sums, are easy to administer.   The cost ratio (expenses of management plus dividends) of the ordinary branches of companies transacting industrial assurance as given in Appendix D, para. 37, is 16·2 per cent. It would probably be reasonable to put the cost ratio for ordinary life assurance apart from annuity payments at about 16 per cent.

B. Industrial Assurance

11.   The cost ratio for industrial assurance is discussed fully in Appendix D. Here only the general figures for all companies and societies engaged in this business is given.   The figures are the mean of the four years 1937–40 ; a mean over a period of years is taken in order to smooth out the effects of bonus distribution to staff, which in some of the offices takes place only every third year or so.   If the figures were limited to years before the war the percentage cost of administration would be slightly higher :—

Industrial Assurance—Mean of 1937–40.

Premiums £000	Expenses £000	Dividends to Shareholders, etc. £000	Total Administration (excluding tax)	
			£000	% of Premiums
72,995	23,809	1,805	25,614	35·1

Dividends to shareholders include all transfers out of the Industrial Assurance Fund to profit and loss account other than items earmarked for specific purposes.   Expenses include commission to agents on introduction of new business.   These figures give the administrative cost exclusive of tax, which, as is explained in Appendix D, should be included to give the total cost from the policy-holder's point of view.

C. Employers' Liability

12.   Provision for the liability of employers to compensate their employees for the results of accident or industrial disease takes two principal forms :—

(1)   Insurance with commercial companies working for profit.

(2)   Insurance through mutual insurance companies or associations.

The second form includes both mutual companies doing a mixed type of business covering different industries and companies or associations confined wholly or mainly to particular industries such as mining, shipping or textiles.   In mining, where the risk of accident is much higher than in other industries, the great bulk, though not all the insurance is done through mutual indemnity companies on somewhat special lines.   This industry is dealt with separately below.   In addition, some large employers, including railway companies and dock companies, carry their own risks and a number of small employers, chiefly in non-hazardous occupations, do not insure. This may be described as a third form—Self-insurance.

13.   Figures representative of each of the first two methods are given below, based on the mean of the two years 1938–39.   One set covers all the offices in the Accident Offices Association other than the Iron Trades Mutual which has now left the Association and joined the Mutual Insurance Companies Association.   The other set relates to fifteen of the principal companies, which are now combined in the Mutual Insurance Companies Association, including the Iron Trades Mutual.

TABLE XXXIII.—EMPLOYERS' LIABILITY INSURANCE—MEAN OF 1938-39

	Premiums £000	Commission £000	Management £000	Legal and Medical Expenses £000	Profit £000	Total Administration	
						£000	% of Premiums
Accident Offices Association	4,600	399	1,235	214	290	2,138	46·5
Mutual Insurance Companies Association	7,182	316	824	385	25	1,550	21·6

14.   In each case the legal and medical expenses are included in the total administrative costs, but are shown separately.   The legal expenses are wholly and the medical expenses are mainly part of the cost of determining whether compensation should be paid. But the medical expenses include in some cases payments which are really in the nature of benefit.   Thus in the Federation of Master Cotton Spinners' Associations in 1941 more than a quarter of the medical expenses, equivalent to about one-twentieth of the total administrative cost and 1 per cent. of the whole expenditure on compensation and administration, was incurred in the provision of treatment or surgical appliances and might be described as a form of benefit to the employee, though it is also a means of reducing the liabilities of the association.   Provision of treatment or appliances, however, is not normally undertaken either by commercial companies or by mutual insurance companies.   Error due to the inclusion of the whole of the medical expenses as part of the administrative cost cannot be large.   The legal and medical expenses attributed to the Accident Offices Association represent the proportion of those expenses to premiums in 1938, viz., 4·66 per cent.

15.   The percentage of costs to premiums in the two years named appears to have been slightly higher for the Accident Offices Association than in the years immediately preceding, owing to the larger allocation to profit.   The members of the Accident Offices Association work under a tariff.   Employers' liability insurance is undertaken also by independent non-tariff companies.   But an analysis of the accounts of a number of these companies in 1937 suggests that there is no substantial difference in the cost ratio of tariff and non-tariff companies.   There is little doubt that, as compared with most if not all of the mutual companies, the commercial companies are less localised in their operations and undertake a greater variety of small risks in non-hazardous employments where the amount of compensation is small and the premiums by consequence relatively low.   Both the scattering of the risks and the relatively low premiums would tend to raise the cost ratio in these offices.   It seems clear that the more costly part of the business falls upon them.

Mutual Indemnity in Mining

16.   In coal mining, insurance has generally, though not universally, been effected, almost from the beginning of workmen's compensation, through mutual indemnity companies which now cover 80 per cent. of the colliery undertakings and probably a larger proportion of the total output.   Insurance by employers against their workmen's compensation liabilities, except in respect of the first 26 weeks of disablement, is now compulsory in this industry under an Act of 1934.   The administrative costs of the companies covering the principal mining districts are set out in the following table distinguishing management expenses and legal and medical expenses.   The percentages vary considerably from one district to another.   The weighted average, according to the numbers employed in each district in 1935, is about 7 per cent., divided as 3¼ per cent. for management and 3¾ per cent. for legal and medical expenses.

TABLE XXXIV.—COLLIERY MUTUAL INDEMNITY COMPANIES

ADMINISTRATIVE COSTS PER CENT. OF COMPENSATION PLUS ADMINISTRATIVE COSTS—1938

Company	Management expenses including staffs, directors' fees and office expenses	Legal and Medical expenses	Total
	%	%	%
Northumberland	2·71	3·01	5·72
Durham	2·47	2·26	4·73
Cumberland	4·87	4·94	9·81
Northern Employers	1·75	3·65	5·40
South West Lancashire	2·40	5·90	8·30
Yorkshire	2·83	3·38	6·21
Midland Mutual	2·85	3·97	6·82
North Staffordshire...	2·82	4·00	6·82
Forest of Dean	3·62	1·11	4·73
South Wales...	3·41	3·63	7·04
North Wales	3·51	4·16	7·67
Ayrshire	5·99	1·40	7·39
Scottish Mine Owners	6·02	6·02	12·04
Weighted Average	3·23	3·73	6·96

17. These figures do not in all cases cover the whole of the administrative costs involved. Except in Scotland, South Wales and Cumberland, where the cost of compensation is shared from the date of the accident, the compensation payable for the first 26 weeks of disability is charged to the individual employer. In one or two areas, including Yorkshire, this means that the indemnity company does not handle claims at all unless disability lasts 26 weeks ; that is to say, the administrative cost is that of long disability cases only. This, however, is exceptional. In most districts, the company handles claims from the outset, even though the individual employer, and not the common fund, will be charged by it with the compensation paid for the first 26 weeks.

18. In another respect the figures may include items which are of the nature of benefits to the injured employee rather than administrative cost such as supply of protective clothing, hospital treatment or treatment in rehabilitation centres. Supply of protective clothing is a large item in Durham, equivalent to ½ per cent. of the amount paid as compensation and is excluded from the figures shown in the table ; elsewhere it is presumably included, but is not nearly so important. Substantial expenditure on treatment before the war appears to have been incurred only in one or two areas.

19. The mutual indemnity companies as stated do not include the whole of the mining industry. Those excluded are insured with a commercial or a mutual insurance company except in the few cases where a " compensation trust " has been set up under the Act of 1934.

Self-insurance

20. Employers who do not insure at all include, on the one hand, certain large undertakings, notably railways, docks and public utilities, which carry their own risks. They include, on the other hand, a number of small employers in non-hazardous industries, who do not think it necessary to insure. The average administrative costs over the nine years 1930–38 of three large undertakings carrying their own risks are given below as percentages of the amounts paid in compensation and administration together.

TABLE XXXV.—SELF INSURANCE FOR EMPLOYERS' LIABILITY

ADMINISTRATIVE COSTS PER CENT. OF COMPENSATION PLUS ADMINISTRATIVE COSTS MEAN OF 1930–38

	Management Expenses	Legal and medical Expenses	Total
Gas company	13·62	1·44	15·06
Electrical engineering firm ...	6·34	2·69	9·03
Iron and steel firm	6·05	4·89	10·94

Average Cost Ratio

21. The cost ratios of the various forms of provision for employers' liability, as given above, vary from over 45 per cent. for commercial insurance to 7 per cent. for mutual indemnity in mining. The average administrative cost of workmen's compensation as a whole depends on the relative importance of the different forms. Employers insured in a mutual association or with a mutual company comprise the great bulk of those in industries with heavy accident risks such as mining, shipping, iron and steel and ship-building and account probably for nearly 70 per cent. of the total compensation. 30 per cent. out of this 70 per cent. is paid in coal mining and 40 per cent. in other industries. As some collieries insure not through colliery indemnity companies but through other mutual companies, it is probably fair to assume that, say, 25 per cent. of the total compensation is paid through indemnity companies in mining with an average cost ratio of 7, and that some 5 per cent. in mining is paid through general mutual companies for which a cost ratio of 22 per cent. has been assumed. Some of the 40 per cent. in other industries dealt with on mutual lines may have a cost ratio materially below this 22 per cent. This is certainly the case in shipping, where the administrative charge is put at 10 per cent. of the compensation. But no figures are available for most industries. The 30 per cent. of compensation which is not dealt with on mutual lines is probably divided fairly equally between employers insured with commercial companies and those carrying their own risks. That is to say, 15 per cent. of the total compensation is paid by commercial companies at a cost ratio of about 45 per cent. For the 15 per cent. paid by employers carrying their own risks it seems reasonable to take a cost ratio of 10 per cent.

22. The foregoing information, which is the best that is available at present, is not sufficient to make possible any close estimate of the average cost ratio of workmen's compensation in all industries. For the purpose of arriving at the best average which can be got of the existing data, it seems reasonable to say that about 15 per cent. of the compensation is paid at a cost ratio of 45 per cent. by commercial companies ; that 35 per cent. is paid at a cost ratio of 22 per cent. by mutual companies mainly doing a mixed business ; that about 10 per cent. is paid by mutual companies in industries other than mining at a cost ratio of, say, 10 per cent. ; that 15 per cent. is paid by employers carrying their own risks at a cost ratio of 10 per cent. ; and, finally, that 25 per cent. is paid by mutual companies in mining at a cost ratio of 7 per cent. Of these figures the average for all compensation works out at a little less than 19 per cent. The sums treated as administrative cost in this calculation include certain expenditures which are not administrative, such as that part of medical expenses which is really benefit to the employee and includes other expenditure which is concerned not with workmen's compensation but with common law liabilities. On the other hand, they do not include expenses incurred by the injured employee or his trade union or association in pressing a claim. These expenses are sometimes substantial and may fairly be set against any error due to inclusion of all medical expenses as administrative and of expenses through common law liabilities. That is to say, the administrative cost of workmen's compensation as a whole may be put at about 19 per cent. of the premiums, though it must be realised that this is an estimate with a considerable margin for error, owing to the lack of comprehensive statistics. The high cost of commercial insurance is offset by the low cost of mutual insurance in coal mining and in other industries with specialised mutual indemnity arrangements.

D. VOLUNTARY INSURANCE THROUGH FRIENDLY SOCIETIES

23. The term " friendly societies " is restricted here and elsewhere in the Report to those societies which do not receive premiums through collectors (*see* Appendix D, para. 6). The societies dealt with here are of two main types, those without branches and those with branches ; the latter are described officially as " Orders." Comprehensive figures are available for the first type in 1935, enabling expenses of management to be compared with contributions. Similar information can be given for the same year for the largest society of the second type—the Manchester Unity of Oddfellows—but not for any others of this type. The sickness and death benefits paid by the Manchester Unity

are about two-fifths of the total of these benefits for all societies with branches. The relevant figures are as follows :—

TABLE XXXVI.—FRIENDLY SOCIETIES' CONTRIBUTIONS AND MANAGEMENT EXPENSES IN 1935

	Contributions £000	Interest £000	Total benefits £000	Management Expenses	
				£000	% of Contributions £000
Friendly Societies without branches	9,738	3,627	7,954	978	10·0
Manchester Unity	1,103	976	1,568	282	(25·6)

24. In considering these figures regard must be had to certain important differences between the two types of society.

First, the Manchester Unity has a very large income from investments and current benefits exceed the current contribution income. Since administration is concerned mainly with benefits, costs of administration cannot be compared with contributions only and the figure of 25·6 per cent. is shown in brackets.

Second, the kind of work done by the two types is different. The total expenditure on benefits in 1935 is distributed between different purposes in the following proportions :—

TABLE XXXVII.—FRIENDLY SOCIETIES' BENEFIT EXPENDITURE, 1935

	Societies without branches		Manchester Unity	
	£000	% of all benefits	£000	% of all benefits
Sickness	2575·4	32·4	1126·7	71·8
Medical Aid	592·6	7·4	37·8	2·4
Death	830·2	10·4	218·6	13·9
Superannuation	1055·7	13·3	18·6	1·2
Endowment, divided, and deposits withdrawn	2259·1	28·4	43·3	2·8
Other benefits	641·0	8·1	123·3	7·9
	7954·0	100·0	1568·3	100·0

A much larger proportion of the work of the Manchester Unity than of the centralised societies consists of the administration of sickness benefit—a relatively troublesome task. The societies without branches pay out large proportions in much simpler ways—on endowments, dividing and withdrawal of deposits ; they do much more also by way of superannuation.

25. Comprehensive figures for both types of society are available for some earlier years and give the following results :—

TABLE XXXVIII.—FRIENDLY SOCIETIES' CONTRIBUTIONS AND MANAGEMENT EXPENSES, 1910 TO 1935

	Contributions (£000)			Management Expenses (£000)			Expenses as % of Contributions		
	1910	1926	1935	1910	1926	1935	1910	1926	1935
Societies without branches	3,456	6,886	9,738	400	780	978	11·6	11·3	10·0
Societies with branches...	3,510	3,435		533	728		(15·2)	(21·2)	

The contribution income of the societies without branches has risen nearly three times from 1910 to 1935 and the expense ratio has fallen slightly. The contribution income of societies with branches fell slightly from 1910 to 1926 ; the rise in expense ratio may represent nothing but greater dependence on interest from investments. The expense ratio is shown in brackets accordingly as with the case of the Manchester Unity ratio in para. 23.

26. The societies without branches are of several descriptions with different cost ratios. A special analysis of a number of relatively large societies in 1935 gives the the following results :—

TABLE XXXIX.—CENTRALISED FRIENDLY SOCIETIES' CONTRIBUTIONS AND EXPENSES, 1935

Number and Description of Societies	Contributions £000	Expenses of Management £000	Expenses as % of Contributions
5 Sickness and Death (Accumulating)	195·7	36·1	18·6
13 Sickness and Death (Accumulating and Deposit)	2742·1	345·9	12·6
4 Sickness and Death (Deposit)	1981·5	204·4	10·3
6 Sickness and Death (Dividing)	174·7	13·9	8·0
5 Death	15·5	3·3	21·3
33—Total...	5109·5	603·7	11·8

The cost ratio decreases as provision for return of deposits and division replaces accumulation. The five societies giving death benefit only are small. The cost ratio for the 33 societies is higher than that for all the societies without branches in para. 23 because it excludes some societies whose cost ratio is reduced by exceptional factors, such as employment in a particular industry or firm.

E. COMPULSORY STATE INSURANCE

27. The table below gives the official costs of administration of the three State schemes of compulsory insurance, with an estimate of the employers' costs in exchanging and stamping insurance documents and making deductions from wages. The contributions are those of the three parties—employee, employer and State. The official costs cover the expenditure of all the Government departments concerned in each case. The unemployment figures cover both the general and the agricultural schemes of insurance.

TABLE XL.—COMPULSORY STATE INSURANCE—ADMINISTRATIVE COST, £000

	Contributions	Interest	Official Costs	Employers' Costs	Total Costs	Costs % of Contributions
Unemployment (1938)	66,247	1,475	6,110	500	6,610	10·0
(1939)	67,521	1,351	5,805	500	6,305	9·3
Health (1939)	37,637	6,464	6,018	350	6,368	16·9
Contributory Pensions (1939)	53,382	942	1,705	350	2,055	(3·9)

28. Estimates of the employer's costs are necessarily rough. Statements obtained from individual employers of the clerical work involved, yielded figures ranging from 0·17d. per employee per week to 0·33d. ; one or two figures were lower, but these apparently took no account of the work of exchanging unemployment books and health cards. Most of the establishments from which statements were obtained were large. The smallest of them, with 2,200 employees, yielded the highest figure given above, namely 0·33d. per employee. The cost per employee clearly rises as the size of the establishment decreases. Where there are only a few employees, the employer presumably does the work himself and there is no recorded expense ; but the employer's expenditure of time in such cases must be reckoned as part of the administrative cost of State insurance. If it is assumed

that the cost per employee rises gradually from 0·17d. per week in establishments of 5,000 and upwards to 0·33d. between 1,000 and 2,500 employees to 0·50d. where the numbers are below 500, including all the employers of one or two men, an average of something like 0·33d. per employee over all is reached. If half of this is attributed to unemployment insurance and one-quarter each to health and pensions insurance, the estimates given in the table are reached, namely about £500,000 for unemployment and about £350,000 a year each for health and pensions. These estimates assume 15,000,000 persons insured against unemployment, and 21,500,000 insured for health and pensions, with 10 per cent. in each case unemployed or sick so that no stamp is required. The statements furnished by employers suggest that use of a single insurance document and stamp for all State insurances would reduce their costs by from 30 to 40 per cent., that is to say, on the estimates given above, by about £400,000 a year.

29. The administration of health insurance is divided between Approved Societies and insurance committies on the one hand and central departments on the other hand. The proportion of the total cost incurred by the former has tended to rise, having been 77·2 per cent. of the whole in 1914 and 82·0 per cent. of the whole in 1939. The following table shows that in relation to contributions the administrative cost of the central departments has remained nearly stationary while that of the Approved Societies and insurance committees has risen from 10·3 per cent. in 1914 to 13·1 per cent. in 1939. The figure of 16·0 per cent., shown as the total excludes the employers' costs and is thus lower than the 16·9 per cent. shown in para. 27. The higher cost ratio of health insurance as compared with unemployment insurance is clearly due, in part, at least, to the lower general rate of benefit. An increase of the benefit rates, and by consequence of the contributions required to pay them, would automatically decrease the administrative cost ratio.

TABLE XLI.—NATIONAL HEALTH INSURANCE

COST OF ADMINISTRATION, 1914–1939

		1914	1920	1925	1930	1935	1939
CONTRIBUTIONS (including Exchequer contributions) ...	£000	22,534	32,894	35,794	33,374	33,948	37,637
BENEFITS	£000	14,447	21,190	27,511	32,931	31,089	34,535
ADMINISTRATION :—							
Approved Societies and Insurance Committees ...	£000	2,316	3,666	3,867	4,594	4,559	4,934
% of Contributions ...		10·3	11·1	10·8	13·8	13·4	13·1
% of Benefits ...		16·0	17·3	14·1	14·0	14·7	14·3
Central Departments ...	£000	686	1,313	1,041	1,066	1,045	1,084
% of Contributions ...		3·0	4·0	2·9	3·2	3·1	2·9
% of Benefits ...		4·8	6·2	3·8	3·2	3·4	3·1
Total Administration ...	£000	3,002	4,979	4,908	5,660	5,604	6,018
% of Contributions ...		13·3	15·1	13·7	17·0	16·5	16·0
% of Benefits ...		20·8	23·5	17·8	17·2	18·0	17·4

30. The administrative cost for contributory pensions shown in brackets in the table in para. 27 is to some extent artificial, in so far as the pension scheme by using a joint contribution card with health, has its contributions collected practically free of charge. But the percentage of 3·9 shown above, while in this respect it slightly understates the administrative cost of contributory pensions, in a more important respect overstates the cost. The sum of £53·4 million shown as the contributions for pensions relates only to pensions under the age of 70, while the pensions over the age of 70, which are given " by virtue " of contributions, are treated as a direct charge on the Customs vote. They amounted in the year in question to £33·9 million and the additional expense of their administration as shown in the Parliamentary estimates amounted to £0·1 million. Making this and certain other minor adjustments, the revised percentage cost of administration of contributory pensions should be put not at 3·9 per cent. but at about 2·5 per cent.

RECEIPTS BY WAY OF INTEREST

31. Most insurance undertakings, in addition to premiums or contributions, receive income as interest on investments. This interest is an important part of the total income in the case of life assurance and sickness insurance. The following table shows for each of these cases the proportion borne by interest to the premiums or contributions.

	Premiums or Contributions (£000)	Interest less Tax (£000)	Interest % of Contributions
Ordinary Life Assurance (1937)	99,739	38,903	39·0
Industrial Assurance (1937)	69,235	17,420	25·2
Friendly Societies without branches (1935)	9,738	3,627	37·3
Manchester Unity (1935)	1,103	976	88·5
National Health Insurance (1939)	37,637	6,464	17·2

CONCLUSION

32. The broad results of the comparison made between the five forms of insurance just before the present war may be summarised as follows :—

(1) Commercial insurance against fire, accidents and motor risks uses nearly 42 per cent. or about 8/5 in every £ of premiums for commission and management. The actual figures range from 36·9 per cent. for accident and general insurance through non-tariff companies to 47·8 per cent. for fire insurance through tariff companies. These figures exclude underwriting profit. Commercial insurance against employers' liability uses about 40 per cent. of the premiums, or 8/- in the £, for commission, management and legal and medical expenses, and another 6 per cent. for profit, making a total of something over 45 per cent., or 9/- in the £. The part represented by commission is substantially less than in other forms of commercial insurance.

(2) Ordinary life assurance, the resource of men of substantial means, uses about 16 per cent. of the premiums or 3/2 in the £ for administration, while industrial assurance, for men of limited means, uses 35 per cent. or 7/- in the £ exclusive of tax in each case. With tax, the total administrative cost of industrial assurance is 37·2 per cent. or 7/6 in the £. (See Appendix D, para. 25.)

(3) Mutual insurance against employers' liability otherwise than in mining, shipping, and perhaps one or two other industries, uses a little more than 20 per cent. of the contributions or 4/- in the £ for administration. Mutual insurance in mining uses in this way about 7 per cent. of the total cost of compensation and administration, that is to say 1/5 in the £. In this industry compensation is heavy. For workmen's compensation as a whole, the most reasonable estimate that can now be made would put the administrative cost at about 19 per cent. of the premiums.

(4) Voluntary insurance against sickness, death, old age and for endowment or saving through centralised friendly societies uses just over 10 per cent. of the contribution or 2/- in the £ for administration.

(5) In compulsory State insurance, administration of health insurance costs 17 per cent. or 3/5 in the £ of contributions, of unemployment insurance costs 10 per cent. or 2/- in the £, and of contributory pensions costs 2½ per cent. or 6d. in the £. These figures include the estimated cost of administration by employers, which is paid not from the contributions but in addition thereto.

(6) These comparisons are not comparisons of the relative efficiency of administration in the different forms of insurance, since the work to be done, and the conditions under which it has to be done, differ from one form of insurance to another. The markedly lower cost of administration in most forms of State insurance, as compared with most forms of voluntary insurance, arises essentially from the economies possible in the obtaining of premiums. If a risk is of such a kind that it can fitly be dealt with by compulsory social insurance, that is as a rule administratively the cheapest way of meeting that risk. But many risks are too varied for compulsion and must be left to voluntary insurance. In that case the cost of administration will normally be higher.

APPENDIX F

SOME COMPARISONS WITH OTHER COUNTRIES

1. The difficulties at the present time of making any detailed comparison between the existing and the proposed schemes of social insurance in Britain and the practice of other countries are obvious. Social and other institutions all over the world are in process of change : price levels are fluid ; the obtaining of accurate information direct from the source is in many cases impossible. But, since social security is a common interest of all peoples in the world and since in the past fifty years or so this interest has led nearly everywhere to the development of national institutions of various kinds for the solution of common problems, some of the principal points of similarity or difference between the schemes of different countries are noted briefly here.

2. Tables XLIII, XLIV, and XLV, provided by the International Labour Office, show, in general terms, the extent to which the main risks of social insecurity are covered in countries other than Britain. The first two of these tables relate to 10 countries which appear to be most relevant for purposes of direct comparison with Britain : for these selected countries the cash benefits for temporary and permanent incapacity, old age and unemployment respectively in 1938 are shown in Table XLIII for a single person, and in Table XLIV for a man with family responsibilities, as percentages of the weekly wage with family allowances where these are given. Table XLV gives information for 20 other countries showing which of them have made provision for sickness, pension insurance, unemployment and non-contributory pensions respectively, without attempting to indicate the scale of this provision in relation to wages. All three tables must be read subject to the comments in the notes upon them. In the Soviet Union, social insurance, like the economic and social system as a whole, is organised on lines so different from those of most other countries that direct comparisons are difficult. Some of the special features are noted in para. 14.

3. *Risks Covered in Selected Countries.* Looking first at the selected countries and considering, not the amount of cash benefits, but the question whether or not any provision is made for the various risks, the following main results emerge :—

(i) Provision for occupational incapacity, that is to say, for incapacity arising out of employment (workmen's compensation in Britain), is found in all ten countries.

(ii) Provision for non-occupational incapacity, that is to say, compulsory sickness insurance, exists in four only out of the ten selected countries, namely, Germany, New Zealand, Roumania and Denmark.

(iii) Compulsory unemployment insurance is found in five of the selected countries, namely, Canada, New Zealand, South Africa, the United States and Queensland from among the Australian States. In Denmark unemployment insurance on a voluntary assisted basis is widespread.

(iv) All ten countries provide old age pensions of some kind, but the pensions are wholly or partially contributory in six cases only—Belgium, Germany, New Zealand, Roumania, Sweden and the United States of America. Non-contributory pensions subject to means test, and representing assistance rather than insurance, are found in Australia, Canada, Denmark, South Africa, and, combined with contributory pensions, the United States of America. The New Zealand pensions plan is dealt with more fully in the Report itself (para. 241) since in its main principle of introducing adequate pensions without means test only at the end of a lengthy transition period, during which needs are met by non-contributory age benefits subject to a means test, it follows a line very similar to that of the plan of the Report for Britain.

4. *Other Countries.* Among the 20 other countries, 16 have compulsory sickness insurance, 18 have some form of contributory pensions and only three have unemployment insurance.

5. *All Countries.* Taking all the 30 countries together, 20 have compulsory sickness insurance, 24 have some form of contributory pension, 8 have unemployment insurance. Three countries only in the 30—New Zealand, Bulgaria and Poland—make provision against all the three risks of sickness, old age and unemployment. That is to say, three countries only aim at covering all the principal forms of social insecurity as fully as Britain. The United States has no sickness insurance ; Germany has now no unemployment insurance.

6. *Benefits Generally Related to Earnings.* Though in Tables XLIII and XLIV an indication is given of the amount of the cash benefits in relation to wages or family income, it is not easy from this to make comparisons between the real value of the cash benefits being paid in Britain or proposed under the plan, and those of other countries. These tables are of interest mainly as illustrating one outstanding difference between the

TABLE XLIII.—BENEFITS AND PENSIONS IN RELATION TO WAGES IN CERTAIN COUNTRIES—SINGLE PERSON WITH DEPENDANTS

Country	Weekly Wage	Temporary incapacity		Permanent incapacity		Old Age	Unemployment	Approx. purchasing power of wages as percentage of U.K. (based on comparative food prices)
		Non-occupational	Occupational	Non-occupational	Occupational			
U.K.	70/-	—	—	—	—	—	—	100
Australia— New South Wales ...	100/-	—	60 (a)	24 (b)	(c)	24 (b)	—	120
Queensland ...	100/-	—	60 (a)	24 (b)	(c)	24 (b)	17	—
Belgium	260 frs.	—	50	—	67	46	—	56
Canada— Ontario ...	$25	—	67	—	67	20 (b)	40	143
Denmark ...	70 kr.	(d)	48 (a)	19 (b)	36 (a)	17 (b)	—	100
Germany ...	30 Rm.	50	50	15	67	30	—	43
New Zealand ...	100/-	20	67	30	(c)	30 (j)	20	—
Roumania ...	560 lei.	50	50	24 / 67 (e)	67	46	—	—
South Africa ...	100/-	—	64 (a)	—	64 (a)	17 (b)	30	127
Sweden	60 kr.	—	67	3 (g) / 14 (h)	67	4 (g) / 15 (h)	—	89 / 114
U.S.A.— New York ...	$25		67	—	67	30 (i)	50	
Pennsylvania ...	$25		67		67 (c)	30 (i)	50	
California ...	$25		65		65	30 (i)	50	

TABLE XLIV.—BENEFITS AND PENSIONS IN RELATION TO WAGES IN CERTAIN COUNTRIES—MARRIED MAN WITH WIFE NOT GAINFULLY OCCUPIED AND 2 CHILDREN UNDER 15

Country	Weekly Wage plus Family Allowance	Temporary incapacity		Permanent total incapacity		Old Age (Married Couple)	Unemployment	Death	
		Non-occupational	Occupational	Non-occupational	Occupational			Non-occupational	Occupational
Australia—									
New South Wales	105/-	5	97 (a)	27 (b)	5 (c)	47 (b)	5	38 (b)	5 (c)
Queensland	105/-	5	78 (a)	27 (b)	5 (c)	47 (b)	43	5	5 (c)
Belgium	297 frs.	7	53	—	70	46	—	21	28 (c)
Canada—Ontario	$25	—	67	—	67	40 (b)	48	40 (b)	60
Denmark	70 kr.	(d)	48 (a)	25	36 (a)	26 (b)	—	12 (b)	(c)
Germany	30 Rm.	70	70	29	80	30	—	23	60
New Zealand (i)	108/-	50	70	55	8 (c)	60 (i)	42	42	8 (c)
Roumania	560 lei.	50	50	24 / 67 (e)	67	46	—	19 (f) / 60 (e)	60
South Africa	100/-	—	64	—	64	34 (b)	30	—	45
Sweden	60 kr.	—	67	3 (g) / 14 (h)	67	7 (g) / 31 (h)	—	—	42
U.S.A.—									
New York	$25	—	67	—	67	45 (i)	50	46	50
Pennsylvania	$25	—	67	—	(c)	45 (i)	50	46	(c)
California	$25	—	65	—	65	45 (i)	50	46	(c)

General Note on Tables XLIII and XLIV

The benefits are expressed as percentages of a basic wage. The figure selected for the basic wage is not an average for the insured group (except in the case of Roumania, for which no other figure was available) but is intended to represent the typical full-time earnings of a moderately skilled male industrial worker (e.g. a fitter in the engineering trade) in 1938. This wage is, of course, somewhat higher than that of the unskilled worker and considerably higher than that of the agricultural worker or female worker. Moreover, because the maximum statutory basic wage fixed by certain workmen's compensation laws is less than the basic wage adopted for these tables, the compensation is shown as less than the nominal percentage of wages prescribed by the laws in question. Where a family allowance is added to wages, as in Australia, Belgium, New Zealand, the benefits in respect of families are expressed as percentages of the basic wage plus the family allowance. Nevertheless, in the case of old age pensions for a married couple, the pensions are related to the basic wage without family allowances.

Detailed Notes

(a) As limited by absolute maximum weekly payment.

(b) Non-contributory benefit.

(c) Lump sum payment.

(d) Voluntary insurance ; rate depends on each individual.

(e) Non-occupational accident.

(f) After qualifying period of 8 years.

(g) Contributory for persons with means.

(h) Contributory component plus non-contributory component for persons with means not exceeding 100 kr. a year.

(i) Since the preparation of this Table, family allowances in New Zealand have been increased from 4/– per head to 6/– per head. The figure of 108/– used in the Table and the percentages based on it do not take account of this increase.

---

practice of other countries and the practice of Britain both in the past and in the plan proposed. Difficulty of direct comparison of amounts of benefit is due not merely to difficulties in determining the money rates of wages and the real value of wages, but to the difference of principle in fixing the amounts of benefit or pension. In Britain these amounts are flat rates irrespective of earnings, and so are the same for all classes of persons, though with a differentiation for sex in some cases and a differentiation between various forms of interruption of earnings. In most other countries the benefits are percentages of the wages, and vary, therefore, from one man to another. There is no general rate with which the British flat rate can be compared. Looking at it from the other side, the British flat rate cannot be expressed as a percentage of wages ; the percentage would vary, being higher for unskilled men with relatively low wages than for skilled men with higher wages. The methods of relating benefit to wages in other countries vary. In Germany the insured population is graded by income classes and this plan has been widely followed. In the United States the amount paid for unemployment and pensions is related to the earnings of each individual insured person. In the Soviet Union the percentage itself varies from man to man with the same wages. In one way or another, in nearly all countries other than Britain, Eire and New Zealand, the man of low earnings, when sick or unemployed or pensioned, normally gets through compulsory insurance a lower payment than a man of higher earnings. He pays, or his employer pays, a lower contribution, also proportionate to his earnings.

7. *Flat Rate in Britain, Eire and New Zealand.* The principle adopted in Britain in the past and proposed to be retained for the future is that of a flat rate of State insurance benefit for all. The difference between existing schemes in Britain and the proposals for the future is that the rates of benefit proposed for the future are all materially higher than the present ones and aim at full subsistence. Social insurance in Eire began as part of the British system, and though it has developed on its own lines in some ways, particularly in relation to medical treatment, it retains the flat rate principle for cash benefits. New Zealand, like Britain, differs from the other countries in providing benefits without relation to previous earnings. It differs from Britain in two important respects :—

(a) that apart from the contributory pensions which are to reach their full rate in 1968, all the benefits in New Zealand are subject to a means test ;

(b) that nearly all the money required for the security scheme in New Zealand is raised by an income tax, adjusted to capacity to pay. In contrast to this, the British systems, both present and proposed, raise funds partly by flat contributions irrespective of earnings and partly by taxation adjusted to capacity to pay.

TABLE XLV.—OTHER COUNTRIES* HAVING COMPULSORY SICKNESS, PENSION OR UNEMPLOYMENT INSURANCE, OR HAVING NON-CONTRIBUTORY PENSIONS WITH MEANS TEST

Country	Sickness	Pension Insurance	Unemploy-ment	Non-contributory Pensions
Belgium	—	X	—	—
Brazil	X	X	—	—
Bulgaria	X	X	X	—
Chile	X	X	—	—
Costa Rica ...	X	X	—	—
Czechoslovakia ...	X	X	—	—
Ecuador	X	X	—	—
Finland	—	X	—	—
France	X	X	—	X
Greece	X	X	—	—
Hungary	X	X	—	—
Italy	—	X	X	—
Japan	X	—	—	—
Netherlands ...	X	X	—	—
Norway	X	†	—	†
Panama	X	X	—	—
Peru	X	X	—	—
Poland	X	X	X	—
Spain	—	X	—	—
Sweden	—	X	—	—
Uruguay	—	X	—	X
Yugoslavia	X	X	—	—

* The list covers most countries other than those in the earlier tables which have social insurance schemes, but is not exhaustive. It omits the Soviet Union and Eire, which are dealt with specially in paragraphs 7 and 14.

† In Norway there is a universal old age tax, and the pension is subject to means test.

8. *Scope.* In most countries most schemes of social insurance are limited in effect to employed persons, as at present in Britain. The outstanding exceptions are New Zealand, the Soviet Union and, less completely, Denmark. For pensions only, Finland and Norway have schemes for all citizens rather than for employed persons.

9. *Industrial Accident and Disease.* The provision made for industrial accident and disease is described in a detailed Memorandum submitted by the International Labour Office to the Royal Commission on Workmen's Compensation which has been published. An extract from this, comparing the rates of compensation in relation to wages with that of Britain, is given in para. 99 of the Report. The general practice of most countries is to place the cost of compensation solely on the employer and thus, through the employer, upon the particular industry in which the workman is engaged. A partial exception to this is found in Denmark and in Germany, where the cost of compensation is borne by the sickness funds for the first 13 weeks and the first six weeks respectively. In these two countries also there is a difference between the scales of benefit at the beginning of incapacity and later. In Denmark victims of industrial accident and disease receive benefit at sickness insurance rates which vary with the different insurance funds for 13 weeks ; after that they receive a pension of three-fifths of the wages lost. In Germany sickness benefit at 50 per cent. of the wages is paid for a minimum of 13 weeks and a maximum of 26 weeks ; the 50 per cent. may be increased after six weeks up to 60 per cent., according to the financial position of the particular sick fund to which the beneficiary belongs. After 26 weeks of wage loss in any case, or earlier, if the need for medical care ceases, sickness benefit is replaced by accident pension equal to two-thirds of the wages lost. There are children's allowances in addition. Nearly all countries include medical treatment for workmen injured by industrial accident or disease as part of the provision for them. Most countries, moreover, as appears from Table XLIII, give markedly higher benefits for occupational than for non-occupational incapacity. To this the Soviet Union is an exception in making no distinction of benefit rates between the two forms of incapacity.

10. *Maternity.* In countries other than Britain, provision for maternity normally includes (a) for female wage-earners periodical cash benefits and medical care, and (b) for wives of wage-earners medical care without cash benefit. For group (a) the international

standard of maternity cash benefit adopted by the Childbirth Convention of 1919 is full and healthy maintenance for the mother and child for six weeks before and six weeks after childbirth, and most Continental and South American countries grant 50 per cent. of the wages for the 12 weeks. These percentages are usually the same as those given for ordinary sickness. The present scheme in Britain falls short of this in providing only a small lump sum for the maternity of female wage-earners. The proposals of the Report go beyond it in providing a benefit 50 per cent. higher than sickness benefit for 13 weeks. For group (b), that is mothers who are not wage-earners, a cash benefit (such as the £2 given in Britain) is not generally found in other countries, but medical care is provided free for the wives of insured men.

11. *Widows.* In respect of widows only one country other than Britain—Belgium— now gives unconditional widows' pensions. All others require a widow, before receiving a pension, either to prove invalidity or to have attained a pensionable age—60 or 65 in most cases, 55 in the Soviet Union. None of the countries appears to provide anything to correspond to the temporary widows' benefit at the specially high rate proposed in the Report as a means of readjustment.

12. *Funerals.* Almost all countries other than Britain which have schemes of compulsory sickness insurance provide as part of their scheme payment of a funeral benefit at the death of the insured person ; New Zealand is an exception. Funeral benefit for dependants of insured persons is given in relatively few countries : in Czechoslovakia, Norway and Poland as a statutory benefit, and in Germany and Hungary as additional or optional benefit.

13. *Health Service.* Nearly all the countries which have a sickness insurance scheme provide medical treatment not only for the insured person, but for his wife and children, including in most cases both general and specialist medical attendance at home, and hospital treatment. Countries which are listed by the International Labour Office as giving a medical service which is materially more extensive than that provided in Britain under national health insurance include Denmark, France, Germany, Hungary, Roumania, Norway, New Zealand and the Soviet Union.

14. *Soviet Union.* The following notes deal only with a few of the salient differences between the practice of the Soviet Union and that of other countries :—

(i) All contributions are collected exclusively from the various undertakings, i.e., there are no contributions by insured persons.

(ii) All benefits are fixed as percentages of wages, but the percentages vary with the importance and arduousness of the work, length of service of the beneficiary and generally with what might be regarded as his value to the community.

(iii) Occupational incapacity is compensated at the same rate as non-occupational incapacity though under easier conditions. Different rates are fixed for temporary incapacity, permanent incapacity and old age respectively. No benefit has been provided for unemployment since 1930, on the ground that there is no unemployment.

(iv) Old age pensions are paid in proportion to wages to men at 60 after 25 years' service (or at 50 in unhealthy occupations) and to women at 55 after 20 years' service. Retirement from work is not a condition of pension.

(v) In respect of disability, three groups are distinguished :—

(a) workers who have completely lost their ability to work and are in need of constant attendance ;

(b) workers who have completely lost their ability to work but are not in need of outside care ; and

(c) workers who have lost their capacity to work in their former occupation, but retain sufficient capacity to engage in casual work, part-time work or definitely less skilled work in another occupation.

These groups are treated alike in dealing with non-occupational and occupational incapacity. In the former case, but not in the latter, a qualifying period is imposed before benefit can be received. In each case the pension is equal to full wages for workers in group (a), to 75 per cent. of wages in group (b) and to 50 per cent. of wages in group (c).

(vi) In sickness, benefits are payable from the first day of incapacity, without a waiting time.

(vii) The main features of the maternity service are described as follows in an officially recommended handbook : " The care of the child begins well before it is born. In every city, in every collective or state farm, there are women's medical consultation centres linked up with hospitals, maternity homes, and the Institute of Mother and Child in the big cities. Here the woman who becomes pregnant is encouraged to come for advice. Here she will be examined and given attention. A place will be reserved for her in the nearest maternity hospital. If she is working, her manager will be informed. From time to time she is examined, and if the doctor considers that her work is too heavy for her, she must be put on a lighter job at the same pay. She must receive 8 weeks' pregnancy leave with full pay, and be taken back at her original job. She will receive a layette and an allowance for the extra need during that period. When she returns to the factory she will leave her baby in the factory crèches and she will be allowed 30 minutes off from work every 4 hours to feed the baby. If the mother is unable to feed it, there are milk kitchens where she can obtain cheaply the proper milk."

(viii) The health service is based on the following principles :—

    (a) Every kind of medical benefit is provided free of charge.

    (b) The families and dependants of insured persons are included.

    (c) Specialist services are included, e.g., dental, ophthalmic, surgical ; drugs, medicines and appliances ; orthopædic treatment and artificial limbs ; hospital and convalescent treatment and maintenance in sanatoria and rest-homes.

    (d) Medicine is designed to be preventive as well as curative by establishment of a network of clinics and polyclinics in towns and villages, and factory and rural health centres, and by the special attention that is paid to the health of children, from infancy upwards, and to ensuring continuity of treatment.

15. *Merits of Present British Schemes.* The existing schemes of social insurance in Britain, in common with the schemes of most other countries, are schemes for employees rather than for all citizens. They make less provision than is made in a good many other countries for medical treatment of others than the insured persons and of the insured persons themselves, for maternity of women who are gainfully occupied and for funerals. On the other hand their total range is greater than that of nearly all other countries. British social insurance, with its allied services, has merits which are summarised by the International Labour Office in the following terms :—

The existing British system " excels in point of (1) its scheme of unemployment insurance, embracing practically the entire employed population, including agricultural workers ; (2) its contributory pensions, comparatively adequate as basic pensions, and granted after a comparatively short qualifying period, at comparatively small cost to insured person or employer ; (3) its unemployment and old age assistance, nationally financed, guaranteeing a tolerable standard of subsistence, and adjusted to the needs of each individual ; (4) the continuity of its medical benefit, granted, from the first day of insurance, during employment, sickness, unemployment, disablement and old age."

16. *Proposals for Britain.* The Plan for Social Security in the Report develops the existing British schemes in four directions : it unifies them while providing for variety of benefit and administration where difference is justified ; it extends the scope of insurance to all citizens ; it raises benefits to subsistence level and makes them adequate in time ; it gives new benefits. While doing this, the plan preserves the main feature of the British system which distinguishes both it and the New Zealand system from the systems of nearly all other countries. This feature is the preservation of a flat rate of benefit not varying with the earnings which have been lost. In planning for social security each country, while it may with advantage learn from the experience of others, needs a scheme adapted to its special conditions and its dominant political ideas. The principle adopted by most other countries of making State insurance benefits proportionate to the earnings which have been lost has advantages and disadvantages. Apart from the greater administrative difficulties, the view taken here is that a system on this principle would not achieve the purposes which for the British people are most important. The reasons for this view may be summarised briefly as follows :—

(1) The flat rate of benefit treating all alike is in accord with British sentiment for equal treatment of all in social insurance—irrespective both of their previous earnings and of the degree of their risk of unemployment or sickness.

(2) A flat rate of benefit, if raised, as it is raised in the proposals of the Report, to subsistence level, is a direct contribution to a policy of a national minimum. Benefits which are proportions of wages do not guarantee subsistence, and are liable in the case of the lower paid workers to be below subsistence level.

(3) Provision by compulsory insurance of a flat rate of benefit up to subsistence level leaves untouched the freedom and the responsibility of the individual citizen in making supplementary provision for himself above that level. This accords both with the conditions of Britain, where voluntary insurance, particularly against sickness, is highly developed, and with British sentiment. But to give the fullest possible encouragement to voluntary insurance and saving, it is important to reduce to a minimum the cases in which assistance has to be given subject to consideration of means. To do this is a central feature of the plan for Britain as set out in the Report.

DETAILED TABLE OF CONTENTS

DETAILED TABLE OF CONTENTS—*Continued.*

APPENDICES

LIST OF TABLES

* Tables in the Memorandum by the Government Actuary forming Appendix A are not included in this list.

For the reader's convenience a Table of Conversion of English to American money has been added to this photographic reproduction of the English proof-sheets. It appears on the reverse of this leaf.

CONVERSION TABLE

(Based on the high quotation of December 4, 1942)

				English Pounds £	American Dollars $
1 Pence	= $.0168			5	20.20
1 Shilling (12 pence).....	= .202			10	40.40
1 Pound (20 shillings)....	= 4.04			15	60.60
				20	80.80
				25	101.00
				30	121.20
Pence	Dollars & Cents			35	141.40
1d	$.0168			40	161.60
2d	.0336			45	181.80
3d	.0504			50	202.00
4d	.0672				
5d	.0840			100	404.00
6d	.1008			200	808.00
7d	.1176			300	1,212.00
8d	.1344			400	1,616.00
9d	.1512			500	2,020.00
10d	.1680			600	2,424.00
11d	.1848			700	2,828.00
				800	3,232.00
				900	3,636.00
				1000	4,040.00
				1500	6,060.00
				2000	8,080.00
Shillings				2500	10,100.00
1/	.202			3000	12,120.00
2/	.404			3500	14,140.00
3/	.606			4000	16,160.00
4/	.808			4500	18,180.00
5/	1.010			5000	20,200.00
6/	1.212				
7/	1.414			10000	40,400.00
8/	1.616			20000	80,800.00
9/	1.818			30000	121,200.00
10/	2.020			40000	161,600.00
				50000	202,000.00
11/	2.222			60000	242,400.00
12/	2.424			70000	282,800.00
13/	2.626			80000	-323,200.00
14/	2.828			90000	363,600.00
15/	3.030				
16/	3.232				
17/	3.434			100000	404,000.00
18/	3.636			200000	808,000.00
19/	3.838			300000	1,212,000.00
20/ (£1)	4.04			400000	1,616,000.00
				500000	2,020,000.00
				600000	2,424,000.00
				700000	2,828,000.00
				800000	3,232,000.00
				900000	3,636,000.00
				1000000	4,040,000.00

3

Date Due